THE BACKYARD BUILDER

PROJECTS for OUTDOOR LIVING

William Hylton

Editor

Rodale Press, Emmaus, Pennsylvania

Margaret Lydic Balitas, Senior Managing Editor

If you have any questions or comments concerning
this book, please write:
Rodale Press
Book Reader Service
33 East Minor Street
Emmaus, PA 18098

Library of Congress Cataloging-in-Publication Data

Projects for outdoor living / William Hylton, editor.
      p.   cm. – (The Backyard builder)
  ISBN 0-87857-884-6 hardcover
  1. Garden structures–Design and construction–
Amateurs' manuals. I. Hylton, William H. II. Series.
TH4961.P762 1990
717–dc20   89-28074
                                         CIP

Distributed in the book trade by St. Martin's Press

2 4 6 8 10 9 7 5 3   hardcover

**David Schiff
Michael Ferrara
Tim Snyder
Walter Jowers
David Sellers
William Hylton**
TEXT

**John Carlance
Frank Rohrbach
Sally Onopa**
ILLUSTRATIONS

Mitch Mandel
PHOTOGRAPHS

**Fred Matlack
Phil Gehret**
KNOW-HOW

Linda Jacopetti
DESIGN

Mary Green
COPYEDITING

Stacy Brobst
EDITORIAL ASSISTANCE

CONTENTS

CONTENTS

A NEW LOOK AT THE OLD BACKYARD

1

You've seen them in magazines and books. Gorgeous gardens! Lush vegetation, colorful flowers and blooming trees, a brick-paved serpentine walkway leading to a cool nook with a comfortable bench. Perhaps there's a trellis or an arbor nearby, a sundial in the center of an adjacent sunny spot, or water running over a rocky fall into a small garden pool.

You want that setting for your own. But after reading the article or a chapter or two of the book, and even though you're a gardener, and a good one—your flowers bloom with the best!—you realize there are key pieces of this setting missing from your backyard. You have no bench, no trellis, no arbor, no brick walkway, no pool. And your book with the pretty pictures doesn't explain how to get those missing pieces.

Well, you can build them—yourself—using the how-to know-how provided in the pages that follow.

Projects for Outdoor Living will tell you how to turn the not-very-special backyard that came with your house into an outdoor living area designed just for you and your family. It'll be a yard *you* can enjoy. It's easy to do. In the chapters ahead you'll find a wealth of general construction information and a tremendous variety of projects with very specific, step-by-step instructions.

All the construction information is here—grading, mixing concrete, selecting bricks, designing and estimating for a deck, constructing a swimming pool, erecting a wall or privacy fence. You'll find a gazebo; arbors and trellises to shade your patio, deck, or terrace; planter tubs; redwood furniture; a mahogany lounge; and much, much more.

But before you forge ahead to learn how to build something, you have to decide what to build. And you have to decide what to build it with. That's what most of this short chapter is about—assessing your needs to come up with a plan for your yard.

In this chapter is a color section you've probably already paged through. It shows dozens of beautiful yards, yards you can live

1

in. Yards you *want* to live in. And in the many pages that follow that color gallery of outdoor living ideas, you'll find the detailed information you need to actually construct those projects.

Design

If you were to hire a landscape architect to design your outdoor living space, he'd hand you a detailed plan showing each element of your yard down to the last bush. The drawing probably would have an overlay so you could flip back and forth between what exists and what he proposes. If you liked the plan, you'd nod your head. A backhoe and a bunch of workers would arrive at your house, and within a few months, you'd have the yard of your dreams.

But few of us can afford this route to our dream yard. We're more likely to build a fence one year, a patio the next. If we get really ambitious, we might even build a pool.

But regardless of your timetable and regardless of who does the construction, it pays to have a plan.

You may be thinking that you don't know anything about making landscape drawings, and you don't see why you need one. You just want to replace that crumbling concrete walk.

Your instinct may be correct. For many projects you may not need to draw a complete site plan. But that doesn't mean you shouldn't plan.

Ask yourself some questions before rebuilding that walk. What material would blend best with your yard? With the character of your house? With your neighborhood? Concrete again? Brick? Flagstone? Is the existing route of the walk exactly right? Would it be nice if it meandered around that tree? Is it wide enough? Or can you think of times you've been forced to continue a conversation over your shoulder because the walk forced you and your companions into single file? And—perhaps most important— are you planning future projects that will change the traffic pattern of your yard, making this walk obsolete?

For some projects it would be foolish not to make at least a rough site plan. If you are planning a deck, for example, you'll surely want a sketch of your yard showing the "footprint" of your house. It's a good idea to sketch in other major elements, such as large trees. This sketch will be an indispensable aid in designing a deck with a shape and size that harmonizes with your yard and home.

Sure, your sketch may not have the polished, professional look of a landscape architect's blueprint. But his blueprint is a sales tool, conveying his concepts to a client, as much as it is a plan of work. Your sketch is a personal record, helping you to organize your ideas; it doesn't have to impress anyone.

Make a Wish List

A good way to start creating your new yard—designed for your kind of outdoor living—is a family brainstorming session. Sit around the kitchen table and have everyone —including the kids—tell what they would like to do outdoors. Have someone write down the ideas. Try to put your ideas in terms of activities—not "We'd like a patio," but rather, "We like to cook and eat outside." You might find, for example, that Junior wants to shoot baskets, Sis would love a playhouse, Mom wants to garden, and Dad would much rather spend Sunday morning reading the newspaper on the deck than mowing a big lawn.

A serene setting for relaxing outdoors is created by this garden pool surrounded by lush ornamentals. A high cedar fence closes out the sight and sound of traffic.

Whether it's reading or sun-
ning, quiet entertaining, or a
boisterous party, this elaborate deck and patio provide
the perfect outdoor setting.

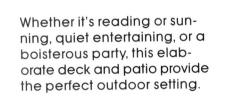

Water in the backyard: a swimming pool and spa; an artificial garden pool with water tumbling over rocks. The scale of your yard, the level of your know-how, your style of life all play a role in the kind of backyard pool you'll have. Or whether you'll even have one.

Consider how evocative your outdoor constructions can be. A new gazebo with turned posts and balusters and modest gingerbread (above) summons feelings of turn-of-the-century prosperity, good times, and family get-togethers. Urnlike turned finials give this gateway (right) a regal stamp.

6

New constructions tend to be Spartan, modern affairs that project more a sense of cost-consciousness than anything else. But the oriental ambience of this outdoor setting is inviting, attractive, and unique. And no more costly to construct than a less-creative design.

Think of a deck as more than a platform with a fence around it. Incorporate a trellis, arbor (left), or gazebo (below). Make it an inviting entryway. Instead of uprooting trees, frame around them, enhancing the deck's role as a transitional element between house and yard.

As often as a deck is a platform (left) from which you can view your world, it is also a stage on which your world can see you perform. For a measure of privacy, your deck may need a fence or trellis or at least, as exemplified by this hot tub pavilion (right and below right), a semi-enclosed area into which you can retreat for restful seclusion.

12

"Rooms" for outdoor living can be delineated with trellises (above), arbors (above right), fences (below), and other open structures (left). The plantings you use will enhance and accent your constructions.

Fabulous decks are character-ized not only by spectacular design features like the sweeping prow, but by the detailing, such as that of the railing and posts, by the quality of the materials used, and by the craftsmanship displayed in the construction.

Who knows what delights lie behind these gateways? If they're as special as the structures that conceal them, they are grand indeed. Perhaps they include a deck or terrace, a pool and spa, a garden bridge, or comfortable furnishings, inviting you to tarry and enjoy.

17

A little bit of everything is incorporated into this deck. The unusual railing has built-in seating, an arbor shelters a table and benches, and, set apart from the main deck area, a raised platform embraces a spa. It's a great design executed with special skill.

The most inviting patios and walks are more than blocks of concrete. The shape and the layout, as well as the combinations of materials selected, all contribute to the ultimate success of paving projects. Don't settle for something pedestrian, when you can have outdoor spaces such as these.

21

Evoking the rays of the sun, this fence (above and right) manages to be simultaneously decorative and utilitarian. Even the shadows it casts are special.

Picket fences (left) are infinitely variable within the parameters of the genre—experiment with picket size, shape, spacing, and length, punctuate fencing runs with stand-out posts, or direct passage through impressive gateways.

Not everyone who wants to do some outdoor living is an adult. Play structures—swings, slides, monkey bars, sandboxes, even playhouses—offer varied fun and exercise. Create a vestpocket playground with a scaled-down project, like the turnstile merry-go-ground (right).

Concrete, stone, and slate may well be
the ideal materials for underfoot in the
outdoors. Durable and long-wearing,
relatively impervious to the weather, they
can be used, alone or in combinations,
in a myriad of attractive ways, in steps,
walks, walls, or terraces.

Outdoor furniture is essential, whether you buy a full ensemble for poolside relaxation or a café table and chairs for the deck, or build a simple Adirondack chair for the yard.

Simple joints, rot-resistant woods, weatherproof finishes—these are the marks of the most durable—and common—outdoor furniture. But such furniture doesn't need to be uncomfortable.

Moderating intrusions is a primary goal of many outdoor building projects. Fences especially are used to limit the scrutiny of neighbors and passers-by. Various designs working around louvers and lattice and slats can offer privacy without completely walling off light and air circulation. Overhead, slats, louvers, and lattice can moderate the harshness of the sun without completely cutting off its light.

A natural building material, stone is most appropriate for outdoor projects. Stone laid up, forming a wall, can hold back the earth or delineate a boundary. It can also serve as paving, or form a bench.

Whether it is overhead, shielding you from the sun, or underfoot, protecting you from the mud, wood is the most versatile material for outdoor projects. It is the basis for all framed structures, such as decks.

33

English-style garden furniture is popular, attractive, and utilitarian. It's also expensive to buy. The skillful and experienced woodworker can not only make his own, but can extend the style to swings, serving carts, and other furniture pieces.

Analyzing the Yard

Now compare the yard you have to the one you want. Analyze the way you currently use your yard. Is there an area where people tend to congregate? Why? Is it sunny? Shady? Does it get a nice breeze? Are there areas that seem really nice to you but which nobody seems to use? Why is that? Perhaps an inviting path would help you capitalize on that corner of your yard.

Take a close look at the pattern of sunlight in your yard at different times of day, and if possible, during different seasons. Think about the patterns of shade and sunlight in relation to when you are most likely to use areas of your yard.

In making this analysis, it's important to think about how your outside space relates to the indoors. Would the trellis you are considering block the view from your favorite chair by your favorite window? Is the spot that seems perfect for a brick barbecue too far from the kitchen? Is the deck easily accessible from the main indoor entertaining space so parties will naturally flow out there in nice weather? What will supervising adults most often be doing while the kids are at the play structure? Should the play area be visible through a kitchen window? A home office window?

Your next step will be measuring your yard to make a base plan. You'll be doing this primarily to give yourself a drawing to work from, but it's also a great opportunity to look at your yard from every angle. Perhaps as you are pushing past a bush to measure a corner of your property line, you'll discover a view you never knew you had.

Design Vocabulary

It's important to think of your yard not as an area, but as a space. Area describes two dimensions: length and width. It's easy to fall into thinking of your yard this way, especially because you'll draw a two-dimensional plan. But your yard is three-dimensional: It also has height.

One aspect of this third dimension is the slope of your land. For many projects—a deck, walk, patio, or retaining wall—it is important to measure slope accurately.

Another aspect is the "ceiling" of your yard. If you're in the middle of a treeless plain, the yard's ceiling could be as vast as the sky from horizon to horizon. On a narrow lot under a canopy of trees, its ceiling will be much more intimate. Obviously, the ceiling is not something you measure, it's just something to be aware of as you determine the scale of elements.

Few of us live in the middle of barren plains, so most yards also have walls. This

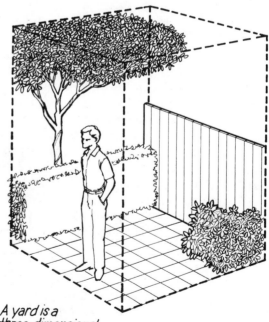

A yard is a three-dimensional space, with walls, ceiling, and floor

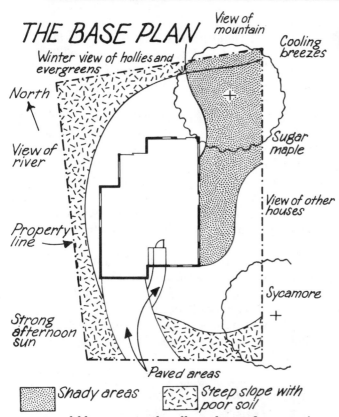

THE BASE PLAN

View of mountain

Cooling breezes

Winter view of hollies and evergreens

North

View of river

Sugar maple

View of other houses

Property line

Sycamore

Strong afternoon sun

Paved areas

Shady areas

Steep slope with poor soil

could be an actual wall, such as a fence, or it could be whatever interrupts your horizontal view, such as neighboring houses.

And of course, every yard has a floor.

Sometimes models and perspective drawings are used to help visualize the yard as a three-dimensional space. For a complex project, you may want to study how to make models and perspective drawings. But for most projects, all you will need is a floor plan. You can always step out your door for a three-dimensional look at your yard.

View Positions

Where are you standing when you view your yard? Some of the most important view positions are inside the house. The

window over the kitchen sink is a typical —and important—view position. When planning a project in the spring, it's easy to forget how much we enjoy our winter yard as viewed from a particular window.

Of course, you also need to consider outdoor view positions. Take a chair to your proposed patio and check the views. Remember that view position is affected by elevation. The view you get when standing by the fence will disappear when you sit down. Give some thought, too, to your neighbors' view positions. Even a 10-foot-high fence won't afford privacy from a neighbor's second-story windows.

The Base Plan

It may have occurred to you by now that all this landscape design talk is nothing more than a lot of common sense. The trick, though, is to organize it so you see how each element of your design affects every other element. That's the purpose of a base plan.

The base plan, drawn to scale on graph paper, shows your yard as it exists at the outset of your project. For mapping areas of one-half acre or less, get paper with four squares to the inch and let each square equal a foot. This scale is expressed as 1:4. If your area is larger, you can use a 1:8 scale, or use two or more pieces of graph paper. You'll also need a 50- or 100-foot tape measure, a ruler, a compass, and a pencil.

The first draft of your base plan probably will be sloppy, because you'll be drawing and making notes as you measure. It's vital that all dimensions be accurate. Double-check your dimensions; it's easy to miss little jogs in a walk or hitches in a fence line.

North should be at the top or left on the base plan; indicate north with a little arrow.

Jot down the scale. Mark a baseline as a reference for the rest of your drawing. If you are mapping out your backyard, the baseline may represent the house's back wall. It could be a fence, or even the property line.

Working from the baseline, plot the perimeter of your property. Go back and embellish the plan with all the elements of your yard that will affect what you want to build. Include tree trunks and leaf canopies, large bushes or groups of bushes, buildings, planting beds, paved areas, paths, and pools, as well as unseen elements like easements and setbacks. If you'll be doing any digging, it's important to locate buried utilities and indicate these on your base plan. Depending on their relevance to your project, you may want to note topographical characteristics, such as steep or rocky areas.

Make notes that will help keep less tangible aspects in mind. Note, for example, areas that get hot afternoon sun or cool evening breezes. Delineate views you want to screen and views you want to preserve and, perhaps, emphasize. When your base plan is complete, take the eraser-smudged mess inside and redraw it on a clean piece of graph paper. You might even want to use some color to indicate elements—gray for shady areas, green for tree canopies, red for walks, and so forth.

A Working Drawing

Now comes the creative part—designing your project or projects to harmonize with your yard. For most people, this will take experimentation, so get a big pad of tracing paper. Lay a sheet of it on your base plan. Begin sketching areas. Don't be too compulsive about this. Just sketch—freehand it!—on successive sheets of tracing paper.

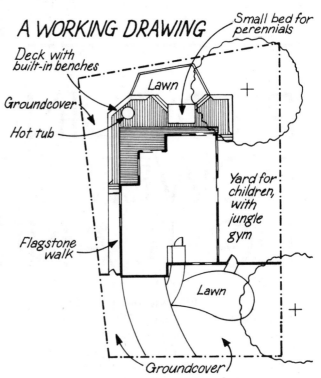

When the project takes a shape that pleases you, when you find a form appealing on a gut level, take a hard look at it in practical design terms. Make adjustments. A fabulous deck, for example, will be a real disappointment if awkward traffic patterns or a total lack of privacy discourage its use.

When you have a design that meets your needs, get out the ruler and compass, if you need one, and draw your project's specific dimensions. For some projects—a flagstone walk, for example—this is the only drawing needed. For other projects, you may need more detailed drawings—the framing plan for a deck, for example.

In the chapters following, you'll learn the specifics of designing, estimating, and actually building all sorts of practical, enjoyable projects for outdoor living.

PROVIDING POWER, LIGHT, AND WATER

2

Few of us live without electricity and running water these days. We have all sorts of electric lights, recorded music, and power appliances for washing and cooking, even exercising. There's running water in the kitchen, the several baths, the laundry room, perhaps even a wet bar in the family room and a hose bib in the garage.

How about the outdoor living space? Is it wired for electrically powered living? Is it lighted? Fitted out with receptacles for a stereo, an electric hedge trimmer, a circular saw? Does it have running water to sprinkle the petunias, fill the wading pool, hose down sweaty ball players?

Here's how to extend the utilities we all find essential to home life into the out-of-doors.

Outdoor Wiring

The difference between indoor and outdoor wiring is in the materials used in the installation. Electrically, everything works the same. Outdoor wiring installations have to survive the elements, so outdoor materials must be water and corrosion resistant.

Today's wiring hardware and procedures are very straightforward and standardized. Few tools are needed and, once you understand what you're doing, the work goes smoothly and quickly. To work safely and effectively, however, it is essential that you understand exactly how to do the job.

Before you start work, call your local building codes administration to find out if you'll need a permit. Whether your town requires a permit or not, make sure your plans and materials meet or exceed local codes. Most codes are drawn from the National Electrical Code (NEC), but some municipalities have more stringent requirements.

Wiring Materials

The simplest way to run an outdoor circuit is to use buried cable. For underground installation, you can choose between simply burying UF cable or installing UF cable

Not security lights, but lights of passage. That's what low-voltage lights are. Unobtrusive in the daylight, it's easy to overlook them in your landscape planning. But try negotiating steps or pathways in the dark. They don't throw much light, but they direct it to just the right spots. A variety of commercial units is available.

in either of two types of conduit.

Type UF cable is the only kind to use underground. It has a solid plastic covering rather than the water-permeable paper insulation you'll find in Type NM, which is designed exclusively for use indoors. For residential branch circuits, the NEC allows burial of UF cable a *minimum* of 12 inches deep.

The easiest way to dig a 12-inch-deep trench is with a small trenching machine, which can be rented. Small trenchers can be operated by one person, but the job is a lot easier with two—one on each side of the trencher's pull handle. After you run an underground cable, cover the cable with rot-resistant boards. This will cut down on the danger of digging through the cable later.

Although UF cable is all right to use underground, it must be protected by rigid metal conduit wherever it is aboveground.

Conduit

Aboveground conduit must be rigid metal. Conduit used underground can be rigid nonmetallic (plastic) or rigid metal conduit. Each type has its pros and cons. Advantages of rigid nonmetallic conduit are that it's easy to install and it doesn't corrode underground. But it must be buried a minimum of 18 inches deep, and the plastic conduit can't serve as a ground. With plastic conduit, the ground wire must be continuous. This requires making ground connections in boxes the same as in indoor wiring. If you use plastic conduit, use gray conduit cement, NOT water pipe cement. And complete joints *before* you pull the wire through, because the cement can attack the insulation of the wire.

Rigid metal conduit is harder to install. It has to be bent with special tools; a begin-

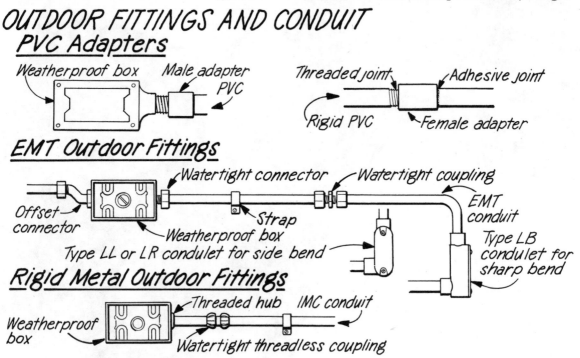

OUTDOOR FITTINGS AND CONDUIT
PVC Adapters

Weatherproof box — Male adapter PVC

Threaded joint — Adhesive joint
Rigid PVC — Female adapter

EMT Outdoor Fittings

Watertight connector — Watertight coupling
EMT conduit
Offset connector — Weatherproof box — Strap
Type LL or LR condulet for side bend
Type LB condulet for sharp bend

Rigid Metal Outdoor Fittings

Threaded hub — IMC conduit
Weatherproof box — Watertight threadless coupling

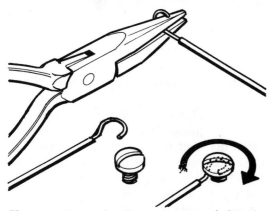

Form a loop in the wire and fit it around the screw so tightening the screw tightens the loop

ner has to buy or rent them, then master their use. When used underground, metal conduit eventually will corrode. The advantage is that it only has to be buried 6 inches deep. Even so, digging a lengthy trench by hand is hard work. And if you use a trencher, you can make the trench 12 to 18 inches deep as easily as you can 6 inches. The upshot is: Where codes permit, nonmetallic is preferable to metal, both for ease of installation and service life.

Thinwall conduit (EMT) shouldn't be used underground. EMT is good for above-ground outdoor applications. It can be used, for example, to protect cable installed along the side of a house.

Both plastic and metal conduit are used with special waterproof fittings for outdoor work.

Cable

Generally, 12-gauge Type UF wire is adequate for outdoor lighting. It will carry 20-amp power, lighting 2,400 watts' worth of bulbs—that's a lot of lights—along a run of 87 feet (figuring a 5 percent voltage drop). For a longer run, or more lights, or a circuit that will demand more than 20 amps, you'd have to upgrade accordingly to 10- or 8-gauge.

You want wire with two conductors and a separate ground wire. To buy it, ask for "Type UF, twelve-two, with ground." For ease

Calculating Circuit Capacity

To determine if a circuit has enough capacity to run additional lights or appliances, find the total amount of current drawn by existing fixtures on the circuit. Here's how.

Read the nameplates on appliances that will be plugged into the existing circuit. The nameplates usually display the amperage consumed by the appliance. With appliances that don't have nameplates—such as lights—divide the number of watts by the number of volts to get the amperage. Add up the number of amps on the circuit.

Suppose, for example, that your TV is rated at 2 amps, the stereo at 2, and the vacuum at 4, for a total of 8 amps. Though it's unlikely that anyone would use all three appliances at the same time, it's best to ignore that fact to ensure your circuits have plenty of capacity. Next add in the four 100-watt bulbs, which is 400 total watts divided by 120 volts, or 3.2 amps. On this theoretical circuit, then, if you turned on everything at once, you'd consume 11.2 amps.

If it's a 15-amp circuit, that gives you 3.8 amps extra capacity, or enough to run 475 watts of outdoor lighting—about 12 40-watt bulbs.

of installation, make sure you get wire that's rated at 90°C. You can use this wire for the entire circuit, according to the NEC, including the portion that's inside the house.

Boxes

There are two types of outdoor boxes: "driptight" and "watertight." Driptight boxes are made of painted sheet metal, with shields to deflect rain water. But they are *not* waterproof; they must be mounted where standing water or rain from hoses or sprinklers can't touch them.

Watertight boxes are made to tolerate *temporary* immersion or dousings from hoses, sprinklers, or rain. Made of aluminum, galvanized steel, or bronze, they have threaded entry holes and gaskets sealing their covers.

Ground Fault Interrupters

The NEC requires that all outside receptacles be equipped with a safety device called a ground fault interrupter (GFI). GFIs are used with receptacles in areas that get wet. A GFI senses a leak of current—as with a faulty ground—and switches off the current to the receptacle.

GFIs can be installed in your service panel in the same space as a typical circuit breaker, or for easy installation of an outdoor receptacle, you can buy a combination receptacle/GFI unit. It fits into the

TYPICAL OUTDOOR CIRCUIT

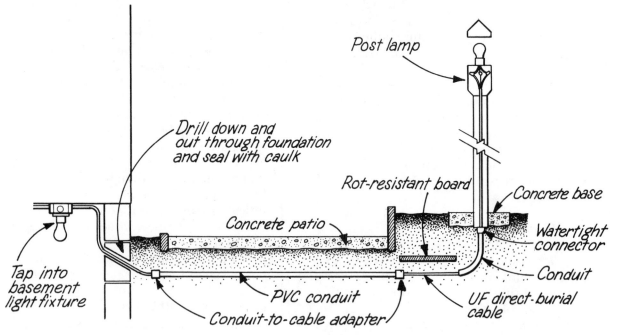

SOURCES FOR OUTDOOR CIRCUITS

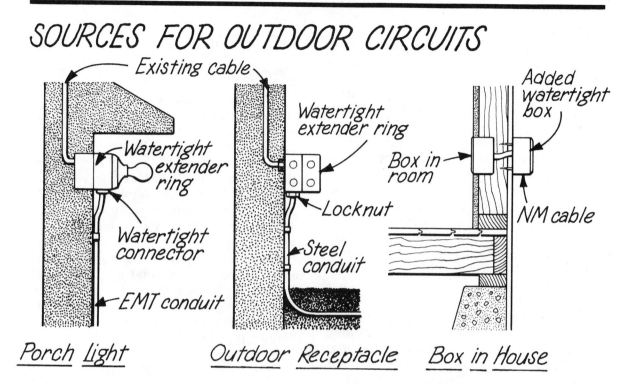

Existing cable

Watertight extender ring

Watertight connector

EMT conduit

Porch Light

Watertight extender ring

Locknut

Steel conduit

Outdoor Receptacle

Added watertight box

Box in room

NM cable

Box in House

same space and is wired in the same way as an ordinary receptacle. GFIs are equipped with test switches and should be tested periodically.

Tools and Tips

The tools you'll need for wiring are simple and few: wire stripper, needle-nose pliers, test light, utility knife, and flat-blade screwdriver.

You can get by without a wire stripper by using your utility knife, but a stripper is inexpensive and speeds the job. With cutters sized to the standard wire gauges, you can cut through the insulation and strip it without nicking the wire.

The needle-nose pliers has three jobs: cutting wire, bending conductors into tight loops for effective connections, and twisting

conductors together for connection with a wire nut.

The utility knife is for stripping insulation off the cable. This is a little trickier with UF cable than it is with the NM cable used for indoor wiring. With UF cable, it's easiest to work against a flat surface, stripping the cable insulation back about 4 inches. Knock out a hole in the box, screw in the cable connector, and put the cable just far enough through it so the connector clamps unstripped cable.

Tapping a Circuit

The easiest way to get power outside is to tap into an existing underused circuit. As mentioned, outdoor lighting generally uses low-wattage lamps, so it won't be demanding much current unless you're planning really extensive lighting. In most houses, branch circuits to rooms other than utility rooms, bathrooms, and kitchens are underused. Dining room, living room, and basement circuits are usually good candidates for expansion.

If you don't have an underused circuit to tap into, you'll have to add a circuit at the service box, and that's usually not particularly difficult.

Once you've decided which circuit to tap into, turn off the power to that circuit at the service panel. Then find a convenient point—a receptacle, lighting fixture, switch, or junction box—to tap into.

If you're extending the circuit from a fixture in your basement or crawl space, you can run wire straight to the trench that runs to your outdoor fixture. Use a carbide bit or star drill to drill through the foundation wall into the trench. Make the hole slant downward toward the outside. After you pull the wire through, seal both sides of the hole with a good-quality silicone or marine caulk to prevent water from running into the basement or crawl space.

You can also run wires from higher points, such as wall-mounted receptacles or attic junction boxes, using the proper fixtures and materials.

Generally, all openings in outdoor boxes, even the ones you don't punch through, should be caulked with a sealant labeled "weatherproof and conductive." Such sealants are available at electrical supply houses.

When mounting boxes on exterior walls or posts, use noncorroding screws, such as stainless steel or brass. Also, be sure to support all wire with cable straps every 4½ feet, and within 12 inches of every metal box. Secure PVC conduit no more than 4 feet from each box.

Hooking Up

Receptacles

The easiest way to extend wiring is to start at the last receptacle on a circuit. The only conductors to it are a black one to the brass terminal and a white one to the silver-colored terminal. If the circuit is grounded, there will also be three bare wires attached with a wire nut. They connect the box, the ground terminal, and the ground wire of the run. To extend the circuit, attach the black wire of the new run to the unused brass terminal and the white wire to the remaining silver-colored terminal. If the receptacle is grounded, the new section should also have a ground wire. Insert the bare ground wire of the new section into the wire nut connecting the other three ground wires. You may need a larger wire nut for this. The jumpers—or, as electricians call them, "pigtails"—between the wire nut, the box, and the receptacle may be green insulated wire or bare wire.

If you'll be starting your branch circuit from a box in the middle of a run, the wiring is the same except the second set of terminals on the receptacle will already be used. Remove one set of black and white wires and, using a wire nut, connect the black wire to the black wire of the new run and to a short piece of black wire. Attach the short wire back to the remaining brass terminal. Then connect the white wire to the new run and to a short piece of white wire. Attach the short white wire back to the silver-colored terminal.

Switches

Extra wiring can be added to a switch in the middle of an electrical run, but not

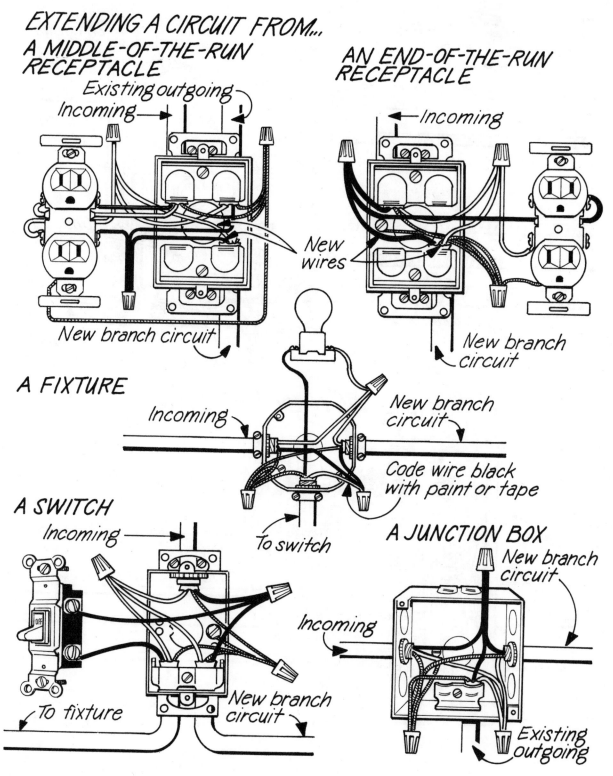

EXTENDING A CIRCUIT FROM...

A MIDDLE-OF-THE-RUN RECEPTACLE

Existing outgoing

Incoming

New wires

New branch circuit

AN END-OF-THE-RUN RECEPTACLE

Incoming

New branch circuit

A FIXTURE

Incoming

New branch circuit

Code wire black with paint or tape

To switch

A SWITCH

Incoming

To fixture

New branch circuit

A JUNCTION BOX

New branch circuit

Incoming

Existing outgoing

SERVICE PANEL WITH FUSES

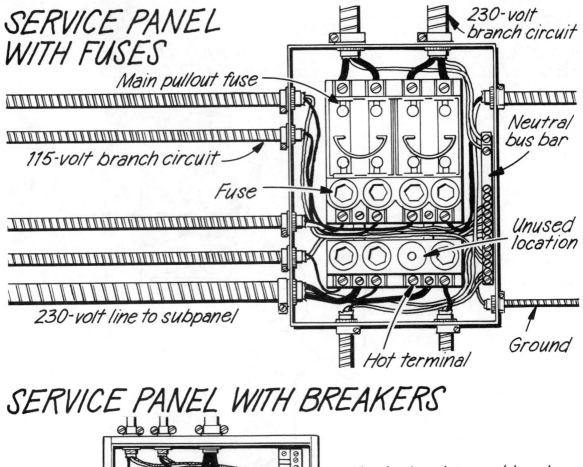

230-volt branch circuit

Main pullout fuse

Neutral bus bar

115-volt branch circuit

Fuse

Unused location

230-volt line to subpanel

Hot terminal

Ground

SERVICE PANEL WITH BREAKERS

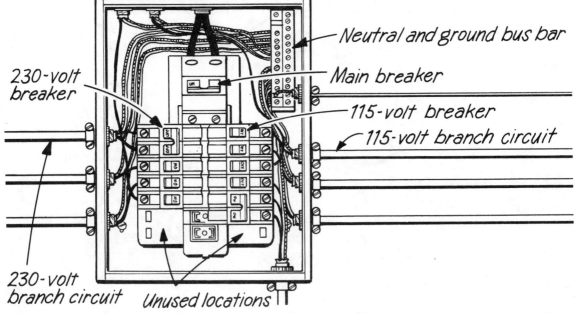

Neutral and ground bus bar

230-volt breaker

Main breaker

115-volt breaker

115-volt branch circuit

230-volt branch circuit

Unused locations

from a switch loop. If the switch is on a loop, one of the wires going to it will be black, the other will be white and should be coded black with paint or electrical tape. If the switch is in the middle of a run, both wires connected to it will be black. You must determine which of the two black wires carries the power from the service panel by shutting off the power, removing the switch from the box, restoring the power, then checking the two wires with a test light. The wire to the box will test hot whether the switch is on or off. Turn the power off again. Disconnect the black wire leading to the panel from its terminal, and attach it with a wire nut to the black wire of the new run and to a pigtail to the terminal. The white wire and the ground wire of the new run are attached to the two existing wire nuts, white to white, ground to ground.

Fixtures

As with a switch, a circuit can only be extended from a fixture in the middle of a run. If the fixture is in the middle of a run, one of the black wires will test hot, even if the switch is off. To extend the circuit, attach the new wires to the existing wire nuts. If the fixture has its own wire leads instead of terminal screws, you'll find the black fixture wire attached to the black switch wire with a wire nut. Nothing more will be added to that connection. There will be three other wire nut connections. Add the new white wire to the two existing white wires and add the new bare wire to the two existing bare wires. The last nut will contain a black wire and a white wire going back to the switch. This white wire should be coded black with paint or electrical tape. Add the new black wire to this connection.

Junction Boxes

If more than one circuit passes through the junction box, determine which one is the circuit you want to tap. First, have someone turn off the the house wiring. Next, remove the wire nuts from the black wires, making sure the exposed wires don't touch the box or any other wire. Have someone turn on all the circuits but the one you want to tap. Use a test light to determine which set of black wires has no current; those are the ones you want to connect the new black wire to. Add the new white wire to the white wires of the circuit you are tapping and add the new ground wire to the wire nut containing all the ground wires.

Service Panel

If you run a new circuit, instead of extending an existing circuit, you will have to attach the cable to the main panel. Adding a circuit to the existing service box is not difficult, but it requires turning off the power throughout the house. Even after you kill the power, the heavy service-entrance wires remain hot. This means you will be working on a panel that is live at two terminals. Usually these terminals are at the top of the panel, well away from the branch circuit terminals.

Each service-entrance wire carries 115 volts of electricity. The breakers are arranged in pairs. The first pair of breakers is served by one 115-volt leg, the second pair by the other 115-volt leg, and so on. This is so a double-width breaker can pick up 230 volts to serve appliances that require it.

Attach the new circuit to an unused fuse or breaker location on the panel. Circuit breaker panels usually have extra spaces at the bottom of the panel. But, if yours doesn't, you can replace single breakers with two half-size breakers of the same amperage.

Installing a new breaker is easy. Remove a knock-out from the box as near as possible to the new breaker location. Put the cable connector over the new cable, pull the cable into the service box, screw the connector in place and tighten it over the cable. Attach the new white wire and bare wire to the neutral and ground bus bar. If you are installing a GFI breaker, it will have a curly white wire to attach to the neutral and ground bus bar. Attach the black wire to the breaker and snap the breaker in place. Restore power to the house.

If your main panel has fuses instead of breakers and there are extra spaces for fuses, the job is simple. You'll find the hot terminal below the fuse socket. The neutral terminal, as in a breaker box, is on the grounding box. The new cable enters and is connected to the box in the same way as in a breaker box. Fuse boxes can have anywhere from two to six main pullout fuses. Pull all of them before working on the box to make sure all power to the house is off.

Lighting Design

Lighting can play an important role in creating a cohesive design for your yard. Many people think of home outdoor lighting as being strictly for security and safety—to discourage burglars, prevent tripping on the front stoop, and allow you to see the keyhole when you enter the front door. But outdoor lighting can do much more than that. Using the darkness as your canvas, you can paint with light, using color, intensity, and direction to emphasize what is most beautiful in your yard and de-emphasize what is not. Most important, outdoor lighting allows you

to use your yard at night. If you have a wonderful yard, why abandon it when the sun goes down?

As you design your outdoor lighting scheme, remember that landscape lighting is a matter of personal taste, just like choosing a fabric for a sofa or a color for a room. The most important design considerations are what you like and dislike about your yard and what you like to do in your yard. Here are some things to consider.

What areas do you want to light to make them useful at night? This might include lighting for patios, paths, entrances, or garage doors. Perhaps you like to shoot baskets or play volleyball in the evening. Take note of any changes in level in your yard such as steps and terraces. People can walk on flat areas or gradual slopes without much light, but abrupt changes should be lit.

Then think about areas that you want to light simply because they are beautiful—a stately old tree, a garden pond, the texture of a stone or brick wall.

Equally important, think about the things you don't want to light. During the day you may have to look at those garbage cans, the back of your neighbor's house, or the swing set rusting in his yard, but at night, you can erase these things from view. (Speaking of neighbors, you'll want to make sure your lighting will not disturb adjacent property owners.)

The distant view is another consideration. Perhaps you overlook a town. Too much light will obliterate your night view of the city lights.

You can, of course, design your lighting to do different things at different times. Switches are inexpensive and can be used to zone your yard. Dimmers cost a few dollars more but allow you to create different moods. For an intimate dinner on the patio,

Outdoor light can take many forms. Cylindrical fixtures direct light onto a deck (above); their color, style, and location make them unobtrusive. The homemade garden light (top left) is unique, relatively inexpensive, and practical; wooden louvers mask the bulbs of the unit and direct the light downward. A commercial fixture mounted on a trio of posts serves as a curbside entry light (left); it is decorative as well as functional.

49

you want only a low light level. For a big outdoor party, more light encourages guests to wander around the yard. Dimmers enable you to have it both ways.

Think how your outdoor lighting will work when you are inside the house, looking out. In a cold climate, imagine how the yard looks covered with snow. Lighting can create dramatic winter views. Remember that the windows in a brightly lit room will act as mirrors, so be prepared to dim interior lights to view your yard at night.

Take time to observe the effects of sunlight. Note the shadows cast at various times of the day, and record the sun's position when you see an effect you like. This information is helpful when you aim your lighting fixtures. In a rural area with little outdoor lighting, spend time observing your yard during a full moon.

One more general design tip: It's usually best to conceal outdoor lighting fixtures and wiring. There are exceptions, but generally, the effect is much more magical if you emphasize the subject rather than the light source.

Now it's time to experiment with light. Use a mechanic's "trouble light" fitted with a shade of aluminum foil or cardboard and several light bulbs (25, 60, and 100 watts). You may need an extension cord. Move around your yard, experimenting with different positions and light intensities. Drive wooden stakes in the ground where you want to place fixtures, and mark the wattage of bulb you liked on each stake. On a scale drawing of your yard, mark the locations you want to light to give you an overview of the lighting plan and to help you calculate how much wire to buy.

One thing you'll notice is you need much less wattage outdoors than indoors. This is because the outdoor environment is so dark

that it takes only a little light to create dramatic contrasts. As a rule of thumb, no residential outdoor light should ever exceed 150 watts.

Lighting Techniques

There are several lighting techniques you may employ. Keep these in mind while you are experimenting with the trouble light.

■ Uplighting is most dramatic, because it is never found in nature. Fixtures set in the ground and pointed up create a focal point—a majestic tree, the house facade, a statue. Uplighting is a practical style. The fixtures are set in the ground, where they are easy to hide and accessible when you need to change bulbs.

■ Downlighting is subtle, imitating nature. Place low-wattage lights high in tree canopies to mimic the effect of a full moon. Use slightly higher wattages and lower angles to emulate the morning sunlight. Downlighting can be difficult to install, since it must be elevated.

■ Contour lighting combines beauty and safety along a walkway. It consists of low-lying fixtures that illuminate limited spots of ground.

■ Area lighting floods specific outdoor areas with light—your patio, deck, or lawn, for example. The intensity of the light and the type of bulbs you use will be determined by what you want to do in an area. Lighting your patio for intimate evening entertaining requires soft, low-intensity lighting. For nighttime volleyball, you'll want floodlamps.

All the lighting techniques you use will fall into these four basic categories, though there are variations.

Grazing lighting, for example, brings out surface textures—the brick of your house, a stone wall, tree bark. Grazing lighting can be uplighting or downlighting. In crosslighting, two light beams cross to create interesting and subtle shadows. Crosslighting most often is downlighting, but it can be uplighting. It is usually done with diffuse light sources like broad floodlights.

Spotlighting is used to draw attention to a particular spot—a statue or sculpture, for example. A more subtle way to accomplish the same end is accent lighting, small fixtures placed near their object of attention. Silhouetting is yet another way to accent objects, especially those near a garden wall or fence. It works well for objects that derive their beauty more from their shape than from their color or texture. To silhouette, hide the fixture between the object and the wall or sink it in the ground with the light shining on the wall.

Choosing a Current

You can power your outdoor lighting with the same 120-volt current you use inside your house, you can install a transformer and use a 12-volt system, or you can combine the systems.

The 12-volt systems are relatively new and are touted as being safer and easier to install, as well as less expensive than 120-volt systems. While it is true that the least expensive lighting systems you can buy are 12-volt ones, that fact is that *good-quality* 12-volt fixtures (constructed of copper or corrosion-proof aluminum) will cost as much as their 120-volt counterparts. You won't need junction boxes and other 120-volt system hardware, and wire for 12-volt systems is less expensive than conduit and wire for 120 volts, but you will have to pay for a transformer. And replacement bulbs for 12-volt fixtures generally cost more than 120-volt ones.

Installation of 12-volt systems is considered safer because the voltage cannot kill you. Connections are simple to make. The only potentially dangerous part of the installation is connecting the transformer to 120-volt service (unless you purchase a system that just plugs into an outlet). But connecting it to the service is the only potentially dangerous part of wiring any electrical circuit, even if it's 230 volts.

One advantage the 12-volt system does offer the do-it-yourselfer is an exemption from permit requirements, since such a system is exempt from the NEC, which governs in most municipalities. The exemption also relieves you of the obligation to bury the wiring, though you'll surely want to avoid having it exposed. (All building codes require you to bury wiring for 120-volt systems.)

A disadvantage of the 12-volt system is that it can be used for lighting only—you can't include an outlet for an electric lawn mower or your portable radio. You can circumvent this shortcoming by running a 120-volt circuit to a junction box in the yard and locating an outlet and the 12-volt transformer there.

In planning your wiring, it's important to know that 12-volt systems are more sensitive to voltage drops caused by long runs. The longer the wire, the greater resistance. Solve this problem by using a heavier-gauge wire.

Lamps

Lamp is the technical term for what most people call a light bulb. Here are the most common lamps for outdoor use:

■ Incandescent lamps are popular for residential use because they give a warm, white light that is closest to natural light. Although incandescent lamps have the widest light spectrum, the one color they are weak in is the predominant outdoor color, green. Though bright incandescent light tends to make green foliage appear gray, it is the best light for flowers, particularly yellow flowers. Incandescent lamps, with or without quartz, are the only type you can use in 12-volt systems and they are the only kind that can be used with a dimmer. They are the cheapest lamps to buy, but they need replacement most often and use more electricity than other types of lamps.

■ Tungsten-halogen lamps, also known as quartz-halogen, are brighter versions of incandescent lamps. They're available for 12-volt and 120-volt systems.

■ Mercury vapor lamps are one of several types of very efficient high-intensity discharge lamps. Each of the several types of mercury vapor lamps available gives off a different hue. Most commonly used in garden lighting are clear lamps, which cast a blue light. This light renders green foliage well but not the color of most flowers.

■ Metal halide and high-pressure sodium are two other high-intensity discharge lamps that are used in the garden, although less commonly than mercury vapor. Few people like their effect on color.

Fixtures

Choosing fixtures should be the last step in designing your outdoor lighting. The fixtures you select should depend on the job you want them to do, the lamps you have decided to use, and of course, your personal taste and budget.

The most expensive, most durable, and to many people, most attractive fixtures are made of copper. The least expensive, least durable, and least attractive fixtures are made of plastic. In between are corrosion-resistant aluminum fixtures, which are less expensive than copper and more durable than plastic.

A lamp holder is the simplest fixture—it's just a socket or two attached to a junction box. It provides no way of directing or shielding the light or protecting the lamp. A better choice is a bullet light, which shields the lamp to cut glare and protect it from debris and water.

A fixture on a stake is another alternative for uplighting. Easy to install and adjust, it is best hidden in a garden bed where people won't trip on it and you won't have to mow around it.

A post light is often used at an entrance or driveway or along a walk. Between 3 and 8 feet tall, it encloses the lamp in a translucent glass or plastic globe to cut down glare. A bollard is a type of post light, usually about 3 feet tall, that encloses the lamp behind a plastic or glass panel built into the post itself.

The mushroom fixture and the pagoda fixture are the two popular choices for low-lying contour lighting, such as you would use to illuminate a garden path. Both get their names from their shapes.

The well light is the best choice for concealed uplighting. Installed flush with the ground and protected by a grille, it can be walked on or mowed over without damage.

A recessed stair light is built right into stair risers or walls. Obviously, such fixtures need to be installed while you are building your garden steps.

These are just a few general categories. Fixtures are available in tremendous variety. The best approach is to design your lighting scheme, and then shop for the fixtures that will meet your needs.

PROJECT
DECK LIGHT

Designed with a deck in mind, this elegant light housing conceals an ordinary 120-volt weatherproof light fixture. Made of rot-resistant cedar or redwood, the housing's shape is very postlike, and the diagonal grooves complement any pattern of decking. The unit is easy to mount on the edge of a deck, on a railing, or even beside a garden path or step.

To make the housing, you cut rows of grooves into opposing faces of the housing parts. The depth of the grooves just slightly exceeds half the material's thickness, so holes are created wherever grooves in opposing faces intersect. Light streaming through these diamond-shaped holes produces a subtle dappled pattern, enough to illuminate your path, but not so much as to be intrusively bright.

Although a 120-volt fixture is used with the housing shown, you can easily fit the housing over a 12-volt fixture.

Shopping List
1 pc. 1 × 6 × 6' cedar
2 #6 × 1" brass wood screws
resorcinol glue

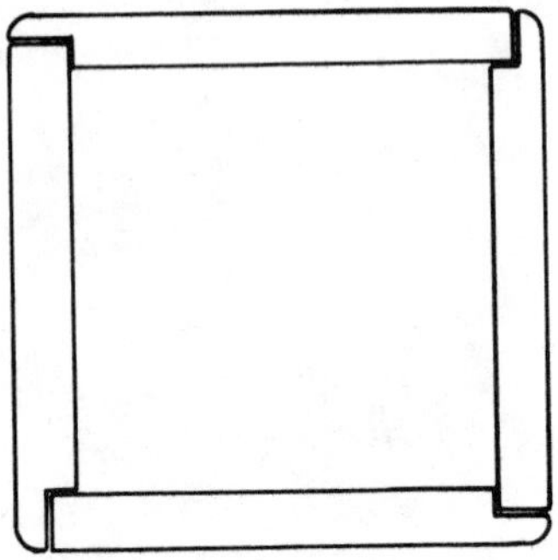

Panel

Top

Stops

Top View

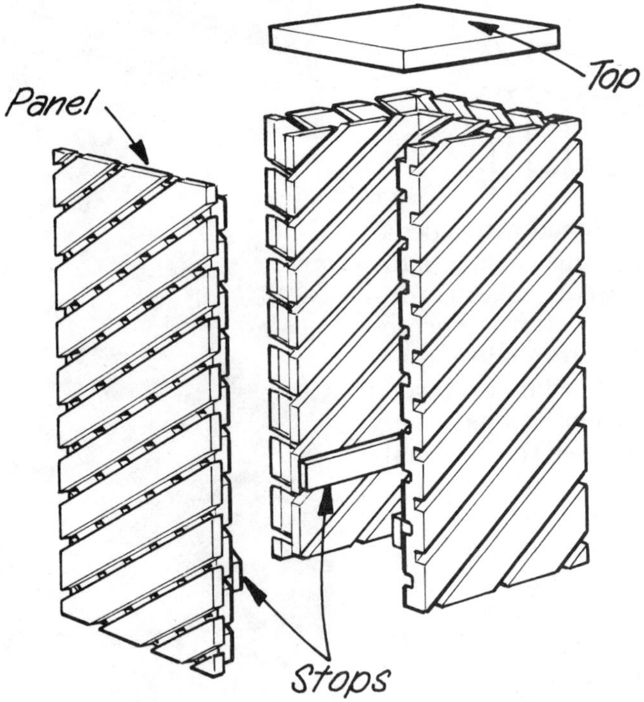

Cutting List

Number	Piece	Dimensions	Material
4	Panels	¾″ × 5½″ × 15″	cedar
1	Top	¾″ × 5⅛″ × 5⅛″	cedar
4	Stops	¼″ × ¾″ × 4⅞″	scrap

1. **Cut and rabbet the panels.** Cut the four panels to size. Make a ¾-inch-wide, ⅜-inch-deep rabbet along the left side and along the top of each panel.

2. **Cut the inside grooves.** The diagonal grooves are cut on a radial arm saw fitted with a dado cutter. Set the cutter to make a ¼-inch groove slightly more than ⅜-inch deep, and set the arm to a 30-degree angle to your right. Position a panel against the saw's fence with the rabbeted side closest to you. Cut a series of grooves, 1³/₁₆ inches apart.

3. **Cut the top.** This piece will fit into the rabbets cut in the top edges of the panels.

4. Assemble the fixture. Make the four stops. Assemble the panels and top with resorcinol glue. Glue the stops inside the assembly, 1¾ inches above the bottom edges.

Secure the stops with tape until the glue dries. To clamp the assembly while the glue sets, wrap large rubber bands around it or use a band clamp.

5. Cut the outside grooves. Crank up your radial arm saw to clear the assembled housing. Then lower the dado cutter to cut a groove just slightly deeper than ⅜ inch.

Cut the first groove, starting at the upper left corner. Roll the housing 90 degrees and make another cut, again starting at the upper left corner. Before you roll the unit again,

make a second cut in this panel, this one starting in the kerf left by the cut on the first side. Now roll the housing 90 degrees. Make the cut beginning at the upper left corner. Make two additional cuts, each beginning in a kerf at the edge of the housing.

Continue this process until you've completed all the grooves.

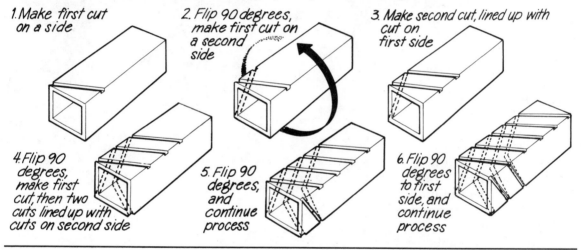

1. Make first cut on a side

2. Flip 90 degrees, make first cut on a second side

3. Make second cut, lined up with cut on first side

4. Flip 90 degrees, make first cut, then two cuts lined up with cuts on second side

5. Flip 90 degrees, and continue process

6. Flip 90 degrees to first side, and continue process

6. Sand the housing. Use a belt sander to sand the housing and round over all edges.

7. Secure the housing to the lamp. Mount a weatherproof electrical box and a lamp holder in position, wire them up, install the bulb, and fit the housing over it. Secure the housing by driving screws through the sides, tightening them against the base of the fixture.

To install the housing at grade in the yard, use a concrete block as a base. Set the block into the ground, and bring the under-ground electrical cable up through one of its holes. Ready an electrical box by putting long machine screws through its mounting holes and threading nuts on them; the nuts should be on the inside of the box. Fill the block holes with concrete. Set the electrical box on the wet concrete and push the heads of the screws down into it. After three days, tighten the nuts, wire and mount the lamp, and install the housing.

PROJECT LIGHT POST

This basic but beautiful light post is flexible enough in design to fit into any yard-lighting scheme. As shown, it is a solitary sentinel. But it can easily be adapted to other lighting requirements by altering its height, its location, or the direction in which it casts its light.

Post one by the street to mark your entryway. Let it announce your house number, and by its light, signal your welcome to guests. Set several by the pathway to illuminate a nighttime stroll. Build one or more into a deck railing, or post the boundaries of a patio or terrace.

Although the light post shown houses a 12-volt fixture, you can use a 120-volt fixture quite easily. An interesting twist to the 12-volt option is that we built this light post using an automotive fixture: a backup light available at any auto parts store. Less costly than a fixture designed for household use, the automotive kind is nevertheless weather-resistant, durable, and 12 volt.

Shopping List

1 pc. 4 × 4 × 4' pressure-treated pine
1 pc. 1 × 6 × 1' cedar
3 pcs. 1 × 4 × 8' cedar
plexiglass as needed
1 automotive backup light fixture and bulb
6-1½'' brass wood screws
6d finishing nails
12-volt wire as needed
waterproof glue

56

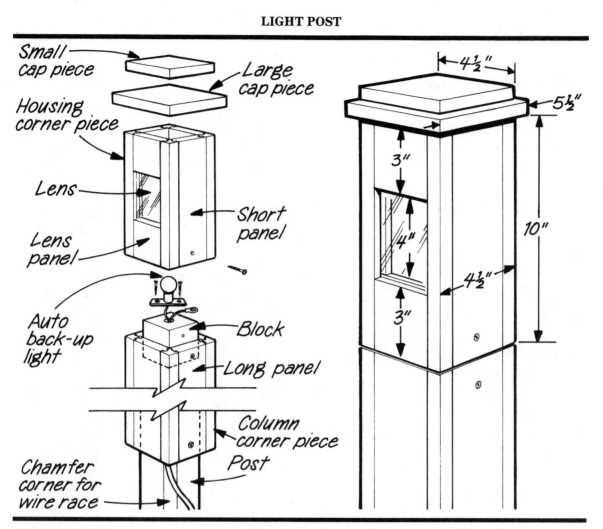

Small cap piece

Large cap piece

Housing corner piece

Lens

Lens panel

Short panel

Auto back-up light

Block

Long panel

Column corner piece

Post

Chamfer corner for wire race

4½"

5½"

3"

4"

10"

4½"

3"

Cutting List

Number	Piece	Dimensions	Material
4	Column corner pieces	¾″ × ¾″ × 38″	cedar
4	Housing corner pieces	¾″ × ¾″ × 10″	cedar
4	Column panels	¾″ × 3¼″ × 38″	cedar
1–4	Housing panels	¾″ × 3¼″ × 10″	cedar
1	Post	3″ × 3″ × 24″	pressure-treated pine
1	Block	3″ × 3″ × 4″	pressure-treated pine
2–8	Lens panels	¾″ × 3¼″ × 3″	cedar
1–4	Lenses	¼″ × 3¼″ × 4″	plexiglass
1	Large cap	¾″ × 5½″ × 5½″	cedar
1	Small cap	¾″ × 4½″ × 4½″	cedar

1. **Cut all the parts to size.** Choose a durable, rot-resistant wood for the light post. We used clear cedar, but redwood is also a good choice. For a striking appearance, you can mix woods, using a dark stock for the corners and light wood for the panels.

Cut the parts to the sizes listed. This will yield a light post that's 4 feet tall. If you want a taller or shorter unit, adjust the lengths of the long corner pieces and the long panels accordingly. All the other parts stay at the dimensions indicated on the cutting list.

2. **Groove the corner pieces.** Using a table saw fitted with a dado cutter, plow $\frac{1}{4}$-inch-wide, $\frac{1}{8}$-inch-deep grooves in two sides of each corner piece, as shown.

If you don't have a dado blade, you can easily cut this groove with a standard table saw blade, which cuts a kerf about $\frac{1}{8}$ inch wide. Set the depth of cut to $\frac{1}{8}$ inch high. Set the fence $\frac{1}{2}$ inch away from the *outside* of the blade. Run the stock through, turn it around, and run it through again, widening the kerf. This technique will ensure that the groove is centered on the stock.

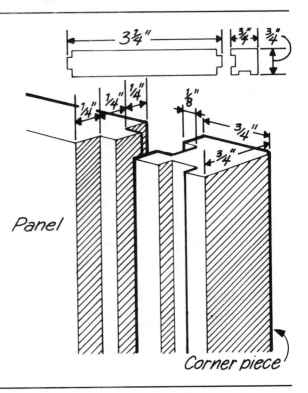

Panel

Corner piece

3. **Cut tongues on the panels.** Machine a $\frac{1}{8} \times \frac{1}{4}$-inch tongue on both edges of each panel.

To do this, set the depth of cut to $\frac{1}{4}$ inch. Then set the fence practically against the blade—be sure you have a wooden facing attached to the fence before you do this. Lay the panel face down on the saw table and slide it along the fence, cutting a $\frac{1}{8}$-inch-wide, $\frac{1}{4}$-inch-deep rabbet along the edge. Flip the panel and cut a rabbet along the opposite face, completing the tongue. Form tongues on the edges of all the panels.

4. **Chamfer the post and bore the block.** You should have ripped both pieces of 4 × 4 pressure-treated pine to 3 inches square.

Bore the block used to join the column and the fixture housing with a $\frac{1}{2}$-inch-diameter hole through the center.

Rip a ½-inch-wide chamfer along one edge of the 24-inch-long post to form a race to run the wiring through when the light post is assembled.

5. **Glue up the column.** Dry assemble the corner pieces and the panels forming the column to check that the joints fit correctly and to rehearse the gluing-up routine. Apply waterproof glue to the mating edges of the pieces and reassemble them. To ensure that the column assembly will be square, you can use the post and the block as forms. Wrap them in waxed paper to ensure that they don't inadvertently get glued inside the column. Use band clamps or rubber bands cut from an old inner tube.

6. **Make the fixture housing.** Before you make the housing, you must decide how many lenses it will have and what their character will be. The lenses can be clear, colored, or frosted, according to your personal preference. And you can have a single lens (for unidirectional lighting), or two, three, or four lenses (for omnidirectional lighting). For each plexiglass lens, you must cut two 3-inch-long wooden lens panels.

Having made your design decision, cut the plexiglass lenses and the wooden lens panels.

Assemble the fixture housing much the way you did the column. Fit 3-inch wooden lens panels above and below each lens and a 10-inch panel on each blank side. Glue up the assembly, insert one of the 3 × 3 pieces inside (wrap it in waxed paper first) to keep the assembly square, and apply band clamps or inner-tube bands.

After the glue sets, nail the large cap in place with 6d finishing nails. Center the small cap atop the large cap and nail it in place.

7. **Wire the light post.** The automotive light fixture will have only one wire connected to it, which may mystify you at first. But remember that in an auto, all the wiring is grounded to the chassis. To wire up the fixture, connect the black (hot) conductor to the fixture's pigtail and ground the fixture by passing one of the mounting screws through a loop in the white (neutral) conductor.

Pull the wire through the column and the drilled block. Fasten the block in the top of the column with brass screws. Two inches of the block should project from the column. Mount the fixture and wire it up.

8. **Install the post.** Plant the 24-inch length of 3 × 3, leaving 6 to 8 inches of it above grade. Run the 12-volt power lines to this stub post. Connect the leads in the column to the power lines, lay the wires along the chamfered corner of the post, and slide the column down over it. Secure the column to the post with several 1½-inch brass wood screws.

Test the light, then slide the fixture housing onto the block. Fasten the top to the block with two brass wood screws.

HOW TO DOWNLIGHT COVER

This cedar fixture cover has a rustic simplicity that makes it perfect for mounting on a wooden retaining wall. You may want to build several to accent the garden or strategically light garden steps.

The light source used with this cover is a 12-volt automobile license plate fixture, which looks obviously automotive with its chrome housing. The wooden cover thus is appropriate. Since these fixtures can vary considerably in size, it's a good idea to buy them before building the cedar covers. The cover shown was scaled to a fixture 2⅛ inches wide.

1. Layout the triangular sides and cut them out. The cover will weather best if the grain runs vertically on the sides.
2. Cut and install the two cleats, each about ¾ × 3½ inches. Near the bottom of each cleat, drill a pilot hole for a 1¼-inch #8 galvanized wood screw. Glue and nail the cleats to the sides, using 3d finishing nails. Position the cleats so the screw holes will be just below the edge of the top, so you'll be able to reach the hole with a screwdriver to install the cover.
3. Cut and install the top. Bevel one end of the top so its fits flush against the wall. The top overhangs the sides about ¼ inch all around.
4. Install the light fixture. Connect the black conductor of the power cable to the fixture's pigtail. Connect the white conductor to the fixture's housing by looping it tightly around a mounting screw. Drive the mounting screws directly into the wall.
5. Mount the wooden cover, making sure its top is high enough to allow removing the metal fixture cap to change the bulb.

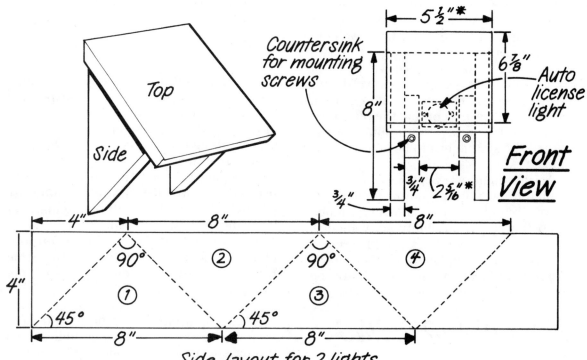

Side layout for 2 lights

**Adjust these dimensions as necessary to clear light fixture*

Materials List

Number	Piece	Dimensions	Material
2	Sides	$3/4'' \times 4'' \times 8''$	cedar
2	Cleats	$3/4'' \times 3/4'' \times 3 1/2''$	cedar
1	Top	$3/4'' \times 5 1/2'' \times 6 7/8''$	cedar

Hardware

1 12-volt automobile license plate fixture
2 #8 × 1 1/4-inch galvanized wood screws
2 1/2-inch galvanized wood screws
3d galvanized finishing nails
resorcinol glue

Outdoor Plumbing

When it's time to wash the car, water the lawn and garden, or bring fresh water to your animals, an outdoor hydrant or two can save the mess and inconvenience of stringing garden hoses all over the yard. Outdoor plumbing is not much different from indoor plumbing, except that the pipe must be suitable for burial and, in much of the country, the system has to be able to withstand a freeze.

You have quite a few options when choosing pipe to bury for an outdoor plumbing project. Your choice should be determined by building codes, durability, convenience, and price. Before you bury any pipe, make sure the materials and methods you choose comply with local codes. Price should be the least important consideration. Your in-

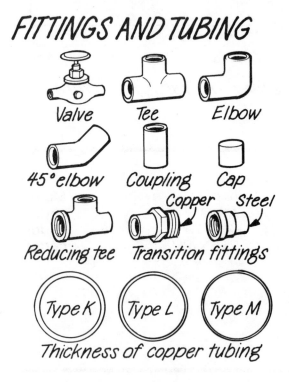

FITTINGS AND TUBING

Valve   Tee   Elbow

45° elbow   Coupling   Cap

Copper   Steel

Reducing tee   Transition fittings

Type K   Type L   Type M

Thickness of copper tubing

vestment in materials will be small compared with your labor.

Copper Pipe

For outdoor plumbing, copper tubing is the best material. It's also the most expensive. Copper tubing, used as described here, meets or exceeds the requirements of the Universal Plumbing Code, from which most local codes are drawn.

For pipe that is to be buried in the ground, use type K; intended for underground use (though it's suitable for interior piping, too), it has the thickest walls of the available types of copper tubing. For exposed outdoor plumbing—for instance, the vertical pipe that runs to an outdoor hydrant—type L copper is required by most codes.

Both of these types of copper tubing can be bought either as rigid hard-temper tubing or bendable soft-temper tubing. Rigid tubing is available in 20-foot lengths, though some dealers may sell you a shorter length. Soft tubing comes in 60-foot coils. For outdoor jobs, the soft tubing is handy: It's forgiving about being bent, and you can install runs up to 60 feet long without joints. In most situations, ½-inch tubing is suitable.

Join copper pipe and fittings by sweating the joints with solder. It's easy, though you do need some special tools and supplies, including steel wool or emery cloth, a container of noncorrosive flux, lead-free solid-core wire solder, and a hand-held propane torch.

Prepare the joint. First, cut the copper pipe to length with a tubing cutter and remove any burrs from the pipe end with the reamer on the cutter. Polish the end of the pipe and the inside of the fitting with steel wool or emery cloth, to remove oxidized copper. With

Outdoor plumbing may connote only a backyard hydrant to facilitate garden watering. But don't overlook water gardens, garden pools, and decorative patio fountains, all of which necessitate the installation of plumbing.

CUTTING TUBING

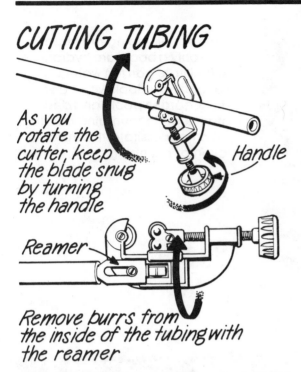

As you rotate the cutter, keep the blade snug by turning the handle

Handle

Reamer

Remove burrs from the inside of the tubing with the reamer

SWEATING COPPER PIPE

Polish pipe with steel wool

Brush on flux

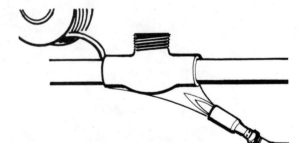

Apply solder to the joint, opposite the flame

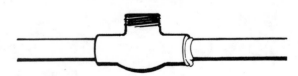

Check that solder has no gaps

most fluxes, this is very important; if the mating surfaces aren't shiny clean, the solder won't adhere properly and you'll have pinhole leaks.

Brush flux onto the polished surfaces. A nice even, thin coating of flux is what you want. Don't apply too much; it may ruin the joint. (And don't bother polishing or fluxing any joints except the one you are working on; the copper will oxidize by the time you're ready to solder them.)

Slide the cleaned and fluxed pipe into the fitting. If you have a helper, have him hold the pipe in place with a gloved hand (it will get hot). If you are working alone, go ahead and put a hanger or two on the pipe to hold it in place while you work. Make sure the pipe fits straight into the fitting.

Sweat the joint. Fire up your torch. The flame is hottest about 1 inch from the nozzle. Play the flame over the fitting, not the pipe. The pipe will get hot, but you want the fitting hotter than the pipe.

When the flux starts to bubble and smoke, remove the flame and touch the solder to the fitting. If the solder melts, the joint is hot enough. Feed solder into the side of the joint opposite the flame, until a rim of solder appears completely around the joint. When this happens, the solder has completely filled the joint by capillary attraction. It works for vertical as well as horizontal joints. Solder will defy gravity and run up into a hot joint.

Once the joint is made, take a close look to make sure there's solder all the way around the fitting. Black spots in the silver ring of solder are usually flux (which can be wiped off), but sometimes they are gaps in the joint. If you suspect gaps, it's best to resweat the joint. Heat the joint and pull it apart. Reburnish the pieces, apply flux, and so forth, repeating the entire sweating process.

PVC Pipe

An alternative to copper is polyvinyl chloride (PVC) pipe, which is easy to work with and less expensive than copper. As with copper, ½-inch pipe should be sufficient for most outdoor jobs. Some codes don't allow PVC to be used as supply pipe; those that do usually require a grade called Schedule 80 PVC pipe. ("Schedule" is terminology used by the plumbing code to indicate wall thickness; Schedule 40 pipe, intended for waste, has a specific wall thickness, while Schedule 80 pipe, intended for water supply, has the thicker walls that a pressured water-supply system requires.) PVC has some practical advantages. You don't need any special tools. A hacksaw will cut it, and joints are made up with a special cement. Though it's a relatively new material, there's little reason to think PVC won't last indefinitely when buried.

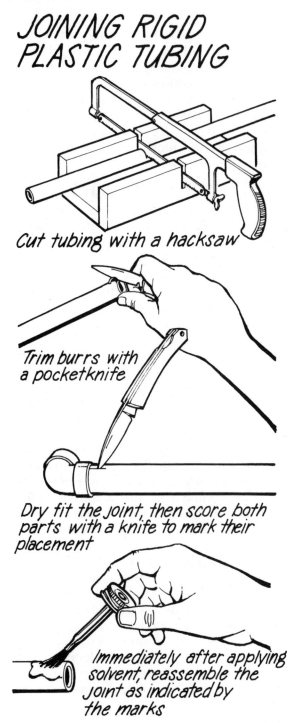

JOINING RIGID PLASTIC TUBING

Cut tubing with a hacksaw

Trim burrs with a pocketknife

Dry fit the joint, then score both parts with a knife to mark their placement

Immediately after applying solvent, reassemble the joint as indicated by the marks

Another type of plastic pipe is flexible polybutylene tubing. Easy to work with, it can be cut with a sturdy knife, and joints are made up with compression fittings. Polybutylene has a couple of advantages for an outdoor job: It'll take some freezing (it stretches instead of bursting), and it bends easily around curves. Unfortunately, some codes don't permit its use.

Outdoor Hydrants

There are essentially three ways to install an outdoor hydrant. Your climate and your winter watering needs will decide which one will work best for you.

If you live in a part of the country that seldom, if ever, gets a hard freeze, the job is relatively simple. You dig a trench for the supply line (check local codes for minimum depth), lay the pipe, then fit the faucet to one end and connect the other to the water supply.

In colder climates, you'd do better to install a system that can be drained through a bleeder valve. To do this, dig a trench that slopes toward your basement wall. Fit the faucet to the pipe. Inside the basement, install a bleeder valve. When the cold season comes, shut off the bleeder valve, then remove its integral plug and bleed the hydrant's supply pipe (you'll have to open the faucet in the yard to allow the water to drain from the pipe). This way, you have a system that won't be hurt by a freeze. The drawback is that it can't be used during a freeze, either.

If you need a year-round freezeproof system, here's how it's done: Dig a trench from your basement wall to the hydrant location. The trench bottom must be below the frost line. Dig about a foot deeper at the hydrant location, and put gravel into this deeper section. Connect the line to the water supply, then install what's variously known as a freezeless hydrant or a yard hydrant.

A yard hydrant is a one-piece unit, from 2 to 5 feet long. When you lift the lever at the top of the hydrant, a long stem inside the casing pulls up a stopper that's situated below frost level. When you push the lever down, the water flow is shut off, and the water left in the pipe drains out through an opening in the bottom of the hydrant and into the gravel.

One of the nice things about a yard hydrant, regardless of your climate, is that the unit is self-contained and self-supporting. The stem is a ¾-inch galvanized steel pipe, sturdy enough to withstand the rigors of outdoor living without additional reinforcement. A copper or PVC pipe rising from the ground would need to be bolstered by a steel or wooden post.

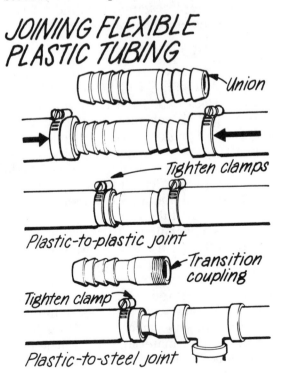

JOINING FLEXIBLE PLASTIC TUBING

Union

Tighten clamps

Plastic-to-plastic joint

Transition coupling

Tighten clamp

Plastic-to-steel joint

PROJECT
HYDRANT WITH DUCK-BOARDS

As you develop your yard into a space for outdoor living, you are likely to discover you need a convenient watering spot. Perhaps you want to be able to get a drink during volleyball without trekking into the house. Maybe you want to fill the kids' wading pool or water the garden without laying hose 50 feet from the house or garage. Is this leisure living or firefighter training?

Well, bringing water out into the yard is not hard to do. The setup here is simple but flexible. Using a yard hydrant allows you to bury the supply line below the frost line for your area and leave the water turned on year-round. The hydrant's valve is at the base of its stem (so it is below the frost line and won't freeze), and any water left in the stem when the valve is closed

drains out, so it won't freeze either. A bleeder valve, located where the outdoor line taps into your home's water-supply system, allows you to shut off water to the line and drain it, when and if you ever need to.

The only drawback to the backyard hydrant is the water hole that tends to

develop around it. The grass drowns, the water puddles, mud appears.

No such worries with this setup. Surrounding the hydrant is a duckboard minideck. Set on a gravel base, the duckboard provides clean footing by eliminating puddles and mud.

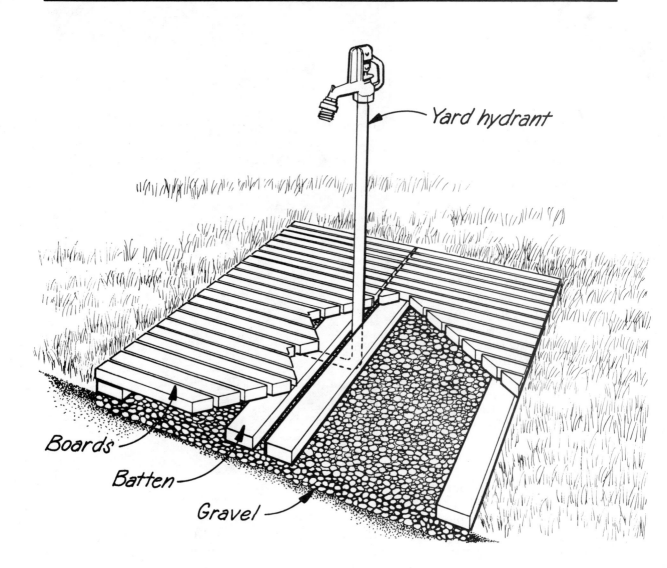

Yard hydrant

Boards

Batten

Gravel

Cutting List

Number	Piece	Dimensions	Material
25	Boards	1½″ × 1½″ × 45″	pressure-treated pine
2	Boards	1½″ × 1½″ × 21½″	pressure-treated pine
4	Battens	1½″ × 3½″ × 48″	pressure-treated pine

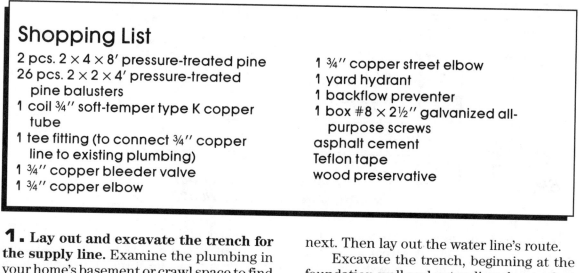

Shopping List

2 pcs. 2 × 4 × 8' pressure-treated pine
26 pcs. 2 × 2 × 4' pressure-treated
    pine balusters
1 coil ¾" soft-temper type K copper
    tube
1 tee fitting (to connect ¾" copper
    line to existing plumbing)
1 ¾" copper bleeder valve
1 ¾" copper elbow

1 ¾" copper street elbow
1 yard hydrant
1 backflow preventer
1 box #8 × 2½" galvanized all-
    purpose screws
asphalt cement
Teflon tape
wood preservative

1. **Lay out and excavate the trench for the supply line.** Examine the plumbing in your home's basement or crawl space to find a spot to tap into a supply line. Next, select the spot where your line to the outdoors will penetrate the foundation wall. Mark the spot on both the inside and the outside.

Establish the location of the hydrant next. Then lay out the water line's route.

Excavate the trench, beginning at the foundation wall and extending about a foot beyond the location of the new hydrant. Exact depth doesn't matter, so long as the trench slopes gently toward the basement wall. A trenching machine, available at rental centers, is usually the best tool for this job.

2. **Drill through the wall.** With a carbide bit, drill through the basement wall. With a star drill or cold chisel, open the hole to accommodate ¾-inch tubing.

3. **Lay the tubing.** Type K is intended for underground installations. Use the flexible soft-temper form. You can lay 60 feet of tubing without joints. Moreover, you can snake the tubing a bit in the trench—give it some slack, in other words—to accommodate settling.

Lay the copper tubing in the trench. Push one end through the hole in the foundation wall and feed enough tubing into the basement to allow you to make the connection to the supply. At the hydrant end, cut the tubing.

4. **Install the hydrant.** Sweat an elbow onto the tubing, then sweat a transition fitting in place, so you can join the threaded galvanized pipe of the hydrant to the copper tubing. (Be sure to use the proper dielectric fitting for this transition, so the mating of copper and galvanized steel doesn't produce galvanic corrosion.) Wrap Teflon tape around the threads of the hydrant, then turn it into the transition fitting. Temporarily brace the hydrant until you backfill the hole.

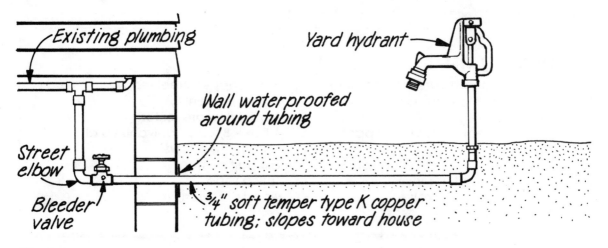

Existing plumbing

Yard hydrant

Wall waterproofed around tubing

Street elbow

Bleeder valve

¾" soft temper type K copper tubing; slopes toward house

5. **Connect the new line to the water supply.** In the basement, sweat a bleeder valve onto the end of the new tubing. Be sure the valve is at the lowest point on the new line. Ensure that the arrow on the valve is pointing toward the water source. Sweat a street elbow onto the bleeder valve. A street elbow has one female end and one male end. Fit a length of copper tubing–long enough to connect to the supply line–into the female end, and sweat it.

Shut off the water in the house and cut into the supply line at the appropriate location. Install a tee fitting in that line, then sweat your new line to the tee. Install strapping to support the new line.

Turn the water back on and check all your joints for leaks. If there is a leak, you'll have to shut off the water, drain the line, and resweat the leaky joint.

6. **Close up the various holes to complete the plumbing installation.** Start by mortaring the hole in the foundation around the pipe. In the trench, coat the exposed part of the basement wall with asphalt cement to waterproof it. Now backfill the trench.

Around the faucet, where the duckboard will be installed, compact each layer of backfill to minimize settling. If your soil is particularly heavy, you may be wise to backfill around the faucet with gravel to promote improved drainage.

7. **Cut the duckboard parts to size.** The duckboard should be built of pressure-treated wood or a naturally rot-resistant wood, such as redwood, cypress, or cedar. We used 2×2 deck balusters–they're readily available at any lumberyard–for decking. These balusters have rounded edges, which are kind to bare feet and less prone to splinter. The

48-inch balusters have 45-degree miters on both ends, so they must be trimmed.

Cut 25 of the 26 balusters to 45 inches. From the remaining baluster, cut two pieces, each 21¾ inches long. Cut four 4-foot lengths of 2×4. After you cut the wood, apply a generous amount of a water-repellent wood preservative.

8. **Assemble the duckboard.** Lay out the 2 × 2 decking, as shown, positioning the pieces about ⅜ inch apart. Note the location of the two short 2 × 2 strips. Lay the 2 × 4 battens in place. Using 2½-inch galvanized all-purpose screws, fasten the two end battens flush along the ends of the 2 × 2s. Drive the screws through the battens into the boards.

Now install the two middle battens. Position them so their inside edges are flush with the ends of the two short 2 × 2s. This leaves space for the faucet pipe.

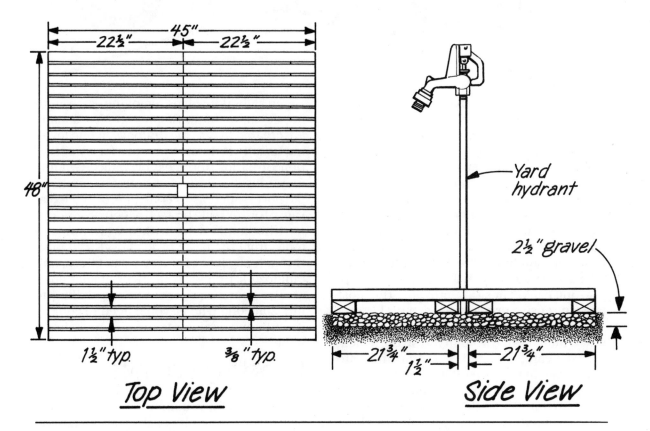

Top View

Side View

9. **Cut the duckboard in half.** Turn the assembled duckboard over and strike a line across the 2 × 2s, midway between the two inner battens. Cut the duckboard in two along this line.

10. **Prepare the base and install the duckboard around the faucet.** Excavate a 4-foot-square area around the faucet. Dig about 4 inches, and backfill with 2½ inches of gravel. Compact the gravel. Set the duckboard in place and settle it into the gravel.

ALTERING THE LANDSCAPE 3

Now that you have mapped out your outdoor living needs, you may realize you need to move the earth around or perhaps do some masonry work to achieve the yard you want. If your plans call for grading or any other form of earth moving, a retaining wall, a patio or walk, or a pond, this chapter will tell you what you need to know.

Landscaping work conjures images of pure, hard labor. It is true, some of these projects—building a stone wall or undertaking major grading work, for instance, require a strong back. These are probably the most labor-intensive projects you can undertake.

But landscape construction involves much more than the ability to swing a pick. It takes careful planning and an intimate understanding of the natural forces that affect your site. Most important, you'll probably be changing the pathways water takes to drain from your site. If you change them without a thorough understanding of what you are doing, you might find you have created a swamp in your backyard or a pond in your basement.

Grading

Grading is the process of creating a smooth landscape that is level or sloping.

Essentially, it involves removing earth, adding earth, or both. Sloping grades usually are created to provide drainage, while leveling usually is done to prepare for construction of patios, terraces, or walks. Grading may also be done for more specialized purposes, such as to control erosion, excavate pools, or build protective berms or ridges.

Grading is done with a wide range of tools, from the basic pick, shovel, and rake, through all sizes of tractors, backhoes, and bulldozers. Unless you are a proficient operator of heavy equipment or are willing to hire someone who is, you'll need to confine your grading projects to the pick-and-shovel scale.

Grading Permits

Most likely, you do not need a building permit for any grading work you can handle with a pick and shovel. Most municipal ordinances don't require permits for excavations of less than 5 feet or fills less than 3 feet high, requiring less than 5 cubic yards of soil.

But for anything more than that, ordinances may require you to submit plans and specifications, secure a permit, and allow inspections. These ordinances prevent grading that causes erosion or undercuts exist-

Your home landscape is defined as much by the man-made elements as by the "landscaping." Plantings alone won't do it. The ashlar stone wall and steps and the flagstone patio (top), the wood-and-flagstone walk and steps (left), and the tiered retaining walls (above) are essential to their respective landscapes.

73

ing foundations. Whatever the size of your project though, it certainly doesn't hurt to check in with your local building inspector before you start.

Also, before you start digging you'll want to make sure your shovel won't strike anything it shouldn't. Check your deed to see if any utility easements run through where you want to grade. If in doubt, check with gas, water, electric, and even cable television companies. They usually will stake out rights-of-way for you at no charge to avoid the possibility of having you cut a cable or pipe. And don't forget about your own utilities.

You'll have to consider your neighbors, too. Because grading changes drainage, you must make sure you're not diverting water into your neighbor's yard or a public roadway.

If you have doubts about your grading plan, get professional advice—from municipal officials, Soil Conservation Service advisers, or a professional engineer.

Cut and Fill

There are two kinds of grading operations —cutting, which is the removal of soil, and filling, which is the addition of soil. Soils and earthwork techniques vary throughout the country, but certain principles are basic to all regions. The degree of possible slope is based on the angle of repose of the material that you are grading. Sand has the lowest angle of repose and rock the highest. Most soils are somewhere in between. Normal maximum angles for ordinary soil are 1 vertical foot to 1 horizontal foot (1:1) for cut slopes and 1 vertical foot to 2 horizontal feet (1:2) for filled slopes. Any structures should be based on undisturbed subsoil, not fill, which may shift and settle enough to crack foun-

dations. If a slope steeper than 1:1 or 1:2 is required, it probably will need a retaining wall.

A newly cut or filled slope will not remain smooth and stable unless surface water runoff is controlled. Water running over the slope will wash soil away. This surface water can be diverted from the top of the slope with berms or ditches that parallel the slope and channel the runoff to lower ground. After you have graded the slopes and established drainage controls, you must cover the bare ground surfaces as quickly as possible. This will protect the surface from the direct impact of rain and wind.

Changing existing grades always disturbs the natural relationship between topsoil, subsoil, and bedrock. This can be avoided by stripping all existing topsoil from areas that are to be graded, built over, or paved, and saving it to be used later. At least 6 to 12 inches of topsoil should be removed, and the grading should allow for this depth of soil to be replaced after the rough grades are made. It takes several hundred years to build a layer of good, natural topsoil, and too often it is buried under tons of subsoil and rubbish where it can't be recovered. Saving the topsoil takes extra work, but you won't have to pay to have new topsoil hauled to your yard.

Rough Grading

The classic cut-and-fill project is one in which you dig into a slope, creating a cliff bounding as many as three sides of the excavation. Even if you are cutting only, or filling only, the general methods remain the same. The material excavated is simply pushed over the edge of the cut, down the slope, broadening the excavation bottom. What's removed from the cut is used as fill, in other words. Depending on the size of the excavation, this sort of project is easily handled with pick and shovel. Just remember to strip the topsoil from both the area to be filled and the area to be cut.

As you build up the fill, tamp it. Spread about 6 inches of soil, then compact it with a heavy roller or, better, with a rented manual or power tamper. Spread more soil and compact that. More soil, more tamping. This compaction process is particularly important if you plan to build anything over the fill, whether it is a shed or a sidewalk. If time isn't a factor, give nature a few months to really settle the fill before you construct anything on it.

Sometimes disposing of material removed from a cut can be a problem. Try working it into the terrain of your yard. If, for example, you're excavating for a pond, consider building a low ridge along one side of the pond. Or use the material to create drainage swales.

Conversely, getting clean fill can be a problem. Avoid fill that's laden with foreign objects, particularly building materials, unless it will be deeply buried.

Finish Grading

Cutting and filling is mostly a matter of hard work. You don't need to measure

CUT AND FILL

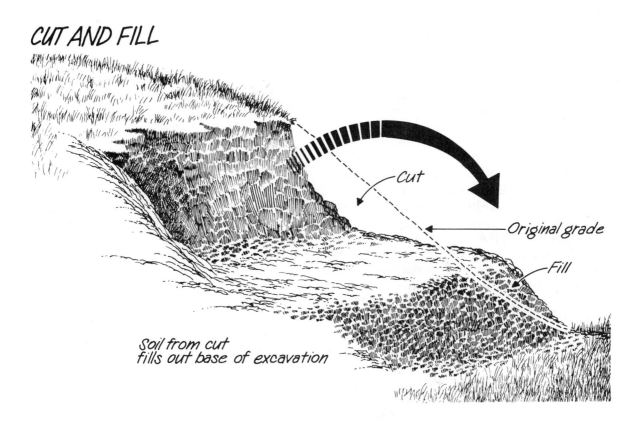

Cut

Original grade

Fill

Soil from cut fills out base of excavation

anything. You just pick and shovel until the ground looks pretty much the way you want it. When you get the ground underfoot roughly level or roughly to the slope you want, you've completed the rough grading.

It is unlikely that you want the ground underfoot absolutely level, and you surely don't want a subtle slope in the wrong direction. You'll get puddles or runoff collecting in the wrong spots—your basement, the patio, where you park the car. You may have to do finish grading. Here's where measuring comes in.

You can get a rough measurement of your yard's contours by using a hand level and a folding carpenter's rule, a yardstick lashed to a board, or even just a board. The hand level is a small telescope with a level built in so that you can be sure you are holding it level when sighting through it. A hand-held device can never be as accurate as a surveyor's transit set on a steady tripod, but a hand level is a lot less expensive and perfectly adequate for sketching out the slopes of your yard. Here's how to use it:

You'll need two people—one to stand down-slope and sight through the level and the other to hold the ruler up-slope. First measure the distance from the ground to your eye. If you are just using a board, mark eye level on the board. Have your helper hold the board plumb at the top of the slope. (Holding a level vertically against the board will increase accuracy.) Now sight the board through the hand level and have your helper mark the point you sight. The distance between the two marks is the change in elevation. If you are using a yardstick mounted on a pole or a folding carpenter's rule, measure your eye level—say 55 inches, for example. When your helper holds the stick at the top of the slope, the measurement you read through the level will be less

−30 inches, for example. The difference, in this case 25 inches, is the change in elevation.

Now measure the distance between where you are standing down-slope and where your helper is standing up-slope. Don't run your measuring tape along the ground. Rather, have your helper stand up-slope and hold the tape at the mark you read through the level (30 inches, in the example). Now pull the tape out to the down-slope point and hold it at eye level when you measure the distance. This measurement is the "run" of the slope. The change in elevation is the "rise." For example, if you were standing 20 feet away from your helper, your slope has a rise of 25 inches in a run of 20 feet.

This rise and run information is useful for more than just grading work. You'll need it if you plan to build steps into a hill, if you are setting piers or posts for a deck built on ground that is not level, or if you are preparing a subbase for a patio.

USING A HAND LEVEL

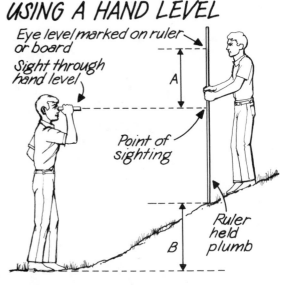

The distance between eye level and the point of sighting, A, is equal to the change in elevation, B

USING A LINE LEVEL

Line level

Establish a slope by moving the string up or down on one stake

If you are measuring grade in preparation for any kind of construction, you'll probably want to measure the rise and run more accurately than you can with a hand level, especially if the slope is subtle and the distance short. For example, patios look level, but actually should be built with a ¼-inch-per-foot slope away from the house so that water will run in that direction.

For this kind of measuring you'll want to use stakes, string, and a line level, which is a spirit level that can be suspended on a string.

As an example, let's use a patio that extends 10 feet from the house. This means the outer edge of the patio should be 2½ inches lower than the inner edge, where the patio meets the house. Drive a stake into the ground next to the house. Measure out 10 feet perpendicular to the house and drive another stake there. Tie a string around the

first stake you placed, securing it at the height of the finished patio. Put the line level on the string and pull it taut and level against the second stake. It's important that the string be as taut as possible; sag creates inaccuracy. Measure 2½ inches down from the level mark on the outer stake and tie the string at that point. The string can now act as a guide for establishing the slope. Of course, if you want to make the area perfectly level, simply tie the string to the second stake when the line level reads level.

Drainage

As mentioned, it's important to consider drainage before altering your landscape, so that your project won't create problems. Beyond that, if you already have drainage problems, this may be the time to correct them. For example, building a patio that is sloped properly away from the house may alleviate that wet basement that has been plaguing you for years.

In general, it is easier to improve surface drainage than to install subsurface drainage systems. If you need to improve the subsurface drainage, you'll use perforated plastic drainpipe. Preferably, this should be done before grading or planting, but after heavy construction has been completed. It should be installed in conjunction with a proper surface drainage system. You should consult the Soil Conservation Service; its experts can make recommendations about drainage systems for your soil type and terrain.

Surface Drainage

Drainage is based on the very simple facts that water flows downhill and that the more confined the area and the smoother the surface, the faster the flow will be. On areas where there is no penetration of water into the soil, such as roofs, patios, walks, or driveways, there will be a lot of runoff, which must be directed to a suitable area.

Drainage from large paved areas, such as a parking area or a driveway, can best be accomplished by the installation of a storm-sewer system at the time of construction.

Although smaller paved areas such as patios or walks cause fewer problems, they still need to be adequately drained. That means ensuring that they slope in the direction you wish the water to go (away from the house) and, if possible, providing a porous surface with adequate drainage underneath.

Surface drainage techniques for planted areas are easy enough to implement, but must be carefully designed. Unwanted depressions or low pockets should be eliminated, and the grade should always direct runoff away from structures and paved areas. Water should flow to a central surface drainage system, such as a swale; to surface inlets of a subsurface drainage system or dry well; or to a street or public storm sewer. It should never be carelessly directed off your land; directing water onto your neighbor's property is not ethical and, in most cases, is not legal.

Retaining Walls

The need for a retaining wall occasionally arises in connection with grading. If a slope is too steep for planting or stability,

SURFACE DRAINAGE

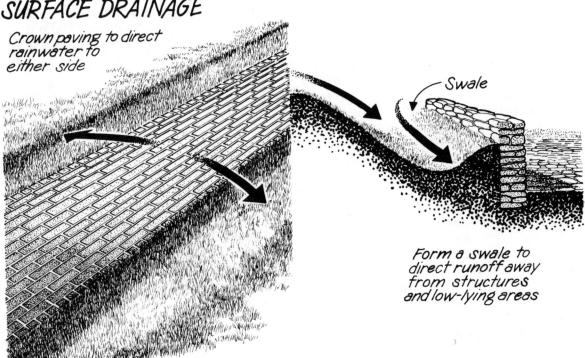

Crown paving to direct rainwater to either side

Swale

Form a swale to direct runoff away from structures and low-lying areas

a properly constructed wall can keep the soil from eroding and provide more useful, level areas.

Because retaining walls must support great weight and accommodate drainage from the slope, they have to be carefully designed and constructed. In many places, building regulations govern the construction of retaining walls. A permit must be obtained, and the construction monitored by a building inspector.

A low wall, such as that required to retain a gentle slope, is easily constructed by a beginner. In fact, if you have a long, steep slope, you may decide to build two or more short retaining walls, one behind the other, instead of one tall wall. As well as being easier to construct, this approach requires less earth moving. Also, a series of retaining walls, rather than one tall one, usually gives the yard a more attractive, natural look.

The materials you use and the method of construction should be determined by the intended use of the wall, your skills, your finances, and the character of your landscape. A concrete-block wall will hold up a bank, but doesn't usually blend well with landscaping. The wall could just as easily be constructed of brick, stone, or landscaping ties and be more in harmony with your landscape.

The details of constructing such walls are discussed at length under the headings Masonry Walls, Stone Walls, and Wooden Retaining Walls, later in this chapter. But first, let's look at paving.

Paving

Designing a patio, walk, or drive can be an opportunity to try your hand at creative design. There are dozens of materials available—the basic types are discussed below—yet the principles of paving are simple, regardless of which materials you use.

Your paving project must be more than aesthetically pleasing, of course. It must be within your budget. It must be convenient and practical to use. It must drain properly and hold up to the elements and to its intended use.

Walks

Plan your walks so they provide a visual, as well as physical, link between elements in your landscape. You don't necessarily want to take the shortest route between two points —a meandering wood-chip path through a grove of trees can be nice. On the other hand, curved walks that have no apparent reason for curving will only encourage walkers to ignore them. You can always tell a poorly planned walk; worn into the earth somewhere nearby will be the route people actually use.

If your house is close to the street, where visitors park, a walk from street to door is often the best. But if the house sits back from the road or if you live in the country, you may need, not a walk from the street, but a walk that directs visitors from a guest parking area to the front door.

Use as few walks in addition to the entrance as possible. Secondary walks designed to ramble through the garden or to lead to a vista or patio need not be paved, since they will be used only in fair weather. Stepping stones, gravel, and grass are frequently more attractive and are cooler and more inviting in summer, while walks leading to the patio are often best paved in the same material as the patio itself.

(continued on page 82)

The material you select for your paving project should enhance your landscape. Among the varieties and combinations you can choose from are concrete with brick edging (far left), cut flagstone and exposed-aggregate concrete (top left), mortared flagstone (bottom left), oversized brick pavers with ties (top), loose aggregate (above), and exposed-aggregate concrete with wood accents (left).

81

Steps: Where a walk leads from one level to another, the usual practice is to install steps at the slope. Ramps may be used if the slope is not too steep, or where it is necessary to wheel conveyances from one level to another.

Patios

The outdoor area you will use most is the patio. There you can relax and entertain. Since tables and chairs will be placed there, a patio should be relatively flat. It should directly connect with the living room, kitchen, or some other room where there are related activities. But this doesn't mean that the patio must be built against the house. You may get more enjoyment from being out in the garden, and you may get a better summer breeze. By connecting the house and the patio with a paved path, you can make the walk to the patio pleasant and convenient. If you provide shade for all or part of the patio, it will get more use on hot, sunny summer days.

Be sure the patio is in scale with the rest of the landscape and will accommodate your desired activities. Think about when and how you will use it. Do you like to eat outside? You might want the patio off the kitchen. Do you like to sunbathe in the afternoon? Then the position of the afternoon sun in relation to your house may be more important.

Paving Materials

There are several points to consider in choosing a paving material. Although you will probably find that no one type meets all of your needs, you should make sure that the color, texture, and pattern blend well with your landscape and with the materials of your home. Is the look formal or rustic?

And is the size of the individual paved area in scale with the other elements in your landscape?

The texture, too, must be suitable for the intended use of the paving. While cobblestones set high are attractive and durable, they are uncomfortable to walk on, and the unwary can trip on them. Smooth-textured concrete, on the other hand, can be slippery when wet or freezing.

Consider also how readily paving will stand up under your use and your climatic conditions? Is it subject to cracking or disintegration? How much skill and effort are needed to lay the material? The material you choose should be suited to its purpose, pleasing to the eye, and priced within your budget.

Loose Aggregates

Loose aggregates range from wood chips to the more familiar crushed stone, often called gravel. The biggest advantage of loose aggregates is that they are pervious. Water soaks right through them, so they don't change the natural drainage patterns of your yard. This consideration is especially important if you plan to pave a large area that might require storm sewers and/or extensive grading if you were to use impervious paving such as concrete, asphalt, or brick.

Another advantage is that using loose aggregates is the easiest way to pave. Compacting the ground usually is the only subbase preparation you need. And if you want your yard to have a natural, casual look, loose aggregates may be the best choice.

There are disadvantages, however, that you should think about. Loose aggregates can be uncomfortable to walk on and very difficult to wheel anything across. Regular rolling is necessary to keep the surface compacted. You may want to install edging to contain the material.

COMMON BRICKS AND PAVERS

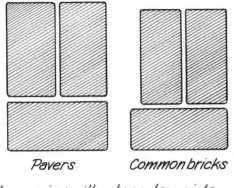

Pavers   Common bricks

When paving without mortar joints, use pavers

Bricks

Bricks are a very versatile and easily laid paving material. They are available in a wide variety of colors, textures, and shapes, and under most conditions, will provide a solid and durable surface. Because bricks are small, they are excellent for making gradual changes of direction or level, and they can be laid in many attractive patterns. The rough texture of bricks reduces glare and gives good traction.

Finish and color are matters of personal taste, but the grade of brick needed depends on the job it is to do. General information on bricks can be found under the heading Masonry Walls, later in this chapter.

There is a special category of bricks known as pavers. These bricks are harder and more resistant to abrasion than ordinary bricks; they are designed to withstand the traffic of city streets. Common severe-weather bricks are more than strong enough

for use in a garden walk or patio or even a private driveway. However, unlike common bricks, pavers are exactly twice as long as they are wide. This allows them to be used without mortar to create a variety of patterns known as bonds. With common bricks, you'll have to stick to the running bond.

In choosing a bond, think about the effect you want to create, but keep in mind that more complex bonds require more brick cutting, which takes more time and creates more waste. Some patterns tend to direct the eye to emphasize the features of the brick. Others can only be laid in large areas; otherwise they look too busy. Sometimes even a large paved area needs a simple bond if the area has a lot of turns and steps. Basket-weave patterns, which have sets of two or three bricks placed in alternating directions to suggest weaving, are a popular choice. Herringbone patterns require some brick cutting, but the results are attractive. Walks and patios can also be laid in the running bond so widely used in walls. You can set bricks flat or on edge.

Materials such as stone, railroad ties, boards, or gravel can be used with brick to add variety and contrast. An attractive walk can be made by combining bricks with concrete paving blocks, slates, or cobblestones. For example, start by laying the bricks down the middle of the path, spacing them about ¼-inch apart. Then lay the blocks or stones along both sides of the bricks.

Concrete Pavers

Concrete pavers are available in thousands of sizes, colors, shapes, and textures. This allows them to be used creatively, either alone or in combination with brick, loose aggregates, or rot-resistant wood. You can butt them together or space them and allow

PAVING BONDS

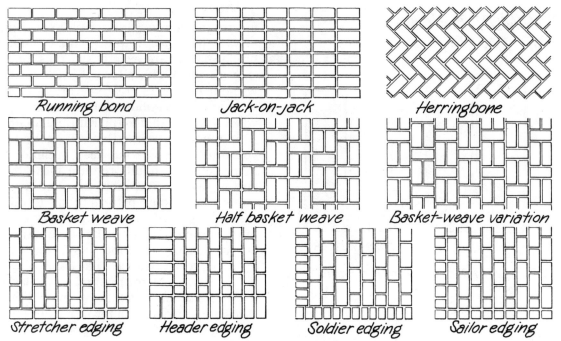

Running bond   Jack-on-jack   Herringbone

Basket weave   Half basket weave   Basket-weave variation

Stretcher edging   Header edging   Soldier edging   Sailor edging

Running bond with four edging treatments

grass to grow between. There is even a type called Turfstone that forms a concrete grid for grass to grow through.

Some concrete pavers are designed to interlock. This makes them resistant to heaving caused by frost. Concrete pavers are laid in exactly the same way as dry-laid brick pavers.

Stone

Natural stone slabs are one of the most durable and attractive paving materials you can use. Because stone is found in nature, it looks appropriate in almost any landscape. Slabs are the best choice for laying directly on the soil or on a bed of sand, because their weight is enough to ensure stability.

The most commonly available paving stone is flagstone, which is cut from any

stone that splits into flat pieces, such as sandstone or slate. Flagstones are available in irregular or rectangular shapes and range in thickness from ½ inch to 2 inches. Uneven chunks of natural stone, gathered from a field or left over from quarrying, can make a rustic and attractive, although uneven, surface. Bluestone, granite, and marble are expensive but beautiful, and they work well in a formal setting. Large irregular pieces of stone require care in laying, as they look best when fitted together like a jigsaw puzzle. With both irregular and rectangular stone, it is a good idea to arrange the pattern before fixing the stones.

Wood

Wood paving can be beautiful, but it has serious drawbacks. One of the best reasons for using wood is its appropriateness in the garden. A wood surface provides an effective link between man-made and natural elements. Unless it is brightly painted, it will never clash with the landscape or the architecture.

Wood is a marvelous accent material when used with other paving materials. Wide edgings or headers made of heavy timbers or railroad ties are popular.

Concrete

To many people, concrete brings to mind harsh, impersonal expanses, not the comfortable, warm and inviting feeling you are trying to create in your yard.

But concrete can be used with taste and imagination. Plastic when wet, it can assume almost any shape and many textures. You can mix in a wide range of color pigments that become part of the concrete, not

a surface coat that can later peel or wear off. And concrete is inexpensive and easy enough to handle if you know what you are doing.

Round pavers are lily pads on the gently rolling seas of your backyard. Below are cut flagstone pavers set in loose aggregate. The homemade pavers marking a path across the grass (below left) are made of stones set in concrete.

You can buy concrete pavers in virtually any shape or size you might want. But making your own is an easy way to save money while enjoying the satisfaction of truly building your patio or walk from scratch.

Two different forms are shown. One is for casting individual, rectilinear pavers; the second for casting a set of four pavers.

Rectilinear Pavers

Square or rectangular forms can be made of 1 × 2s or 2 × 4s, depending on how thick you want the blocks to be. In either case, hinge three corners with butt hinges. Install a hasp and staple on the fourth corner to close the form while casting.

Paver Set

The form shown yields a set of four pavers from a single casting. Cut the parts to the lengths listed. Nail the 2 × 2 frame together. Nail the dividers together, then fit them into the frame and nail them in place.

The form can be lifted from around the pavers after the concrete has been cut free and has set for a couple of days.

Casting Pavers

When you are ready to cast pavers, you can do it on a cement floor if you place tar paper under the form. An even cheaper alternative is to just put newspaper between the floor and the pour. Some of the newspaper may become embedded in the bottom of the blocks, but that won't matter if you put that side down in your patio or walk.

Another alternative, useful if you don't have a flat concrete floor to pour on, is to make your forms ½ inch deeper than you want the blocks to be. Fill this ½ inch with sand and pour the concrete over that.

Whichever type of form you use, follow these steps for making paving blocks.

1. Lay and smooth the sand bed, if you'll be

SQUARE PAVER FORMS

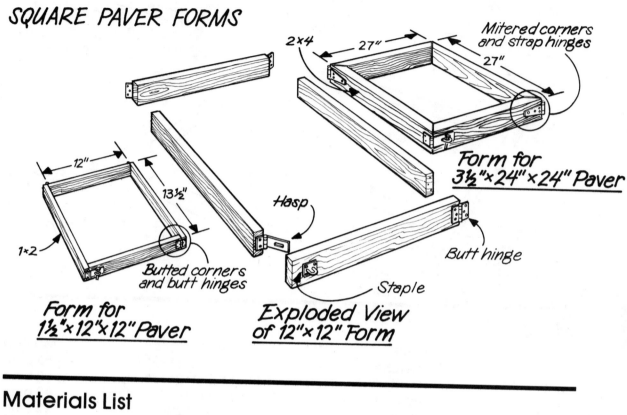

2×4

27″

Mitered corners
and strap hinges

27″

Form for
3½″×24″×24″ Paver

12″

13½″

1×2

Hasp

Butt hinge

Butted corners
and butt hinges

Staple

Form for
1½″×12″×12″ Paver

Exploded View
of 12″×12″ Form

Materials List

Number	Piece	Dimensions	Material
2	Headers	¾″ × 1½″ × 13½″	#2 pine
2	Stretchers	¾″ × 1½″ × 12″	#2 pine

Hardware
3 pr. 1½″ butt hinges
1–1½″ hasp and staple

using one. Wet the inside faces of the form and put it in place. Cut a piece of reinforcing wire mesh to fit the form.

2. Mix the concrete and pour it into the form, stopping about ½ inch from the top of the form. Embed the wire mesh. Finish the pour and screed the concrete even

with the top of the form.

3. If you want a smooth surface, wait until the sheen of the water has disappeared and the concrete is firm enough to hold the shape of a trowel run along the edge of the form. Run a mason's trowel around the inside of the form to cut the concrete

PAVER SET FORM

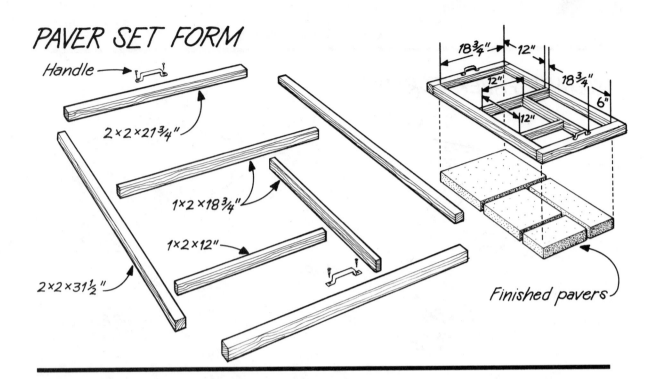

Handle

2×2×21¾″

1×2×18¾″

1×2×12″

2×2×31½″

18¾″   12″   18¾″

12″

12″

6″

Finished pavers

Materials List

Number	Piece	Dimensions	Material
2	Stretchers	1½″ × 1½″ × 31½″	#2 pine
2	Headers	1½″ × 1½″ × 21¾″	#2 pine
2	Dividers	¾″ × 1½″ × 18¾″	#2 pine
1	Divider	¾″ × 1½″ × 12″	#2 pine

Hardware
12d galvanized nails

free of the form. Then float the concrete. If you want an even smoother surface, trowel the concrete after floating. Finally, run an edging tool around the perimeter of the form to round the top edges.

4. Cover the newly cast pavers with sheets of plastic or damp burlap sacks; protect from direct sun and freezing. Wait at least four days before removing the forms.

5. Stand the blocks on edge for two or three weeks for complete curing.

Getting Started

Once you have decided on your materials and planned your paving on paper, you are ready for the first physical step–to lay out the paving on the ground. This involves staking out strings that will delineate the perimeter and finished height of the paved area. In addition to string and stakes, you'll need a line level and a measuring tape.

Begin by establishing the grade using the methods previously described. Now lay out the perimeter of the patio with stakes and string, remembering to include the thickness of your forms. For a rectangular patio, you can begin with either the length or the width, just make sure the strings delineating the sides are parallel and the stakes are planted at least 2 feet beyond the ends of the patio. Then lay out the perpendicular

sides, again with the stakes planted a couple of feet beyond the patio border. The point at which strings cross will show the actual corners of the patio plus forms, if they are to be temporary.

Use a framing square to check that the corners form right angles. Another way to check that your patio will be a rectangle and not a trapezoid is to measure diagonally from corner to corner. Both diagonals should be the same. A third way of checking–the so-called 3-4-5 method–is to measure 3 feet from the corner along one side and 4 feet along the other. If the 3-foot and 4-foot points are exactly 5 feet apart (along the hypotenuse of the triangle), you've got a right-angled corner. Multiples of the 3-4-5 measurements will also work.

With the boundaries set, adjust the vertical alignment of the strings, so you have a

LAYING OUT A PATIO

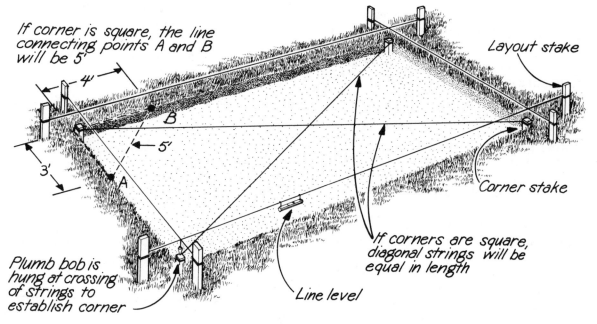

If corner is square, the line connecting points A and B will be 5'

4'

B

5'

3'

A

Layout stake

Corner stake

If corners are square, diagonal strings will be equal in length

Plumb bob is hung at crossing of strings to establish corner

Line level

reference point for the depth of the excavation. When you dig, excavate enough room to work easily and efficiently with forms or header boards. This means you should dig a foot beyond the perimeter of the area to be paved; hence the need to have the stakes well back from the perimeter.

Subbases

Don't confuse subbases with footings. Both are types of foundations, but they have different functions and design considerations. Like the roots of a tree, a footing is designed to anchor a vertical structure to the ground. A concrete footing is buried below the frost line—as deep as 4 feet in cold climates—so the moisture in the surrounding earth can't freeze, expand, and crack the footing.

A paved area, because it is horizontal, doesn't need an anchor deep in the ground. But frost is still a consideration, because when moisture near the surface freezes and expands, the ground surface moves to accommodate it. This movement will crack concrete and heave bricks. This is where the subbase comes in. Rather than an anchor, the subbase may be thought of as a drain. Subbases for concrete slabs are made of gravel, while subbases for brick or other paving units are made of gravel and sand. Either provides a firm base that won't hold water. Without water, there is nothing to freeze and expand, so the subbase doesn't move when the weather gets cold.

In short, the depth of your subbase is determined not by the depth of the frost line, but by the depth needed for adequate drainage. Therefore, the nature of the soil under your paved area is the most important consideration in designing a subbase. If you have a large percentage of clay in your soil, you may need a subbase of 9 inches of gravel topped by 2 or 3 inches of sand. If your soil is very sandy, you may need only a couple of inches of gravel under the sand.

One way to get a rough idea of how your soil drains is to dig a hole about a foot or so deep. Fill the hole with water. If the water drains away within a few hours you've got good drainage, and you'll need only 4 or 5 inches of gravel under 2 or 3 inches of sand. If the water is still there when you come back a day later, you'll want a 12-inch gravel subbase.

Buying Gravel

Gravel is sold by the ton. But different types of gravel have different weights, and the type you buy will depend on what's available in the area. The best approach to figuring out how much gravel you need is to calculate the volume you want to fill, then let the supplier determine how many tons you need.

Here's a formula for determining cubic yards:

$$\text{width} \times \text{length} \times \text{thickness} \div 27 = \text{cubic yards}$$

All three variables—width, length, and thickness must be expressed in feet (or fractions thereof). For a 6-inch gravel subbase for a patio that's 10 feet wide and 20 feet long, you'd multiply $10 \times 20 \times .5$ (half a foot) to get 100. Divide 100 by 27 (the number of cubic feet in a cubic yard). You need 3.7 cubic yards of gravel.

It's also a good idea to learn about common subbase practices in your area. Subbases for paving are not usually covered in building codes, but your local building inspector probably knows the usual practice for your area. Another good source of information is the local Soil Conservation Service office.

For a subbase to provide solid support, it must be compacted. The best tool for the job is a gasoline-powered tamper, which can be rented. You can also use a hand tamper or a lawn roller. First, compact the excavation. Then put in the gravel and compact that. If you are using paving units, add the sand, wet it, and compact it.

Some builders like to lay plastic sheets, tar paper, or Typar landscaping fabric in the subbase. Laid between the sand and the gravel, it is intended to prevent the sand from slowly filtering into the gravel layer, prompting uneven settling of the pavers. Typar, a durable synthetic fabric, will block sand filtration and the growth of weeds, but not inhibit drainage. The other materials must be perforated to allow water to drain out of the sand layer, which is somewhat contradictory to the point of laying them in the first place.

Drainage

A proper subbase takes care of the water beneath the paving, but you still must concern yourself with what happens to the water that falls on top of the paved surface.

SUBBASE DRAINAGE

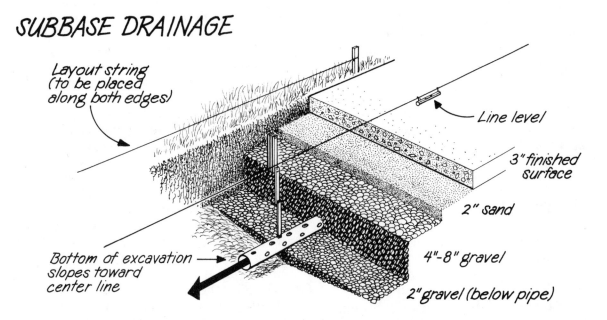

Layout string (to be placed along both edges)

Line level

3" finished surface

2" sand

Bottom of excavation slopes toward center line

4"-8" gravel

2" gravel (below pipe)

Measure from level line to establish the pitch of the drainpipe. The pipe should drop at least 1 foot in 100.

Estimating Sand

Subbases for dry-laid paving usually have about 2 inches of sand under the paving material. This works out to about 1 cubic yard of sand per 150 square feet of paving.

You don't want the water to lay on top of your paved area. Wet pavement can be slippery, and of course, icy pavement is even worse. Slope the surface at least 1 percent to allow water to run off. Paving sloped up to 3 percent (3-foot drop per 100 feet) looks flat to most people, but slopes beyond 4 to 5 percent are too slanted for use in patios, although walks and drives may go up to 10 to 12 percent.

If you are paving a large area and if your soil doesn't drain well, you may need to install 3- or 4-inch-diameter perforated drainpipe under the center or around the edges of the paved area.

Utilities: Plan and install utility lines before you begin paving. Plan for sanitary sewer, storm drains, drainpipes, water pipes, gas lines, and electrical conduits. This will save time and money and will eliminate the need to dig up pavement for a utility line later.

Forms

How deeply you dig and what sort of forms and base you construct depend upon the material you chose for paving, your climate, and the nature of your soil.

Concrete slabs require the strongest forms because they must withstand the outward thrust of wet concrete. For concrete, your forms may be temporary or a permanent design feature. Forms for bricks laid without mortar need not be as strong as concrete forms, but they must be permanent to contain the loose brick.

Forms are most commonly made of boards or dimensional lumber. If the forms are to be permanent, you'll want a rot-resistant wood. If the forms are to be removed, then green—newly sawed, unseasoned—wood is best. Dry wood will suck moisture out of concrete, which may prevent it from curing properly.

Begin setting up your forms by driving 2×2 stakes into the ground, spacing them about 2 or 3 feet apart. Line up each stake so its inside face touches the layout string and pound it in until its top is level with the string.

Now nail through the stakes into the form boards. Use duplex nails, which have two heads; sometimes called scaffolding nails, they are made for temporary construction, such as scaffolds and forms. Try not to knock the stakes out of alignment as you nail the forms into place. Holding a hand sledge or a large rock behind the form board when nailing can help.

If your layout includes curves, the easiest solution is to use 1/16-inch sheet-metal garden edging instead of wood at the curves. Begin by laying out the curves with string. Now install stakes at 1- or 2-foot intervals along the string. Remember, here you don't need to allow for the thickness of wooden forms, and the thickness of the metal is not significant enough to worry about. Cut the sheet metal about 6 inches longer than the curve. Nail the metal to the form board at one end of the curve, overlapping the board about 3 inches. Nail the metal to each stake in the curve, then overlap the form board at the other end of the curve and nail it in place. Make sure the top of the metal is level with the top of the form boards.

BUILDING FORMS

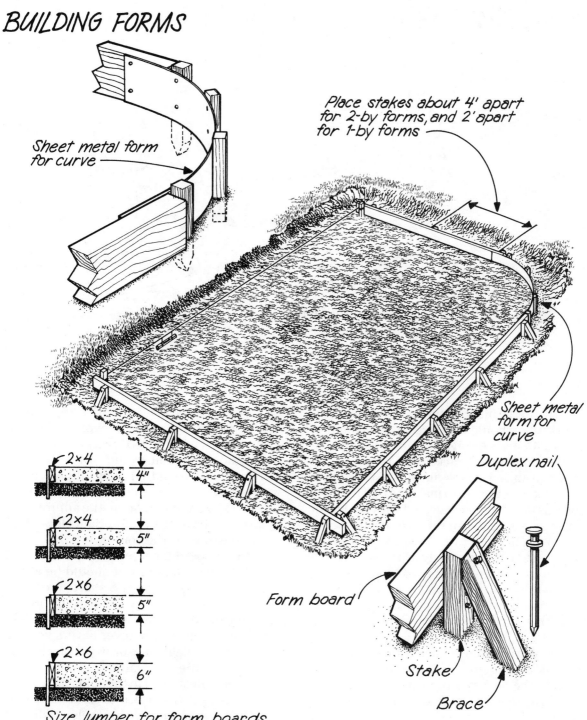

Sheet metal form for curve

Place stakes about 4' apart for 2-by forms, and 2' apart for 1-by forms

Sheet metal form for curve

Duplex nail

Form board

Stake

Brace

2×4 — 4"

2×4 — 5"

2×6 — 5"

2×6 — 6"

Size lumber for form boards according to thickness of slab

93

SCREEDING SAND

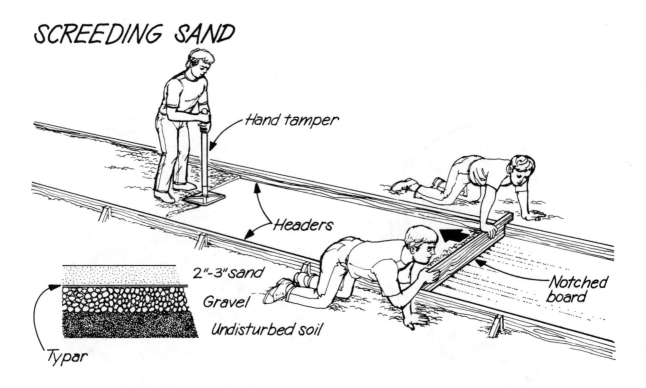

Hand tamper

Headers

2"-3" sand

Gravel

Undisturbed soil

Typar

Notched board

If the forms will be used for concrete work, they should be braced. Cut an angle of about 45 degrees on one end of each brace stake. Pound the braces in at an angle and nail the angled end to the other stake. After bracing, check again to make sure all the form boards are plumb and aligned with the layout strings. Now you can remove the strings.

With the excavation completed and the forms set up, you are ready to proceed according to the dictates of the materials you are going to use.

Using Headers

If you are going to use wooden headers, that is, permanently installed boards which define the edges of the walk or patio, you can use them as a guide for leveling the sand bed.

For headers, use 1 × 4 pressure-treated pine, or redwood, cedar, or cypress that has been treated with a wood preservative. Install the headers as you would forms, but use galvanized nails rather than duplex nails, and shorten or bevel the stakes so they don't show. They should be set to the appropriate depth and have the appropriate slope. Nail them together at the corners.

Cut a board for screeding the sand bed and leveling the bricks. It should be about 12 inches longer than the shortest dimension of the area to be paved. In each end, cut a notch about 6 inches wide and ½ inch less than the depth of whatever pavers you are using—brick, flagstone, or wood blocks.

Screed the sand after you have compacted it as described in the subbase section. To screed, set the board over the headers, notches down, and with a helper, slide it back and forth along the headers. Thus, you'll be able to create a nice, level sand bed.

By making the notches slightly smaller than the depth of your pavers, you allow for a modest amount of settling. Otherwise, the pavers would eventually sink below the headers. If that's the effect you want, of course, you can adjust the size of the notches accordingly.

If your plan calls for the use of brick headers, dig a narrow trench around the perimeter of your paved area. Set the headers in the trench vertically. As you set each one, tamp soil against the outside and sand against the inside. Use your layout strings as a guide and check with a level to make sure the headers are level and plumb.

You can set the headers more solidly by using mortar. This means you'll have to dig the trench a little deeper and add a couple of inches of gravel. Mix a batch of mortar as described under the heading Masonry Walls, later in this chapter. Trowel mortar onto the gravel and set the bricks. If you want mortar joints between the bricks, butter the bricks as you go.

If you use brick headers, you won't have wooden headers to act as a guide when screeding. Instead, place two 1-inch-thick boards parallel to each other on the sand and work them in to the level you want the sand to be. Then run an unnotched screed board over these boards. This method also is useful for patios that are too wide to screed from header to header.

LEVELING HEADER BRICKS FOR EDGING

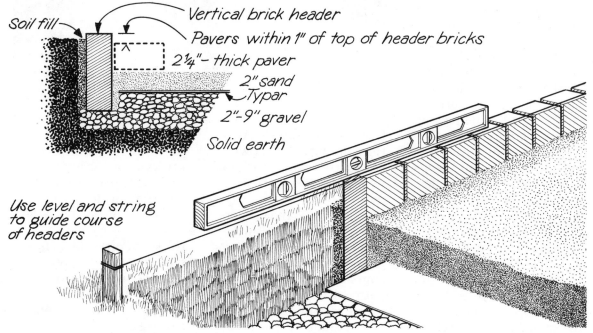

Soil fill

Vertical brick header

Pavers within 1" of top of header bricks

2¼"- thick paver

2" sand

Typar

2"-9" gravel

Solid earth

Use level and string to guide course of headers

PROJECT
BRICK WALK

The simplest and most common way to pave with bricks is to lay them in a bed of sand without mortar. A big advantage of this method is that you can easily remove the bricks later. This is especially important to the novice because it means you can correct mistakes. But it also means you can replace broken bricks, remove bricks to install or repair utility lines, or even remove the patio if you decide you don't want it.

This brick walk has a border of raised "soldier" bricks that make it particularly well-suited for paving around planting beds—the border keeps dirt from the beds off the walk and keeps walkers off the beds, which are raised 2 inches above grade. The walk is laid without mortar, so the border also serves to keep the bricks in place.

The running bond pattern is simple and economical because you only need to cut six bricks for each end of the walk no matter

how long the walk is. Also, the running bond allows you to use common bricks, which are cheaper than pavers.

Excluding the borders, this path is 12 bricks wide—that's about 45 inches if you use common bricks. Of course, the length of your path will depend on your own yard. For our example, we'll assume the path is 50 feet long.

You can easily revise the borders. Set the border bricks as sailors instead of soldiers for a narrower border requiring fewer bricks. If you don't like the raised border, you can sink the soldiers or sailors flush with the walk. Or you can use pressure-treated wood flush with the bricks as a permanent form to retain the walk.

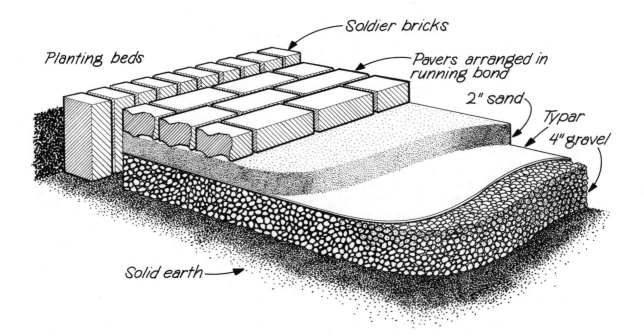

Soldier bricks

Planting beds

Pavers arranged in running bond

2" sand

Typar

4" gravel

Solid earth

1. **Lay out the walk with string and stakes.** The strings will be 2 inches above grade, which is flush with the planned height of the planting beds. The strings will be 50 inches apart (45-inch width of the walk plus 2½ inches for the thickness of each border.)

Shopping List
1,031 common severe-weather bricks
9 tons of gravel
1 ½ cubic yards of sand

2. **Excavate the walk.** Dig a trench 6 inches below grade and 2¼ inches wide for the border bricks. To calculate the depth of the sub-base of the walk, allow 2 inches for sand and 2¼ inches for the thickness of the bricks, plus the depth of gravel dictated by your locale and soil, less ¼ inch for settlement.

3. **Set the border bricks.** These bricks are in the soldier position. As you set each one, tamp soil against the outside and sand against the inside. Use your layout strings as a guide and check with a level to make sure the headers are level and plumb.

4. **Build the subbase.** Spread gravel evenly in the excavation, wet it down, and compact it. Spread sheets of Typar, then spread sand evenly over them. Wet down the sand, and compact it. After it dries, screed the sand.

5. **Lay the bricks.** With the subbase and headers in place, this is simple work. Start at one corner and work out, setting the bricks in the pattern you've picked. In the case of this project, you must cut three bricks in half. Begin the running bond at one end of the walk by alternating six full bricks with six half bricks across the width of the walk.

If you are going to have any kind of joint between bricks, use a piece of plywood of the appropriate thickness as a guide. If there won't be joints, just butt the bricks together. For paving, you'll need about 5.5 bricks per square foot.

Each brick should be tamped into place and leveled. As a practical matter, you probably will not use a level on each and every brick. Rather, you'll use the headers and the screed board to level the bricks in aggregate. Set the board on the headers and sight beneath it to determine if the bricks are level.

6. **Settle the bricks to complete the project.** To do this, wet down the bricks once they are all in place.

If you've chosen to have a joint between bricks, dump fine sand or sand and cement mix on the bricks—*before wetting them*—and sweep it into the joints. Then wet the bricks. You'll need to repeat this process two or three times. Adding cement to the sand will give you a mortarlike joint.

Another option is to seat the bricks with a vibrating compactor, which you can rent.

HOW TO FLAGSTONE PATIO

This patio of 1-inch-thick rectangular flagstone ties together several partitions off the back of the house. It is laid in sand on a subbase of gravel.

1. Lay out the patio with stakes and string.
2. Excavate subbase. To calculate the depth, allow 2 inches of depth for sand, 1 inch for flagstone, and the depth of gravel dictated by your locale and soil.
3. Compact the subbase.
4. Add gravel and compact.
5. Add 2 inches of sand and compact.
6. Place flagstone with joints of approximately ½ inch and no wider than 1 inch.
7. Tamp down flagstone with a 2 × 4.
8. Sweep sand or mixture of sand and dry cement into joints. Repeat as necessary.

Shopping List
(For a 500-square-foot patio with a 4-inch gravel base)

2.5 tons of flagstone
24 tons of gravel
4 cubic yards of sand

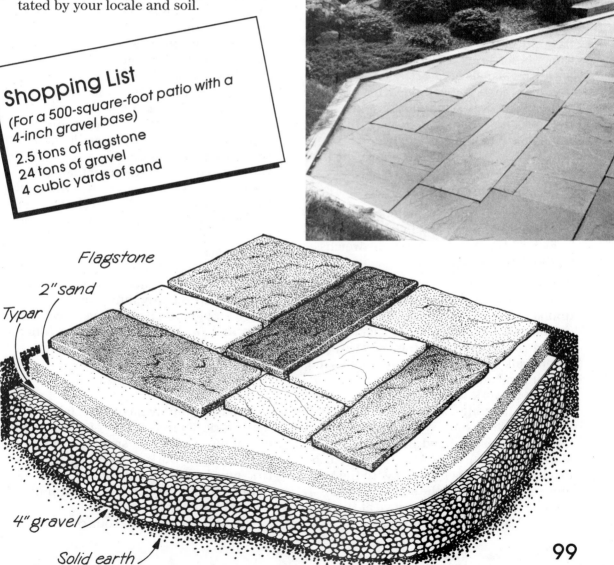

Flagstone
2" sand
Typar
4" gravel
Solid earth

99

Laying Stone

Stones laid on soil should be at least 2 inches thick to ensure stability and strength. Fill the joints between the stones with soil and plants. To lay the stones on soil, simply dig to a depth slightly less than the thickness of the stones and fit them into place. Sometimes a little sand can be helpful in leveling the stones.

Thinner flagstone may be laid in a bed of gravel and stone or set into a concrete base. In either case the procedure is the same as for brick. Of course, if you work with irregular flagstone, the joints will be irregular too. If you will be laying irregular stone on concrete with mortar joints, keep the joints less than 1 inch wide by using small pieces of stone where needed.

Whatever method you choose, the final

Buying Flagstone

Flagstone most commonly is about 1 inch thick. As a rule of thumb, 1 square foot of 1-inch-thick flagstone weighs about 10 pounds.

---

grade should be evenly sloping for proper drainage. Lay the stones in place, and after establishing the pattern, tamp them in place with a rubber mallet so they don't wobble when walked on. Fill the joints with sand, soil, or sand mix.

Try to work with the natural size and shape of the stones, as cutting is difficult. If you have to cut some, you can do it with a broad cold chisel, a hand sledge, and a 2 × 4. Mark where you want to make the cut by making a 1/8- to 1/4-inch groove with the hammer and chisel. Place the stone on the 2 × 4, holding the chisel in the groove at the middle of the stone, and hit it sharply.

Concrete

Concrete is a durable material. If not properly mixed and handled, however, it can crack and buckle, and the surface can flake and break up. Because it sets quickly, it must be handled with speed, and any one slab—whether it's a single paver or an entire patio—must be completed in one pour. A large job can be designed as a series of small blocks that can be poured one or two at a time to spread out the work.

There are three ways you can get concrete. The most expensive is to purchase premixed bags; all you do is add water. This approach is practical if you need a small batch—to set a post or two, for example.

The second option is transit-mixed concrete. This involves the least labor, and if you are ordering more than 3 to 5 cubic yards, it may even be cheaper than the third option—buying the ingredients and mixing the concrete yourself. Ordering transit-mixed concrete requires careful planning and preparation. You have to work fast, and it helps to have assistance when the truck arrives.

Most transit trucks have about 22 feet of chute. If you're lucky, the driver will be able to pour directly into your forms. More likely, though, you'll need several wheelbarrows and pushers to spread the concrete throughout the forms.

Mixing Concrete

Mixing your own concrete takes lots of hard work. The advantage of this approach is that it is cheaper for small batches, and it allows you to work at your own pace. You *can* mix by hand, but for anything more than a batch-a-day project, you'll probably want to rent a mixer.

In almost all cases, your concrete mixture will begin with portland cement—a type, not a brand. Portland cement is used in more than 80 percent of modern concrete mixes. In the United States, it comes in standard 1-cubic-foot bags weighing 94 pounds. Cement absorbs moisture readily, and when it does, it lumps up. If a bag seems hard, roll it around a bit. If it doesn't loosen up easily, the cement is no good.

When you add water to cement, it forms a paste that binds the aggregates—sand and gravel—into concrete.

The sand must be clean or the concrete will not bind. Do not use seashore sand. Mortar sand is another, finer variety, and it should not be used for mixing concrete.

When buying gravel, you can specify the maximum size you want, or you can order what is known as "bank run," or unscreened gravel, which includes gravel of all sizes and some rock dust.

The water you use must be clean. If you can drink it, it is fine for concrete. Seawater should not be used.

Mix your concrete only after all your forms and other equipment are ready and in place. When it comes to mixing your ingredients, keep in mind the proportions and the relative consistency of the product you want. The chart shows the proportions to use: for a floor, one quantity of cement to two like quantities of sand and three like quantities of gravel. You can use a can or bucket to measure your quantities. Masons oftentimes measure by the shovelful, but use containers for accuracy until experience gives you a sense of the right proportions.

When preparing a small batch in a wheelbarrow, mix the cement and sand first. They must be blended to a uniform color, showing neither light nor dark streaks. Add water little by little, until the entire mixture is evenly moist. Mix in the gravel last. If you

Concrete Proportions

If you are mixing concrete yourself, here are recommended proportions for common home projects.

	Cement	Sand	Gravel
Driveway	1	2½	3½
Floor	1	2	3
Footings	1	2	4
Sidewalk (light traffic)	1	2	4
Sidewalk (heavy traffic)	1	1½	3
Stairs	1	2	4

add gravel before the water it will be too difficult to mix by hand.

If your mixture is too wet, add small amounts of cement, sand, and gravel in the same proportions you used in the original mix. If it is too dry, sprinkle only small amounts of water across the heap.

If you use a mixer, first measure the ingredients to the proportions you need. With the mixer stopped, load in the gravel and some water. Start the mixer, and while it is running, add the sand, cement, and more water. Keep the mixer running for at least three minutes, or until the mixture is of uniform color. Add water a little at a time until you get a mix of the right consistency. Use the concrete as quickly as possible.

Clean up promptly when you are done. Once the concrete hardens on tools, it's all but impossible to get off. A stiff-fiber brush is a big help in cleaning up, and unless you're looking forward to swinging a 200-pound shovel someday, what little time it takes is

Estimating Concrete

Transit-mixed concrete is sold by the cubic yard. Estimate the amount of concrete you need using this table:

Thick-ness (in.)	Area (sq. ft.)					
	10	**25**	**50**	**100**	**200**	**300**
4	0.12	0.31	0.62	1.23	2.47	3.70
5	0.15	0.39	0.77	1.54	3.09	4.63
6	0.19	0.46	0.93	1.85	3.70	5.56

For example, to find the amount of concrete required for a 4-inch-thick patio that is 10 × 15 feet, first calculate the area (10 × 15 = 150). Turn to the table and note that 100 square feet at a 4-inch thickness requires 1.23 cubic yards, and 50 square feet 0.62 cubic yard. Add the amounts; for a 150-square-foot slab 4 inches thick, you need 1.85 cubic yards of concrete. It's a good idea to add 5 or 10 percent for spillage and/or an uneven subbase; round up to 2 cubic yards.

Batch-mixed concrete: If you are mixing your own concrete, you need to calculate how much of each ingredient to buy. Use the table below, which lists how many pounds of each ingredient to use to produce 1 cubic foot of concrete.

Size Aggregate (in.)	Cement (lb.)	Sand (lb.)	Coarse Aggregate (lb.)
⅜	29	59	46
½	27	53	55
¾	25	47	65
1	24	45	70
1½	23	43	75

For example, let's say we've determined by using the estimating table that you need 2 cubic yards of concrete. There are 27 cubic feet in a cubic yard, so you need 54 cubic feet of concrete. All you need to do is multiply the weight of each ingredient by 54. If you'll be using a maximum aggregate size of ⅜ inch, you'll need 1,566 pounds of cement, 3,186 pounds of sand, and 2,484 pounds of gravel.

Cement is sold by the bag—1 cubic foot weighs 94 pounds. Gravel and sand are sold by weight or volume. As a rule of thumb, a cubic foot of sand weighs 90 pounds and a cubic foot of gravel weighs about 100 pounds.

Thus, you should buy 17 bags of cement (1,566 lbs. ÷ 94 lbs. = 16.66 cu. ft.); 1⅓ yards of sand (3,186 lbs. ÷ 90 lbs. = 35.4 cu. ft. ÷ 27 cu. ft. = 1.31 cu. yd.); and a yard of gravel (2,484 lbs. ÷ 100 = 24.84 cu. ft. ÷ 27 cu. ft. = 0.92 cu. yd.).

worth the trouble. A good hard stream of water will do a pretty good job on the mixer, but throw in 5 or 6 shovelfuls of gravel, add water until it's really sloppy, and let it thrash around for a while. Then rinse it out with the hose until the water runs clean.

Controlling Cracking

There is no way around it; concrete slabs will crack. The material expands and contracts with changes in temperature and humidity, and these forces inevitably crack the concrete. Since it can't be prevented, reinforcing mesh and joints are used to control cracking so it will result in the least structural and aesthetic damage.

Mesh reinforcement: In all concrete projects it's a good idea to use some kind of mesh reinforcement to distribute the cracks and keep them tightly closed, thus preserving the strength of the slab.

A special transit-mixed concrete called fiber mesh has ¾- to 2½-inch fibers in it. If you are mixing your own, you'll have to use the traditional wire mesh. For patios and walks, use a 6-inch mesh of 10-gauge wire. For drives, use heavier 8- or 6-gauge wire mesh. The mesh is sold in rolls 5 feet wide × 150 feet long. To cover wider areas, overlap the mesh one square. Position the mesh a few inches shy of the perimeter and expansion joints.

To be effective, the mesh must be centered in the slab. You can pour half the

MESH REINFORCEMENT

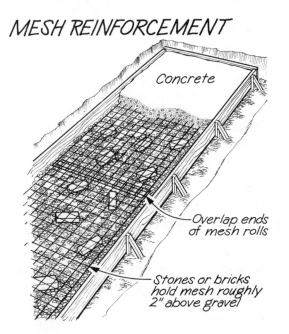

Concrete

Overlap ends of mesh rolls

Stones or bricks hold mesh roughly 2" above gravel

slab's thickness, lay the mesh, and complete the pour. Or you can lay the mesh on the base, pour all the concrete, and pull the mesh to the center with a rake. Or you can lay the mesh on small stones to hold it above the base and pour around it.

Concrete joints: The three kinds of joints used in concrete work are expansion, control, and construction joints.

Expansion joints allow movement where concrete abuts a building or another concrete element. Usually consisting of a ½-inch-thick strip of resilient fiber material, the joint compresses and expands with movement in the slab. For slabs on grade, the strips extend the full depth of the slab. Expansion joints are not *required* at regular intervals in sidewalks, patios, or driveways—that's where control joints come in.

A control joint provides a weakened section to induce cracking where it won't be obvious, in the seam of the joint. A crevice, penetrating to one-fourth the slab's thickness, is usually hand-tooled into fresh concrete as a control joint. For driveways, sidewalks, and patios, control joints should be spaced at intervals equal to not more than 30 times the slab's thickness—about every 10 feet for a 4-inch slab.

A construction joint is purely a matter of logistical necessity. Inserted where a pour is suspended for 30 minutes or more, it makes it possible for one man to build a large patio or drive. To make a construction joint, cut a piece of 2 × 6 to fit between the forms, and support it with stakes placed outside the pour. After the concrete has set, remove the board and continue the pour. Usually, a construction joint is placed where it can act and look like a control joint.

If your slab is more than 6 inches thick, a construction joint should be tongue-and-groove to provide load support across the

103

CONCRETE JOINTS
Control Joints

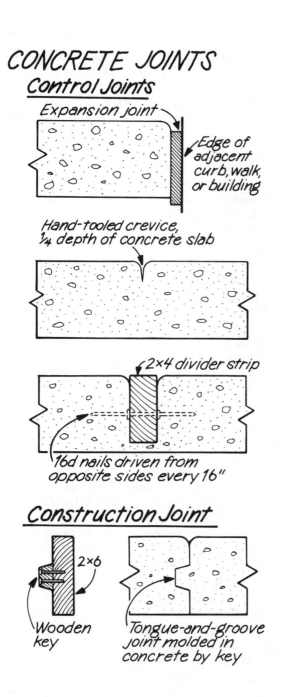

Expansion joint

Edge of adjacent curb, walk, or building

Hand-tooled crevice, ¼ depth of concrete slab

2×4 divider strip

16d nails driven from opposite sides every 16"

Construction Joint

2×6

Wooden key

Tongue-and-groove joint molded in concrete by key

joint. To create the groove, fasten metal, wooden, or premolded key material to the inside of the joint board. When you remove the board and continue the pour, the tongue will be formed as the concrete flows into the groove.

You don't necessarily have to remove boards used for construction joints. Use rot-resistant wood, and feature them in the design. This is an excellent strategy for a person working alone with a cement mixer. Set up all the boards before you do any pouring, nailing them together where they intersect and supporting them with stakes kept below the surface of the pour. Use any rectangular pattern you like, but keep the sections no larger than about 25 square feet, an amount one person can handle in a day. It's a good idea to put plastic tape on top of the boards to protect them from concrete stains during the pours.

Tools for Concrete Work

It's clear by now that working with concrete requires some special tools. Striking off, or screeding, is one of the first smoothing operations. It can be performed with a 2×4 cut a few inches longer than your job is wide.

Other tools include a wooden float or leveling trowel; a bull float, which is a large float with a long, broomlike handle; an edging trowel or edger; a jointer; a finishing trowel; and a mason's trowel.

You'll also need a shovel or two, a hoe, perhaps a rake, and, of course, a hammer and saw for setting up forms. If you use wire mesh reinforcement, you'll need wire cutters.

Knee boards are useful for distributing your weight over a broad area of the concrete and are used in floating and troweling broad expanses of concrete. Use 1- or 2-foot-square pieces of plywood.

CONCRETE WALK

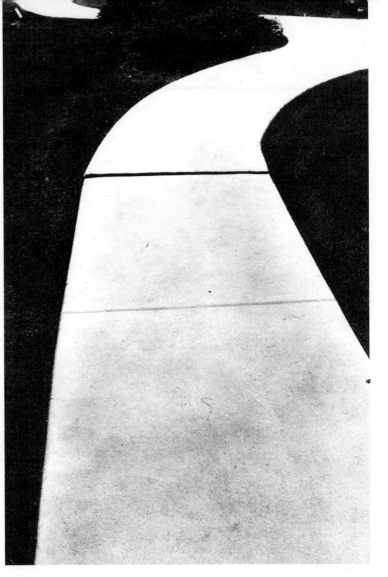

This walk offers an excellent example of how creative use of concrete can add texture and interest to the landscape.

With any concrete project, some careful planning is necessary. First, develop your specifications. Measure the area to be paved or the volume of the form to be filled, and compute how much material you will need.

Most municipal building codes require 4-inch-thick slabs for walks, patios, and private drives. If your drive will welcome the oil delivery truck regularly, you may want a 6-inch slab.

This walk is 4 inches thick. Though this thickness requires a control joint only every 10 feet, for the sake of appearance, the joints are spaced 4 feet apart.

Shopping List

(For a walk 50 feet long and 36 inches wide, with concrete 4 inches deep over gravel 4 inches deep)

48 pcs. 2 × 2 × 2′ (stakes and braces)
100 linear feet of 1 × 4 (forms)
2 cubic yards of concrete
7 tons of gravel

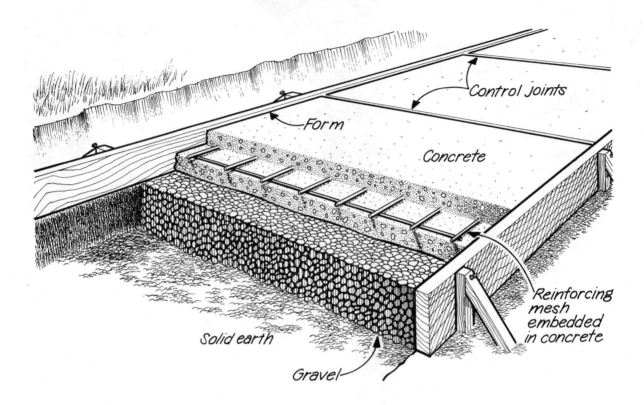

Control joints

Form

Concrete

Reinforcing
mesh
embedded
in concrete

Solid earth

Gravel

1. **Excavate for the walk.** First, lay out the sides of the walk with stakes and string. Excavate to the proper depth, and compact the excavation.

2. **Construct the forms.** In constructing the forms, consider the weight of the concrete. For a sidewalk, 1-inch stock will be adequate. For a patio or wall, the extra strength of 2-inch stock is advisable. Stake and brace all forms securely. Trying to repair a broken or uprooted form while your concrete sets will age you quickly.

For this walk, use 1 × 4 for the forms. One side should be slightly lower for drainage.

3. **Prepare the subbase.** Add gravel to ½ inch below the bottom of the forms. That's 4 inches below grade. Compact gravel. Lay wire mesh reinforcement.

4. **Mix and pour the concrete.** To prevent sticking, wet the forms where they will touch the concrete. Mix the concrete, using the proper proportions of ingredients for the walk. Work as quickly as possible, placing the concrete as accurately as you can with a shovel or hoe, leaving it about an inch above the top of the form. Knead the concrete with the shovel blade to work out air pockets.

5. **Screed and smooth the concrete.** Use a straight 2×4 as a screed. Rest the edge on the top of the forms. The object is to skim off the excess concrete so the surface is flush with the top of the form boards.

Next you smooth the concrete with a bull float or a darby. A bull float has a long handle and is used to smooth large areas you can't reach with a darby. Work the bull float as you would a sponge mop. As you push the tool away from you, hold the front up so it will compact the concrete without digging in. As you pull the bull float back toward you, run it flat on the concrete to cut off bumps and fill holes. The darby is short and low-handled, giving you more control in the easy-to-reach areas. It is moved across the concrete in a sawing motion.

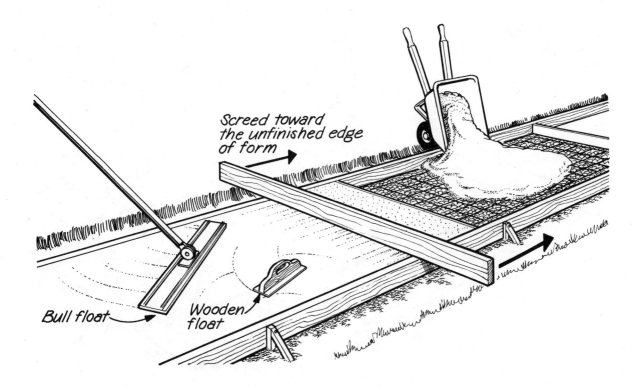

Screed toward the unfinished edge of form

Bull float

Wooden float

Smoothing should work up a small amount of cement paste, but overworking the concrete will weaken it.

After smoothing, use a pointed trowel to cut the concrete away from the forms to a depth of about 1 inch.

6. Complete the finishing operations. Wait until water rises to the surface of the concrete and evaporates. Check the concrete periodically. After the sheen of water has disappeared, try edging it. If it holds the rounded shape of the metal edging tool, finish the first edging operation with a firm, steady pressure. You'll edge again after each finishing step.

The next step is adding your control joints. Use a 1 × 6 or wider board as a straight-edge to guide the jointing tool and to kneel on as you work.

Floating usually is the last step in finishing outdoor concrete. You'll use a wooden or metal hand float to further smooth the surface. Work the float flat on the concrete, in wide arc motions. But don't press too hard. It is hard to erase gouges made at this point.

Sometimes concrete is troweled to make it even smoother and more dense. But this

FINISHING OPERATIONS

Use a trowel to cut concrete away from forms

Run edging tool along form

Slide jointing tool along straightedge to cut control joint

extra smoothness is not desirable for outdoor concrete because it can become slippery when wet. An alternative is to trowel to make the concrete denser and then use a stiff-bristled brush after the last troweling to make the surface skid-resistant.

The first troweling is done immediately after floating. If you need to kneel on a board to reach areas, you can float an area and then trowel it before moving the board. Hold the trowel flat against the concrete. The second troweling should be done later, when your hand leaves only a slight impression in the concrete.

TROWELING AND BRUSHING

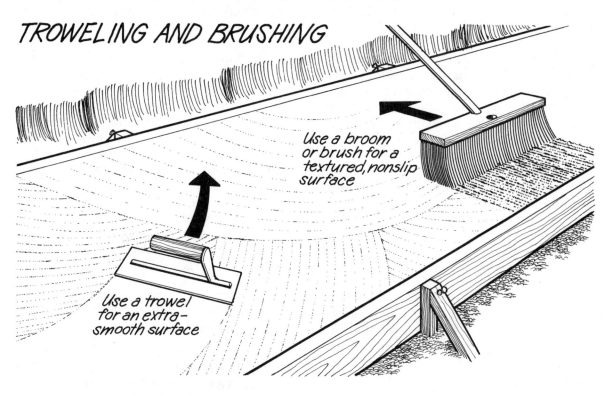

Use a broom or brush for a textured, nonslip surface

Use a trowel for an extra-smooth surface

7. **Keep the concrete damp while it cures.** It takes 29 days for concrete to cure to its full strength. The first 5 to 7 days, depending on the weather, are the most crucial. During this time, you must make sure the concrete has a chance to cure slowly by keeping it moist. Cover it with plastic sheets, damp burlap, or straw and sprinkle it periodically. The forms can be removed after several days. For best results, allow a few more days before using it.

Exposed Aggregate

An exposed-aggregate surface can be a particularly appropriate finish for a garden walk or patio. The texture and color of the aggregate makes the concrete surface blend into a natural setting. Exposed-aggregate finishes are not only attractive, but they can be rugged, slip-resistant, and highly immune to wear and weather.

Ready-mix: One way to obtain an exposed-aggregate surface is to order ready-mixed exposed-aggregate concrete brought in by truck. This mix contains pea or river gravel instead of the usual crushed stone.

Pour and screed the concrete. Float it well but not so much that you bury all the aggregate deep into the concrete. Wait until the concrete will bear your weight on a knee board without sinking. Then lightly brush the concrete with a stiff nylon-bristled broom to remove excess mortar. If this brushing dislodges any aggregate, delay the operation until brushing doesn't make this happen.

After an initial brushing, brush the surface again while simultaneously flushing away loosened mortar with a fine water spray. As the slab continues to set, washing and brushing can proceed at a more vigorous pace. (Soft- and hard-bristle brooms and special exposed-aggregate brooms with attached water jets are available for this job.) The washing and brushing should continue until exposure is uniform and at the proper depth, the flush water runs clear, and there is no noticeable cement film on the aggregate.

Seeding: Another common way of exposing aggregate is the seeding method. In this method, special aggregates are seeded into the top of the slab rather than mixed throughout the concrete. Because of the extra working time required with exposing aggregates, you may want to use a surface retarder for

better control of the exposing operations; however, this step is not essential.

Begin by setting forms for a conventional concrete slab. If the slab is large you may need to add construction joints, since seeding concrete takes about three times longer than normal finishing and you'll need to work on smaller sections at a time. When building the forms for a seeded slab, set the height $\frac{1}{8}$ to $\frac{7}{16}$ inch lower than the finished required height of the slab to allow for the added thickness of the seeding aggregate.

Use a maximum $\frac{3}{4}$-inch size of coarse aggregate to ease embedment of the seeding aggregate. The aggregate to be exposed must be carefully selected to ensure that it does not contain such substances as iron oxides and iron pyrite, since these stain concrete surfaces. For best results, select rounded river gravel and avoid crushed stone.

After the slab is struck off and darbied or bull-floated in the usual manner, spread the aggregate over the slab by hand or shovel so that the surface is completely and uni-

---

Screeding Allowance for Seeding

If you plan to pour concrete and seed it later with exposed aggregate, you have to pour a little below the top of your forms to allow for the volume of the aggregate you'll be placing on top. Here's how much to allow for various aggregate sizes:

Aggregate Size	Allowance
$\frac{3}{8}$–$\frac{5}{8}$"	$\frac{1}{8}$"
$\frac{1}{2}$–$\frac{3}{4}$"	$\frac{3}{16}$"
$\frac{3}{4}$–1"	$\frac{1}{4}$"
1–1$\frac{1}{2}$"	$\frac{5}{16}$"
1$\frac{1}{4}$–2"	$\frac{7}{8}$"

MAKING AN EXPOSED-AGGREGATE SURFACE

Seed stones evenly

Embed stones flush or 1/16" below surface

Expose stones with fine spray and brushing

formly covered with one layer of aggregate.

The seeded aggregate is embedded in the concrete by tapping it with a wood hand float, a darby, or a straightedge. Final embedment is done by using a magnesium float until all of the aggregate is entirely embedded and mortar completely surrounds and slightly covers all particles. The surface appearance after all the aggregate is embedded will be similar to that of a normal slab after floating, with all voids and imperfections removed.

Ideally, all the embedded aggregate should be worked down until it is covered with a layer of mortar about 1/16 inch thick. Care must be taken not to embed the aggregate too deeply and to ensure that the finished surface remains flat and is not deformed.

None of the seeding aggregate should become intermixed with the aggregate of the base concrete during the embedment. If this happens, the coarse aggregate in the base concrete will show up on the finished surface. Any need for additional mortar to embed the aggregates is generally due to an improper mix design or delaying the seeding and embedment operation.

Exposing seeded aggregate follows the same brushing and washing procedure as exposing ready-mixed.

Steps

Steps can be made of the same materials used to build walks. In fact, if you are building a walk, you'll probably want to do

Steps in the landscape can guide your entrance to the home (right), welcome your ascent (above), or suggest an intriguing detour.

112

just that. One very popular approach is to build landscaping-tie risers like a series of one-course retaining walls. The treads are filled in with more landscaping ties, brick, stone, cement, or compacted gravel or earth. Just follow the procedures outlined here for paving with each material.

Regardless of the materials you use, you must follow basic design rules if your steps are to be safe and comfortable to use. The rules are based on the fact that the higher you have to step up (the rise), the shorter the horizontal distance (the run) your foot can travel. For a comfortable stride, the sum of each step's rise and run should equal 17 to 20 inches.

How you apply this sum-of-rise-and-run guideline depends on where and how the stairs will be used. Interior stairs, which are always dry, accompanied by a handrail, and subject to space limitations, can have rises of as much as 8 inches. Consequently, each tread depth (the equivalent of the run) can be 9 to 12 inches. A step or two up from a patio into the house or up from the yard onto a porch can also have a rise of 7 or 8 inches. However, if you are planning steps to accommodate a slope in your yard, chances are you'll have a lot more run per rise. As a result, you'll want a maximum rise of 6 inches per step. This is comfortable where there is no handrail. Moreover, it makes using 6 × 6 landscaping ties convenient.

Steps to accommodate gentle outdoor slopes usually have landings—runs where you take at least one horizontal step between steps up or down. In fact, sometimes it is practical to let every step be a landing—two steps out for every step down. For layout purposes, landings should be thought of as two or more steps without rises. In other words, make each landing depth equal to the rise plus two times the run (if you are using 6-inch rises that would equal 6 plus 22 to 28, yielding a landing depth of 28 to 34 inches).

The first thing you'll need to know in designing steps is the total rise and run. This is easy to determine using a line level and stakes, as described under the heading Finish Grading, earlier in this chapter.

Planning outdoor steps is a trial-and-error process. An example will clarify.

Suppose you have a rise of 10 feet in a run of 27 feet. You've decided to use full-dimensional rough-sawn 6 × 6s for risers. That means you need 20 steps up. Divide 27 feet by 20 steps, and you discover the treads would be 16.2 inches deep. Awkward. The treads are too deep for one step and too shallow for two. The 6-inch rise demands a tread 11 to 14 inches deep and/or a landing at least 28 to 32 inches deep.

Cogitate. If you need 20 steps, each 11 to 14 inches deep, you can eat up 220 to 280 inches of your 27-foot (324-inch) run with normal steps. Consequently, landings of 28 to 32 inches must consume a total of 44 to 104 inches. Either two or three landings will give you steps of the proper size. Two 32-inch landings would eat up 64 inches of your 324-inch run, leaving you 260 inches to be traveled by 20 steps of 13 inches each. Or, three landings of 30 inches each will eat up 90 inches, leaving 234 inches to be traveled by 20 steps of 11.7 inches each.

Which combination of steps and landings should you use? Let the slope decide. Chances are it doesn't slope down in a straight line but includes some areas that are flatter than others. These are good spots for landings. You'll have to move the least amount of earth and the steps will blend most naturally into your landscape.

PROJECT
GARDEN STEPS

This simple, elegant stairway is an excellent design for a gentle slope. It is not hard to build, and the materials are relatively inexpensive.

Since most backyard slopes aren't as steep as the stairways you'll find in a house, this one has a gentler pitch. In this design, a gentler pitch means that the treads are wider than usual. And instead of wood treads, this stairway has treads of compacted gravel. The risers act as retaining walls, and the gravel steps provide excellent drainage as well as solid, durable footing.

Shopping List

3 pcs. 4 × 4 × 8' pressure-treated posts
2 pcs. 2 × 6—each 12 inches longer than the slope
1 pc. 2 × 4—12 inches longer than the 2 × 6s
18-5½ × ½" carriage bolts w/nuts and washers
20d galvanized nails
5 or 6 60-pound bags of ready-mix concrete
Approx. 3 cubic feet of gravel per step (Remember, if you order a truckload, there are 27 cubic feet in a cubic yard.)

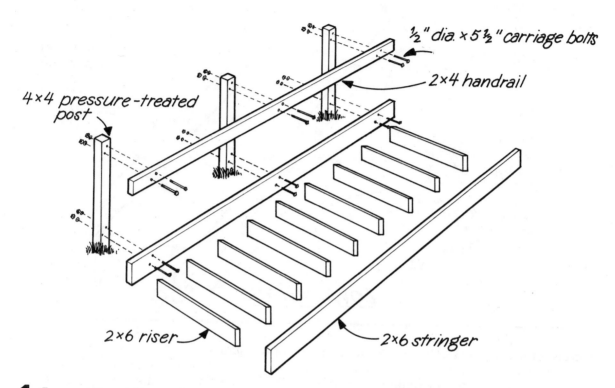

½" dia. × 5½" carriage bolts

2×4 handrail

4×4 pressure-treated post

2×6 riser

2×6 stringer

1. Lay out the stringers. Use two pressure-treated 2 × 6s for the sides of the stairway. These stringers support the steps. Select 2 × 6s that are about 12 inches longer than the slope where the stair will be built. Decide on the width of the stair. It should be at least 24 inches wide; 30 to 36 inches would be better.

To hold the stringers parallel, nail up two temporary braces—one near the top of the stair, one near the bottom—as shown. Place the stringers on the slope.

Using a level to determine plumb, mark plumb lines at the ends of the stringers where the stringers meet the finished grade. Remove the stringers from the slope, and make the four plumb cuts.

2. Locate the postholes. First, determine the locations for the holes. Place the stringers back on the slope, and use them as a guide to positioning the posts. Six should be enough for most stairs—two at the top, two at the bottom, and two at midspan. For long stairs, though, spans between posts should not exceed 6 feet. The posts butt against the outside edges of the stringers.

Move the stringers out of the way and dig the postholes 24 inches deep. Keep the holes as nearly plumb as possible.

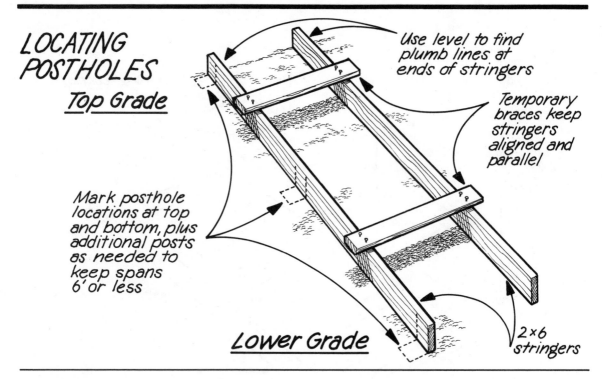

LOCATING POSTHOLES
Top Grade

Use level to find plumb lines at ends of stringers

Temporary braces keep stringers aligned and parallel

Mark posthole locations at top and bottom, plus additional posts as needed to keep spans 6' or less

Lower Grade

2×6 stringers

3. **Set the long posts.** Cut 30-inch lengths from three 8-foot 4 × 4s. That will yield three 66-inch posts for the railing side of the stair, the proper length to sink the posts 2 feet in the ground, clear the stringer, and provide a 32-inch railing height. The 30-inch cutoffs are the short posts for the other side of the stairway.

Set the long posts on the railing side of the stair (typically the right side as you descend the stair). Place the posts in the holes, brace them for plumb in both directions, and fill the holes with concrete.

4. **Attach the stringer and handrail to the posts.** After the concrete has set—about a day later—butt the rail-side stringer against the posts, and attach it to the posts with ½-inch carriage bolts that are 5½ inches long. Use two bolts at each post. Separate the bolts in each post by as much as possible to get maximum stability. Place the nuts and washers on the outside of the posts as shown, so they can be tightened as necessary after the stair treads are backfilled with stone.

Now check to see if all the posts extend the same height above the stringer. If not, trim as necessary with a hand or power saw. With the same size carriage bolts, attach a 2 × 4 handrail to the inside of the posts. The top of the handrail should be 32 inches above the top of the stringer; the handrail should be parallel to the stringer. If necessary, trim the post tops so they don't protrude above the handrail. Plumb cut the ends of the handrail as you did the stringers earlier.

5. **Install the second stringer.** Drop the short posts into their holes on the other side of the stair (but don't set them yet). Attach the posts to the stringer with carriage bolts as described above. Check to be sure that the stair stringers are parallel and aligned on the slope; install braces as necessary to get them parallel and aligned. Now, fill the remaining postholes with concrete. Let the concrete set.

6. **Install the risers.** To do this, use a 2-foot level to establish a level line extending from the top of the grade. At the point where this line intersects the top of the stringers, draw a vertical line. This vertical line is where you install the topmost riser. From the point where this vertical line intersects with the bottom of the stringer, draw a level horizontal line. Where this line intersects with the top of the stringer is where you install the second riser. Continue this layout to the bottom of the stair.

Cut each riser individually from treated 2×6 stock after measuring at its designated point on the stair. (This allows for a good fit despite slight discrepancies in the stringers.) Plumb and square each riser with the stringers. Fasten the risers into place with four 20d galvanized nails per side. It's best to drill pilot holes for the nails; it helps to keep the banging of the hammer from knocking the risers out of square.

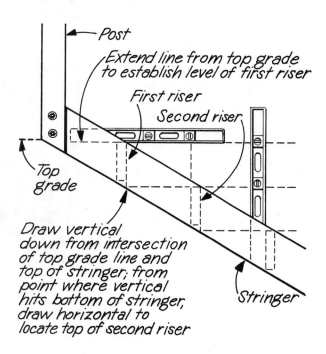

Post

Extend line from top grade to establish level of first riser

First riser

Second riser

Top grade

Draw vertical down from intersection of top grade line and top of stringer; from point where vertical hits bottom of stringer, draw horizontal to locate top of second riser

Stringer

7. **Fill in the tread spaces with gravel or crushed stone.** Washed gravel or stone, 1 inch in diameter, makes the best fill. Pack the stone firmly in place (a hand tamper is good for this). If necessary, pack stone in at the bottom of the stair up to the level of the bottom edge of the bottom riser. (You can buy gravel in bags at most home centers, or you can buy it by the truckload from local suppliers.

8. **Stain the stairway.** Wait a few months for it to weather before you stain the treated wood. For best results, use a water-repellent stain.

PROJECT

LANDSCAPING- TIE STEPS

These rugged stairs use a mix of materials—railroad ties and exposed aggregate —to create a rustic effect. For an informal garden or backyard, they offer an attractive alternative to poured concrete steps or wooden stairs.

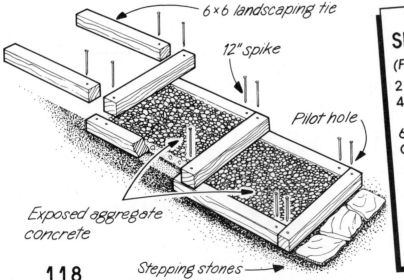

6×6 landscaping tie

12" spike

Pilot hole

Exposed aggregate concrete

Stepping stones

Shopping List

(For a 3-foot-wide stair)

2 landscaping ties per step
4-12" galvanized spikes per step
6-12" anchor bolts (optional)
Concrete—Figure the amount needed by multiplying the depth of the tread space by its width and length Then multiply that figure by the number of steps. That will tell you th number of cubic feet of concrete you'll need.

118

1. **Measure the rise and run of the slope.**
Use two boards and a level as shown. (For a
lengthy horizontal run use a line level.) The
distance from A to B is the rise; the distance
from A to C is the run.

Determine the number of steps by dividing the rise by the riser height. The riser
height will be 6 inches, because the typical
landscaping tie is 6 × 6. The best run for a

single step with a 6-inch rise is 14 inches.

The steps in the photo are 3 feet deep.
That allows walkers to step up, then step
horizontally before they step up again. That's
good for long, gentle grades. Unfortunately,
there are no foolproof ratios for such steps;
you just have to step off the run and see if it
works for you.

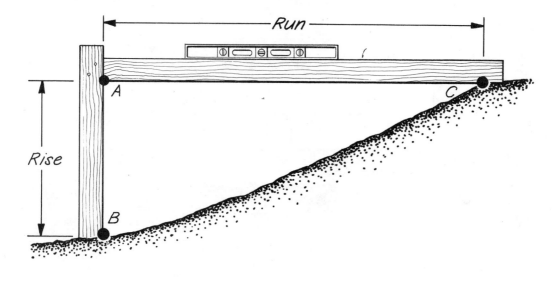

2. **Excavate as necessary to accommodate the stair.** The steps shown are 3 feet
wide. The minimum width for a utility stair
is 2 feet; a stair that will allow two people to

walk abreast should be 5 feet wide. Maximum width would be 8 feet; that's as long as
landscaping ties come.

3. **Measure and cut the ties to fit.** A chain
saw would be best, though two passes with
most circular saws would do the job. Wear a
dust mask and gloves when you do the cut-

ting; you don't want to inhale any chemical-
laced dust or have prolonged skin contact
with the pressure-treated wood.

4. **Place the ties.** After ensuring that it is level, anchor the first step using 12-inch galvanized spikes. Driving the spikes will be easier if you first drill pilot holes.

For a somewhat sturdier fastening, you can use 12-inch anchor bolts, as shown. Use four to secure the bottom step and two to finish off the top step. To do this, dig to the depth of a posthole digger blade and fill the

hole with concrete. When the concrete has stiffened slightly, push the bolts in. With a spade bit, drill countersinks in the ties as shown. Two days later, after the concrete has set, set the ties, then install washers and tighten the nuts.

Place the ties for the remaining steps, check for level, and spike the ties into place.

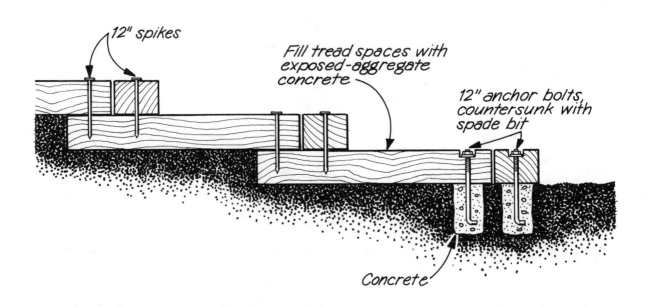

12" spikes

Fill tread spaces with exposed-aggregate concrete

12" anchor bolts, countersunk with spade bit

Concrete

5. **Fill the tread spaces with exposed-aggregate concrete.** Details on mixing and finishing exposed-aggregate concrete can be found under the heading Exposed Aggregate, earlier in this chapter. (For a large project, you might want to order exposed aggregate from a concrete contractor; most truck deliveries have a 3- or 4-cubic-yard mini-

mum. For a smaller job like this one—in which each roughly 3 × 3-foot tread space contains about 5 cubic feet of concrete—you can site-mix the concrete.)

A few hours later, clean any cement off the ties with a wire brush. Then backfill around the steps to achieve the finish grade.

Masonry Walls

Brick walls can be made of single, double or triple thickness, and there are a variety of ways of arranging or bonding the bricks. For a retaining wall, you should use at least a double thickness of brick. A single thickness won't be strong enough.

You can use blocks, though the wall won't be terribly attractive. Blocks are used extensively in construction these days for two very practical reasons. One is that they are significantly less expensive than bricks. The other is that block goes up a lot faster than a brick wall because the structural units are larger. You can achieve a thick, attractive, and reasonably inexpensive result by building a brick-veneered block wall. In this situation, you build a block wall, then lay up bricks in front of the block, leaving about ½ inch of working space for your fingers between the block and bricks. The two walls are tied together with brick ties—strips of corrugated galvanized steel that are mortared into the brick-and-block joints. Or you can use an ashlar veneer. For a retaining wall, veneering isn't a bad approach.

Additional strength can be gained with a block wall by pouring concrete into the cores of the blocks after the wall is laid up. The strength can be bolstered further by embedding reinforcing bars in the footings so they project vertically out of the concrete about 10 inches. These bars will fit into the cores of the first two courses of block. When the cores are filled with concrete, all the elements of the wall—footing, blocks, and concrete—will be securely bonded together.

Laying block is similar to laying brick. There are, however, a few extra things to consider. First, make sure the block is dry when you lay it. Block is very absorbent. If it gets wet and then dries in place, it may contract, cracking the joints. Second, block is more brittle than brick, so handle it carefully. Finally, be aware that the top of each block has wider edges than the bottom. This provides more surface for mortar.

Bricks

A wide variety of bricks is available, differing not only in texture and color, but also in grade. While finish and color are matters of personal taste, the grade of the brick you choose should depend upon the job it is to do and your climate.

The least expensive variety of brick is building or common brick. Building brick is as strong and durable as the more expensive variety known as face brick. The difference is that common bricks do not have to meet standards for color, design, or texture. This is not necessarily an aesthetic disadvantage, especially for outdoor building projects where you may prefer the more rustic look of a variety of colors and textures. Common bricks are about 8 inches long, 3¾ inches wide and 2¼ inches thick. However, the dimensions of common bricks can vary as much as ½ inch within a single load. When

Buying Brick

When buying common bricks for walls, you'll need approximately 7 bricks per square foot. When buying common bricks for paving, you'll need 5 bricks per square foot if you use a mortar joint, or 5½ bricks per square foot if you use no joint between the bricks. If you use pavers without a mortar joint, you'll need 5 bricks per square foot.

BLOCK WALL

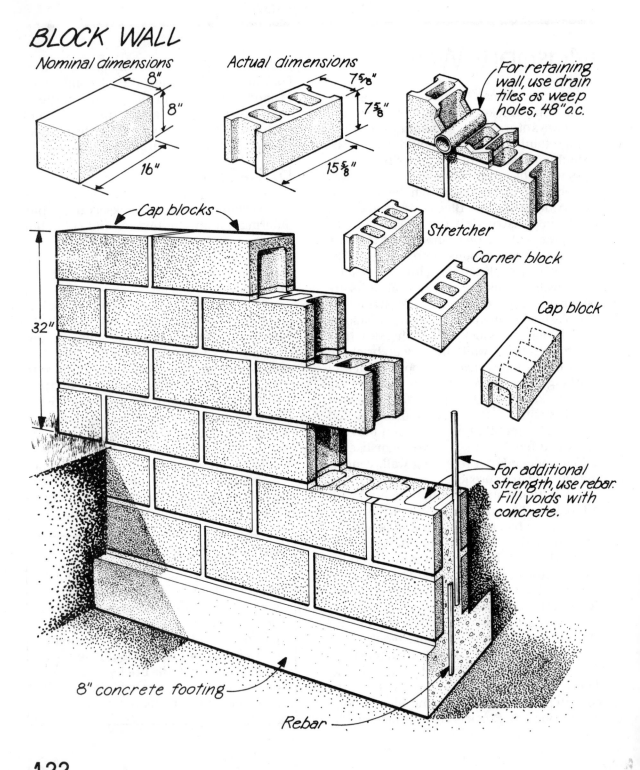

Nominal dimensions

8"
8"
16"

Actual dimensions

7 5/8"
7 5/8"
15 5/8"

For retaining wall, use drain tiles as weep holes, 48" o.c.

Cap blocks

Stretcher

Corner block

Cap block

32"

For additional strength, use rebar. Fill voids with concrete.

8" concrete footing

Rebar

calculating the number of bricks needed for a wall, use dimensions that take into account a ½-inch mortar joint. In building a wall, you'll be putting mortar on the top bed joint and one side head joint of each brick, so you would work with dimensions of 8½ inches × 3¾ inches × 2¾ inches in calculating the number of bricks you need. As a rule of thumb, you can figure on 7 bricks per square foot. This allows for waste.

Regardless of climate, severe-weathering bricks (SW) are the only choice if the bricks will be in contact with the ground, as they will be in a retaining wall or patio. You may also choose SW bricks if you have severe winters and the brick will be subjected to moisture. Moderate-weathering (MW) bricks can withstand freezing weather, but not if they will be in contact with the ground. If the bricks will be used in a veneer over a block retaining wall, you could get by with MW bricks in most climates. Stay away from nonweathering bricks (NW), as these are designed for interior work.

Whether laid in well-defined patterns (top) or arresting randomness (bottom), bricks are an attractive material for landscape constructions.

Mortar

Let's begin by defining terms. Portland cement consists of silica, lime, iron, and alumina. Concrete consists of cement and aggregates—gravel or crushed stone and sand. Mortar technically is a form of concrete but the only aggregate is sand. In addition, mortar contains hydrated lime. Most masons buy masonry cement which already contains hydrated lime, so all they need to add is sand and water. Mortar is gray-white, but you can purchase dyes at masonry yards.

To mix mortar, combine 1 part portland cement, 3 parts sand, and ¼ part hydrated lime with water. If you are using masonry

Brick Positions

Here are the six positions in which bricks can be laid:

Stretcher

■ The stretcher is the most common position. It is laid horizontally with the longest, narrowest side of the brick exposed to the face of the wall.

Shiner

■ The shiner is laid horizontally like the stretcher, but with its longest, *widest* side exposed to the face of the wall. The shiner is the most common position for paving.

Header

■ The header is laid horizontally with its wide sides at top and bottom and its 4-inch face exposed at the front of the walls. Structurally, headers are used to tie together walls that are two or more stretchers thick, although sometimes their purpose is simply to vary the bond. They can be used to cap walls.

Rowlock

■ The rowlock, like the header, is laid horizontally with its 4-inch face exposed to the front of the wall. But the rowlock is laid with its narrow sides at top and bottom.

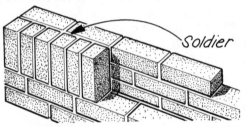

Soldier

■ The soldier brick stands vertically on end with its narrow side exposed to the face of the wall.

Sailor

■ The sailor also stands on end but with its wide side exposed to the face of the wall.

cement, the proportions are 1 part cement to 3 parts sand.

You can do the mixing with a cement mixer, but if you are working alone, as opposed to working with a whole crew of experienced bricklayers, it's probably more efficient to mix small batches of mortar by hand. Mix it in a wheelbarrow or a metal or plastic trough especially made for the job. A regular hoe will do for mixing, but a special mason's hoe, which has a couple of holes in the blade, is better. Use a bucket for measuring out the ingredients. A flat-bladed shovel is useful for shoveling cement and sand into the bucket and for shoveling mortar onto your mortarboard. Keep your tools hosed off; the mortar will dry on them surprisingly quickly, and once dried, it won't come off.

Mix your dry ingredients first. Then slowly add water. It is too easy to overdo the water, giving you soup rather than what masons call mud. For block work, you want fairly dry, sticky mortar, while for brickwork, the mortar can be wetter. But in no case do you want a runny mix. So mix the dry ingredients, then add water a little at a time while mixing.

If you do go too far, you can always add more sand, cement, and lime to soak up the excess moisture and, in the bargain, give you a larger batch. Just be sure the proportions of sand, cement, and lime are consistent with your original mix.

Start by mixing a small batch. It will take a little experience to get an idea of how much mortar you can use up before it begins to set. Your batch sizes will increase when you get into the rhythm of handling building units and mortar. You can revive a batch that's drying by working in a little water, but if you find yourself doing this routinely, you probably ought to cut back on the amount you are mixing in the first place.

Masonry Tools

Masonry work requires several basic tools beyond the mixing tools mentioned above. To apply the mortar, you will need a trowel. Choose one with a substantial wooden handle, since you will use the end of it to tap the bricks into alignment on the mortar bed. Some masons twist a rubber crutch tip on the handle to extend the life of the tool. If you use the metal trowel blade, the blocks or bricks could crack.

Another indispensable tool is a 4-foot level that can be laid on several courses or several blocks or bricks in a course to check for level and plumb. Most masons also have a 24-inch level.

String and line blocks help keep entire courses running level and plumb. A line block is simply an L-shaped scrap of wood. You start laying up a wall at the corners or ends, building up courses with a diminishing number of bricks in each. A level is used here to get the corners square and plumb. Then a string with a line block tied to each end is stretched from one corner to the other, lined up with the front top edge of the first course. The line blocks hook over the end bricks and tension on the string holds them in place. The space between the courses is then filled in, using the string rather than a level to check the alignment. As one course is completed, it's easy to move the blocks and string up to the next, one end at a time.

A mason's rule could also be handy, although you can cobble up a story pole to use instead. A mason's rule looks, at first glance, like an ordinary folding rule, and it does have standard inch and foot increments marked on one side. But the other side is marked at standard spacings for bricks, blocks, and mortar joints. The ruler is a guide to ensure that the thickness of your mortar

Bonds for Walls

The most common bricklaying bond, for walls as well as paving, is the running bond. Using only stretcher bricks, laid one over two, the running bond is the simplest to lay, requiring cut bricks only at the ends or corners.

The American bond is the same as running bond except that a header course is incorporated at a regular interval, usually every fifth, sixth, or seventh course. This bond is particu-

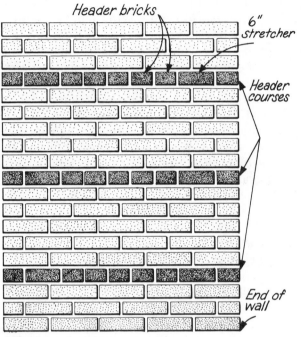

American bond

larly well suited to two-wythe walls, because it binds them together. To get the proper overlapping of joints, each header course has a 6-inch piece of brick (called a three-quarter) laid in the stretcher position on or against each end or corner.

An attractive variation on the American bond is the Flemish bond. In it, each brick in a course alternates from

Running bond

joints remains consistent. If you don't want to spend the money for this rule, make a story pole by marking your brick or block and mortar spacings on a narrow board.

You'll need a jointer, also called a striking tool, and a dust brush. The jointer is used to finish off the mortar joints so they are uniform in appearance and shed water.

This is sometimes called striking off the joint. You'll use the brush to dust the sandy mortar off the wall as you strike off the joints.

A mason's hammer, or brick hammer, and a brick chisel are tools you may want to invest in, though you could get by without them, depending on the job. First of all, it is possible that you won't need to cut any bricks

header to stretcher—making for a very strong two-wythe wall. The headers in every other course are aligned vertically. Every other course will end in a header brick. There are two ways to begin and end the alternate courses. You can use a three-quarter in what is known as a Dutch corner, or you can use a header and a 2-inch piece called a plug to form what is known as an English corner.

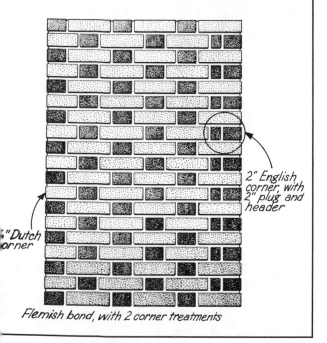

2" English corner, with 2" plug and header

3/4" Dutch corner

Flemish bond, with 2 corner treatments

or blocks to do your job. Or you could use a claw or ball peen hammer, if you already own one, to break the few bricks you have to cut for your job. If you cradle a brick in one hand and give it a sharp rap in the center with a hammer, it probably will break just about in half. If the rough edges can be concealed in a mortar joint, and they usually

can, there's no need for further chiseling. You can use the edge of the trowel to whack off ragged edges.

Finally, you'll need something to hold your mortar as you work. Perhaps you can work right out of the wheelbarrow you use to mix the mud. A square piece of exterior plywood can be set on sawhorses or blocks. Or you can buy a mud pan, made specifically for the purpose.

Footings

Concrete footings are an important preliminary step in building any mortared wall. It doesn't matter how well you build the wall if the footing isn't solid. Footings must always be set below the frost line so they can protect the structures built upon them from frost-heaving damage. Many specifics about footings—how deep? how wide? how thick?—are spelled out in your local building code.

As a rule of thumb, a footing should be twice the width of the wall it supports. A footing thickness of 8 inches is enough to support a one-story house and more than enough to support any project in this book.

Determine if local code requires a particular location and type of reinforcement. Usually, a minimum of three horizontal steel rods called rebar are placed in the lower third of the footing's thickness. Some walls require vertical reinforcing bars, which must be anchored in the footing.

The depth of the footing will be determined by the frost line in your area. In Bangor, Maine, for instance, the depth is 4 feet. In Tampa, Florida, which has no real frost line, it is 6 inches. Depending on where you live, excavation for footings can be a major task.

PROJECT
BRICK WALL

Build a brick wall; it's a good practical project to initiate you into bricklaying. The wall doesn't have to be high or long, but it certainly will be handsome. The sort shown is ideal for the beginner.

Built of common bricks, the wall is about 3 feet high and demarcates an entry patio, a semi-public area. Two wythes of bricks are laid in the running bond—it is the easiest, least troublesome bond to use, and minimizes cutting—and capped with a rowlock course. (The wall shown actually has half-bricks laid in rowlock, but a course laid using full bricks will be stronger and

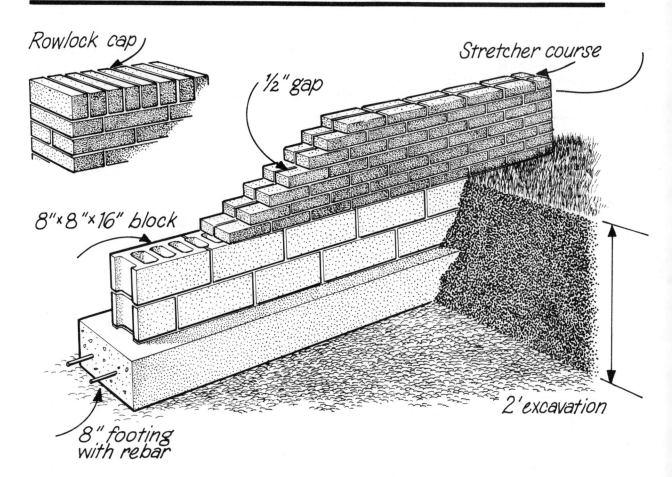

Rowlock cap

Stretcher course

½" gap

8"×8"×16" block

8" footing with rebar

2' excavation

will bond the wall better.) To accommodate both the mechanics of setting the bricks and their size, the wythes are set ½ inch apart.

A wall of this construction needs to be built on a footing poured below the frost line. The entire wall can be brick, but you can economize in terms of materials and labor if you lay masonry blocks to bring the wall up to grade. Above grade, of course, you use bricks. The illustration depicts the wall built on two courses of block. Add or eliminate courses to suit the frost line depth in your area.

Shopping List
420 common severe-weather bricks
14 8-inch blocks
2 sash half blocks
7 bags of masonry cement
1 ton of sand

129

1. **Pour a footing.** Start by digging a trench that will be wide enough to work in. Dig as deep as you must to get below the frost line. At the base of the trench, excavate for the footing and use the walls of the excavation as the form for the footing. Pour a third of the concrete, place your horizontal rebar, and then complete the pour.

2. **Lay a block foundation.** When the concrete has cured at least 24 hours, lay a block foundation to bring the wall almost to grade—in this case, two courses of nominal 8 × 8 × 16-inch block. Begin opposite ends of each course with a nominal 4-inch "sash block" to create a structurally strong running bond. The block should be centered on the footing with 4 inches all around.

Start by snapping a chalk line on the footing where you want the face of the wall to be. Now lay out the first course of blocks, working without mortar. You should leave a gap of about ⅜ inch between blocks to allow for mortar joints. Use a lumber crayon or a carpenter's pencil to mark the gaps where the mortar joints will go. Now remove the blocks and set them near the footing.

Spread a bed of mortar on the footing, long enough for a block or two, and set an end block firmly in it, establishing a ½-inch mortar joint. The wider edges of the block should be up. Make sure the block is level and plumb and aligned with the chalk line. Take the next block and smear mortar on one end with your trowel. Push this "buttered" end against the first block, carefully squeezing the vertical (or head) joint down to ⅜ inch, and settling the block into the mortar bed. Spread mortar on the webbing of the two blocks, and start the second course by setting an 8-inch sash block in place. Repeat the process at the other end of the footing, setting three blocks forming the end of the foundation.

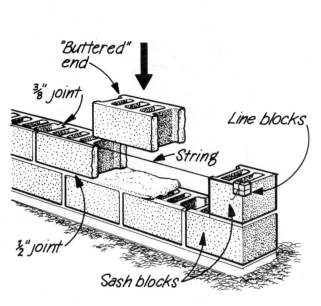

With the ends plumb and level, set up the line blocks and string and fill in the first course. Follow the spacing you marked on the footing, and align the blocks with the string. Move the line blocks up, and lay the second course.

3. **Make a dry run of the first brick course.**
Lay out the bricks on the foundation, working without mortar. You should leave a gap of about ⅜ inch between each brick to allow for mortar joints, but you can use joints of ¼ or ½ inch if this will allow you to make the whole wall of whole bricks. Remember that common bricks are only roughly standard in size and mortar joints will compensate for the differences. Since this is a two-wythe wall, you will have two rows of bricks set out atop the block foundation. The rows should be aligned with the edges of the blocks, with a gap of about ½ inch between them. Mark where the mortar joints will go. Now remove the bricks, and stack them near the footing.

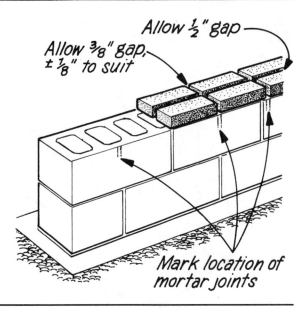

Allow ½" gap

Allow ⅜" gap, ± ⅛" to suit

Mark location of mortar joints

4. **Build up the corners.** Set an end brick in a bed of mortar. Set it carefully, making sure the mortar joint is ½ inch thick and that the brick is level across its length and width. Be sure, too, that it is flush with the face of the foundation.

Take the next brick and smear mortar on one end with your trowel. A bricklayer will do this, then with three more flicks of his trowel, shape the mortar into a tidy, four-sided pyramid, in a process called buttering. Push the buttered end against the first brick, carefully squeezing the vertical (or head) joint down to ⅜ inch and settling the brick into the mortar bed. Check the alignment with the level. Repeat the process for a half-dozen or so bricks.

Start the second course. As you work, check frequently with your level to ensure that each new course is level and plumb; use your story pole or rule to keep the mor-

Alternate courses begin with header bricks

Use a level to check for alignment and plumb

½"-thick horizontal joint

⅜"-thick vertical joint

tar joints uniform. As you build up the ends, each course should be a half-brick shorter

BUTTERING A BRICK

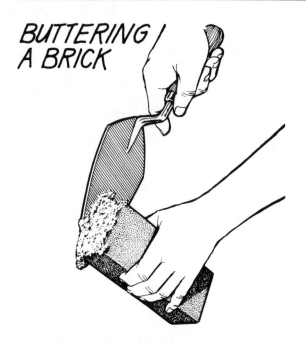

USING A STORY POLE

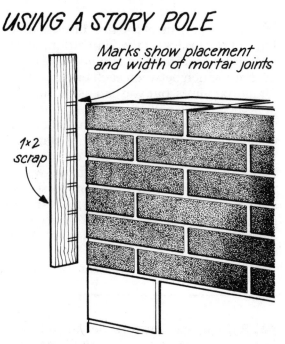

Marks show placement and width of mortar joints

1×2 scrap

than the previous one, giving the work a stepped appearance. Your last course should be only one brick long. Repeat the entire process at the other end of the wall.

5. **Fill in the courses.** Adjust the line blocks so the string will be a guide for the first course. The gap in the course is now filled in, using the string, rather than a level, to check the alignment of the individual bricks. When you get to the last brick in the course, butter both ends and ease it into place.

Move the blocks up one course, and repeat the process. Do this until all the courses are complete. If necessary, build up the ends of the wall again, and fill in the courses.

As you work, use the trowel to scrape excess mortar from the mortar joints. If you do it properly, you'll be pressing the brick into the mortar bed and cleaning up the squeeze-out at the same time. The little gobs can be tossed back into the mortar pan. Try to avoid smearing the faces of the bricks with mortar, since it is very difficult to clean off.

6. **Lay up the sixth course.** Begin by cutting two bricks to a length of 6 inches and placing them as "three-quarter" stretchers on each wythe at one end of the wall. Lay the rest of the sixth course as headers.

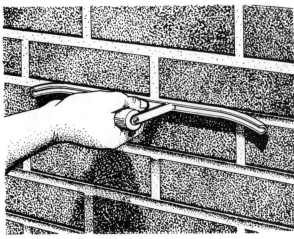

Striking a horizontal joint

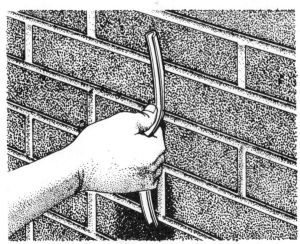

Striking a vertical joint

7. **Periodically, strike all the mortar joints.** You don't have to do this immediately after each brick is laid, but it should be done after every few courses. To test whether the mortar is ready to strike, press your thumb in it. It's ready if the mortar doesn't come off on your thumb but your thumb impression remains. To strike, just slide the broad face of the striking tool along the joint. Concave joints are most often used.

If you've got little pockets in your joints that need more mortar, hold a trowel with a bit of mortar on it by the pocket and use the jointer to push the mortar off the trowel and into the pocket. Strike horizontal joints before vertical joints.

After the joints are finished off, use the dust brush to clean the wall.

8. **Cap the wall with a rowlock course.** The bricks are in the rowlock position when laid on edge and oriented to bridge the two wythes.

Spread a mortar bed, and set the first brick in place. Butter the *top* of the next brick, set it on edge, its buttered top against the first brick. Continue until the entire wall is capped. Keep checking the bricks for level and plumb using the 2- and 4-foot levels.

9. **After the wall has been completed and the joints have cured, do the final cleanup.** Get a small bottle of muriatic acid at the building-supply company, and mix a very dilute solution according to the directions on the bottle, usually an ounce or two in a bucket of water. Wash the wall with the solution, using a stiff brush. For hard-to-clean spots, a scrap of brick can be used, though you don't want to deface the wall by scratching up the bricks. Wear rubber gloves for this job, and don't splash the acid solution around. It may be diluted, but it is still acid, and it can still burn.

Stone Walls

Stone is the most naturally beautiful and durable material you can use to build a garden wall, whether it is to be a retaining wall or a freestanding wall. It looks and works great in contact with the ground because, after all, that's where it comes from. If you use an indigenous stone, it can be inexpensive or even free for the taking.

There is nothing technically complicated about stonemasonry; you don't even need mortar. But you do need to use care in placing stones to ensure a strong and attractive wall. Stonemasonry, particularly dry laying natural stone known as rubble, is a very low-tech, visceral pursuit. Nobody can tell you exactly how to do it because nobody can predict exactly what your pile of stones will be like. We can just provide basic principles and techniques to work with. After that, it's a matter of getting the hang of it. If you are planning to work with rubble, it might be a good idea to get yourself a pile of small irregular rocks and pebbles and try your hand at a miniature wall.

The same inexactness that makes rubble stonemasonry impossible to learn from a book makes the work forgiving and easy to learn on the job. If you are dry laying a wall and it just doesn't look right, you can take some of it down and start again. And if the wall is really unsound it will let you know in no uncertain terms: It will fall down before you finish it.

There may be abandoned or ruined stone buildings in your area. Seek out the owner and bargain. Construction crews often consider the stones they have to excavate a nuisance. Offer to take them off their hands. Abandoned quarries seldom are picked clean, so check at the bottom of slopes for usable rubble. But keep in mind that stone that has been exposed for a long time can crack or crumble to the point where it no longer is usable. Be especially careful if you take stone from a building that has been destroyed by fire. Stone that has been subjected to extreme heat can develop internal cracks that may cause it to crumble later. A test for the soundness of any stone is to hit it with a hammer. A sound stone will ring, a cracked stone will give off a dull thud.

If you have to buy stone from a working quarry, keep in mind that unless the quarry is close to your home, hauling costs may exceed the cost of the stone itself.

Building with Rubble

Once you have the stone at the building site, you must sort it. A word on stone-handling safety: Don't overtax yourself. You are building a wall that might last centuries, so if you become tired, it doesn't matter at all if you leave the next stone for tomorrow. When lifting, let your legs do the work, not your back. Always keep the stone close to your body. Watch your footing. A pair of tough-skinned mason's gloves would be an excellent investment.

Separate your pile of rocks. In one pile, put the flattest, squarest, and most regular pieces. These will be needed for ends, corners and top. Put stones whose length is equal to the wall's width in another pile. These will be the "tie" stones. Also, make a pile of small, wedge-shaped stones to use as shims.

In working with rubble, it is generally easier to find a stone that fits rather than cut one. If you are building a retaining wall, you may be able to avoid cutting altogether because only one face needs to be regular; the other is covered with dirt. But some stonecutting might be inevitable. This is done

Stone walls look a part of whatever landscape they find themselves in, whether they're retaining planting beds (left) or defining a seemingly impregnable garden haven (above).

with a cold-tempered chisel and a sledgehammer. To cut a slab, score a groove about ½ inch deep where the stone is to be cut. If possible, make the score along the grain of the stone. Cut by one of three methods: Lift one end of the slab and strike along the groove with a hand sledge; lay the slab on a bed of sand and strike along the groove with the sledge; or place an angle iron beneath the slab and strike it from the top with the sledge.

Although you can use mortar to bind the stones together, cultures all around the world have built walls without mortar. There are practical advantages—the stones can ride out frost heave, eliminating the need for a foundation, and spaces between the stones allow natural drainage.

PROJECT
STONE RETAINING WALL

One reason rubble-stone retaining walls are so beautiful is that no two are the same. Each has its own character and contour as it nuzzles up to the earth it retains. In an age when most building materials are perfectly regular in dimension, the irregularity of rubble encourages the builder to work in harmony with the landscape.

While every wall is different, they are all built according to the same procedure summarized here. We'll assume this wall is about 2 feet thick, 10 feet long, and 3 feet high.

Tar paper wrapped around joint

Rubble wall

Perforated plastic drainpipe

Gravel

Shopping List
8 tons of stone
1.5 tons of gravel
3″ perforated PVC drainpipe,
as needed

1. Lay out the wall. Stake the two front corners, and then the two back corners. For a wall 3 feet or less in height, the minimum width is 24 inches. For each 6 inches higher than 3 feet, add 4 inches to the bottom width. Build the wall with a bit of taper. A good guideline is that the top should be one-fifth narrower than the bottom.

2. Prepare the foundation. Walls 3 feet high or less generally can be built right on ground level. You can make a stronger base for taller walls by digging down a foot or so and leveling the bottom of the trench.

3. Lay the first course. This layer must provide a sound, level base for the wall. Instead of using valuable slabs of rock below ground, dig holes to fit rocks with only one flat face so the flat face is up. These faces need not be exactly level but should dip slightly toward the back of the wall. This will turn gravity in your favor by having all the pieces of the wall pull inward. Place all the stones that are below ground level a few inches apart, and fill in the spaces with smaller rocks and gravel for drainage.

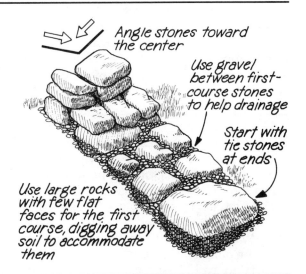

Angle stones toward the center

Use gravel between first-course stones to help drainage

Start with tie stones at ends

Use large rocks with few flat faces for the first course, digging away soil to accommodate them

4. Install a drainage system behind the retaining wall. Even though water can weep through gaps in dry walls, you should also provide for lateral drainage along the base of the wall. Along the back of the wall, excavate a shallow trench, then fill it with gravel. Lay perforated plastic drainpipe on the stone, perforations down. Cover the entire run with more gravel. As the wall is laid up and as you backfill, this drainage system will be buried in the hillside.

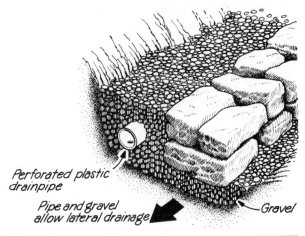

Perforated plastic drainpipe

Pipe and gravel allow lateral drainage

Gravel

5. **Lay the first aboveground course.** Use the biggest rocks you have so you don't have to lift them off the ground. Lay the ends or corners of each course first, using your squarest, flattest stones. Use as many long rocks as possible to tie the ends into the wall. Use tie rocks on every other course. Then work toward the center. At this point, you will begin to apply a basic principle of all masonry: one over two, two over one. This is exactly the way a brick wall is laid, and it ensures that there is no vertical fissure where the wall can separate. So, position stones so that the one going on top always covers the space between at least two stones beneath it.

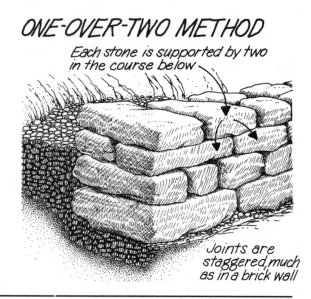

ONE-OVER-TWO METHOD

Each stone is supported by two in the course below

Joints are staggered, much as in a brick wall

6. **Add more courses.** Check the stones with a level as you go. If a rock wobbles, see if you can knock off a knob or point to make it fit more solidly. If not, use small, wedge-shaped stones to shim it up. These shims should always be placed toward the inside of the wall, pointed end out. If they are placed near the outside, they tend to work out.

Try to avoid using round stones; they simply don't provide a stable building unit.

If you have a lot of irregular stones, start each course by placing the worst stones down the middle of the wall so they won't be exposed at either face of the wall, placing and shimming them so they do not wobble. Then, place rocks with at least one flat side along the wall's exposed faces. In this type of arrangement, each stone should touch five others: rocks to each side, two rocks beneath, and at least one core stone.

7. **Incorporate tie and riser stones.** On any wall, you must place tie stones every 6 to 8 feet. Tie stones are as long as the wall is wide and are set across the width of the wall to add to its transverse strength. It's also a good idea to use a riser stone every six to eight feet, staggering the positions from course to course. A riser is a stone that's

TIE STONES

No more than 8' apart

Tie stones run between faces

RISER STONES

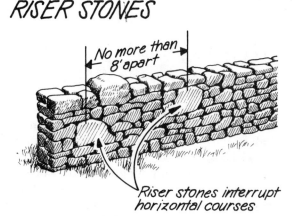

No more than 8' apart

Riser stones interrupt horizontal courses

FILLING VERTICAL SPACES

Weak alternative

Good alternative

about twice as thick as the other stones; it helps to knit the wall together by breaking the horizontal line of the courses.

If you need to fill a space in the wall that is longer vertically than horizontally, resist the temptation to fill it by setting a stone on its narrower side. It's much better to fill it by stacking several smaller flat stones.

8. **Incorporate batter.** Dry-laid stone retaining walls should be battered, but not by stepping the stones back. This would create ledges that the frost heave could push against, pushing the wall forward. A better approach is to make the face of the wall roughly plumb but make the first few courses thicker so that you actually fill on top of them. It's also a good idea to include a few extra-wide stones in the first few courses with the extra width extending into the hill as deadmen.

As you work with rubble, keep in mind that what you are trying to do is build something straight and regular with irregular materials—a goal that can never be perfectly accomplished. As a result, stonemasonry is a process of constant adjustment and compromise. If a layer of stone strikes you as slightly unstable, span it with a good solid rock that will take the load.

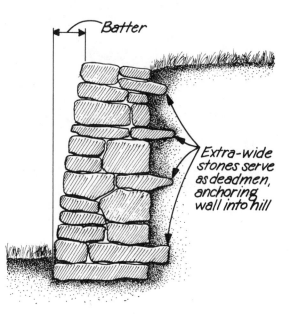

Batter

Extra-wide stones serve as deadmen, anchoring wall into hill

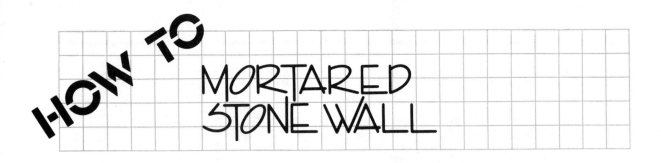

HOW TO MORTARED STONE WALL

Think of all the mortared stone walls you've seen. Obviously, you can mortar stones together. But the truth of the matter is that all you'd really be doing is making more work and expense for yourself.

To build a sound mortared stone wall, you should dig down below the frost line and pour a concrete footing. Then you should follow all the procedures you would for building a dry wall. But in addition, you must mix mortar, with all that entails.

For outdoor projects such as a retaining wall or garden wall, the reason to use mortar with stone is because you like the way it looks. Only you can decide whether or not the reward offered by the mortared stone wall will make the effort and extra expense of constructing it worthwhile.

1. Pour a footing.
2. Mix a batch of mortar and lay the first course. Build from the corners first, and fill in the middle. Spread a 2-inch mortar

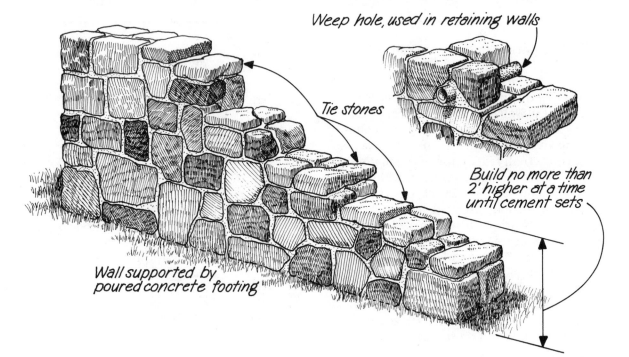

Weep hole, used in retaining walls

Tie stones

Build no more than 2' higher at a time until cement sets

Wall supported by poured concrete footing

bed, and set stones in it, each on its broadest face. Fill in the gaps behind the face of the wall with smaller stones, both to add strength and to save mortar.

3. Run a string from one corner to the other, along the face of the wall. As you set the stones that form the face of the wall, line them up with this string.

4. Set the second layer of stone. Spread 2 inches of mortar along an area 4 to 5 feet long. Place stones following the two-over-one method. Gently rest each stone on the mortar bed, pressing it to ensure good contact. If a stone must be moved after it has been set in the mortar bed, it should be lifted out entirely and reset to ensure a good bond.

5. With the front stones in place, fill in the back of the wall. The back may be filled with a cheaper class of masonry or be poured concrete known as backing, to save cost. Every few feet you should place a stone that runs entirely through the width of the wall, to tie the different layers together and to add strength.

6. Due to the weight of the stones, you should not add more than about 2 feet in height to the wall at a time. Allow the mortar to dry completely, usually for about 24 hours, before adding another layer.

Wooden Retaining Walls

Wooden timbers have become an increasingly popular material for building retaining walls. They are quicker and easier to use than stone or brick and blend well with a natural setting. You can expect a wall to last at least several decades if you use railroad ties or pressure-treated landscaping timbers.

In building any retaining wall, the first steps are to lay out the wall and to acquire your materials. Obviously, when you will be purchasing materials, you want to be able to estimate accurately what you'll need. Knowing the size of the wall, in length and height, is important in doing the estimating. Lay out the wall in place, to be sure the calculations you've done on paper actually hold.

The timbers you'll use are commonly sold in 8-foot or longer lengths of 6×6 and 8×8. You can get rough-sawn, full-dimensional wood, in which a 6×6 really measures 6 inches by 6 inches and an 8×8 really is 8×8. Or you can get dressed timbers, which have been planed after sawing. These timbers are smoother and their actual dimensions are ½ inch less than their named dimensions—a 6×6 actually measures $5½ \times 5½$. You can also get $3½ \times 5$ or $3 \times 4½$ pressure-treated timbers with two rounded sides and two flat sides for a log-cabin-like look.

Look for southern pine that has been treated to a retention level of at least 4.0 pounds per cubic foot.

You'll need to buy spikes to hold the wall together. You'll need 12-inch spikes that have been galvanized with zinc. Sometimes these spikes are referred to as log home or barn spikes. You'll need three spikes per landscaping tie—one for each end and one for the middle.

As you build up the courses, offset each course toward the cut by at least ¼ inch, so the wall leans into the hill. This offset is called batter. It helps the wall resist the pressure of the soil mass. To give the wall even more lateral strength, build anchors called deadmen at each end of the wall and every 6 to 8 feet in between. Deadmen are tied into the third course of a wall. They consist of 2- to 3-foot pieces of tie called crossplates which are located 8 feet from the wall and parallel to it. The crossplate is connected to the wall by an 8-foot timber. The deadmen at the ends of the wall become the first course of end walls. The deadmen in between will be buried. All these timbers and spikes have to be figured into the bill for materials for your wall.

Tools for Wooden Walls

You will need some tools that aren't always a part of the home handyman's collection. If you need to rent a saw, get a chain saw, which can zip right through any dimension of timber in one pass. Though it makes a neater cut, the circular saw is less convenient. The common 7¼-inch size can't cut all the way through a 6×6 in one pass. Moreover, with a circular saw, you won't be able to trim timbers after they have been spiked into place.

You'll need a two-pound sledge for driving the spikes. Driving 12-inch spikes without bending them takes a bit of a knack. If you have trouble, predrill the holes.

PROJECT

LANDSCAPING-TIE RETAINING WALL

Here's a retaining wall constructed of nominal 6 × 6 pressure-treated landscaping ties. This particular wall is 3 feet high and 20 feet long. It consists of eight courses of ties, including one course below grade. Of course, the height and length of your retaining wall will be determined by your terrain. This wall has four deadmen buried in the slope.

3'

20'

12" spike

6×6 tie

Top of slope

Deadman

Cross plate

Perforated plastic drainpipe

Gravel

Shopping List
30 pcs. 6 × 6 × 8' pressure-treated landscaping ties
102–12" galvanized spikes
1 ton of gravel
3" perforated PVC drainpipe, as needed

1. Lay out the wall and excavate. The first course of your timber retaining wall should be laid about 6 inches in the ground. After laying out the wall, dig a trench about 6 inches deep. The bottom of the trench must be level. If you are working with a complex slope, your trench may be more than 6 inches deep in places; it must be that deep at the shallowest point. If your soil is impermeable, so that drainage is a problem, you may want to dig deeper and add 6 inches or so of gravel in the bottom of the trench. In addition to improving drainage, the gravel will make it easier to level your first course. In any case, no footing is necessary, nor is it necessary to begin below the frost line.

LAYING THE FIRST COURSE

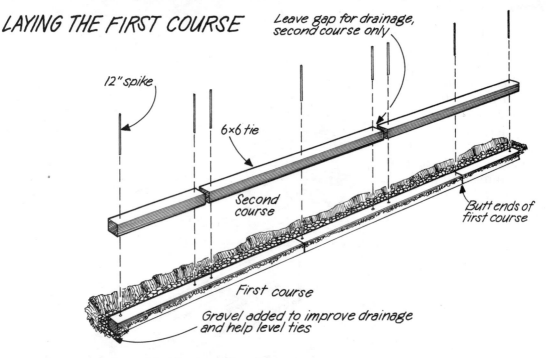

Leave gap for drainage, second course only

12" spike

6×6 tie

Second course

Butt ends of first course

First course

Gravel added to improve drainage and help level ties

2. Lay the first course of ties. Butt the ends together, and level them from end to end. From front edge to back edge, however, the ties should have a ¼-inch pitch. Use a level and ruler to establish this pitch.

3. Add the second course. The front edge of the ties making up this course should be ¼ inch back from the front edge of the first-course ties. Rather than butt the ends tightly together, leave a gap between them to allow for drainage. Stagger the joints from course to course. Spike each tie to the one below using one spike about 6 inches from each end and one in the middle.

4. **Excavate for behind-the-wall drainage and for the deadmen.** The drainage trench is created by simply widening the trench in which the first course of ties rests, then backfilling with gravel. Lay perforated plastic drainpipe atop the stone, a couple of inches from the second-course ties. Make sure the perforations are facing down. Cover the pipe with more gravel.

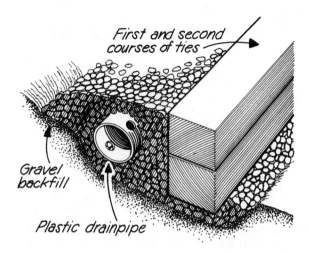

First and second courses of ties

Gravel backfill

Plastic drainpipe

5. **Install the deadmen.** Mark the position of each deadman's crossplate and ready a trench for it, if necessary. Cut the crossplates and spike them to their connecting timbers. Now spike the deadmen to the second course of timbers. The internal deadmen are now complete, but the end ones will be the foundations for end walls.

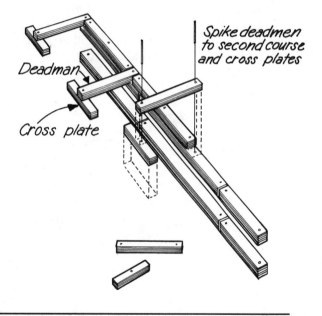

Deadman

Cross plate

Spike deadmen to second course and cross plates

6. **Add the remaining courses of ties.** Each new course is pulled back ¼ inch toward the hillside. Spike ties at each end and at least every 4 feet in between. That means three spikes for every 8-foot tie; two spikes for a 4-foot section of tie. The end-wall ties, joining the main wall at right angles, are also spiked at right angles to the end of the adjacent tie.

You can backfill as you build, or wait until the wall is complete. Just remember to backfill in layers and tamp each layer.

Protecting Plants

Earth moving can be dangerous to plants. When heavy earth-moving equipment is used, it is almost inevitable that some plants you wanted to save will be scraped, broken, crushed or uprooted. Even a careless pick swinger or wheelbarrow pusher can injure plants. Moreover, regrading often can present special dangers for trees, either by exposing their roots or by burying them too deeply.

Consequently, if your landscaping plan calls for the preservation of existing plants, and at the same time requires grading, drainage work, or other construction projects, you've got to take some precautions.

First of all, if a bulldozer, backhoe, or other earth-moving equipment will be used, make sure the operator understands the value you place on trees and shrubs that are to be preserved. If possible, fence off areas that are not to be encroached upon.

If you are doing work yourself with pick and shovel, you are in control. Avoid cutting too many roots when trenching or cutting. Think about where you are routing paths or swales. Don't run a heavily laden wheelbarrow over tree roots again and again; vary your passage if you can't avoid the roots altogether. Don't store mounds of materials— gravel or bricks or boards—on those roots, either. Again, try to fence off the preservation area from the *immediate* work area.

These cautions are largely common sense. What you might overlook is the sensitivity of trees, especially, to grading that exposes or buries roots. What you might not realize is that you *can* save that beautiful tree.

CUTTING AROUND TREES

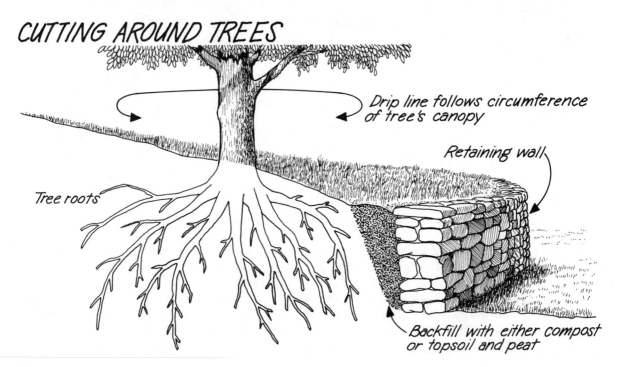

Drip line follows circumference of tree's canopy

Retaining wall

Tree roots

Backfill with either compost or topsoil and peat

Cutting around Trees

Ordinarily, cutting at a spot occupied by tree roots would remove the roots, thus killing, or at least severely injuring, the tree. You can save the tree if you are willing and able to compromise the cutting and build a retaining wall around the specific area containing the tree roots.

Doubtless, the value you place on the tree will dictate whether or not the grading plans can be altered to allow for a hummock harboring a tree. And your building skill will determine whether or not you can construct a retaining wall to gird the hummock.

Here's how to do it.

Start by marking the tree's drip line on the ground. The drip line is the circumference of the tree's canopy. Use stakes and string or a trail of lime to mark the perimeter of the cut. Some people have successfully tightened that perimeter by one-third by combining root pruning and branch pruning. If you've never done it before, you probably will want to avoid risking the tree.

After the regrading is roughly done, construct the retaining wall, just as you would any other retaining wall. In backfilling, use compost or a mixture of topsoil and peat, rather than subsoil. As you would in any backfilling operation, be sure to put down the soil in shallow layers, compacting each layer.

Creating Tree Wells

Tree wells with drainage systems are necessary if you plan to add more than 8 inches of soil around the base of a tree. This is because adding fill changes the oxygen content of the soil that was already in place. Moreover, in some situations it can raise the water table. Both of these results can be harmful to trees. Consequently, you have

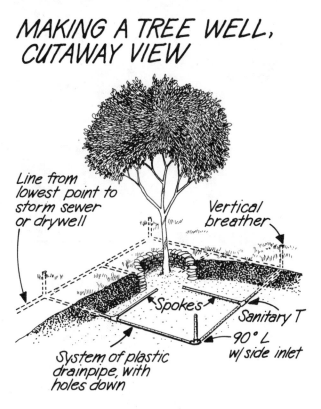

MAKING A TREE WELL, CUTAWAY VIEW

Line from lowest point to storm sewer or drywell

Vertical breather

Spokes

Sanitary T

90° L w/side inlet

System of plastic drainpipe, with holes down

to take special precautions in filling over tree roots.

Start by stripping the sod from around the tree, extending the stripped area several feet beyond the tree's drip line. Spread compost or other organic fertilizer over the area, loosening the soil and working the amendment into the top 2 or 3 inches. Be careful not to sever or nick the tree roots while doing this. Now lay down 2 to 3 inches of crushed stone.

Next, assemble the drain system. It will look like a wagon wheel, with the tree as the hub. Use perforated plastic drainpipes, positioned with the holes down. These pipes easily snap together. The spokes of the system should extend beyond the drip line; you should have four to six of them. In most cases, the pipes can be laid on the original

147

Save those valuable trees if you regrade your property. These unusual wooden tree wells have decorative value well beyond their function. Topping the vertical board walls are seatlike caps.

grade, but you should have at least ⅛ inch drop per foot of run *away* from the tree trunk. The ends of the pipes should be 6 inches to a foot from the trunk; an older, slow-growing tree can be crowded a bit.

Install pipes around the perimeter of your system, connecting the spokes. Vertical breathers are the last elements of the system to be added. Place one at each intersection between spoke and rim. A line should next be extended from the system's lowest point to a storm sewer or a dry well. If neither is within practical distance, you can make a french drain by digging a hole about 3 feet wide and 3 or 4 feet deep. Fill the hole with crushed stone.

As you lay the pipes, snap the ends of the pieces together; you need not cement them. After the whole system is laid out, spread crushed stone over all the spokes and the rim, to a depth of 8 to 12 inches.

The last step before filling over the system is to construct a retaining wall around the tree trunk, to hold the fill away from the trunk, creating a tree well. As with any retaining wall, it's helpful if water can weep through, so this is a good place for a dry-laid stone wall. Another relatively easy method is to use concrete blocks laid down with the cores facing the trunk. Create a funnel-shaped well, placing the blocks as you add fill and packing the blocks with soil. This way, water can move through the wall. Very little of the block remains visible, and you can plant groundcover in the soil in the cores.

In any case, the fill is put down only after the drain system is in place and the retaining wall has been started and finished. As with all fill operations, the fill should be put down in layers and compacted.

You don't, of course, have to encircle the tree for either approach to work. If you are cutting or filling at one side of a tree, you have only to build half or a quarter of either system. You do, however, have to do the preservation work *before* you do the grading. Once the tree shows the symptoms of root injury, it is too late to save it.

PROJECT
BRICK
PATIO

That extra space you need may be right around the corner. This 480-square-foot patio proves that.

The owners wanted more outdoor patio space. The yard, shaded by a huge elm surrounded by an attractive planting bed, already had a small patio. Positioned two steps below the back door and a step or two above the yard, the patio was retained by landscaping ties.

One option for gaining more space for entertaining was to cover the patio with a deck built around the elm. Another option was to extend the patio out into the yard. But eventually, the extra space needed was discovered just around the corner. By extending the patio around the side of the house, the owners were able to achieve their space goal and create a nook for some outdoor solitude, while preserving the existing planting beds and interesting multilevel design.

A new patio was chosen instead of the deck because it was judged to be both more durable and more in keeping with the character of the house and the older, residential neighborhood. Brick and landscaping ties were chosen for much the same reasons.

Because the layout itself provided plenty of visual interest, there was no need to lay the bricks in a fancy pattern. Except for borders, the bricks are laid in run-

149

ning bond, the most economical pattern in terms of materials and labor. The bricks can be laid very quickly; there's no time-consuming cutting and fitting. Few bricks need to be cut, and those that do are cut at 90 degrees. Given the bond, any size bricks would have worked. It is important to use pavers or severe-weather bricks, especially in colder climates. This patio uses replicas of colonial paving bricks.

Access from the yard is gained via a 9-by-6-foot brick landing. It is just a step up from the lawn, four steps up from the driveway. Step up twice more, and you are on the patio. The overall effect is cozy and unassuming. There's plenty of space, but there are also corners and turns that deflect the boredom of large, uninterrupted expanses of brick.

To finish off the entire project, a new cedar fence was installed to separate the new patio from the side street. A shed built into the fence beside the gate shelters (and conceals) trash cans.

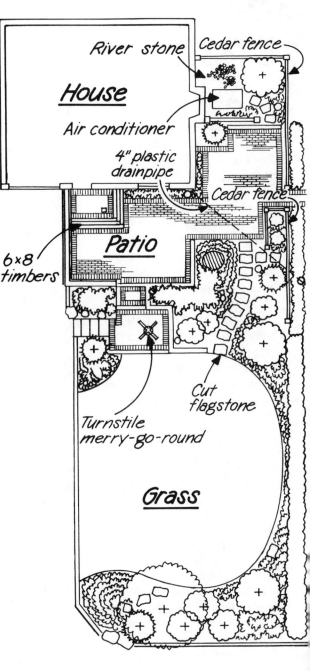

Shopping List
260 linear feet of 6 × 8 landscaping ties
60d galvanized spikes
2,400 brick pavers
25 tons of 2-A modified stone
6 tons of fine screenings

1. **Lay out the patio with stakes and string.** Because the patio isn't a simple rectilinear shape, layout is particularly critical.

2. **Excavate the patio area.** The subbase excavation for this patio was 12 inches deep; yours will vary depending on climate and the nature of your soil. If your land slopes away from your house, as was the case with this patio, you may be excavating in some areas or filling in others to create even grades. Excavate less where landscape timbers will border the patio.

3. **Place the first course of landscaping ties.** Check that the first course is level. Add or remove earth under the ties as necessary to achieve a level first course.

4. **Lay additional courses of ties.** In cutting and placing the ties forming the second course, overlap the joints, giving you good attachment at the corners.

Toenail the courses together using 60d spikes on the inside, where they'll be concealed. Use one spike every 3 feet or so. The base materials and brick will exert outward pressure on the retaining ties. By nailing in the same direction as the pressure, you are assuring that the nails can never loosen.

Lay additional courses of landscaping ties where necessary to compensate for grade. Continue overlapping corner joints as you did in the first two courses. Also continue the same pattern of toenailing. Where corner joints are exposed because of a step down, drive additional nails through the tie's exposed side and end into the ties it rests on.

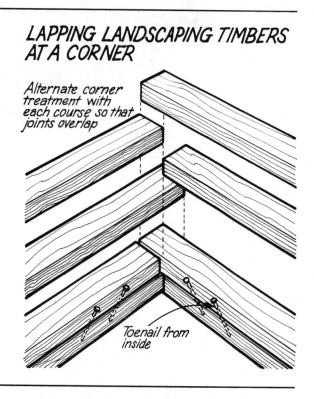

LAPPING LANDSCAPING TIMBERS AT A CORNER

Alternate corner treatment with each course so that joints overlap

Toenail from inside

5. **Spread and compact the patio base.** Start by compacting the bottom of the excavation. The best way to do this is with a gasoline-powered compactor. The tool has a flat foot that bounces on the ground.

Add the subbase next. Spread an 8-inch layer of gravel, wet down the stone, and compact it with the compacting tool.

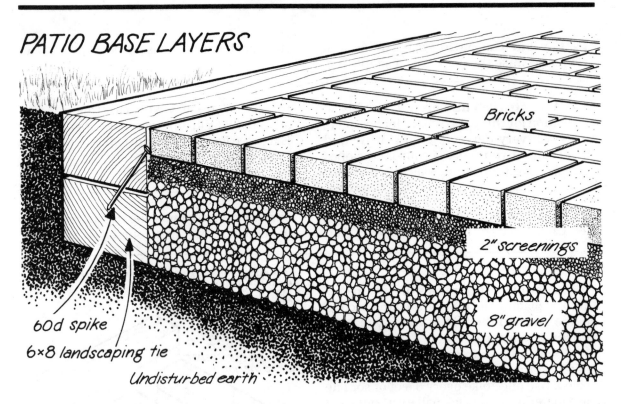

PATIO BASE LAYERS

Bricks

2" screenings

8" gravel

60d spike

6×8 landscaping tie

Undisturbed earth

Add the base. Spread a little less than 2 inches of fine screenings, a powdery by-product of stone crushing that's generally available from the quarry. (If screenings aren't available, you can use sand.) Wet down the base and compact it with the compacting tool. Add more fine screenings for a total of 2 inches and screed it smooth.

6. Lay the bricks. The opposing borders of the patio consist of bricks laid at right angles to the running bond. On the ends, full bricks are laid parallel to the running bond. Then the running bond begins by using half bricks for every other course.

Compact the bricks with a hand com-pactor or vibrating compactor. The bricks are 2½ inches thick, so they will sit about ½ inch higher than the landscaping ties. Compacting the bricks will work them into the base, seating them firmly and leveling them with the ties.

7. Brush dry sand between the bricks. Complete the patio work by grouting the bricks with sand. To do this, spread dry sand on the patio and sweep it back and forth. Wet the surface to settle the sand in the seams between bricks. After it dries, repeat the process. Repeat as many times as neces-sary to fill the seams completely.

PROJECT
BRICK PATIO AND FIRE TABLE

This outdoor space is quintessentially southern Californian. In a climate that is comfortable year-round, people often use their outdoor living spaces as much as, or more than, they use their houses.

Builder Gary Peterson wanted an outdoor living area that would lend itself to small family gatherings, or to entertaining a large group. Landscape architect Michael Kobayashi designed this sunken patio, which meets both demands. With its built-in food preparation area and barbecue, it can function as a large outdoor kitchen and dining area. Smaller groups tend to gather near the built-in fire table, which has a cozy wooden bench nearby.

The fire table is not a cooking device—it's more like an outdoor fireplace. A gas burner heats lava rock placed on a grill above the flame. The rocks, once

153

Shopping List

5,000 severe-weather common bricks
80 firebricks
250–6" concrete blocks
28 cubic yards of concrete
32 bags of masonry cement
18 cubic yards of gravel
lava rock
8 tons of sand
7' × 3" dia. cast iron drainpipe
½" dia. black iron pipe, as needed
    (for gas plumbing to fire table)
10' × 3" dia. PVC drainpipe (to stub in
    drains)
3" dia. perforated PVC drainpipe, as
    needed
1 gas ring log lighter
7 patio drains
1 metal grill

heated, will stay hot for quite a while. Warm but not smoky, the fire table is a pleasant gathering spot on cool nights.

The food preparation area is much like an ordinary kitchen base cabinet; it is built to standard dimensions from resawed cedar. The countertop is 6 × 6 quarry tile, laid over a subbase of ¾-inch marine plywood overlaid with a waterproof concrete-tile backer board. The tile is mated to the backer board with an epoxy thinset adhesive. The sink is a typical stainless steel kitchen sink. The built-in barbecue is a typical gas-fired unit. A fireproof gasket separates the barbecue from the plywood base of the countertop.

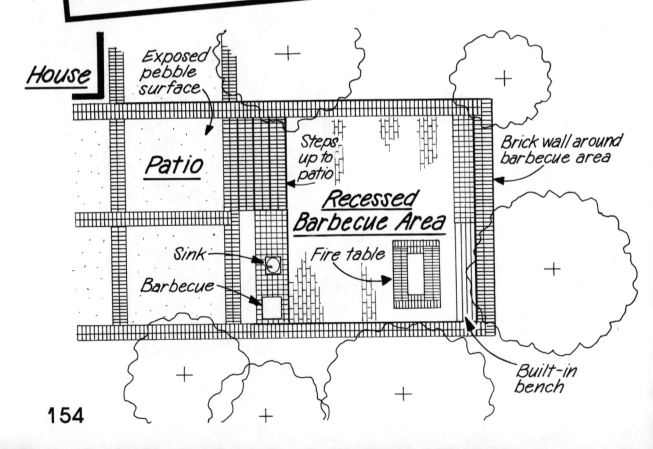

House

Exposed pebble surface

Patio

Steps up to patio

Brick wall around barbecue area

Recessed Barbecue Area

Sink

Barbecue

Fire table

Built-in bench

1. Start with the excavation. The patio is 24 feet square, and its floor is 2 feet below grade. This project calls for moving more than 60 cubic yards of earth—about the same as a foundation trench for a good-size house. The excavation will almost surely require a permit. Check with your local building codes administration. By even the most ambitious do-it-yourself standards, an excavation of this size is a job for earth-moving equipment.

Footings for the outside walls, the fire table, and the steps should be dug below the frost line. For the outside walls, the footings are 20 inches wide by 12 inches deep. For the fire table wall, the footing is only 12 inches wide. Excavate the trenches so the footings can be poured in place without forms.

2. Install drains and utilities. With a sunken patio such as this one, drainage is critical. This patio drains from seven points—four floor drains and three drains at the tops of the walls. The drainpipes are 3-inch PVC for the vertical pipes, and 3-inch perforated PVC, with the holes facing down, on the horizontal runs. In this case, the pipes connect to a large drainage system that serves the entire site; the system drains to daylight at the curb. Some municipalities allow drainage to the street; others require an on-site disposal system, such as a system of dry wells. Be sure to check with your local building codes administration. Slope on the drains should be no less than 1 foot in 100. Trenches for the drainpipe were dug by hand on this job. Alternatives include digging with a narrow backhoe bucket, or using a trenching machine.

NOTE: For the fire table drain, specifications call for 6 feet of cast iron drainpipe underground *before* it mates with any PVC. This is so if rain hits the hot lava rock on the fire table, the hot water will have a chance to cool before it hits the PVC.

Ensure that provisions have been made for all utilities. Besides the drain plumbing, all supply plumbing—both for immediate and any future use—should be in place. Gas plumbing for the barbecue and fire table should be stubbed in, and any conduit for outdoor lighting—present or future—should be stubbed in now.

After installing the plumbing and conduit, backfill the drainage trenches and carefully level the excavated area. Work on the rest of the project should continue as soon as possible, before wind and rain have a chance to significantly disturb the soil.

3. Pour the footings. Pours for both the exterior walls and fire table walls are reinforced with #3 rebar, as shown on the following page. Footings for the steps are a solid concrete pour, reinforced with #4 and #3 rebar.

4. Pour the patio slab. After the forms from the first pour are removed, the slab for the floor of the patio is poured. It is a 6-inch-thick concrete slab, reinforced with 6-inch wire mesh. Typically, such a slab is poured over 2 to 4 inches of gravel, depending on local soil conditions. As with any pour that is to be covered with brick, the surface should be left a little rough—not troweled smooth—so the concrete will form a strong bond with the mortar that holds the brick.

5. **Lay up the walls.** The exterior walls are laid up of 6-inch concrete block and reinforced with #3 rebar every 32 inches. The cells of the block wall are filled with concrete. The outsides of the walls are waterproofed with asphalt cement, and drain tile is run along the footing. The interior is veneered with brick in running bond. The top of the wall is brick in a doubled running bond, mortared in place. The outside walls of the fire table are laid up similarly.

NOTE: The brick for this patio was salvaged from an old winery. As a result, the bricks are slightly larger than modern standard sizes. Construction would be essentially the same using modern, severe-weather common brick.

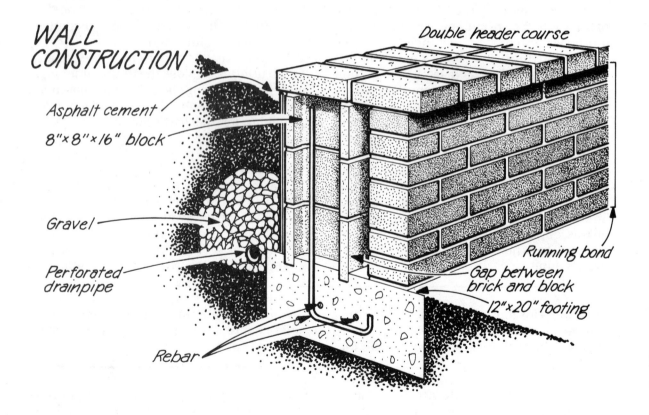

WALL CONSTRUCTION

Double header course

Asphalt cement

8"×8"×16" block

Gravel

Perforated drainpipe

Rebar

Running bond

Gap between brick and block

12"×20" footing

6. Complete the fire table. After the walls of the fire table are built, a 6-inch-thick concrete floor is poured for the floor of the fire table. Then an interior wall of firebrick is installed. A gas ring log lighter—standard fireplace hardware—is installed next. A metal grill is placed over the top of the fire table, and lava rock is placed on top of the grill.

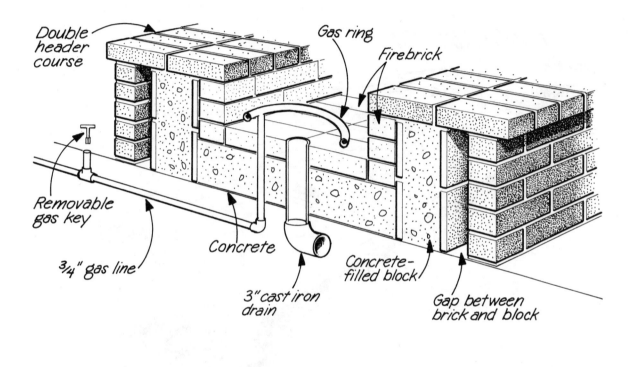

Double header course — Gas ring — Firebrick — Removable gas key — ¾" gas line — Concrete — 3" cast iron drain — Concrete-filled block — Gap between brick and block

7. Lay the brick floor and steps. Pour and screed a ½-inch bed of masonry cement over an area of the slab. Mix only as much cement as you can use in about an hour. Half-inch plywood can be used as edging for the screed; after the floor is laid, the plywood is removed and the joint is filled with cement.

The bricks are laid in running bond with ½-inch joints. Although it is tempting to lay the bricks then go back and grout them, it is a lot easier said than done. The approach professional masons use is to butter the bricks and lay them as if a wall were being built. Gently tap the bricks in place as you go. Using a mason's line and level, check the surface frequently, and adjust the bricks as necessary. If a brick is low, lift it out, scrape up the bedding and relay it, rebutter the brick, and reset it.

Strike the joints with a concave jointer. A few hours later, after any cement on the bricks has developed a haze, scrub the bricks with a burlap sack to remove excess cement. If necessary, cement spills can be cleaned off later with a muriatic acid solution.

The steps are laid up similarly; the only difference is that the bricks used on the risers are buttered and laid into place just as bricks in a brick wall.

STEP CONSTRUCTION

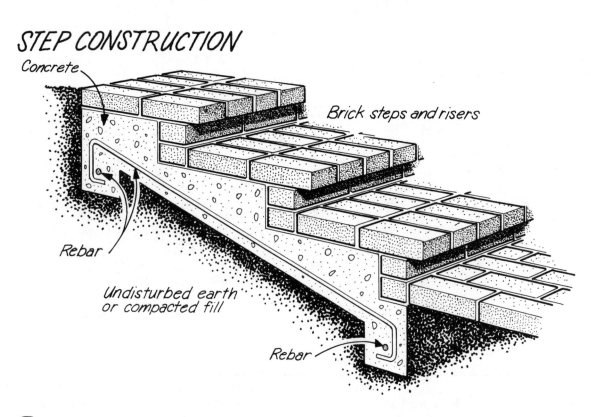

Concrete

Brick steps and risers

Rebar

Undisturbed earth or compacted fill

Rebar

8. **Finish the plumbing and electrical installations.** Once the masonry cement has cured and the brick is cleaned, 3-inch patio drains are mated to the drainpipes, and all electrical fixtures, such as outdoor outlets and lights, are installed.

FENCES, GATES, AND TRELLISES

Fences haven't changed much over the years, but the need for them is more apparent than ever. With the trend toward smaller lots and homeowners with less time to care for them, a fence can help you maximize the enjoyment of your property. Properly designed, a fence is an integral part of your family's outdoor activities.

First and foremost, a fence can provide privacy, and if thoughtfully planned, it doesn't have to be unneighborly or unsightly. A well-designed fence can help you keep your children and pets off a busy street, or serve as a windbreak in a treeless backyard. A fence can provide welcome shade on a hot, sunny day, while providing support for climbing vegetables or flowers. A fence can muffle a noisy neighborhood as it defines your property's boundaries. A fence can do all these things or none of them: It might just add interest to an otherwise barren landscape.

We are basically territorial animals. That's why we establish property boundaries in the first place. Fences are a permanent, physical expression of those boundaries, and it's a good idea to have everyone in agreement about where those boundaries are before building starts. So before you turn a shovelful of soil, talk to your next-door neighbors about the proposed fence. They may have been thinking of putting up a similar structure, and you may be able to split costs. At the least, agree on a design that will look good on both sides.

Letting your neighbor know about your plans before the fact is simply common sense and avoids any problems after the fence is up.

Before building the fence, visit your local building code official to check on any ordinances concerning fences. You may find height limits or materials restrictions.

Finally, make sure you know exactly where your property's boundary lines are. Check the deed for a description of the property.

That done, use some graph paper to

create a scale drawing of where the fence is to go.

Types of Fences

Here are the basic types of fences that you can customize for your particular needs.

Modern post-and-rail fences, usually made of naturally rot-resistant cedar, can be purchased with precut rails that slide into precut holes in the post and are secured with nails. If allowed to weather, this type of fence blends beautifully into the landscape, and can be a neighborly way of breaking up the monotonous expanse of suburban lawns. Although they combine nicely with shrubbery that can act as screening, you won't get much privacy or security value out of a post-and-rail design.

The picket fence has a traditional quality about it. Because it uses a minimum of materials, it remains one of the easiest and least expensive fences to construct. It's the fence of choice when you want to contain small kids and delineate your yard without seeming to turn your back on your neighbor.

The standard picket fence consists of horizontal stringers (also called rails) attached to the posts. The pickets are vertical boards attached to the stringers. Picket fences are mostly used as a decorative feature of your landscape, and offer little privacy and security value.

A board fence is built up from a frame consisting of a set of horizontal stringers joined to posts. A variety of boards (diagonal, vertical, horizontal) of varying widths can then be fastened to the frame. A basket-weave fence is a variation, with horizontal lattice boards 4 to 6 inches wide "woven" around 1 × 1 strips of wood. Board fences make excellent privacy borders, and can serve as windbreaks and sound barriers.

Building a Fence

Building a fence is not difficult. Lumberyards and building centers offer prefabricated fencing sections in a number of different styles. One of these fences can be put up quickly with a modest investment of time and money. But it won't come close to the quality look of a well-built custom-designed fence. A custom-built fence will also highlight the home it surrounds, adding to its resale value, so the extra money spent is well worth it.

The work of building a fence can be divided almost equally between the shop and the site. With few exceptions, the fence "panels" can be prefabbed in the shop; the stringers can be laid on the floor and the fence "siding" nailed or screwed in place. With the fence panels constructed, the posts are set and the panels hung.

The common fence unit is a nominal 8 feet long. With posts set 8 feet on center, the actual length of the stringers will vary according to the joint used to connect the fence panel to the post. If the stringers are attached to the posts with lap joints, for example, they can be a full 8 feet long. If they are to fit between the posts, they must be trimmed by an amount equal to the thickness of one post.

The Tool Chest

A circular saw is invaluable when building a fence, saving time and effort when trimming fence posts or cutting stringers and pickets. A saber saw is another versatile power saw that you will appreciate having if

Setting posts is a prelude to a range of outdoor building projects—erecting a boundary-line fence (above), setting up a gateway arbor (left), and, by fencing out distractions, establishing a nook for quiet contemplation (below). Each project has a different appearance and involves a different range of skills, yet all have a common base.

you decide to shape pickets with a unique cutout. If the fence is extensive, a band saw is an even better saw to use for cutting pickets.

Other valuable power tools include a variable-speed reversible drill. A power screwdriver is almost essential if you assemble your fence with screws.

Some hand tools that will come in handy include a 50- to 100-foot chalk line, a plumb line for marking true vertical lines, a carpenter's square and carpenter's level, and a 50- to 100-foot flexible steel tape.

Important digging tools required for any type of outdoor project include the proper posthole digger for your particular soil, a serviceable shovel, and a hoe for mixing a cement mix. A sturdy wheelbarrow is handy not only for carting away excess soil and rocks, but also for mixing concrete.

Laying Out the Fence

Once you've settled on the kind of fence you want, and you know where you want the fence to go, make sure the posts will be correctly aligned—the mark of a professionally installed project. Use furring strips chisel-pointed with a hand ax or saw to stake out the area, and stretch mason's cord from stake to stake. (Mason's cord is preferable to string, since it won't stretch and sag.) Start with the corners of your lot. Drive stakes into the ground a foot or two beyond the corner points, so the true corners will be located where the cords cross. Pull the line taut and secure it to the opposite stake. If you need a 90-degree corner, a carpenter's square can serve as a guide.

To achieve a perfect 90-degree angle at the corners, try the builder's 3-4-5 method: Measure 3 feet from the corner along one cord and 4 feet along the other. If the diagonal between the two points is 5 feet long, you have a perfect right angle.

Measure along the layout line from the corner posts to find the points for the other posts. (This is when that 50- to 100-foot steel tape is handy.) Mark each spot with a

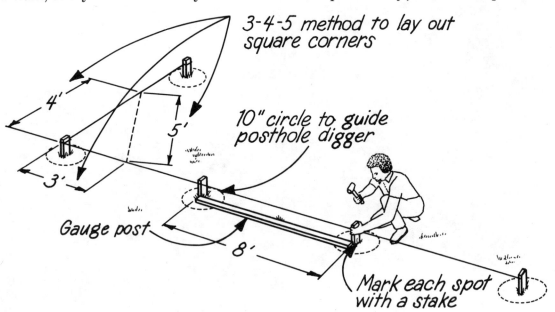

3-4-5 method to lay out square corners

4'

5'

3'

10" circle to guide posthole digger

Gauge post

8'

Mark each spot with a stake

stake centered in a 10-inch circle of lime or spray paint. The stake will mark the center of your hole, and the circle will help guide your posthole digger. An 8-foot span between the centers of the posts is best, since this span will avoid wasting materials, while providing adequate strength for most fences. Be as accurate as possible, since a standard 4 × 4 post only has an actual face width of 3½ inches. If you plan on butting or mortising the fence sections together along each post's centerline, that leaves only 1¾ inches for each section. (A good procedure to double-check your measurements is to use a gauge post—a piece of straight 1 × 2 cut to the length of the fence sections—set against your mason's cord to determine the locations of the intermediate posts.)

Live with the layout. Before you go out and purchase materials for the fence, live with the layout for a few days or even longer. You may decide to change the location of a gate, or an entire span of fence. It's much easier to move a few stakes now than to reposition a post later.

Dealing with Sloping Ground

If you're forced to deal with sloping ground, there are two basic approaches you can use. You can allow the fence to follow the slope, or keep the fence level by stepping the sections. Although the decision is an aesthetic one, on a gentle slope, you're better off following the grade of the slope. Just be sure the posts are plumb, but don't be concerned with keeping the rails level. This approach works well with simple fences, and gives the fence a more casual appearance. On a steep hill, it's better to step each section. You may decide to step the frame, but allow the fence boards to follow the contour of the land. On the other hand, you can slope the frame but step the boards. It all depends on what type of fence you're building and what you think looks best.

Sloped fence for gentle grades

Stepped fence for steep grades

Fence Posts

Assuming you are happy with the layout, you're ready to plant corner posts. A good rule of thumb is that one-third of the posts' length should be sunk in the ground. If your fence is to be 6 feet tall, you're going to need 8-foot-long posts (4×4 posts should be adequate for most fence designs, although 6×6 posts are better for hanging a gate).

Even if you're not planning to use pressure-treated wood for the rest of the fence,

Custom Post Tops

One of the easiest ways to personalize your fence is with customized post tops. Shown below is a sampling of ways to enhance the appearance of your fence's posts. The alterations have a practical value, too, since the end grain of a square-cut, wooden post should not be exposed.

Cutting a 45-degree bevel on the

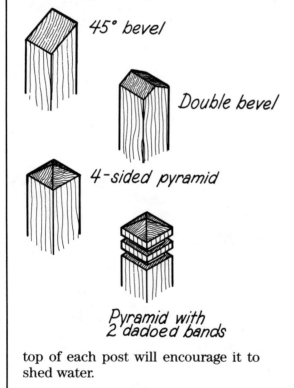

45° bevel

Double bevel

4-sided pyramid

Pyramid with 2 dadoed bands

top of each post will encourage it to shed water.

The quickest alteration is a double bevel formed on the top—like a miniature gable roof. Make two cuts with a circular saw.

Making four passes with a circular saw set to bevel yields a four-sided pyramid.

Using a router, you can machine decorative dadoes and grooves around each post. A ¾-inch straight bit, for example, can be used to cut a band or two around the top of the post. Line up the posts and cut all of them at the same time. Clamp a guide to the posts, and in one pass, cut a dado across one face of each post. Remove the guide, rotate each post a quarter-turn, reclamp the guide, and make another pass with the router. Repeat the operation until all faces are dadoed.

Study a router bit chart to see what ideas come to mind. Imagine what a v-groove would look like. Or a groove cut by a core-box bit. Or combinations of these. Experiment with short pieces of 4×4 until you find a pattern you like.

Yet another approach to post customization is to apply caps and trim. A square of 2×6 can be nailed atop a square-cut 4×4 post. A square of 2×4 can be added atop that. Cove molding can be added, as shown. To reduce water penetration, caulk seams.

You can go one step further and

pressure-treated posts (rated for ground contact) make a lot of sense, since most are guaranteed against rot for up to 30 years. Soaking posts in wood preservative yourself can't compare with commercial methods.

The end grain of the post tops must be

create a boxed post that will cover up the greenish tinge of a standard pressure-treated 4 × 4 post. Cut two 1 × 4s and two 1 × 6s to length. Apply the 1 × 4s to the post, then apply the 1 × 6s, overlapping the 1 × 4s. The wider boards will stand proud of the narrower ones, creating a subtle vertical accent line. Finish the job by topping the post with a square board or with two boards forming a miniature gable roof. Again, seams should be caulked.

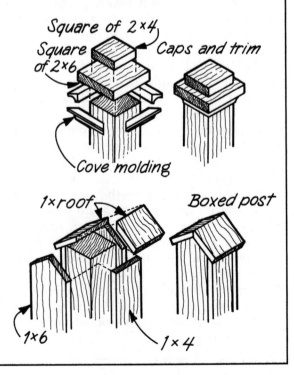

Square of 2 × 4
Square of 2 × 6
Caps and trim
Cove molding
1 × roof
Boxed post
1 × 6
1 × 4

protected from water. Water soaks easily into the porous end grain and hastens rot. Shaping the tops so they shed water or covering them with some sort of cap are two approaches that will work. The tops can be beveled on one, two, or all four sides. They can be sculpted. Turned caps are also available. If you're willing to spend a little time and imagination on the problem, you can fashion your own custom post caps. To accommodate a shape cut into the post itself, you should add 6 to 12 inches to the length of each post. If you apply caps and trim, brush extra waterproofer on the post ends and the applied wood trim.

Make sure you wear goggles and a mask when cutting the posts—the sawdust is toxic.

Digging Postholes

For a post set in concrete, make the hole at least three times the post width; for posts set in tamped earth, dig a hole that is twice the post width. To dig the postholes, use a clamshell-type posthole digger. This tool does a good job with most soils. There are several blade designs for different types of soils. (Soak the soil with water beforehand for easier digging.)

If you hit a rock near the maximum depth of the hole, trim the bottom of the post with a small chain saw.

Setting the Posts

After the holes are dug, it's time to line up your posts. Get the largest carpenter's level available and use it often when setting your posts. Setting the posts is the most crucial part of the fencing job. You don't want to get lazy now and end up with a wavy fence. After the posts are all plumbed and set, putting up the fence panels will go quickly.

DIGGING A POSTHOLE

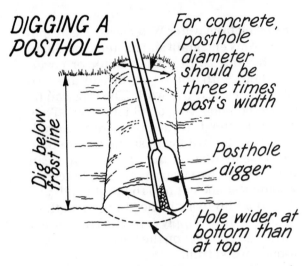

For concrete, posthole diameter should be three times post's width

Dig below frost line

Posthole digger

Hole wider at bottom than at top

Posts don't necessarily have to be set in concrete to assure a good footing. If the soil in your area is not sandy, you can probably set the posts in a footing of a few inches of pea gravel (available in 50-pound sacks—and larger quantities—where you buy concrete).

BRACING A POST

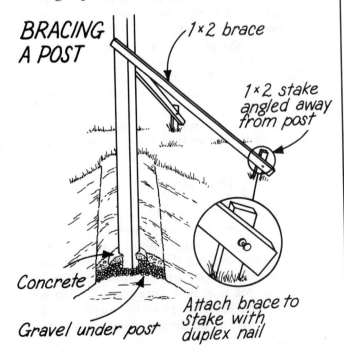

1×2 brace

1×2 stake angled away from post

Concrete

Gravel under post

Attach brace to stake with duplex nail

Using a Power Auger

Power augers can make quick work of digging holes. One- and two-man augers use a two-cycle engine adapted from a chain saw. They weigh between 15 and 40 pounds and can sink a 12-inch-diameter hole 40 or more inches deep in few minutes. Both types are available at tool rental centers. Before taking the auger home, make sure that you fully understand the unit's operation, that you have the proper fuel and oil, and that you have the size of auger bit you want (several different diameters and lengths are available).

Use caution when digging in rocky ground—the auger may kick out of the hole unexpectedly. For this reason, a two-man auger with two large wrap-around handles is far safer and easier to control than a one-man unit.

To use a power auger, measure the depth of the posthole on the auger bit and mark the spot with a large piece of tape. Drop the auger point into the ground so that it will stand on its own. Start up the power unit's engine. Set the chuck onto the auger shaft and lock it into place. Adjust the speed with the handle-mounted throttle (two-man units have dual throttles that must both be engaged before drilling can begin) and exert downward pressure. After digging a few inches, raise the bit to clear the soil from the hole, then continue digging until the tape marker on the auger shaft disappears. If you hit a large rock, stop the engine and use a pry bar to remove the obstruction before proceeding.

Firmly tamp the earth around each post.

Begin with the end posts, so you can use them as a guide to set the intermediate posts. Prepare enough stakes (1 × 2s about 18 inches long) and braces (furring strips 2 to 3 feet long work well) to plumb all your posts.

Drive two stakes a few feet away on adjacent sides of the posthole, and nail a 1 × 2 brace to each stake with a single nail so that the 1 × 2 can pivot. Set the post in the hole, and twist it into the gravel. When the hole is about one-quarter filled, the post can be aligned and braced. Plumb a side adjacent to a brace. When that side is plumb, nail the upper end of the brace to the post. Then plumb the side adjacent to the other brace and nail the brace to the post.

While a helper holds the post plumb using a carpenter's level, fill the hole with earth. Put it in about 4 inches at a time, and tamp each layer with a long 2 × 4 or an iron digging bar. Continue until the hole is overfilled. Form a cone of earth around the post to promote runoff.

The gravel underneath the post should provide adequate drainage. Wooden cleats (2 × 4 scraps) attached horizontally near the base of the post can be used to provide lateral stability. Lag screws partially driven into the bottom of the post can do the same job as the cleats when the posts are set in concrete.

When do posts need to be set in concrete? Primarily when the soil doesn't compact well. In any situation, you may want to set the corner and gateposts in concrete, since they generally are under the most stress.

Never pour concrete into a hole, then try to force the post into the mixture. An untreated post will quickly rot away from the lack of drainage. Instead, set the posts at the proper height in a footing of gravel as described above. Mix one part cement, three parts sand, and five parts gravel. Distribute the concrete mix evenly around the post, periodically kneading it to work out any air pockets. Align and brace the post when the hole is one-quarter filled. Overfill the hole and, with a trowel, form a concrete collar sloping away from the post. This will prevent the concrete from holding water around the post. After about 20 minutes, make sure the posts are still plumb, readjusting the braces if necessary.

Don't try to set all the posts in one day—it's far better to gain experience setting the end posts, letting them cure for 48 hours, and using them as a solid foundation to align the intermediate posts. After the end posts are up, stretch mason's cord between them, one strand at the top, another close to the ground. Put the cord on the side the fence will be attached to. Make stand-off blocks out of scrap wood so you'll have an inch or

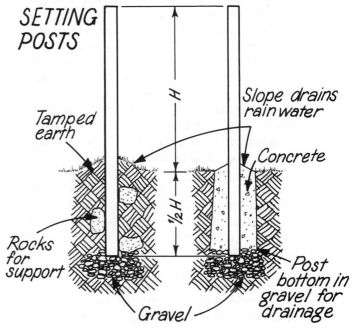

SETTING POSTS

Tamped earth

Slope drains rain water

Concrete

H

½H

Rocks for support

Gravel

Post bottom in gravel for drainage

FORCING A POST INTO LINE

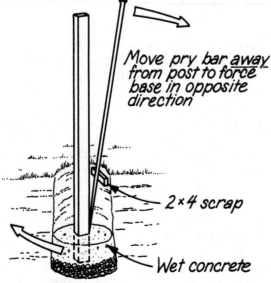

Move pry bar *away* from post to force base in opposite direction

2 × 4 scrap

Wet concrete

so of clearance between the posts and the string. After partially filling the holes with dirt or concrete and making sure the intermediate posts are plumb, sight along the top string to see if any height adjustments are necessary, and along both strings to see if any posts are askew. If a wayward post needs attention, shove a long crowbar, digging bar, or 2 × 4 into the hole to the base of the post. Set a scrap of wood between the pry bar and the side of the hole. A firm push outward with the pry bar should force the post into line. Work quickly before the concrete sets.

To double-check your post spacing, use an extra fence stringer. Test fit this stringer between pairs of posts. If one post is too close or too far away from another, adjust it now with your pry bar, before it's too late. When all the posts are aligned, finish filling the holes with earth or concrete and brace them. Don't remove the braces and install the fence panels until the concrete cures (at least 48 hours).

Picket Fences

A picket fence conjures up pleasant memories for many people. It is the fence that surrounds the stereotypical American dream house. White and pure, yet a symbol of security. The pickets, with their points, have their belligerent antecedents, yet they are clearly unthreatening, too low to turn aside any but the most diffident.

While relatively economical of materials, a picket fence—especially an elaborate one—can be time-consuming to cut out and assemble. It nevertheless offers plenty of flexibility for the homeowner in both rural and urban settings.

As you design a picket fence, you have dozens of options to weigh. Picket fences are infinitely varied. Picket dimensions can vary—wide, narrow, alternating wide and narrow. Picket thickness can vary. Obviously, picket shape can vary. Pickets can even be fashioned from dowels or square stock instead of flat boards. Consider also that picket height can vary, yielding effects from castellated to gently rolling. The gap between pickets can also vary.

In addition, there are the posts to consider. The simplest way to install the fence sections is to butt the stringers against the fronts of the posts. This will create an unbroken line of pickets. But the stringers can be fastened to the backs of the posts. The posts thus become towers punctuating the rank of pickets. In this arrangement, taller posts can be used. A third way to install the sections is to mount them *between* the posts. The posts are a part of the design, without being a dominant element.

In any of these variations, the posts can blend with the rest of the design, or be finished off with turned finials and molding.

Think about the proportions of the fence. A fence that's too long or short for its height may look stretched out or squat. For variation, you can stagger pickets of two sizes, or experiment with the shape of the picket

POST-TO-STRINGER JOINERY

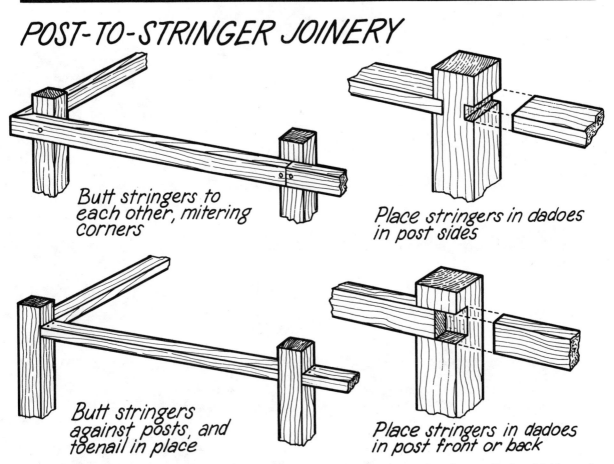

Butt stringers to each other, mitering corners

Place stringers in dadoes in post sides

Butt stringers against posts, and toenail in place

Place stringers in dadoes in post front or back

tips. You can also lay out a pattern on the pickets—single or double diamonds, for example—to add some flair to a potentially boring design.

Before settling on a design, you may want to lay out one full section in the shop to see how it looks.

Building a picket fence will involve a fair amount of shop time. Provided you set the posts accurately, you can cut and assemble all the fence sections in the shop.

Cut a picket template from hardboard. Then use a saber saw or band saw to cut out the pickets. You can stack and cut several at a time. To save money, make the pickets out of pine, the stringers out of fir. If your design

uses a bottom trim piece called a skirt board, be sure to make it from pressure-treated wood rated for ground contact. Fasten the pickets to the stringers with galvanized all-purpose screws (they won't pop out like nails and are far easier to remove without damaging the wood). Make some gauge blocks from scrap wood to space the pickets evenly.

Use galvanized all-purpose screws, instead of nails, to secure the fence sections to the posts. If you can't get anyone to hold the fence sections up while you level them and screw them into place, you can nail cleats made from scraps to the posts to support the sections while you drive the screws.

169

Don't fence in your creativity. Picket fence building should be a creative challenge. Don't just point the tops of the pickets; shape them like spearheads (top right), or vary their length (top left), or use wider (above) or square (right) stock. Use the posts as a counterpoint (above and right) or a harmonizing element (top left and top right). Just don't let the fence be boring.

170

PICKET FENCE

Picket fences have their roots in colonial days. Visit any colonial restoration or reconstruction, and you'll see lots of picket fences, lots of picket gates.

The fence and gate shown are faithful to the Williamsburg style of fence. Before settling on the specifics, the homeowners visited Colonial Williamsburg and studied the fences and gates they saw there, taking notes and measurements. The design they settled on doesn't just reflect the character of the colonial picket fences, it *duplicates* it, right down to the scale of the materials.

All the lumber is at the colonial dimensions. The posts are a hefty 5 inches square, the stringers 2½ × 3½ inches, the pickets 1¹/₁₆ inches thick. (The colonial settlers didn't have redwood, which is specified here, but they surely would have used it if they did.) Square-cut nails are used to secure the pickets; they aren't obvious, but the discerning eye picks them out.

The gate hardware is hand forged.

The obvious colonial element is the shape of the post finials, which is echoed in the shape of the picket tops. Not immediately obvious, until you use the gate, is the colonial gate closer—a ball and chain suspended between the inside of the gate—which only opens out—and a chain post, set a couple of feet behind the fence. The weight of the ball on the chain gets the gate pulled closed. No latch necessary.

171

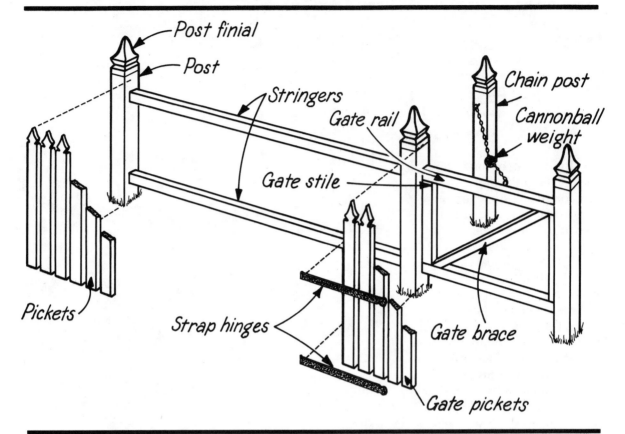

Post finial

Post

Stringers

Gate rail

Chain post

Cannonball weight

Gate stile

Pickets

Strap hinges

Gate brace

Gate pickets

Cutting List

Number	Piece	Dimensions	Material
3	Posts	5″ × 5″ × 68″	redwood
1	Chain post	3½″ × 3½″ × 60″	redwood
3	Finials	5″ × 5″ × 10½″	redwood
2	Fence stringers	2½″ × 3½″ × 91″	redwood
22	Pickets	1 1/16″ × 2½″ × 39½″	redwood
2	Gate rails	1½″ × 3½″ × 43½″	redwood
2	Gate stiles	1½″ × 3½″ × 21″	redwood
1	Gate brace	1½″ × 3½″ × 45⅝″	redwood
2	Pickets	1 1/16″ × 2½″ × 39½″	redwood
2	Pickets	1 1/16″ × 2½″ × 38⅛″	redwood
2	Pickets	1 1/16″ × 2½″ × 37¼″	redwood
2	Pickets	1 1/16″ × 2½″ × 36¼″	redwood
2	Pickets	1 1/16″ × 2½″ × 35⅞″	redwood
1	Picket	1 1/16″ × 2½″ × 35¾″	redwood

1. **Cut the posts and the finial blocks.**
The posts are a nonstandard girth. The 6×6
stock must be planed or ripped to reduce it
to 5×5 inches. When the desired dimensions are achieved, cut three posts and three
finial blocks.

Chamfer the top edges of the posts and
the bottom edges of the finial blocks with a
block plane. When the finials are eventually
installed atop the posts, the chamfers will
form a modest V-groove, which conceals the
joint between the two pieces simply by high-
lighting it.

Shopping List

3 pcs. $6 \times 6 \times 8'$ construction heart
redwood
1 pc. $4 \times 4 \times 8'$ construction heart
redwood
2 pcs. $3 \times 4 \times 8'$ construction heart
redwood
1 pc. $2 \times 4 \times 16'$ construction heart
redwood
11 pcs. $\frac{5}{4} \times 3 \times 10'$ construction heart
redwood
1 pr. hand-forged strap hinges,
$2\frac{1}{4}'' \times 25\frac{1}{2}''$
1 pr. hinge pintles
2–3'' screw hooks
1 hand-forged gate latch
5 feet of 1'' steel chain
1 cannonball w/eyebolt
12d galvanized finishing nails
3'' cut nails
exterior-grade paint

2. **Lay out and cut the finials.** Cutting
the finials is a band saw operation.

Lay out the cuts first. Enlarge the pattern for the finials onto a heavy piece of
cardboard. Cut out the pattern, forming a
template, and trace the pattern onto each
side of all three finial blocks.

To completely cut out the finials, you
must save the waste from the first two cuts,
which must be made into opposite—not
adjoining—sides of the block. To provide a
flat bearing surface for the second two cuts,
tape the waste back to the workpiece using
double-sided carpet tape. Complete the remaining cuts, then pull off the taped-in-place
waste. (You don't need to save the waste
from the broad V-groove, just from the con-
toured top.)

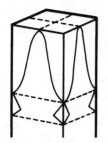

Lay out the cuts

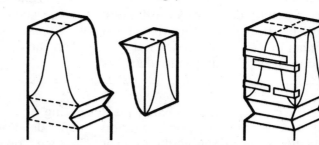

Make the first cuts

Tape the waste back on
to make remaining cuts

1 square = 1/4"

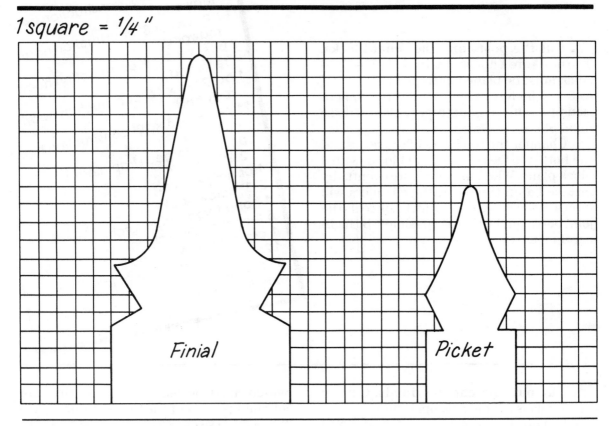

Finial

Picket

3. **Lay out and cut the pickets.** The pickets can be cut on a band saw or with a saber saw. If you use a band saw, you can stack two or three picket blanks and cut them together, reducing the repetitions necessary to form all the pickets.

First, cut the picket blanks to length. Use 5/4 stock for the pickets. Since there are a great number of like-size pieces to cut, you can expedite the work using a radial arm or a cutoff saw. Clamp a stop block to the saw's fence 39½ inches from the blade; by butting the stock against the stop, the picket blanks can be cut to a uniform length without measuring each piece.

Enlarge the pattern for the picket top on a scrap of sturdy cardboard, cut it out, and use it as a template to trace the contour on each picket blank. Then cut them out.

4. **Make the chain post.** The chain post is an essential element in the colonial method of keeping the gate closed, as you'll see after it is set and the gate is hung.

The post is a length of 4 × 4. After cutting it to size, reduce the pattern for the finials enough to fit the slighter stock and trace it on the post. Then cut the contour in the same fashion that you cut the finials.

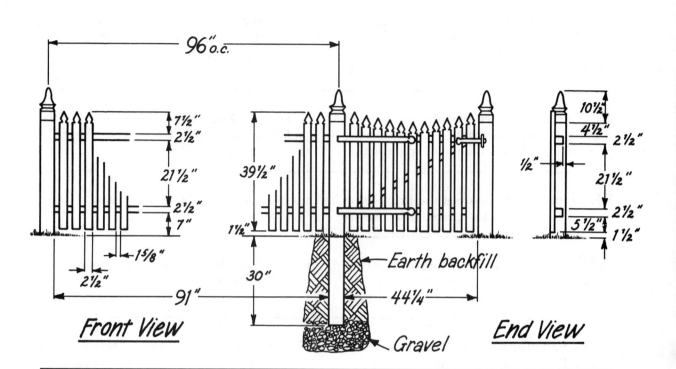

Front View

End View

5. Build the gate. Complete the gate in the shop, before moving to the fence site.

Cut the rails and stiles and nail them together. Cut the brace to rough length, then scribe it to fit the gate's perimeter frame. Miter the ends, then nail it in place. Before nailing the pickets to the frame, establish its proper orientation, so the brace will function as a compression brace. That is, it should extend from the top on the latch side to the bottom on the hinge side.

Trim seven pickets to the lengths speci-fied on the cutting list (two are used uncut). As you lay them on the frame, line up their bottoms in a straight line, parallel with the rail; their tops will form a concave contour. Space them about 1½ inches apart. In keep-ing with the colonial character of the project, use cut nails (hand-forged, preferably) to fasten the pickets.

Install the strap hinges across the pickets, overlaying the rails. The latch can also be installed. It is fixed, serving as a stop, rather than a true latch.

6. Dig the postholes and set the posts. Now the outdoor work begins. Lay out the positions of the postholes, excavate them to the depth of about 3 feet, and backfill them with about 6 inches of gravel. Set and plumb the posts, aligning their tops, and temporar-ily brace them. Backfill with soil, tamping with a scrap 2 × 4. Don't forget to set the chain post.

175

7. **Cut and install the fence stringers.** Cut the stringers to fit and toenail them in place. The stringers are set back from the front of the posts 1 inch. (Because the pick- ets are just over an inch thick, they'll stand proud of the posts about $1/16$ inch, a subtle but classy touch.)

8. **Install the fence pickets.** Use the cut nails to install the pickets. To expedite the installation, make a couple of spacers that you can hook over the stringers and butt the pickets against. Make the spacers $1\frac{5}{8}$ inches thick.

9. **Install the finials.** Set the finials atop the post and toenail in place. Countersink the nails and putty over the holes.

10. **Paint the fence and gate.** The time to paint the fence is before you install the hardware to hang the gate. Remove the hinges and the latch from the gate. Apply two coats of exterior paint.

11. **Hang the gate.** After the paint dries, reinstall the hinges and the latch. Set the gate between the gateposts and shim it up into position. Mark the locations for the hinge pintles on the post, then remove the gate. Drill pilot holes, then turn the pintles into the post. Fit the gate into the pintles.

Drill a pilot hole for one of the screw hooks into the gate's top rail, about 13 inches from the latch edge. Turn the hook into the hole, orienting the hook horizontally, the open end facing the latch.

Drill a pilot hole in the chain post, about 28 inches above grade, and turn the other hook into it. The hook should face up.

Install the chain. Use enough chain to allow the gate to open fully without stretching it completely taut. Close the gate and hang the cannonball from the chain with an S-hook. The idea is to hang it high enough that it will be clear of the ground when the gate is closed.

Try it out.

When the gate is open, the chain is pulled, lifting the cannonball. Release the gate, and the cannonball plunges earthward, pulling the gate closed.

Board Fences

Board fences have a lot of attractive characteristics, but when you consider this fence style, think how your neighbor is going to feel on the other side of your new fence. Remember that a well-designed board fence doesn't have a bad side, and aim to install a well-designed fence.

The most basic board fence is just that: individual boards set edge to edge and fastened to the stringers. Depending upon how you look at it, this is the board fence that can have a bad side. It offers maximum privacy, but presents an expressionless face to both you and the outside world. Cutting the boards picket-style can considerably enhance the appearance of such a fence.

Of course, having the so-called bad side exposed to your yard can have distinct advantages. The exposed posts can serve as supports for climbing plants, and you may want to use part of the exposed fence frame to support a shelter for garbage cans, firewood or garden tools.

Variations on the solid-board fence include the panel fence and the diagonal-board fence. In these latter styles, the panels or boards are set into a perimeter framework, which is then mounted on the posts. These fences can look the same on both sides; nice for you *and* the neighbors.

Alternating the boards from one side of the stringers to the other yields a fence that looks the same on both sides. You give up some—but definitely not all—privacy, but you get better airflow and less dense shadow. Variations on this less-than-solid board fence include the louvered fence and the lattice fence. Louvers can be angled vertically or horizontally, and a louverlike effect can be achieved simply with slats. Lattice can be purchased in prefabricated panels—choose redwood or cedar—and incorporated in a fence. If you make your own lattice, which isn't difficult, you have the options of running the slats horizontally and vertically, or weaving the slats, or altering the size of the lattice openings. These little touches can distance your fence from the stock styles of your neighbors.

With a little imagination, lattice can be successfully combined with a board fence. A few selected panels of lattice can be used to break up a boring expanse of solid fence. Or, you can run a band of lattice across the top of a board fence for more privacy without additional loss of light and breeze.

A final board fence—is it a board variation, or a lattice variation?—is the basketweave fence. It is available in prefabricated panels, but you can easily make your own. Like so many other fence styles, the basket weave offers privacy without completely cutting off airflow.

Building a Board Fence

While many board fences are prefabricated in the workshop, they are site-built with equal frequency.

Most site-built board fences start with a standard frame consisting of the posts and stringers. The posts are set, then the stringers are installed between them. The simplest way to nail the bottom stringers to the posts is to butt them in place and toenail them. (Remember to use galvanized nails for a lasting installation and to avoid rust streaks on the wood.) Metal L brackets can be installed to reinforce the joints and yield a more rigid frame. For a stronger fence, cut dadoes in the post to accept the stringers. The top rails can be simply butted together on top of the posts and mitered at the corners.

(continued on page 180)

177

Privacy and security don't have to mean unsociable and ugly. Ornamental board fences can provide both privacy and security, while enhancing the appearance of the yard and the neighborhood.

SITE-BUILDING A BOARD FENCE

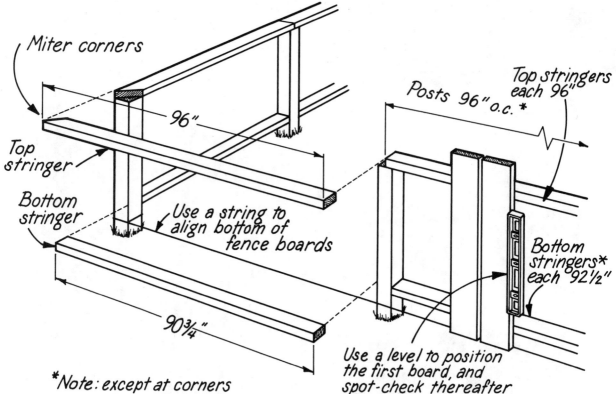

Miter corners

Top stringer

Bottom stringer

96"

Use a string to align bottom of fence boards

90¾"

*Note: except at corners

Posts 96" o.c. *

Top stringers each 96"

Bottom stringers* each 92½"

Use a level to position the first board, and spot-check thereafter

Regardless of the kind of board you're using, use a level to make sure each one is plumb before nailing or screwing it in place. It's not a bad idea to stretch mason's line across the top of the posts to ensure the boards all line up.

Shop-built board fences are constructed much the same way that picket fences are. The boards are cut to size and shape, then nailed or screwed to precut stringers.

Certain board fences can most easily be constructed if a perimeter frame is used. The basket-weave fence is a good example. The fence panels can be prefabricated, the posts set, and the panels installed between posts by driving nails or screws through the vertical frame members into the posts.

If you've decided to opt for a pure privacy fence, don't butt the boards right next to each other. Allow a ¼ inch or so for expansion. Of course, spacing the boards a few inches apart will allow some light and air through. A trick for keeping the boards evenly spaced is to use a scrap of wood the width of the desired space as a gauge. Nail a cleat to one end. Hang the gauge on the top stringer up against the first board, butt the next board against the gauge, and fasten it to the stringer. Slip the gauge out, and repeat the process for the next board. For fence boards of widths 4 inches and less, use one nail (or screw) per stringer. For wider fence boards use two nails (or screws) per stringer.

PROJECT

CUSTOM BOARD FENCE

Despite its one-of-a-kind appearance, this fence is easy to build. It doesn't involve tricky woodworking techniques—just some simple cuts with circular and saber saws. Once completed, the fence provides privacy and security to your yard or garden.

The essential parts of the fence are simple—vertical posts set in the ground, horizontal stringers attached to the posts, and many individual pickets fastened vertically to the stringers. A fence's horizontal stringers can be attached to the posts in a number of ways. For this fence, half-laps cut on the ends of the stringers fit into dadoes cut in the posts. The result is a rank of boards rhythmically accentuated by the heavy, protruding posts.

You can add design details to these basic elements to afford any level of decoration from plain to fancy. The pickets are easy

to customize by changing their shape and style. The tops of the posts also offer design options.

The design shown offers options for passage. A traditional hinged gate is sized for people and smaller tools, while a lift-out fence section allows garden machinery or even a small pickup truck passage.

To build this fence, you can use a decay-resistant wood like redwood or cedar, or a pressure-treated wood. Used as is, these woods will weather naturally to a silver gray color. But if you apply a good outdoor paint, stain, or wood preservative, ordinary fir 2×4s can be used for the stringers and #2 pine for the pickets.

Shopping List*

3 pcs. $4 \times 4 \times 8'$ pressure-treated pine
5 pcs. $2 \times 4 \times 8'$ fir
17 pcs. $1 \times 4 \times 10'$ #2 pine
2½'' galvanized all-purpose screws
1¾'' galvanized all-purpose screws
2 pr. lag-and-eye hinges
1 gate latch
exterior-grade paint, stain, or wood
    preservative

*The materials on this list will yield the parts for a single 8-foot section of the fence, the gate, and the three posts necessary to support them.

181

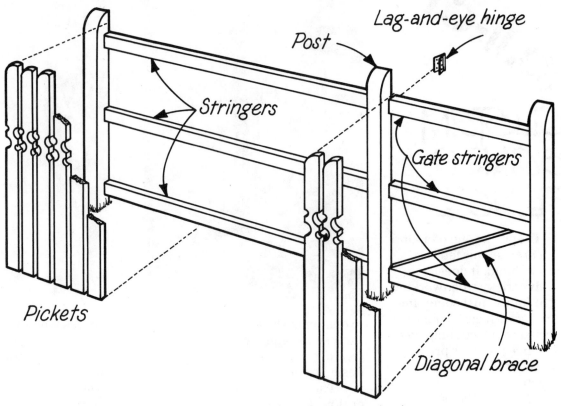

Lag-and-eye hinge

Post

Stringers

Gate stringers

Pickets

Diagonal brace

Gate pickets

Cutting List

Number	Piece	Dimensions	Material
3	Posts	3½″ × 3½″ × 96″	pressure-treated pine
3	Stringers	1½″ × 3½″ × 96″	fir
23	Pickets	¾″ × 3½″ × 59″	pine
3	Gate stringers	1½″ × 3½″ × 43½″	fir
1	Diagonal brace	1½″ × 3½″ × 52½″	fir
11	Gate pickets	¾″ × 3½″ × 54″	pine

1. **Lay out the line of the fence with wooden stakes and mason's cord.** At each corner, put the stakes a foot or two beyond the corner point so the true corner will be located where the strings cross. For a perfect 90-degree corner, use the 3-4-5 rule: Using any unit of length (foot, yard, etc.), adjust the cords until one leg of the right angle formed by the corner equals three units, the other leg equals four units, and the diagonal (or hypotenuse) equals five units. Measure along the layout line from the corner post locations to find the points for the other posts. Drive small stakes to mark them.

2. Cut the posts, stringers, and pickets.
The fence shown is 5 feet tall, with 59-inch pickets. After cutting the essential fence parts to length, lay out any decorative features on the pickets and/or post tops using a template. Cut out the pickets using a saber saw with a conventional blade. To cut out the posts, fit a 6-inch blade in the saw.

Dado the posts to accept the stringers. Cut the three ¾-inch-deep dadoes, centered at 8, 29½, and 51 inches, measured from the post top.

Cut a half-lap on each end of the stringers, 1¾ inches long and ¾ inch deep.

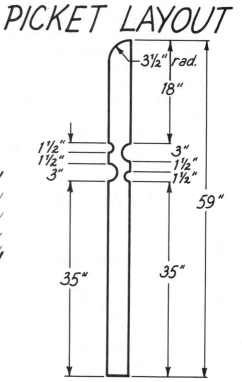

PICKET LAYOUT

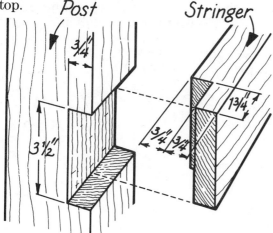

3. In the shop, assemble each 8-foot section of the fence. Lay out three stringers on the shop floor. Position them carefully, so they will fit the dadoes in the posts when the time comes. Nail a scrap 2 × 4 to the floor to set the bottoms of the pickets against. Fasten the pickets to the stringers with 1¾-inch galvanized all-purpose screws. Make gauge blocks from scrap wood to space the pickets evenly.

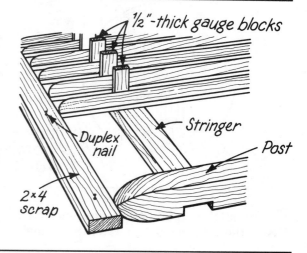

4. **Plant all the posts.** Dig holes for the posts at each stake location. Make the holes a bit deeper than the frost line in your area. Generally, sink about one-third of the post in the ground. To get the tops of the posts the same height aboveground, adjust the depth of the hole. If you hit a rock, trim the bottom of the post with a small chain saw.

Plant the posts in their holes, backfilling and tamping as you go. Plumb the posts with a level as the holes are filled.

Since you've precut the stringers and posts, it's important for you to get all the posts *exactly* in line and at the same height. Use this method: Plant the corner posts first, making sure they are plumb. Run two lines— one at the top and one near the bottom— from one end post to the other. Use mason's line blocks to offset the cords from the posts. Now plant the intermediate posts, using the cords as guides for locating the posts. Use a tape measure to adjust the exact position of each post relative to the cords. Plumb each post with a carpenter's level. Done this way, the intermediate posts will never accidentally push the cord out of line.

SETTING A LINE OF PRECUT POSTS

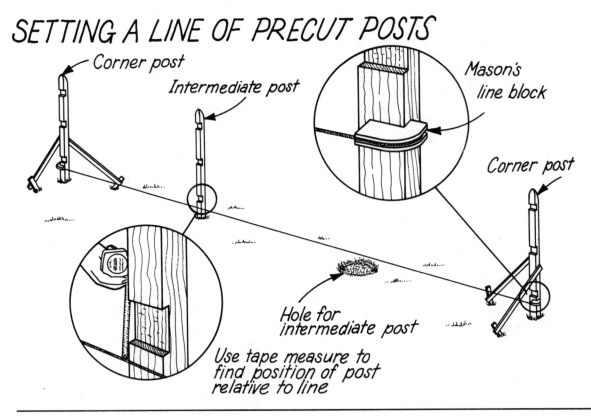

Corner post

Intermediate post

Mason's line block

Corner post

Hole for intermediate post

Use tape measure to find position of post relative to line

5. **Install the prefabbed fencing sections.** Fasten the stringers to the posts with 2½-inch galvanized all-purpose screws. Drill pilot holes to prevent splitting. The stringers' half-lapped ends fit neatly into the notches in the posts.

At the corners, fasten adjoining fence sections together using galvanized angle brackets. Fasten the brackets to the stringers using 2½-inch galvanized all-purpose screws.

6. **Build and hang the gate.** The post center-to-center spacing for the hinged gate is 48 inches, with a stringer length of 42 inches to allow space for hinge pins and swinging clearance. Omit the center stringer. Cut a diagonal compression brace to fit between the top stringer on the latch side and the bottom stringer on the hinge side. Attach hinges and latch hardware.
OPTIONAL: The lift-out gate is built just like the other fence sections—the post center-to-center spacing is 96 inches, just like the main fence sections. Cut the stringers to length so they will fit *between* the posts with a little clearance to spare. Make six ⅛ × 3 × 3-inch aluminum plates and drill two holes in each. Mount the plates on the posts so their upper third overlaps the bottom of the notches. Cut a notch out of the ends of the stringers for the lift-out section. Now the narrowed ends of the stringers can be easily lifted in or out of the notches in the posts.

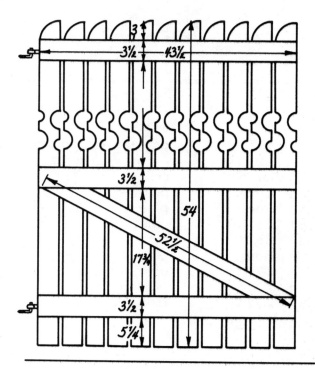

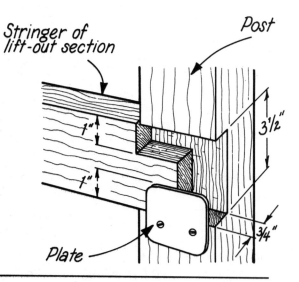

LIFT-OUT FENCE SECTION

Stringer of lift-out section

Post

Plate

SOLID BOARD FENCE

Board fences tend to be bland, blank affairs. This one is different, with its arched-top sections and finial-topped posts. The fence boards extend to the ground, just kissing the river stones spread beneath them.

The fence shown surrounds a large yard with a swimming pool, providing privacy and, equally important, security for the pool. The owners chose to orient the fence's good side toward their living space.

In building this fence, the stringers were simply butted against the posts, so on the good side, the posts stand proud of the fence. The stringers could instead be set into dadoes cut into the posts, which would reduce the relief, or they could be fitted between the posts, which could eliminate the relief.

1. Dig postholes 8 feet on center and approximately 3 feet deep using a posthole digger or power auger.

Materials List

Number	Piece	Dimensions	Material
2	Posts	3½″ × 3½″ × 108″	pressure-treated pine post w/finial
3	Stringers	1½″ × 2½″ × 96″	fir
2	Fence boards	¾″ × 5½″ × 62″	pine
2	Fence boards	¾″ × 5½″ × 64″	pine
2	Fence boards	¾″ × 5½″ × 66″	pine
2	Fence boards	¾″ × 5½″ × 67″	pine
2	Fence boards	¾″ × 5½″ × 69″	pine
2	Fence boards	¾″ × 5½″ × 70″	pine
2	Fence boards	¾″ × 5½″ × 71″	pine
3	Fence boards	¾″ × 5½″ × 72″	pine

Hardware
8d galvanized nails
exterior-grade stain or wood preservative

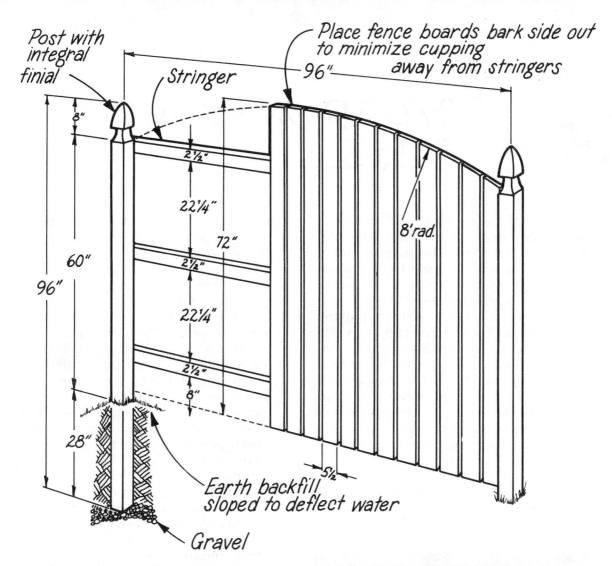

Post with integral finial

Stringer

Place fence boards bark side out to minimize cupping away from stringers

96"

8"

2½"

22¼"

72"

2½"

22¼"

2½"

8"

60"

96"

8'rad.

28"

Earth backfill sloped to deflect water

Gravel

5½

2. Cover the bottom of the holes with gravel for drainage. Set the posts 3 feet in the ground and refill the holes about halfway.

3. Brace and plumb the posts. Refill the holes completely, tamping down the earth around each post. Create a berm with the earth around the post, so it sheds water.

4. Cut the stringers to length (if necessary) and cut the fence boards to the lengths specified on the Materials List.

5. Lay the stringers on a flat surface, and align the boards on top of them. The longest three boards should be in the middle, with the rest arranged in descending order of length, with the shortest on the outsides.

Align the bottoms, so they are in a straight line and parallel with the stringers. Allow ⅛ inch between boards for expansion. Nail the boards down.

6. Scribe the arch on the top of the fence section. The curve is an 8-foot radius; it can be scribed using a string-and-pencil compass, a plywood or hardboard template, or by tracing along a ¼-inch strip of wood flexed to the arc. Cut the arc with a saber saw.

7. Set the fence section against the posts and nail it in place.

8. Apply a finish, even if it is only a water repellent.

HOW TO BOARD-ON-BOARD FENCE

A board-on-board fence offers several advantages over a simple board fence. Although it offers almost the same amount of privacy, this type of fence lets in ample amounts of light and air and has a more interesting three-dimensional look. It also presents the same face on either side of the fence—you don't have to accept the ugly side in deference to your neighbor.

The design here yields a 6-foot-high fence—fairly typical—but it has touches that set it apart from the prefab styles that are so commonplace. The posts and cap are redwood, the stringers and fence boards pine; the result is a fence with natural color accents. An additional accent to the post is lent by a 1 × 4 nailed to either side.

In the landscape pictured, the fence steps up a hill. This requires longer posts that the 8-footers specified in the Materials List. In addition, the cap can't bridge the posts; instead, it caps the lower post and is notched to fit around the higher post.

1. Dig postholes 8 feet apart and approximately 3 feet deep using a posthole digger or power auger.
2. Cover the bottom of the holes with gravel for drainage. Set the posts 3 feet in the ground and refill the holes about halfway.
3. Brace and plumb the posts. Refill the holes completely, tamping down the earth around each post. Create a berm with the earth around the post, so it sheds water.
4. Extend a string with a line level from post to post; if necessary, trim all the posts to the same height.
5. Cut the stringers and the fence boards.
6. Lay out the stringers in proper alignment. Lay ten fence boards on the stringers. The first should be flush with the ends of the stringers, the others about 3½ inches apart. The space between the last board and the stringer ends will be about 4½ inches. Nail the boards in place.
7. Turn the assembly over. Lay out the remaining ten boards in the same sequence, but alternating with those already secured. Nail the boards in place.
8. Cut the post trim, and nail it to the ends of the fence assembly.
9. Fit the fence assembly between the posts, flush with their tops. Nail through the post trim into the posts.
10. Cut and install the cap.
11. Apply a finish, even if it is only a water repellent.

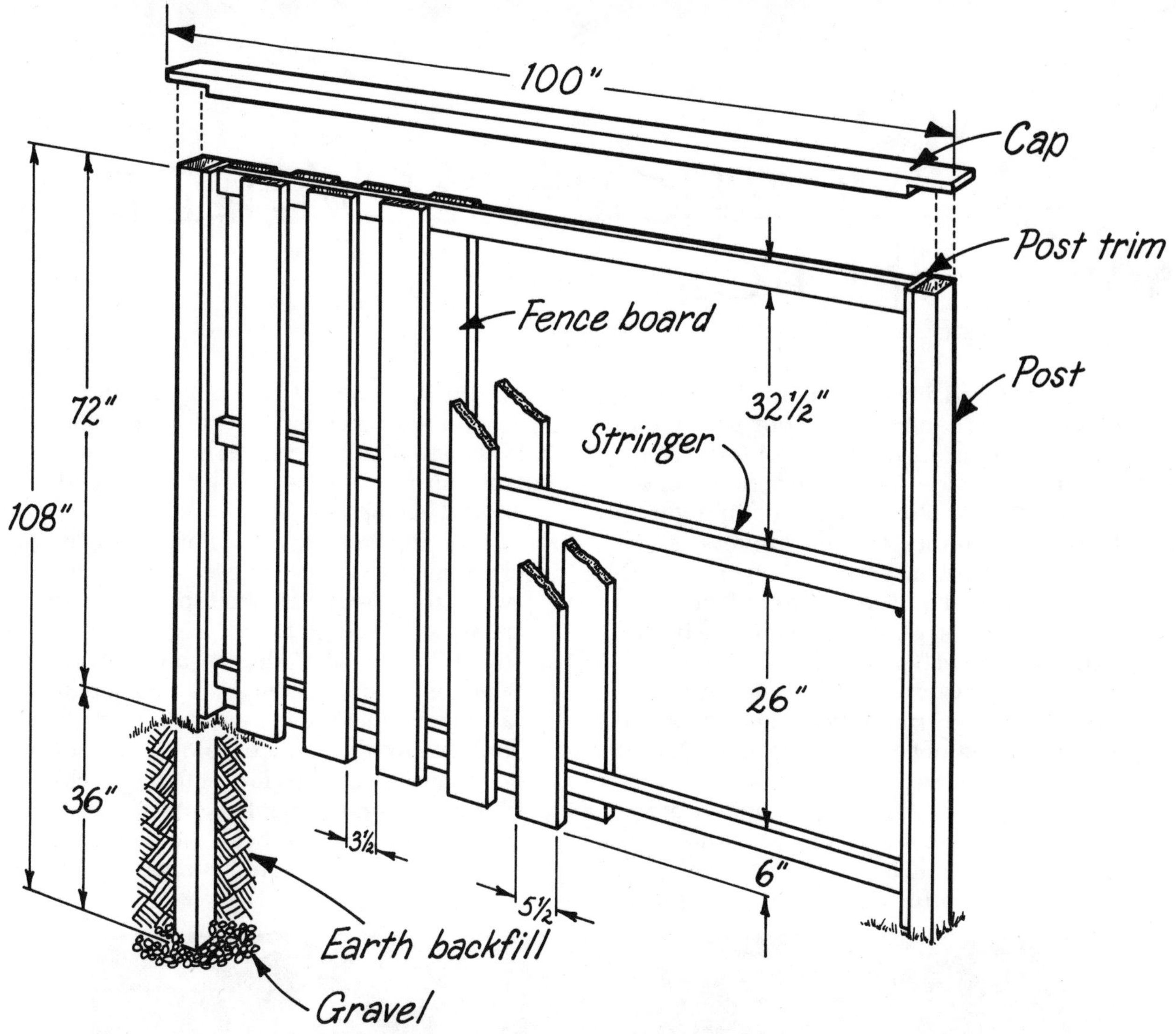

100"
Cap
Post trim
Fence board
Post
72"
108"
32½"
Stringer
26"
36"
3½
6"
5½
Earth backfill
Gravel

Materials List

Number	*Piece*	*Dimensions*	*Material*
2	Posts	3½" × 3½" × 108"	redwood
3	Stringers	1½" × 2½" × 91"	fir
20	Fence boards	¾" × 5½" × 72"	pine
2	Post trim	¾" × 3½" × 72"	pine
1	Cap	1½" × 5½" × 100"	redwood

Hardware

10d galvanized nails
8d galvanized nails
exterior-grade stain or wood preservative

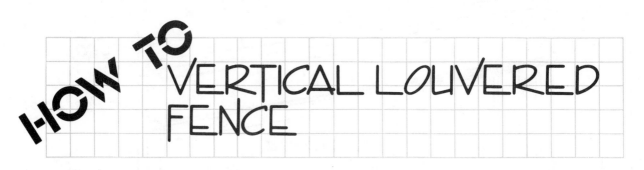

VERTICAL LOUVERED FENCE

A louvered fence is a sophisticated way of letting light and air into your yard while maintaining an adequate amount of privacy. A louvered fence does require more wood, and it's a good idea to use premium grade, kiln-dried lumber for the louvers, since cheaper varieties may twist during the weathering process. For a short run of fence, this design provides pleasant relief from a boring expanse of solid board fence. This plan calls for a true privacy fence, one nearly 8 feet high. The louvers run vertically and are placed at a 45-degree angle. There are two different lengths of louvers.

1. Dig postholes 8 feet apart and approximately 2½ feet deep using a posthole digger or power auger.
2. Cover the bottom of the holes with gravel for drainage. Set the posts 2 feet in the ground, and refill the holes about halfway.
3. Brace and plumb the posts. Refill the holes completely, tamping down the earth around each post.
4. Cut the intermediate and bottom stringers to length. Toenail these stringers between the posts. Nail the top stringer to the tops of the posts.
5. Cut 1 × 4 at a 45-degree angle every 3 inches for spacer blocks. Cut 8 triangular spacer blocks to use against the posts. Nail triangular spacer blocks to the stringers. Nail the first louver to the blocks. Install the first pair of regular spacers, add a louver, and repeat the sequence until all the louvers are installed.

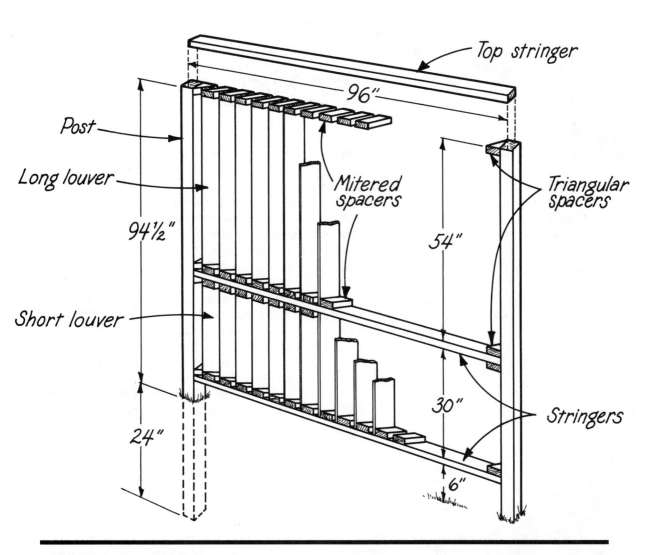

Top stringer

96"

Post

Long louver

Mitered spacers

94½"

Triangular spacers

54"

Short louver

30"

24"

Stringers

6"

Materials List

Number	Piece	Dimensions	Material
2	Posts	3½" × 3½" × 120"	pressure-treated pine
1	Top stringer	1½" × 3½" × 96"	fir
2	Stringers	1½" × 3½" × 92½"	fir
8	Triangular spacers	¾" × 3½" × 3½"	pine
88	Mitered spacers	¾" × 3½" × 3"	pine
23	Short louvers	¾" × 5½" × 30"	pine
23	Long louvers	¾" × 5½" × 54"	pine

Hardware
12d galvanized nails
8d galvanized nails

Building a fence is one way to shield your yard from a busy street. But a solid fence can be too private, making you feel cut off from the world. The solution: a fence made with vertical slats that act like a venetian blind. Landscape architect Mike Taylor designed this fence for a Portland, Oregon, suburban home. An arbor for vines was added near the post tops for visual interest and extra screening.

The fence is constructed of pressure-treated southern yellow pine, except the vertical slats, which are clear heart red cedar. The pressure-treated wood was finished with a water-repellent stain to achieve a more uniform color. Dimensions of the fence pieces can be varied, changing the proportions to please your taste.

1. Plan the location and dimensions of your fence carefully, and sketch the layout on graph paper.
2. Carefully measure and lay out the locations for the fence posts. Dig the postholes deep enough to go below the local frost line. Pour an inch or two of gravel in the holes to help drain water away from the posts' end grain.
3. Chamfer the top edges of the posts, and use a router to cut a decorative dado near the tops of the posts. Set the posts in the holes. Use a level to check for plumb on adjacent sides. Hold the posts vertical with scrap wood braces. Backfill with soil or concrete.
4. Cut upper and lower screen stringers to length and fasten onto the posts with carriage bolts. For a clean appearance, counterbore holes for the nuts and washers. Cut rail end caps to fit rail ends with miter joints, and install with galvanized all-purpose screws.
5. Cut red cedar slats, and toenail through the ends into the screen rails with galvanized finishing nails.
6. Cut arbor stringers so they'll extend 18 inches beyond the end posts and chamfer the edges of the ends. Fasten the stringers to the posts with carriage bolts.
7. Cut and fasten arbor crosspieces with galvanized all-purpose screws.
8. Apply finish.

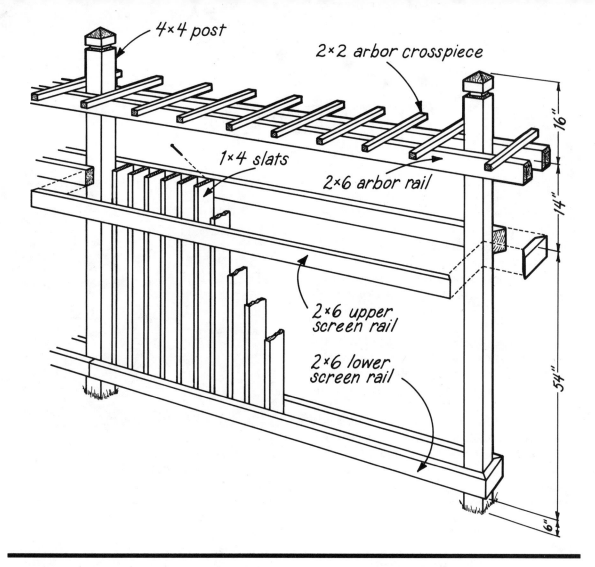

4×4 post

2×2 arbor crosspiece

2×6 arbor rail

1×4 slats

2×6 upper screen rail

2×6 lower screen rail

16″

14″

54″

6″

Materials List

Number	Piece	Dimensions	Material
2	Posts	3½″ × 3½″ × 120″	pressure-treated-pine
2	Upper screen stringers	1½″ × 5½″ × 96″	pressure-treated-pine
2	Lower screen stringers	1½″ × 5½″ × 96″	pressure-treated-pine
19	Slats	1″ × 4″ × 54″	western red cedar
2	Arbor stringers	1½″ × 5½″ × 96″	pressure-treated-pine
8	Arbor crosspieces	1½″ × 1½″ × 20″	pressure-treated-pine

Hardware

1 box #8 × 1½″ galvanized all-purpose screws
1 box #8 × 2½″ galvanized all-purpose screws
6–6″ × ⅜″ galvanized carriage bolts w/nuts and washers
12d galvanized finishing nails

LATTICE FENCE

This unusual fence is ideal for the rose gardener. What's captivating is that the fence has all the positive characteristics of lattice, without the commonplace appearance of prefab diagonal lattice.

In addition, the brick pillars that support the lattice panels harmonize with an older brick house, or even with a brick walkway or patio. It's unlikely your neighbors will have something like this.

1. Lay out the locations and size of footings for the brick pillars. Excavate below the frost line and pour the footing to within a couple of inches of grade. Allow the concrete to cure several days.
2. Lay up the brick pillars. Each pillar is a square, rising 23 stretcher courses above grade, with each course composed of four bricks. The pillars are topped with a shiner course.
3. Construct the lattice panels. Use brass escutcheons, which won't rust, to tack the lattice strips together.

Materials List

Number	Piece	Dimensions	Material
16	Vertical strips	¼″ × 1½″ × 60″	cedar
15	Horizontal strips	¼″ × 1½″ × 64½″	cedar
4	Inner frame rails	1″ × 3½″ × 68½″	cedar
4	Inner frame stiles	1″ × 3½″ × 64″	cedar
2	Outer frame stiles	1″ × 4½″ × 70½″	cedar
2	Outer frame stiles	1″ × 4½″ × 65½″	cedar

Hardware
#8 × ¾″ galvanized screws
12-2″ × ¼″ galvanized lag bolts w/washers
12-¼″ lead shields
8 flat corner braces
⅜″ brass escutcheons
10d galvanized nails
6d galvanized nails
exterior-grade stain or wood preservative

Masonry
225 common bricks
concrete
masonry cement

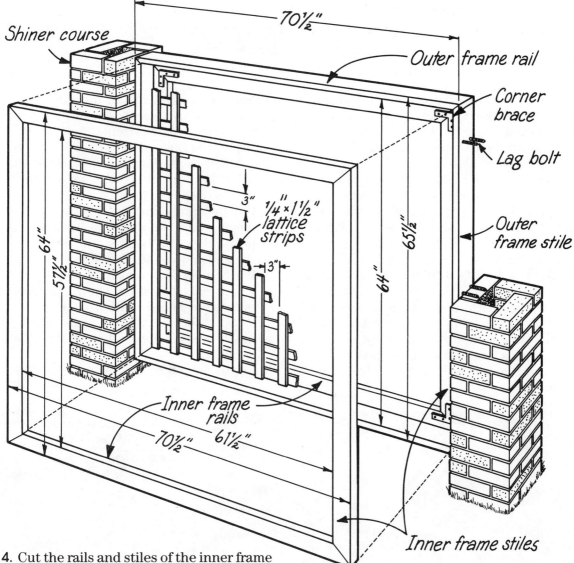

Shiner course

70½"

Outer frame rail

Corner brace

Lag bolt

Outer frame stile

3"

¼"×1½" lattice strips

3"

64"

57½"

65½"

64"

Inner frame rails

70½"   61½"

Inner frame stiles

4. Cut the rails and stiles of the inner frame and miter the ends.

5. Assemble the two inner frames. Drive galvanized nails through the edges of the miter joints to tie the rails and stiles together. Then screw a flat corner brace to the inner surface of the frames to reinforce each joint.

6. Lay the lattice panel on an inner frame and nail it in place. Set the second inner frame atop the lattice and nail the two frames together. Drive nails into both sides.

7. Cut the outer frame parts, mitering the ends.

8. Nail the outer frame around the inner frame assembly.

9. Apply a finish to the assembly.

10. Mount the fence panel between the pillars. Drill holes in the pillars, insert lead expansion shields, then secure the fence panel to the pillars by driving lag bolts through the outer frame into the shields.

195

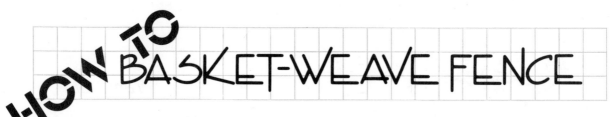

HOW TO BASKET-WEAVE FENCE

The basket-weave fence is a familiar style. Though available from lumberyards and fencing contractors in prefab versions, it is so easy to build you ought to do it from scratch. Doing so will enable you to make your fence higher (or lower) than the prefab units or to vary the spacing between posts.

The key element is the ¼ inch (to ⅜ inch) thick stock required to weave the fencing. If you can't find it at your lumberyard, try buying from a fencing contractor.

1. Dig 2½- to 3-foot-deep postholes, align and plumb the posts, and set them. After they are backfilled, extend a level line from corner post to corner post and trim all the posts to the same height.
2. Toenail a 2 × 3 between the posts, aligning its top face 58 inches from the tops of the posts.
3. Nail two 1 × 1 strips to the side of each post, leaving a gap between them wide enough for the horizontal fence boards. Drive pilot holes in these nailers to avoid splitting them. The strips should extend from the bottom stringer to within 3½ inches of the post tops.
4. Cut the horizontal fence boards ½ inch longer than the distance between the posts. Flex the boards enough to slide the ends down into the slots.
5. Weave a vertical weaver among the horizontal fence boards, as shown, passing it behind one board and in front of the next. Weave a second one into place, alternating the weave set with the first strip. Each 8-foot section should have five weavers.
6. Finish the job by nailing on a 2 × 3 cap.

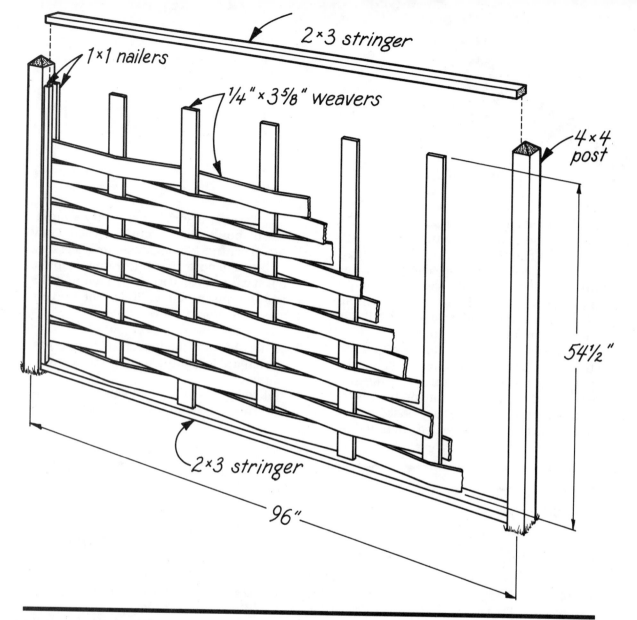

2×3 stringer

1×1 nailers

¼" × 3⅝" weavers

4×4 post

54½"

2×3 stringer

96"

Materials List

Number	Piece	Dimensions	Material
2	Posts	3½″ × 3½″ × 96″	pressure-treated pine
2	Horizontal stringers	1½″ × 2½″ × 92½″	cedar
2	Vertical nailers	¾″ × ¾″ × 54½″	cedar
14	Horizontal fence boards	¼″ × 3⅝″ × 93″	cedar
5	Vertical weavers	¼″ × 3⅝″ × 54½″	cedar

Hardware
8d galvanized nails

HOW TO HORIZONTAL LOUVERED FENCE

Looking for a fence that offers privacy without the look of a maximum security stockade? This fence might fit your bill.

It is a deceptive fence. The proportions are such that you don't realize until you approach it just how BIG it is. The posts are a foot square and more than 6 feet tall. The louver boards are 14 feet long.

The fence is unusual, and so is its construction. The posts are 6 × 6s that are cased in 1 × 12 stock. Because of the distance between the posts, the louver boards get extra support from auxiliary posts cut like stair stringers and concealed "behind" the fence. Though it may seem pretty complicated to build, that is not the case. Only basic carpentry skills and tools are necessary.

One final note: If your terrain is sloping, you'll have to deal with it by stepping the fence sections, as shown here. The louvers themselves must be level.

1. Make the intermediate board supports, which are laid out like stair stringers, as shown.
2. Set the posts on 15-foot centers and the intermediate supports on 5-foot centers in between. Dig the postholes 3 feet deep

Materials List*

Number	Piece	Dimensions	Material
2	Posts	5½″ × 5½″ × variable	pressure-treated pine
2	Intermediate supports	1½″ × 5½″ × 96″	pressure-treated pine
24	Packing	1½″ × 5½″ × 7″	pine
24	Packing	¾″ × 5½″ × 9¼″	pine
24	Packing	¼″ × 5½″ × 10¼″	plywood
8	Post sheathing	¾″ × 5½″ × 73″	pine
7	Boards	¾″ × 5½″ × 168″	pine
8	Crown molding	3″, scribed to fit	pine

Hardware
10d galvanized nails
8d galvanized nails
6d galvanized finishing nails
resorcinol glue
exterior-grade paint or stain
silicone caulk

*This list includes all the pieces necessary to construct one 14-foot section of fence.

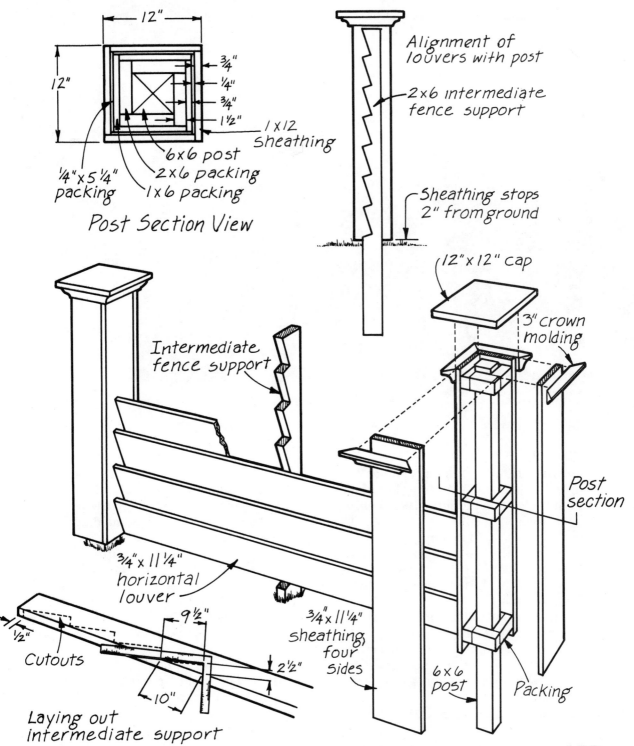

12"

12"

3/4"
1/4"
3/4"
1 1/2"

1 x 12
sheathing

6x6 post
2x6 packing
1x6 packing

1/4" x 5 1/4"
packing

Post Section View

Alignment of louvers with post

2x6 intermediate fence support

Sheathing stops 2" from ground

12" x 12" cap

3" crown molding

Intermediate fence support

Post section

3/4" x 11 1/4" horizontal louver

3/4" x 11 1/4" sheathing four sides

6x6 post

Packing

Cutouts

1/2"

9 1/2"

2 1/2"

10"

Laying out intermediate support

and the intermediate support holes 2 feet deep. Set and plumb the posts. Lay a board in the notches of the supports to help you align them. Backfill the postholes. Cut each post off at 75 inches.

3. "Pack out" the posts in three places, as shown, to increase their cross-sectional dimension (at those three spots) to 10½ inches square.

4. Sheathe the posts with four 73-inch lengths of 1 × 12. Nail the boards to the packing, keeping their tops flush with the post tops. The bottoms of the boards should be 2 inches shy of the ground as protection from rot.

5. Make post caps. Each is a 20-inch square of 1-inch stock, which has to be glued up using resorcinol glue. Sand and prime both sides before nailing it atop the post.

6. Cut and attach the crown molding around the post beneath the cap.

7. Install the louvered boards. Face-nail through the boards into the intermediate supports, and toenail the ends of the boards to the posts.

8. Paint or stain the fence. For a better-looking job and further weather protection, apply silicone caulk where the louvered boards meet the posts. Also caulk above and under the crown molding and any gaps in the crown molding miters.

Gates

A gate can be made to blend into your fence or to stand out. The most important considerations when planning a gate are where it's going to be located and how wide an opening it should provide. You determined your family's traffic patterns before you laid out the fence on paper, so you know *where* the gate needs to be.

How wide does it need to be? A gate for foot traffic is usually between 3 and 4 feet wide. If the gate must provide access for a riding mower or lawn tractor, measure the vehicle in question first and allow plenty of extra inches for accessories such as deflector chutes and bagging attachments.

Building a Gate

Bear in mind that a gate gets more wear-and-tear than a fence. It should be sturdily constructed on level ground. For a gate, the key to long life is bracing.

A gate can be framed in either of two ways. In the first, the gate is constructed like a short fence section, with a diagonal brace added. In the second, a perimeter frame is constructed, fence boards (or pickets) are installed, and a diagonal framing member is added.

The brace is important. Unlike a section of fence, the gate is supported along one edge only. It must be rigidly constructed so it doesn't sag; if it sags, it may drag on the ground or bind between the gateposts—serious performance shortcomings.

If there's one best way to brace the gate, it is with a compression brace. Here the brace angles from the top of the latch side to the bottom of the hinge side; the weight of the gate settles on the top of the brace, which

transfers it to the bottom hinge. The brace is under compression. It doesn't *have* to be fastened to the frame, so long as it is fastened to facing that's attached to the frame. The weight of the gate tends to wedge it tightly in place.

If the brace angles the opposite way—from the top of the hinge side to the bottom of the latch side—it must be fastened to the stringers, because the weight of the gate will *hang* from it. If it isn't securely attached to the stringers, the gate will sag, brace or no brace. This is the tension brace, so-called because the weight of the gate is pulling on it; the brace is under tension.

A third bracing option used frequently is the X brace, which combines the compression and tension braces. The two brace members mate in a cross-lap joint.

A perimeter frame is constructed of the same stock as the fence stringers using simple butt joints held together with galvanized screws. The butt joints can be reinforced with L-shaped plates at each corner. A diagonal brace is then fitted inside the perimeter frame. When the facing is applied, fasteners are driven through the facing into the frame members and the brace.

The principal advantage of the perimeter frame is hinge-placement flexibility. The

---

An Adjustable Brace

A commercial turnbuckle brace kit, which usually includes some wire and corner brackets with eyescrews, can be purchased and used to brace the gate. Although not as attractive as a wooden brace, the turnbuckle can be adjusted easily if the gate sags.

Most fences—and some hedges—call for a gate. While it should harmonize with the fence design, it shouldn't hide. Above all else, it should be well built, so it functions easily.

hinges can be located anywhere along the vertical frame member, rather than only at the stringers. Moreover, the hinge fasteners are driven into long grain, where they have more secure purchase. Under stress, fasteners driven into end grain pull quite easily.

The disadvantage of this design is the additional framing. In most situations, a three-piece frame—top and bottom stringers and a diagonal brace—is all that's necessary for a long-lasting gate.

The easiest way to build the gate—regardless of the frame style—is to set the gateposts, then measure for the gate. Make sure you allow space for the hinge pins and swinging clearance. Build the gate in the shop, with gravity and leverage in your favor, instead of trying to assemble it in place.

Hinges and Latches

A visit to the local hardware store or home center will reveal a wide choice of hinges and latches. It is a really good idea to have your hardware in hand when you build your gate. Before you build, you must know how the gate will swing, how it will latch, and how much clearance you need.

In buying hinges and a latch, your money will be well spent if you purchase heavy-duty hardware designed to stand up to the elements. Two hinges are adequate for most standard-size gates, but if your gate is more than 5 feet tall, use three. No matter what style hinges you choose, make sure they have a weather-resistant coating on them, even if you plan on painting them.

The simplest and least expensive type of hinge is the lag and eye. This hinge is best suited for post-and-rail gates with thick rounded or square posts. It allows the gate to swing in both directions.

The most familiar hinge type is the butt

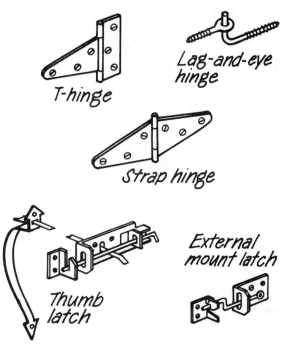

T-hinge

Lag-and-eye hinge

Strap hinge

Thumb latch

External mount latch

—two rectangular plates pinned together. But the most common hinge type seen on picket and board gates is the strap hinge. It features long, permanently joined hinge plates that distribute the weight of the gate over a broad area. The T-hinge combines a leaf from a butt hinge with a leaf from a strap hinge. Butts and straps are like the door hinges in your house—they allow the gate to swing open only one way.

Just as there are different styles of hinges available, so are there many factory-made latches. Probably the easiest to install is the so-called external mount latch. A latch bar attaches to the gate, a catch to the post. The shortcoming—and simultaneously the advantage—of this type of latch is that it can only be opened easily from the side on which it is mounted. Many of these types are made to accept a padlock.

For a garden or entry gate, you surely will want a latch with a through-the-gate thumb latch.

HOW TO COMPRESSION-BRACE PICKET GATE

This is the Basic Garden Gate. Constructed with a modicum of care and hung with sound hinges on a well-set gatepost, this gate will last for generations, even with kids climbing on and swinging back and forth.

The gates people tend to remember are the gates that don't quite work right. The ones that sag. The hinges are sound, the gatepost is set solidly, but the gate itself is loosy-goosy. The latch side drags on the ground and bangs into the latchpost. You need to lift it to latch it.

The gate needs to be braced. Properly. Then the kids can swing themselves loose in the head.

The most popular way to brace a gate is

with a compression brace. The brace and cross members form a Z, with the brace angling from the latch side down to the hinge side. The gate's weight is transferred through the brace to the bottom hinge. The brace is under compression.

1. Cut the rails and the stiles. Cut half-lap joints on the ends of all pieces.
2. Drill and countersink pilot holes, then fasten the frame together using two carriage bolts with nuts and washers for each joint. Ensure the frame is square when bolted together.
3. Cut the brace and lay it across the frame, running from the bottom corner of the hinge side to the top corner of the latch

Materials List

Number	Piece	Dimensions	Material
2	Rails	1½″ × 3½″ × 36″	fir
2	Stiles	1½″ × 3½″ × 34″	fir
1	Brace	1½″ × 3½″ × 39¾″	fir
2	Pickets	¾″ × 2½″ × 39″	pine
2	Pickets	¾″ × 2½″ × 37″	pine
2	Pickets	¾″ × 2½″ × 35″	pine
2	Pickets	¾″ × 2½″ × 33″	pine
2	Pickets	¾″ × 2½″ × 31″	pine

Hardware
8–1¾″ × ¼″ carriage bolts w/nuts and washers
2 strap-type exterior gate hinges
1 exterior gate latch
4d galvanized nails
exterior-grade enamel, stain, or wood preservative

side. Mark and cut the ends of the brace to fit inside the frame.

4. Cut 10 pieces of 1×3 for pickets. Make the 2 longest pieces 39 inches each and each succeeding pair 2 inches shorter than the pair before. With a saber saw, cut a 1¼-inch radius on the upper end of each picket.

5. Place the gate frame on a flat surface and fit the brace in position. Space the pickets evenly across the front of the frame, aligning their lower ends flush with the bottom edge of the frame. The upper ends form a concave curve across the top. Fasten the pickets to the brace and frame using 4d galvanized nails.

6. Finish the gate with exterior-grade enamel or stain, and mount it on a gatepost using a pair of strap-type exterior gate hinges. Install your choice of latch.

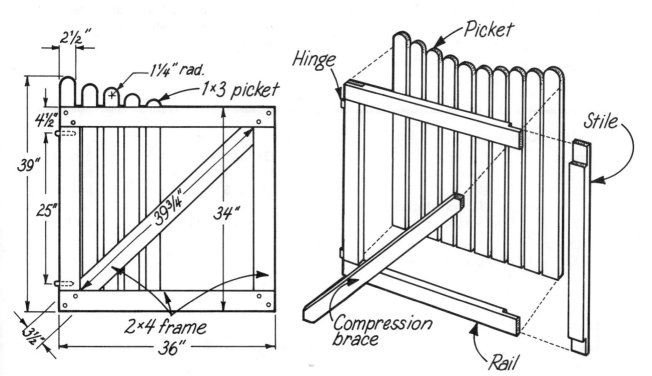

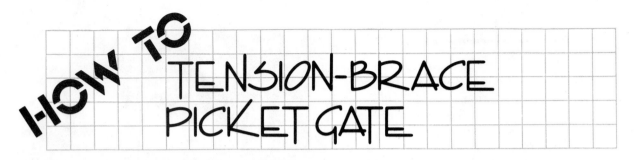

HOW TO TENSION-BRACE PICKET GATE

An alternative to the compression-brace gate is the tension-brace gate. In this design, the diagonal brace is bolted in place, and extends from the hinge side down to the bottom corner of the latch side. The weight of the gate "hangs" from the top hinge.

Building this sort of gate framework is, perhaps, a bit more involved than the compression-brace gate. The assembled perimeter frame must be mortised to accept the brace, which is cut with mitered half-laps. Then the brace is bolted to the frame.

When completed, the frame can be fitted with pickets to match the fence. The design shown provides just one more picket idea.

1. From 2 × 4, cut two 36-inch rails and two 34-inch stiles. Cut half-lap joints on the ends of all pieces and fit them together without fastening them.
2. Cut a 44⅝-inch piece of 2 × 4 for the brace. Lay it across the frame from the top corner of the hinge side to the bottom corner of the latch side. Mark the ends of the brace for cutting as shown. Also mark the bottom rail along the lower edge of the brace, and the top rail along the upper edge of the brace.
3. Miter the ends of the brace as marked, then cut half-lap joints on them. Extend one half-lap on each rail, as marked, to receive the ends of the brace. Fit the five

Materials List

Number	Piece	Dimensions	Material
2	Rails	1½″ × 3½″ × 36″	fir
2	Stiles	1½″ × 3½″ × 34″	fir
1	Diagonal tension brace	1½″ × 3½″ × 44⅝″	fir
10	Pickets	¾″ × 2½″ × 39″	pine

Hardware
10–1¾″ × ¼″ carriage bolts w/nuts and washers
2 strap-type exterior gate hinges
1 exterior gate latch
4d galvanized nails
exterior-grade enamel, stain, or wood preservative

frame pieces together, then drill and countersink pilot holes for 10 bolts, positioned as shown in the plan view. Bolt the frame together.

4. Cut 10 pickets, each 39 inches long. Cut the top of each picket as shown in the picket layout (or to whatever shape is desired). Space them evenly across the front of the gate with their lower ends flush with the bottom edge of the frame, and nail them in place.

5. Finish the gate with exterior-grade enamel or stain. Then fasten it to a gatepost using a pair of exterior gate hinges. Attach a latch to the other side.

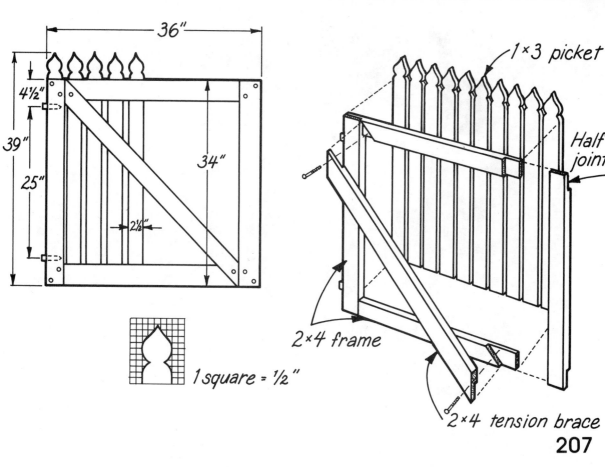

36"

4½"

39"

25"

34"

2½"

1 square = ½"

1×3 picket

Half-lap joint

2×4 frame

2×4 tension brace

207

HOW TO PLYWOOD-PANEL GATE

This gate doesn't have a brace, because the plywood panel is its own brace. The plywood used, called texture one-eleven (or simply T1-11), is designed for siding buildings, so it will weather without delaminating. To spruce up the edges, 1×2 edge bands are applied.

1. Cut one piece of ⅝-inch T1-11 plywood to 34½ × 34½ inches for the gate panel. From 1×4, cut two 34½-inch pieces for the stiles and two 27½-inch pieces for the rails.

2. Lay out the frame with the rails between the stiles, set the plywood panel on top, as shown, and nail it in place.

3. Cut a 36-inch piece of 1×2 for the top edge band, a 34½-inch piece for the bottom edge band, and two 35¼-inch pieces for the side edge bands. Center these pieces on the frame and panel edges, lapping them as shown, and nail them in place.

4. Finish the gate with exterior-grade enamel or stain. Hang the gate on a post using a pair of strap-type exterior gate hinges, then install a gate latch.

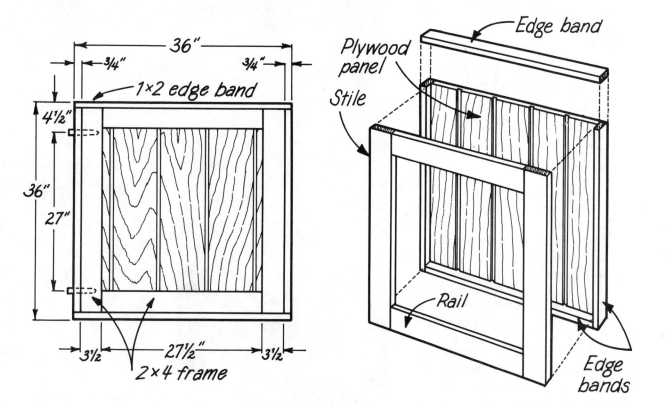

Materials List

Number	Piece	Dimensions	Material
2	Stiles	¾″ × 3½″ × 34½″	pine
2	Rails	¾″ × 3½″ × 27½″	pine
1	Top edge band	¾″ × 1½″ × 36″	pine
2	Side edge bands	¾″ × 1½″ × 35½″	pine
1	Bottom edge band	¾″ × 1½″ × 34½″	pine
1	Gate panel	⅝″ × 34½″ × 34½″	T1-11 plywood

Hardware
2 strap-type exterior gate hinges
1 exterior gate latch
1¼″ aluminum nails
exterior-grade enamel, stain, or wood preservative

PROJECT

ARCHED REDWOOD GATE

Sturdy, yet friendly—that's what this arched redwood gate is.

It clearly bespeaks privacy and security. Yet there's something about this gate that piques a visitor's curiosity. Maybe it's the spaces at the curved top that offer a hint of what's behind. Perhaps the handsome architecture suggests the yard is equally compelling. In any case, the visitor is inexorably drawn to this entrance.

Shopping List

1 pc. 4 × 4 × 16′ redwood
1 pc. 2 × 4 × 10′ redwood
6 pcs. 2 × 4 × 8′ redwood
2 pcs. 2 × 3 × 8′ redwood
1 pc. 2 × 2 × 16′ redwood
1 pc. 1 × 4 × 8′ redwood
5 pcs. 1 × 3 × 12′ redwood
2 pcs. 1 × 2 × 12′ redwood
1 pc. 1 × 2 × 10′ redwood
1 pc. 1 × 2 × 8′ redwood
1 pc. ½ × 8 × 14′ tongue-and-groove redwood
6 pcs. ½ × 8 × 12′ tongue-and-groove redwood

1 pc. ¾ × 5¼ × 2′ maple
1 pc. 36″ × ¾″ dia. hardwood dowel
3 #8 × 3″ oval-head brass wood screws
4 #6 × 1½″ galvanized screws
1 pr. strap-and-pin hinges
50d galvanized nails
8d galvanized finishing nails
8d galvanized nails
6d galvanized finishing nails
resorcinol glue
exterior construction adhesive
water-repellent or water-repellent stain

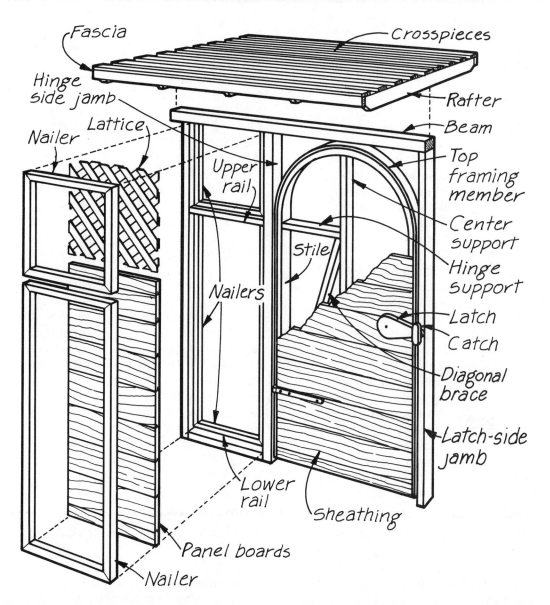

Fascia — Crosspieces

Hinge side jamb

Rafter

Beam

Nailer — Lattice

Upper rail

Top framing member

Center support

Hinge support

Stile

Nailers

Latch

Catch

Diagonal brace

Latch-side jamb

Lower rail

Sheathing

Panel boards

Nailer

And when the visitor does approach, he is impressed by the craftsmanship it displays. Indeed he should be; the construction requires more than basic carpentry skills. To build one like it, you'll need to invest patience and care, but the dividend will be some new techniques in your bag of carpentry tricks.

The 3½-inch-thick gate, identical on both sides, is strong enough to take more than a little hard use, thanks to its sound design and construction. And the handcrafted maple latch is simple and foolproof in its operation.

211

Cutting List

Number	Piece	Dimensions	Material
1	Top framing member	1½″ × 3½″ × 70½″	redwood
2	Gate stiles	1½″ × 3½″ × 48″	redwood
1	Bottom rail	1½″ × 2½″ × 33″	redwood
1	Center support	1½″ × 2½″ × 69″	redwood
2	Hinge supports	1½″ × 2½″ × 15¾″	redwood
1	Diagonal brace	1½″ × 2½″ × 39″	redwood
24	Sheathing	½″ × 7¼″ × 35½″*	redwood
1	Latch-side jamb	1½″ × 3½″ × 74¼″	redwood
1	Hinge-side jamb	3½″ × 3½″ × 120″*	redwood
1	Side-panel post	1½″ × 3½″ × 120″*	redwood
1	Beam	3½″ × 3½″ × 63″	redwood
5	Rafters	1½″ × 3½″ × 48″	redwood
2	Fascia	¾″ × 2½″ × 63″	redwood
1	Middle crosspiece	¾″ × 3½″ × 63″	redwood
8	Crosspieces	¾″ × 2½″ × 63″	redwood
2	Vertical stops	1½″ × 1½″ × 72¾″	redwood
1	Horizontal stop	1½″ × 1½″ × 37½″	redwood
2	Upper and lower rails	1½″ × 3½″ × 18″	redwood
4	Nailers	¾″ × 1½″ × 21″	redwood
8	Nailers	¾″ × 1½″ × 18″	redwood
1	Lattice panel	18″ × 21″	redwood lattice
4	Nailers	¾″ × 1½″ × 62″*	redwood
9	Panel boards	¾″ × 7¼″ × 18″*	redwood
2	Latches	¾″ × 5¼″ × 10″	maple
2	Spacers	¾″ × 4″ × 4″	maple
1	Catch	¾″ × 1½″ × 4¾″	maple
1	Latch shaft	4⅛″ × ¾″	dowel
1	Catch spacer	1½″ × ¾″	dowel

*The exact length should be determined during construction and these pieces cut to fit.

1. Cut the framing for the gate. The gate is constructed somewhat like a hollow-core door. The frame is formed of 2-by stock. A perimeter frame is supplemented with a center support. Horizontal framing members underlie the hinges, and a compression brace running between them helps prevent sagging.

Cut the framing members to the sizes specified in the Cutting List. Because the top framing member must be bent, it's essential that it be cut from clear stock; any knots could cause the piece to snap when you bend it.

Cut 1¼-inch-wide by ½-inch-deep rabbets into the edges of the stiles and the top member, as shown. These rabbets are most easily cut on a table saw.

FRAMING PLAN

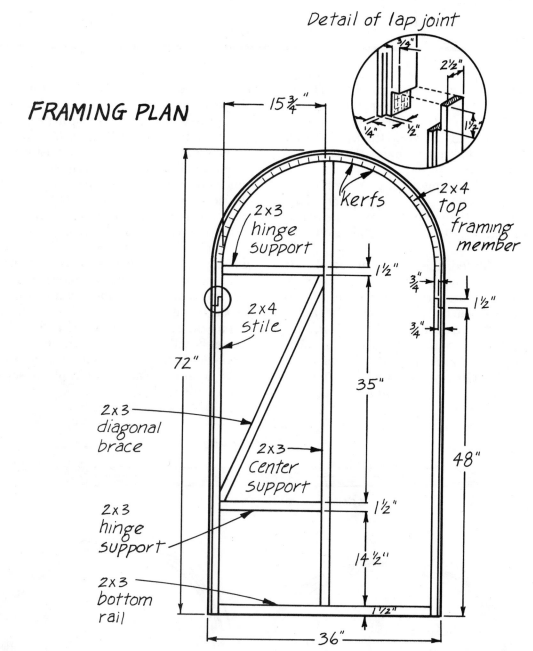

Detail of lap joint

¾"
2½"
¼"
½"
1½"

15¾"

kerfs

2x3 hinge support

2x4 top framing member

2x4 stile

1½"
¾"
1½"
¾"

72"

35"

48"

2x3 diagonal brace

2x3 center support

2x3 hinge support

1½"

14½"

2x3 bottom rail

1½"

36"

Cut laps to join the top framing member to the stiles. The top member is notched on both ends, each stile on one end. The laps are essentially rabbets, each 1½ inches wide and ¾ inch deep, as shown. Cut the laps into the inside face of the top member and the outside faces of the stiles. (Though it seems sensible to orient the laps so the stiles "hook" the ends of the top framing member, the orientation specified will shed water, rather than collecting it. In the final assembly, the sheathing boards reinforce the joint.)

2. Bend the top framing member. This is a two-step process. In the first step, you kerf the back of the piece. Then you soak the piece in water to limber up the uncut wood fibers, allowing you to bend them to the necessary curve.

Start by making a series of kerfs just under 1¼ inch deep and spaced ⅝ inch apart. Begin the kerfs 6 inches from one end of the member and end them 6 inches from the other.

Once kerfed, the piece will bend, but probably not enough. Bend it as much as possible by hand, then fit a band clamp around it. As you tighten the band, the radius of the arc should decrease. The goal is an arc with a 18-inch radius. It's easiest to measure the gap between the ends—it must be 36 inches. Most likely, the stock won't bend nearly this much without breaking. Tighten the clamp slowly, and *stop* if you hear the slightest crack.

Now—with the band clamp in place—soak the piece in water overnight. If your bathtub isn't large enough, make a vat using heavy plastic and bricks. Make a perimeter of bricks large enough to accommodate the piece. Put plastic over the bricks and hold it in place with another layer of bricks. Add enough water to cover the workpiece.

You'll probably be able to complete the curve after an overnight soak. But be careful. You may have to bend the piece in stages, tightening the clamp and soaking, tightening the clamp and soaking. What you'll have when you are done won't be a semicircle. Rather it will be a catenary curve—one that becomes more gradual as it approaches the ends. With the clamp still in place, set the piece aside to dry.

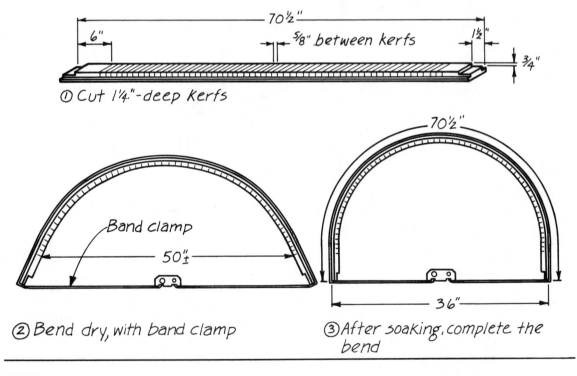

① Cut 1¼"-deep Kerfs

② Bend dry, with band clamp

③ After soaking, complete the bend

3. Begin the door assembly. While the top member is soaking, you can proceed with the door assembly.

First, nail the stiles to the bottom rail with 8d galvanized finishing nails. (Use finishing nails wherever you nail through the side of the door.) Then, position the center support against the bottom rail, and face-nail through the rail into the support. Position the hinge supports, and nail them in place (the top hinge support can only be nailed to the center support, since its outer end attaches, eventually, to the top framing member).

Next, cut the diagonal brace to fit. Set the piece you cut earlier in position and scribe the ends to fit. Trim it, then nail it in place.

4. Cut the sheathing for the gate. With the gate frame nearly complete, it is time to cut and install the sheathing. Use ½-inch-thick tongue-and-groove stock for this.

First, measure the door frame width to determine exactly how long to cut the sheathing pieces. Cut 24 pieces.

Nominal 8-inch boards usually measure 7¼ inches wide (although this varies slightly). Of that width, about ¼ inch is the tongue, so the board is effectively 7 inches wide. The bottom board must be installed flush with the bottom of the door. Since the top board should be 6½ inches wide, you will need to rip the bottom board to an effective width of about 2½ inches.

With all this in mind, lay out your stock and determine the width of the bottom board, then rip two pieces (one for each side of the gate).

5. Begin to sheathe the gate. Check to ensure that the gate frame is square, then fit the bottom piece in place—tongue up, flush with the gate bottom—and nail it, using 8d galvanized finishing nails. Install five more boards, but don't face nail them. Instead, conceal the fasteners by blind-nailing through the base of the tongues into the stiles and center support with 6d finishing nails.

Turn the assembly over and install the same number of sheathing boards on the back of the gate.

6. Attach the top framing member. Remove the band clamp from the top framing member. It will probably spread open a bit, but not so much that you won't be able to pull it closed by hand. Spread resorcinol glue on the lap joints. Lay the top member in place, the arc against the center support, the laps loosely joined. Assemble one of the lap joints, and drive two 1½-inch-long screws through the stile into the top framing member. Now use a C-clamp to join the second lap tightly, and secure it with screws.

7. Attach the top tongue-and-groove boards. Attach additional sheathing boards to the gate. When you reach top framing member, you must scribe the ends of the boards to fit the curve.

Place a large piece of cardboard over the top of the gate, its bottom edge carefully aligned along the edge of the uppermost sheathing board. Scribe the outside curve of the top framing member on a piece of cardboard. Then set a compass to ¼ inch and trace the arc, scribing another inside the first. Cut the cardboard along this second curve. Check to see that the template fits into the rabbet and adjust it if necessary.

Fit three tongue-and-groove boards together, lay the template on them, and scribe the arc. Cut the boards with a saber saw, then install them. Apply construction adhesive to the rabbet and fit the first of the

three boards in place. Blind-nail through the tongue. Install the second board in like manner. The third board isn't nailed; the adhesive will secure it. Clean off any adhesive that squeezes out.

Repeat the process on the other side of the gate. Check the template on the second side and see if it fits properly. If it is too small, make a new one. If it fits, use it to lay out the top three sheathing boards, cut them, and install them.

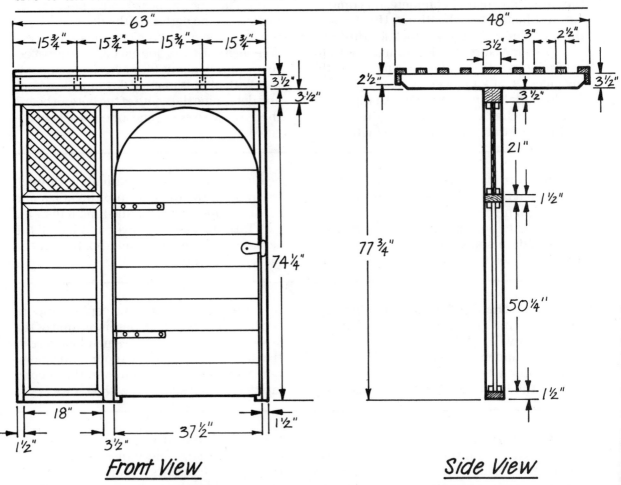

Front View   Side View

8. **Lay out the gateway.** The gateway shown adjoins a house wall at the top of a two-step stoop. The latch-side doorjamb is a 2 × 4 fastened to the house framing, while the hinge-side jamb is a 4 × 4 post set in the ground. In this project, the assumption is that the gateway will be constructed at ground level, but will adjoin a house (or other structure).

Cut the latch-side jamb to length and attach it to the house wall. The bottom of the jamb sits on the ground. Be sure it is plumb; if necessary, use wooden shingles as wedges to shim the post from the wall to make it plumb. Nail directly into the house framing; if the house walls are masonry, use lead expansion shields and lag bolts to attach the jamb.

Using the latch-side jamb as a reference, lay out the postholes for the hinge-side jamb and the side-panel post. Dig the holes about 1 foot in diameter and at least 3 feet deep (deeper if necessary to get below your frost line). Put a couple of inches of gravel in the holes, then put in the posts. Make sure the posts are higher than the latch-side jamb. Plumb them and secure them with temporary braces. Backfill the jamb hole with concrete, the side-panel posthole with earth.

9. **Install the beam.** After the concrete has set, extend a level line from the top of the latch-side jamb across the other two posts, mark them, and trim them. Then cut the beam, set it in place atop the posts, and nail it with 50d nails.

10. **Build the trellis.** The trellis consists of five rafters and nine crosspieces. It is trimmed along the front and back with fascia boards.

Cut the rafters. At the end of each rafter, make a mark 2 inches down from the top side. Strike a 45-degree line from this point to the bottom edge, and trim along the line. Center the rafters on the beam and toenail them in place, spaced 15¾ inches on center.

Install fascia boards next. Cut two, and nail them across the rafter ends, flush with the top edges of the rafters.

Install the crosspieces. The middle crosspiece, the 1 × 4, is positioned directly above the beam. Position a 1 × 3 crosspiece across each end of the assembly, so it overlaps the fascia board. Space the others at 3-inch intervals.

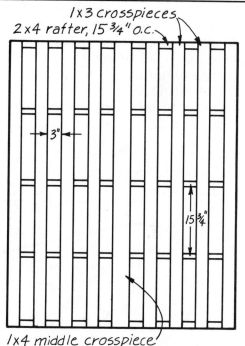

1x3 crosspieces
2x4 rafter, 15¾" o.c.
3"
15¾"
1x4 middle crosspiece centered over 4x4 beam

11. Install stops and hang the gate. The stops for the gate are nailed around the inside of the jambs, flush to the front or back, depending on which way you want the door to swing.

The strap hinges must be installed along the supports incorporated in the gate frame. Drill through the sheathing and supports, and bolt the hinge straps in place. Line up the gate in the frame by shimming under it so you'll know where to drill in the 4 × 4 post for the top hinge pintle. Install the top pintle pointing up. Hang the door on the top pintle, then line up and drill for the bottom pintle. To make it impossible to lift the door off, install the bottom pintle pointing down. (To do this, you must unbolt the strap from the gate, fit it over the pintle, then rebolt it.)

12. Fill in the side panel. The side panel is filled in after the gate is hung, so that joints between its tongue-and-groove boards can be aligned with those of the gate sheathing, a subtle but telling touch.

Complete the lattice panel first. Cut the upper rail. Position it between the posts, 21 inches below the beam; face-nail through the 2 × 4 post, then toenail into the 4 × 4 post. Cut two sets of lattice nailers with mitered ends. Use 6d galvanized finishing nails to fasten one set in place, recessed ¾ inch from face of the assembly. Cut the lattice, place against the nailers, and install the second set to hold it in place.

Cut two sets of nailers for the solid panel and miter the ends. Install one set of these nailers as you did the lattice nailers.

Now cut and install the tongue-and-groove boards. Cut seven boards to length and rip the top one to the width necessary to align its bottom with that of the adjacent gate board. Install that board, groove down, followed by the five below it, tacking them to the nailers with one finishing nail on each side of each board. Rip the bottom board so it is 1½ inches wider than the gate's bottom board. Tack it in place.

Now cut and install the lower rail, as you did the upper rail, fitting it snugly against the bottom tongue-and-groove board. Install the remaining nailers.

13. Cut the parts for the latch and catch. The door latch can be made from any light-colored, tight-grained hardwood—maple, beech, madrone.

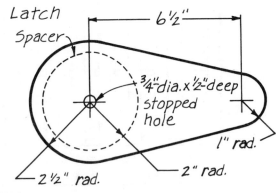

Latch
Spacer
6½"
¾" dia. x ½" deep stopped hole
2½" rad.
2" rad.
1" rad.

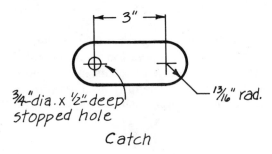

3"
¾" dia. x ½" deep stopped hole
1³⁄₁₆" rad.
Catch

The latch and catch are easy to lay out with a compass, as shown. Cut two latches, two spacers, and a catch from ¾-inch stock. From ¾-inch-diameter hardwood dowel, cut a latch shaft and a catch spacer. Drill ¾-inch holes through the center of the latch spacers. With the same bit, drill ½-inch-deep stopped holes in the latches and the catch, as shown.

14. **Install the latch assembly.** Lay out the location of the latch shaft on the gate, 47 inches from the bottom and 5½ inches from the edge. Drill a ¾-inch-diameter hole through the door.

Spread resorcinol glue in the hole in one latch, and insert the latch shaft. Drill a pilot hole, and drive a 3-inch brass screw through the latch and into the dowel. Slip a spacer on the dowel, and insert the dowel through the gate from the outside.

Glue the catch spacer in the stopped hole in the catch. Position the assembly on the jamb, flush against the wall, so it will catch the latch when it's horizontal. Drill a pilot hole, then drive a 3-inch brass screw through the catch assembly into the jamb.

Complete the installation from the other side of the gate. Close the gate and latch it. From the inside, slip the second spacer over the latch shaft, then glue on the remaining

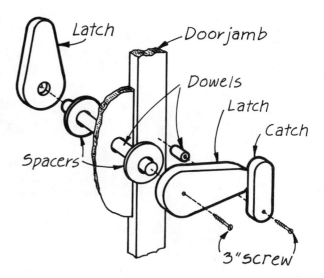

latch and drive a screw into it. Align the latch pointing up, so it won't hit the stop as the gate swings open.

15. **Apply a finish to the gate and gateway.** The entire assembly doesn't need a finish to give it color or character. The redwood used in the project has enough of that.

But to weather well, the entire project should be carefully coated with a water repellent or water-repellent stain.

Lattice walls, gate-way arches, graceful garden backdrops. The trellis's utilitarian function is aesthetic: to make the garden, and its plants, look better.

Trellises

The word trellis comes from an old French word—*treliz*—meaning a fabric of coarse weave. It makes sense. Think of the woven effect of wooden slats on many trellises, or the way vines weave their way through. Whatever the origin of the word, it's certain that a trellis "woven" with your favorite vine can add the finishing touch to your yard or garden.

A trellis can be a simple piece of framed lattice, or it can be part of an arbor or pergola, which are essentially more elaborate overhead trellises to support climbing vines and flowers. What you call it isn't as important as the pleasure this type of structure can add to your outdoor living. A trellis can shelter you from the wind and create a cozy private place. An integral part of Victorian architecture, more and more contemporary homeowners are realizing the value a trellis has in linking their yards with nature.

A simple latticework trellis can be placed in a corner of your yard, by the side of your house, or along a walkway. A trellis can become part of your fence plan as well, particularly as an enticing gateway.

Whatever type you decide to build, make it out of decay-resistant materials like cedar or pressure-treated pine that will just need an occasional application of clear water repellent. Use galvanized screws, not nails, since screws are quicker and easier (with a drill and screw bit) to install on delicate lattice.

What you're going to plant is going to influence what type of trellis you need. Some annual and perennial vines can get too heavy for a thin-lathed trellis to support. Stay away from ivy plants that have rootlike suckers that will be hard to control. Choose plant vines that climb by twining their stems around the wood. Flowering vines range from climbing roses to honeysuckles to grapes. There are many different designs possible, but the trellis should match the overall style of your house. The final location of the trellis is important if you want a particular vine to grow on it. Most vines like their roots in the shade and their heads in the sun.

Arbors

When the sun is too bright, you shade your eyes with your hand. A homemade arbor does the same—and more—for a sunburned gardener. A simply built wooden arbor offers viny plants a place to wind, and it adorns in a natural way your backyard landscape. Figuratively speaking, you could call an arbor an "architectural tree." Literally, the word arbor is derived from the Latin word for tree.

With a hand shading your eyes then, survey your property and decide where your arbor ought to be situated. Before planning construction, though, remember these secrets of backyard shading:

- Keep it light.
- Make it strong.
- Let the air blow through.

Arbors are most often successful when they are combined with other architectural features. They can cover a walk, gate, garden bench, or terrace paving. Many arbors double as roofs for tool sheds, porches, or patios.

Most arbors and pergolas utilize 4×4 or 6×6 posts with a framework of 2×4 or 2×6 beams. Decorative accents, as well as prefabricated lattice or heavier wooden slats, can be added to the basic frame.

Simple is beautiful and this arbor proves it. Just six posts straddled by beams and topped with rafters, it truly adds a new dimension to the small ground-level deck it covers. The arbor provides some shade, but more important, it adds intimacy. Instead of feeling like you are *out* on a deck, exposed, you feel like you are *in* a room, protected yet outdoors and pleasantly unconfined.

Because of the configuration of the house and deck, the posts had to be set in a trapezoid, not a rectangle. Yet the beams and

rafters form a rectangle and are square and level.

Of course, this basic arbor could just as easily be built to conform to our conventional expectations: square and solid, a post at each corner, set over level ground. The alterations necessary are trivial and easily made. In fact, one of the changes is already incorporated; the Materials List assumes you'll build on a level site.

1. Use short stakes to stake out the two middle posts, positioning them 103½ inches apart on center. Tie string tautly between the stakes.

2. Use slightly longer stakes to stake out the end posts on the side that has the posts spaced 98 inches on center. Tie a string between these end posts, ensuring that it is perpendicular to the first (by using the 3-4-5 method, for example) and that it passes through the centerpoint of the middle post on that side.

3. Stake out the remaining two end posts, spacing the posts on that side 61 inches on center. Tie a string between these stakes, ensuring that it is perpendicular to the first and parallel to the second.

4. Excavate the postholes, then place a post in each hole. Plumb the posts and temporarily brace them in position. Backfill the holes with soil.

5. Cut the post at the lowest grade to 9 feet. Run a line around the remaining posts to mark this level. Cut the posts off.

6. Cut the beams. The beams are just under 20 feet long, not an uncommon length in redwood. Trim the 2×10 beams to length. To miter the ends, measure 2 inches across the end. From that point, mark a 60-degree

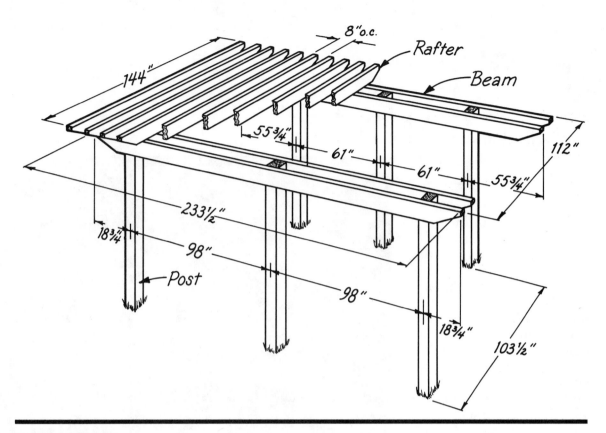

Materials List

Number	Piece	Dimensions	Material
6	Posts	5½″ × 5½″ × 132″	redwood
4	Beams	1½″ × 9¼″ × 233½″	redwood
29	Rafters	1½″ × 5½″ × 144″	redwood

Hardware
2 boxes #8 × 2″ galvanized all purpose screws
10d galvanized nails
water repellent or water-repellent stain

miter (60 degrees from the butt end). Cut along this line.

7. To install a beam, rest it on nails driven into the posts, 9¼ inches below the top. Level it, then drive 10d galvanized nails through it into the posts. Remove the support nails. Install all the beams in this fashion.

8. Cut and attach the rafters. The arbor uses 29 rafters, each 12 feet long. Miter the ends, as you did the beam ends. Toenailing rafters set this close together is difficult, so the rafters are "toe-screwed" to the beams with 2-inch galvanized all-purpose screws.

9. Finish the arbor by applying a penetrating water repellent, or a water-repellent stain.

PROJECT
FREESTANDING TRELLIS

This L-shaped trellis can be used as a privacy screen or wind screen. It's strong enough to support heavier, woody vines.

To soften the angularity of the structure, several pieces—the rafters, short braces, long braces, and decorative ends—have curvilinear profiles. You can customize the overall proportions of the trellis to your liking by varying the spacing of the posts. Remember, though, that spacing the posts differently from the plan will change the dimensions of some key parts.

You can precut the posts, rafters, and braces in the shop, but it's best to wait until the posts are set before measuring and cutting the beams, horizontal lath, and stringers. Measuring on-site will take care of the fact that the actual dimensions between posts will probably vary from the plan a bit.

The trellis was built from cedar, which naturally resists decay. Redwood, cypress, and pressure-treated wood are also good choices.

Shopping List

4 pcs. $4 \times 4 \times 10'$ clear cedar
5 pcs. $2 \times 4 \times 8'$ clear cedar
3 pcs. $5/4 \times 2 \times 8'$ clear cedar
1 pc. $5/4 \times 2 \times 10'$ clear cedar
21 pcs. $1 \times 2 \times 10'$ clear cedar
5 pcs. $1 \times 2 \times 12'$ clear cedar
68 #8 × 3'' galvanized all-purpose screws
152 #8 × 1½'' galvanized all-purpose screws

224

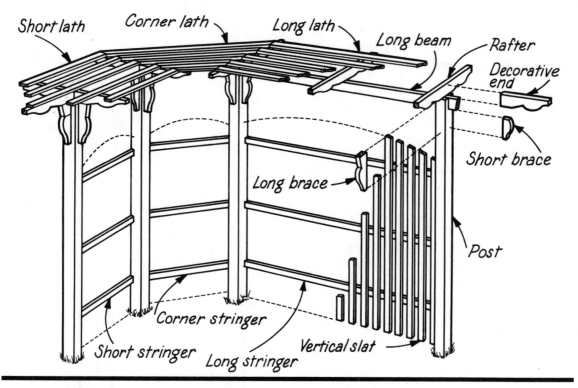

Short lath · Corner lath · Long lath · Long beam · Rafter · Decorative end · Short brace · Long brace · Post · Corner stringer · Short stringer · Long stringer · Vertical slat

Cutting List

Number	Piece	Dimensions*	Material
4	Posts	3½″ × 3½″ × 120″	cedar
1	Long beam	1½″ × 3½″ × 82½″	cedar
1	Short beam	1½″ × 3½″ × 46½″	cedar
8	Long braces	1½″ × 3½″ × 10¾″	cedar
8	Short braces	1½″ × 3½″ × 7¼″	cedar
5	Rafters	1½″ × 3½″ × 31″	cedar
5	Long lath	¾″ × 1½″ × 83¾″	cedar
5	Short lath	¾″ × 1½″ × 47¾″	cedar
1	Corner lath	¾″ × 1½″ × 8″	cedar
1	Corner lath	¾″ × 1½″ × 18″	cedar
1	Corner lath	¾″ × 1½″ × 25½″	cedar
1	Corner lath	¾″ × 1½″ × 36″	cedar
1	Corner lath	¾″ × 1½″ × 44″	cedar
2	Decorative ends	1½″ × 3½″ × 14½″	cedar
3	Long stringers	1¹⁄₁₆″ × 1½″ × 72″	cedar
3	Short stringers	1¹⁄₁₆″ × 1½″ × 36″	cedar
3	Corner stringers	1¹⁄₁₆″ × 1½″ × 24″	cedar
39	Vertical slats	¾″ × 1½″ × 60″	cedar

*All dimensions are based on 72″ post spacing center to center, long side; 36″ post spacing center to center, short side; and 25″ post spacing at corner.

225

1. **Taper the posts, then set them.** Each of the four 10-foot posts tapers. Mark a line 4½ feet from one end and, using a plane, shave off wood on each side of the post from this line to the nearest end. Shape the taper by eye from 3½ inches square at the line to 2½ inches square at the end.

Cut a notch in the top of each post 1½ inches wide by 3½ inches deep.

Locate and dig holes for the posts in the desired locations. Put a layer of stones or gravel in the bottom of the holes. Plant the posts and backfill, keeping the posts 2½ feet deep and plumb.

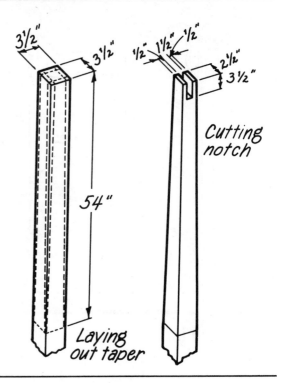

Cutting notch

54"

Laying out taper

2. **Measure and cut each beam to length.** Since you're building on site, the beam length can be measured exactly from the posts. This is equal to the outside-to-outside dis-tance at the tops of the posts plus 7 inches. Cut the ends of each beam to a 15-degree angle.

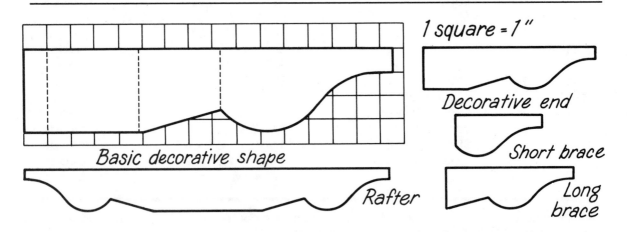

1 square = 1"

Basic decorative shape

Decorative end

Short brace

Rafter

Long brace

3. Lay out and cut the braces, rafters, and decorative ends. Use the pattern as a guide for laying out the appropriate part of the decorative shape on the pieces. The profiles can be sawed on site using a saber saw, or in the shop on a band saw.

4. Assemble the framework. Fasten the beams in the notches in the posts, leaving 3½ inches extending beyond the posts. Fasten the long braces to the front and back of each post flush with the top. Fasten the short braces to the sides of the posts up against the bottom of the beams.

Fasten the rafters, evenly spaced, to the beams. Following the post spacing shown, there are two rafters on the short side and three on the long side. Fasten the decorative ends on top of the beams, perpendicular to the end rafters.

For fasteners, use galvanized all-purpose screws. Galvanized nails will work, but using a drill and screw bit is easier on delicate trellis parts than a hammer and nails. Predrilling for fasteners will prevent wood splitting. Use 3-inch screws for the framework.

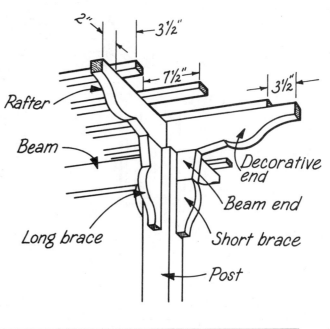

5. Cut and install the lath, stringers, and slats. Cut and fasten pieces of 1 × 2 horizontal lath, evenly spaced, to the top of the rafters. The center lath is cut 3½ inches shy of the tip of the decorative end. The outer lath should overhang the rafters 3½ inches at the ends, while the strips between the center and outer lath strips should overhang the rafters 7½ inches. The corner lath strips will be five different lengths. Miter them on both ends to make good joints with the lath abutting on either side.

From ⁵⁄₄ × 2 stock, cut long stringers, short stringers, and corner stringers to fit between the posts. Lay out notches in the posts to accept the stringers, as shown. Space the notches at 2, 3½, and 5 feet off the ground. Cut out the notches using a chisel and mallet. Fasten the stringers in the notches.

Cut 1 × 2 slats to 60-inch lengths and fasten to the stringers, spacing them evenly. Trim the ends of the slats to a pleasing arc. To do this, cut a piece of wood to ¼ × 1 × 70 inches, bow the wood into an arc, and hold it up to the slats. If you're working alone, use a piece of mason's cord to hold the bow archer-style. Following the arc, scribe a line and cut the stringers at the line with a saber saw. For fasteners, use 1½-inch screws on the lath and slats, and 3-inch screws on all other joints.

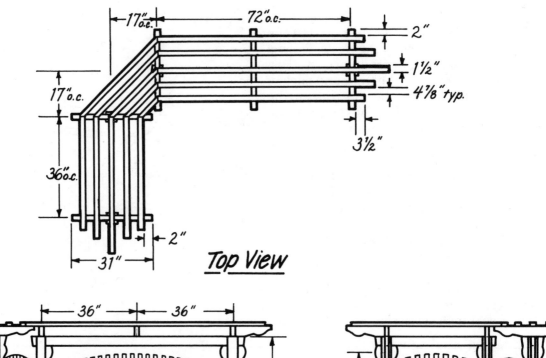

Top View

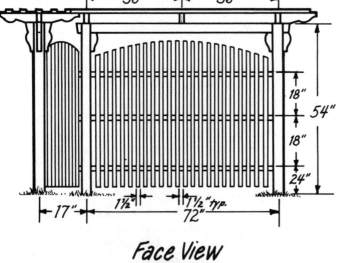

Face View

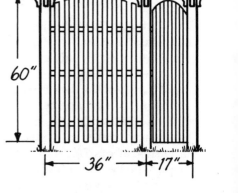

End View

PROJECT
ADJUSTABLE SHADE TRELLIS

The simple fact is the sun doesn't stay in one place. That can be a problem when you're planning a deck. How can you compensate for periods of too-cool shade and brutally hot sun that vary depending on the deck's orientation and the time of day?

This project offers a solution. Architect Brian Zita designed and built this clever trellis, which features louvers that can be adjusted, venetian blind fashion, to block out the sun or let it shine through.

The trellis is composed of 2 × 8 rafters with 1 × 6 redwood louvers fitted between them. The louvers pivot on ¼-inch hardwood dowels, allowing them to rotate up to 180 degrees. A 2 × 2 control rod fastened to all the louvers in a "bay" enable you to move them in unison. The trellis is held up by freestanding 4 × 4 posts carrying doubled 2 × 10 beams, and 2 × 8 ledger strips lag-bolted to the house's framing. Zita added 1 × 2 redwood trim

229

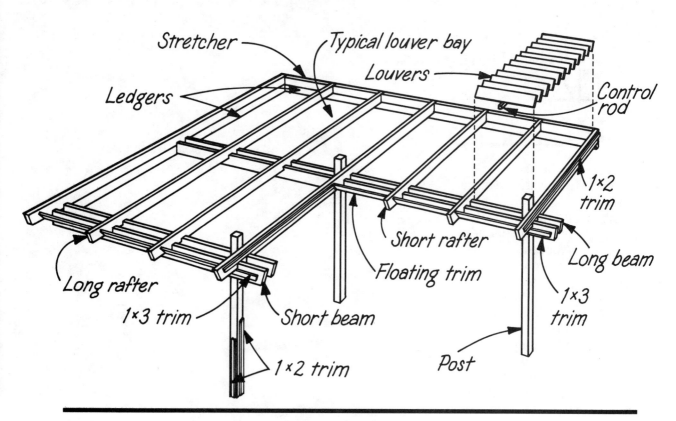

Cutting List

Number	Piece	Dimensions	Material
3	Posts	3½″ × 3½″ × 144″	redwood
2	Ledgers	1½″ × 7½″ × 120″	redwood
2	Ledgers	1½″ × 7½″ × 144″	redwood
2	Beams	1½″ × 9½″ × 144″	redwood
4	Beams	1½″ × 9½″ × 162″	redwood
4	Rafters	1½″ × 7½″ × 103″	redwood
7	Rafters	1½″ × 7½″ × 120″	redwood
144	Louvers	¾″ × 5½″ × 46⅛″	clear heart redwood
6	Stretchers	1½″ × 7½″ × 46½″	redwood
9	Control rods	1½″ × 1½″ × 84″	clear heart redwood
112	Interior rafters	5½″ × ¼″	dowel
64	End rafters	3½″ × ¼″	dowel
6	Floating trim	¾″ × 5½″ × 46½″	clear heart redwood

pieces to the posts and rafters, and 1 × 3 trim to the beams, helping to embellish the utilitarian look of the structure. Open beam and rafter ends were cut at a 45-degree angle for visual interest.

Zita used construction heart redwood for all the structural pieces of his trellis. To ensure the dimensional stability of the louvers and their control rods, he made them of clear heart redwood. It's a good idea to treat the redwood with a water repellent to help prevent warping and cracking as the wood weathers.

The trellis pictured is L-shaped, covering a deck located where exterior walls meet in an inside corner. Using the basic plans shown here, you can tailor the design to match the geometry of your own house and deck. To alter the size of the trellis, you can vary the number of rafters and the spacing between them. The length of the louvers should be limited to 4 feet to make adjusting them manageable.

Shopping List

- 1 pc. 2 × 2 × 8' clear heart redwood
- 4 pcs. 2 × 2 × 14' clear heart redwood
- 50 pcs. 1 × 6 × 12' clear heart redwood
- 3 pcs. 4 × 4 × 12' construction heart redwood
- 4 pcs. 2 × 10 × 14' construction heart redwood
- 2 pcs. 2 × 10 × 12' construction heart redwood
- 4 pcs. 2 × 8 × 12' construction heart redwood
- 13 pcs. 2 × 8 × 10' construction heart redwood
- 30 pcs. 36" × ¼" dia. hardwood dowel
- 66-4½" × ⅜" galvanized lag screws
- 8-6" × ⅜" galvanized hex-head bolts w/nuts and washers
- 288-⁵⁄₁₆" galvanized flat washers
- 144-¼" galvanized screw hooks
- 144-¼" galvanized eyescrews
- 4 joist hangers for 2 × 10s
- water-repellent stain

1. Lay out the louvered roof. Look at the overall view of the trellis, and plan your trellis, adapting the design elements to fit your house and deck. Try to utilize the standard louver bay dimension of 48 inches. Gang together several bays to achieve the necessary overall size. Plan, measure, and mark the locations for posts and ledger strips.

2. Set the posts. The posts for the trellis shown run long enough to project about 18 inches above the rafters. They should be set in postholes dug below the frost line for your area.

Dig postholes to the depth appropriate for your area, and throw an inch or two of gravel into them to promote drainage away from the post bottoms. Plant the posts and plumb them. Cut temporary braces from scrap 2 × 4s and nail them to the posts to hold them in position. Nail the braces to stakes driven in the ground.

3. Install the ledger strips. Mount the ledger strips using ⅜-inch lag screws driven into the framing of the house (not simply into the siding and sheathing). If necessary, use shims to straighten ledgers being installed against beveled wood siding. If the house is sided with aluminum or vinyl siding, consider removing a strip of it, bolting the ledger flush against the sheathing, and installing flashing under the siding and over the ledger.

4. **Install the beams.** Trim the 2×10 beams to length, and cut ⅞-inch-deep, 1½-inch-wide notches in their top edges to receive the rafters. Miter the beam ends, if desired, at 30 degrees off plumb. Mount the beams in position using joist hangers at the ledger strips and $6 \times$ ⅜-inch hex-head bolts with nuts and washers at the posts. If your beams are long enough to require the use of two boards to span the distance, size the pieces so they meet at a post.

Next, cut a couple of rafters and temporarily nail them in place to help hold the structure in alignment. Then backfill the postholes with earth or concrete. Remove the temporary rafters and braces.

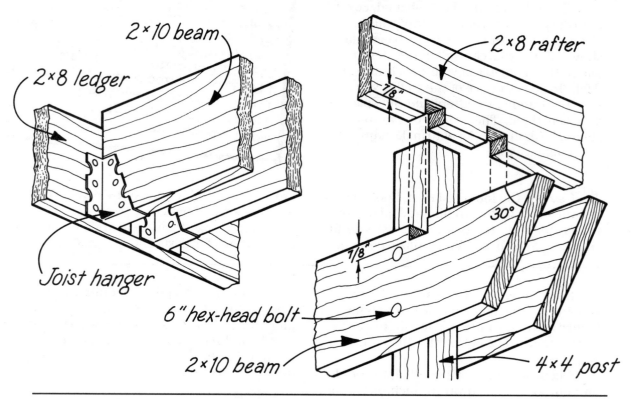

5. **Fashion the rafters and louvers.** Cut the remaining 2×8 rafters to length. In the bottom edge of each rafter, cut two ⅞-inch-deep, 1½-inch-wide notches to match the notches cut in the beams. If desired, miter the rafter ends to match the beam ends. Finally, lay out and drill ¼-inch-diameter holes through the rafters for the pivot dowels.

Select the end rafters. Tap 3½-inch-long dowels into the holes in these rafters; 2 inches of the dowel should protrude. Drive the 5½-inch dowels into the holes in the other rafters; 4 inches of the dowel should protrude on one side of these rafters.

Cut the louvers to length. Drill ⅜-inch-diameter, 2-inch-deep holes in the ends of the louvers. Use a doweling jig, centering each hole across both the thickness and the width of the louver.

6. **Install the rafters and louvers.** Mount an end rafter in position against the house, nailing into the house framing above the ledger strip.

Slip a flat washer on each dowel protruding from the end rafter. Then slide louvers onto the dowels, supporting their free ends with a 2 × 4 resting on the ledger and beams. Move the next rafter into position, and finish tapping the dowels through the

rafter into the holes in the louvers. Be sure to place a flat washer between the louver and rafter on each dowel.

Toenail the rafter into the ledger and beam. Remove the temporary 2 × 4 support. Cut a 2 × 8 stretcher, position it above the ledger and between the first and second rafters, against the ledger, and nail it in place.

Repeat the process, mounting louvers and rafters in turn, to construct all the bays.

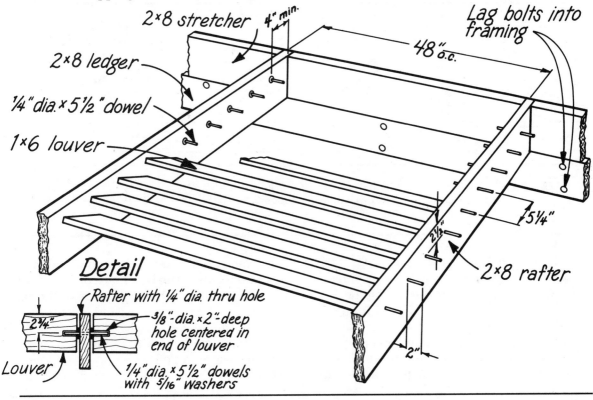

2×8 stretcher   4" min.

2×8 ledger

¼"dia.×5½"dowel

1×6 louver

Lag bolts into framing

48" o.c.

15¼"

2×8 rafter

2"

Detail

Rafter with ¼"dia. thru hole

⅜"-dia.×2"-deep hole centered in end of louver

2¾"

Louver

¼"dia.×5½"dowels with ⁵⁄₁₆" washers

233

7. **Install the control rods.** Cut the 2×2 clear redwood control rods to length; cut one for each bay. Lay out screw-hook positions on the control rods; drill a pilot hole at each location, then turn a screw hook into the hole.

Drill a pilot hole on the lower edge of each louver, midway along its length. Turn an eyescrew into each hole. Hold the rods up to the louvers, engaging the screw hooks in the eyescrews. Bend each hook closed with a pliers or vise grip.

Depending upon how much play each louver section has, you may need to make a stop system to "lock" the louvers at a given position. The stop is simply a wooden dowel inserted into a hole in the side of a rafter; one of the louvers in the set bears on it, preventing any of them from moving beyond that point. If you need the stop system, pick an accessible louver, trace the arc of its movement on the rafter, then drill a series of stopped holes inside the arc.

CONTROL ROD SYSTEM

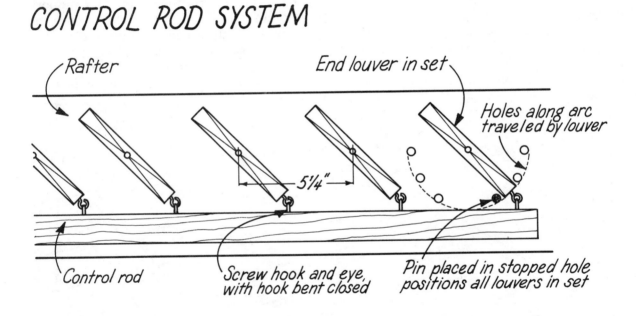

Rafter

End louver in set

Holes along arc traveled by louver

5¼"

Control rod

Screw hook and eye, with hook bent closed

Pin placed in stopped hole positions all louvers in set

8. **Install trim pieces.** Cut and fasten 1×6 floating trim pieces near the outer ends of the rafters, just beyond the double beams. Mount the floating trim 6 inches from the rafter tips and at an angle that parallels the angle cut on the rafter and beam ends.

As an option, you can cut and install additional trim pieces on the main struc-

tural members of the roof to add visual interest and to cover the bolt holes on the posts. On the posts and the lower edge of the rafters use 1×2 trim pieces, and on the lower edge of the beams, use 1×3 trim pieces.

Finish the trellis by applying a penetrating water repellent or water-repellent stain.

PROJECT

GATEWAY ARBOR WITH PICKET GATE

This gateway arbor will announce the entrance to your yard more elegantly than a simple gate. Designed to complement a picket fence, it gracefully assumes the picket motif in the pointed tops of its four posts.

This arbor entrance is so handsome as it stands here—newly built and devoid of vines, that you may decide not to plant any climbing vegetation around it. But a vine-covered arbor provides a more intimate and romantic entrance. This arbor's four posts and two hefty intersecting arches provide structure enough to support the heaviest varieties.

The arbor is a good band saw/saber saw project, since one or the other of these saws is essential for cutting out the arches and for shaping the post tops and pickets. The project is not difficult, although the arch supports may be tricky to visualize at first.

The project can be built of a variety of materials. Pressure-treated pine is best for the posts, regardless of what material you use for the other parts. A naturally rot-resistant wood like redwood or cedar will weather well if you plan to give the arbor a natural finish. But the colonial style seems to call for paint, in which case, a good grade of board lumber will prove satisfactory. The project can be fastened together with galvanized nails or all-purpose screws.

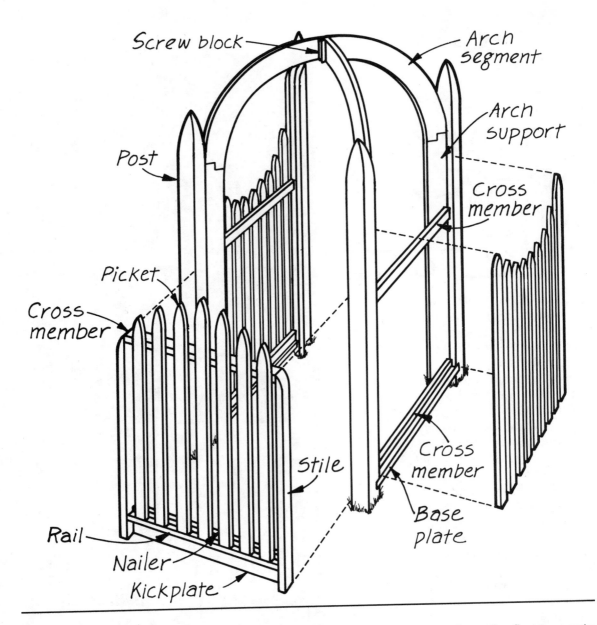

Screw block

Arch segment

Arch support

Post

Cross member

Picket

Cross member

Cross member

Stile

Base plate

Rail

Nailer

Kickplate

1. Prepare the posts. The arbor has four posts, each dadoed near ground level for the base plates, and each given a so-called Williamsburg cap on top.

Cut the posts to length. Then cut a 1½-inch-wide, 1-inch-deep dado to house the base plate; the dado is 40 inches from the bottom of the post.

Forming the Williamsburg caps involves making four identical saber saw (or band

saw) cuts. The waste from the first two cuts must be saved and taped back in place to provide bearing for the saw when making the third and fourth cuts.

To lay out the cuts, make a template. On a 1¾ × 8-inch rectangular piece of plywood or cardboard aligned vertically, draw an arc from an upper corner to the opposite lower corner. It should approximate the arc of the post top. Cut the template along the line

Shopping List

4 pcs. 4 × 4 × 10' pressure-treated posts
2 pcs. 2 × 12 × 8' western red cedar
4 pcs. 2 × 6 × 8' western red cedar
3 pcs. 2 × 4 × 8' western red cedar
2 pcs. 2 × 3 × 8' western red cedar
4 pcs. 1 × 3 × 10' western red cedar
9 pcs. 1 × 3 × 8' western red cedar
1 pc. 1 × 1 × 8' western red cedar
12 #7 × 4" galvanized all-purpose screws
12d galvanized nails
8d galvanized nails
6d galvanized nails
1 pr. gate butt hinges
1 colonial thumb latch
exterior-grade paint, stain, or wood preservative

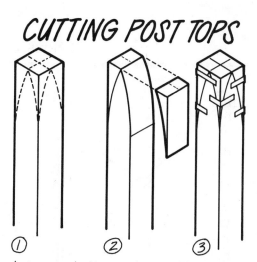

CUTTING POST TOPS

1. Lay out the cuts. 2. Make the first two cuts. 3. Reattach scrap for the final cuts.

you've drawn. By flipping the template over you'll be able to mark out the left-hand as well as the right-hand curve on each side of each post.

Cutting List

Number	Piece	Dimensions	Material
4	Posts	3½" × 3½" × 114"	pressure-treated pine
2	Base plates	1½" × 3½" × 42"	cedar
4	Arch supports	1½" × 5½" × 62½"	cedar
4	Arch segments	1½" × 11¼" × 36"	cedar
4	Cross members	1½" × 2½" × 40"	cedar
4	Screw blocks	¾" × ¾" × 5½"	cedar
2	Stiles	1½" × 3½" × 40"	cedar
1	Kickplate	1½" × 5½" × 33"	cedar
2	Rails	1½" × 3½" × 30"	cedar
1	Nailer	¾" × ¾" × 30"	cedar
4	Arbor pickets	¾" × 2¼" × 58½"	cedar
4	Arbor pickets	¾" × 2¼" × 50½"	cedar
4	Arbor pickets	¾" × 2¼" × 47"	cedar
4	Arbor pickets	¾" × 2¼" × 45½"	cedar
2	Arbor pickets	¾" × 2¼" × 45"	cedar
2	Gate pickets	¾" × 2¼" × 38"	cedar
2	Gate pickets	¾" × 2¼" × 40½"	cedar
2	Gate pickets	¾" × 2¼" × 41½"	cedar
1	Gate picket	¾" × 2¼" × 42"	cedar

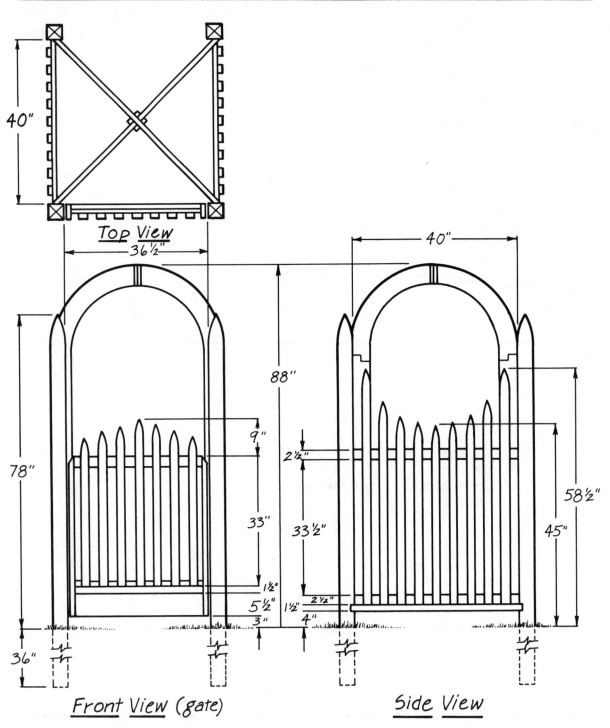

40"

Top View
36½"

88"

78"

9"

33"

1½"
5½"
3"

36"

Front View (gate)

40"

2½"

33½"

2½"
1½"
4"

58½"

45"

Side View

Use a saber saw with a 4-inch blade to cut the curves. It may be helpful to place a mirror beneath the cut so you can monitor the blade's progress along the curve marked on the post's underside. Remember to save the waste from the first two cuts and tape them back in place. After completing all the cuts, clean them up with a belt sander. Don't worry if they aren't perfectly regular; you are reproducing the look of a hand-cut Williamsburg post.

2. **Set the posts.** The front posts must be aligned with the fence posts—assuming you are placing the arbor in a run of picket fence —and spaced 36½ inches apart. Lay out the postholes and excavate them to a depth of 36 inches. Place the posts in the holes, but don't backfill them yet. The dadoes must be positioned to accept the base plates.

Cut the base plates, fit them into the dadoes, and toenail them in place.

Plumb the posts and level the base plates. Then backfill the postholes about halfway, and tack temporary braces from post to post across the front and back of the arbor.

3. **Make the arch supports.** The arch supports are attached to the inside faces of the posts to hold up the crossing arches that top the arbor. They have to be beveled along one edge so they project from the posts at the proper angle to properly support the arches, and they must be dadoed to fit around and support the cross members that hold the arbor's pickets.

As you lay out and cut the supports, you must bear in mind that the arbor requires *two mirror-image pairs* of them. If you make them all the same, two of them will be wrong.

Cut the 2 × 6 supports to length first. Each support has a 1½ × 1-inch notch on top to interlock with projecting tabs on the arch segments. Lay these out, as shown, and cut them.

Next, lay out and cut the wedge-shaped dadoes that house the 2 × 3 cross members. These can be cut on a band saw or with a saber saw that's capable of cutting bevels. With only a little extra effort, they can be cut with a hand saw and a chisel.

The last step in making the supports is

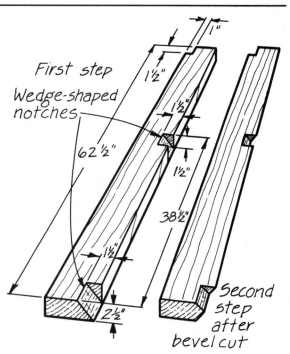

to rip the 45-degree bevel along one edge. If your table saw's blade tilts toward the fence, as is the case with most saws, position the fence 5½ inches from the blade before tilting the blade.

4. **Install the supports.** Rest a support on the base plate with the beveled edge against the post. Align it so the cross members, when installed, will be ¾ inch shy of the post edge. This is so the pickets will be flush with the posts. When the support is in proper alignment, nail or screw it in place.

5. **Cut and install the upper and lower cross members.** Cut four 40-inch lengths of 2 × 3 for cross members. Fit them in place and nail them to the posts, the supports, and the base plates, as appropriate.

6. **Cut and install the arch segments.** Cut four 36-inch lengths of 2 × 12 stock. Enlarge the pattern for the arch segments onto a piece of cardboard, cut it out, then trace the pattern onto the 2 × 12s. Cut out the arch segments on a band saw or with a saber saw.

Mount a pair of arch segments atop two of the supports, forming the first full arch. Fasten the segments to each other and the supports with screws.

Trim ¾ inch from the top end of the second pair of arch segments and install them.

Make and install screw blocks at the apex of the arches to reinforce the joints. Rip a 45-degree bevel along a 2-foot scrap of 1-by stock. Cut 5½-inch lengths of the resulting triangular stock. Screw these blocks into place.

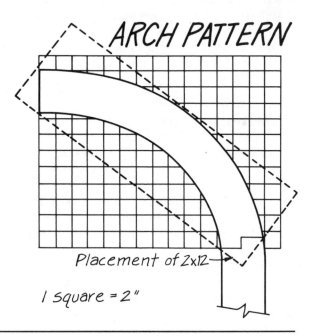

ARCH PATTERN

Placement of 2x12

1 square = 2"

7. **Fill the postholes with concrete.** With the arches in place, it is time to set the arbor permanently. Use concrete, allowing it to set for several days before removing the temporary braces.

8. **Frame the gate.** While the concrete is setting, complete the gate. Begin by cutting two stiles from 2 × 4 stock. To carry the Williamsburg cap theme through the project, lay out a curve on the top edges of the stiles, as shown, and cut them with a saber saw.

Cut a 2 × 6 kickplate and two 2 × 4 rails. Screw one rail to the kickplate, with its face centered over the edge of the kickplate, as shown. Use eight 4-inch screws to fasten this assembly between the stiles. The kickplate should be flush with the bottoms of the stiles. Fit the other rail between the stiles at the top, broad face out and centered front to back, so the pickets will be flush with the stiles. Screw it in place.

Cut a 1 × 1 nailer and screw it to the bottom rail. It must be recessed ¾ inch from the front of the frame.

GATE CONSTRUCTION

Picket lengths:
42"
41½"
40½"
38½"

2x3 cross member
2½"

2x4 stile

49"
40"

1x1 nailer

Recess nailer ¾" from front of rail

2x4 rail Center on Kickplate

2x6 kickplate
33"

9. Cut the pickets. Begin by ripping ¾-inch stock to a 2¼-inch width. For the side panels, you'll need four pickets of each of the following approximate lengths to create the concave curve: 58½ inches, 50½ inches, 47 inches, and 45½ inches. Cut two 45-inch center pickets.

For the gate, you'll need two pickets of each of the following lengths: 38 inches, 40½ inches and 41½ inches. The center picket is 42 inches long.

Cut curves on the tops of the pickets.

10. Attach pickets. The pickets must be spaced evenly across the sides of the arbor. The best approach may be to install the center picket first, and work out from there.

Attach the gate pickets. Again, install the center picket first and work toward the edges.

11. Mount the gate. You can mount the gate on either side of the arbor entrance, but the gate must swing outward. Use butt hinges. Mount a colonial thumb latch.

12. Paint the arbor and gate. Although you can use any finish, the style of the project cries out for paint—white or a colonial color. If the wood you've used has any knots, apply shellac or a shellac-based sealer to them. Then apply two coats of paint.

HOW TO SLATTED SUNROOF

There are a number of ways to control the amount of sun exposure on a deck or patio. One solution is to build a permanent overhead sunshade.

This slatted sunroof filters the sunlight through a series of parallel slats which form a partial roof over the area you wish to protect. The size of the structure and the spacing of the slats can be varied to accommodate whatever effect you're looking for.

This particular roof is constructed of ordinary pressure-treated southern yellow pine. It's a simple structure consisting of four posts supporting a network of 2×10 rafters. Slats made of 1×3 stock are nailed across the top, and over a short perimeter roof overhang. The most complicated joint is the compound miter cut on the slats where they meet at the corners on the overhang. The dimensions in the cutting list and draw-

242

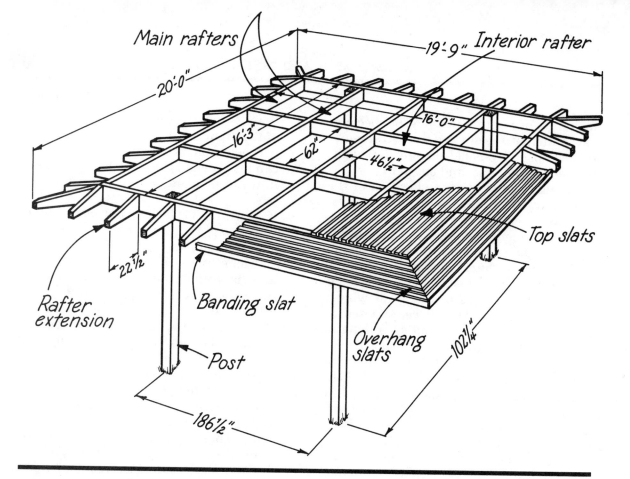

Main rafters

19'-9" Interior rafter

20'-0"

16'-0"

16'-3"

62"

46½"

22½"

Rafter extension

Banding slat

Post

Overhang slats

Top slats

102¼"

186½"

Materials List

Number	Piece	Dimensions	Material
4	Posts	5½" × 5½" × 144"	pressure-treated pine
7	Main rafters	1½" × 9¼" × 192"	pressure-treated pine
8	Interior rafters	1½" × 9¼" × 46⅛"	pressure-treated pine
36	Rafter extensions	1½" × 9¼" × 23"	pressure-treated pine
4	Corner rafter extensions	1½" × 9¼" × 31¹³⁄₁₆"	pressure-treated pine
55	Top slats	¾" × 2¾" × 192"	pressure-treated pine
56	Overhang slats	¾" × 2¾" × variable*	pressure-treated pine
8	Banding slats	¾" × 2¾" × 114½"*	pressure-treated pine

Hardware

16–8" × ⁷⁄₁₆" galvanized carriage bolts w/nuts and washers
16d galvanized nails
8d galvanized nails
water repellent or water-repellent stain

---

*The exact length should be determined during construction and these pieces cut to fit.

ings are as accurate as possible, but because of variations in the dressed sizes of pressure-treated wood, you should measure the lengths needed as you build, and cut to fit.

1. Carefully determine the location of the sunroof. Measure and lay out the post locations. Be certain the roof's overhang will clear adjacent buildings or other objects.
2. Dig postholes, plant the posts, and plumb them. Brace them temporarily, until the main rafters are installed. The posts for this sunroof are 12 feet long, allowing 3 feet in the ground and 9 feet exposed.
3. Cut the 2×10 main rafters to length. Four are bolted to the posts, using $8 \times \frac{7}{16}$-inch galvanized carriage bolts with washers and nuts. These rafters can be held in place with C-clamps while holes are drilled for the bolts. Put four bolts in each post, two each through the adjacent 2×10s.
4. When the rafters are securely fastened in position, check the posts for plumb again and backfill the postholes with concrete or soil. Remove the temporary braces and stakes.
5. Nail the remaining main rafters (those not touching a post) in place with 16d galvanized nails. Cut and nail the interior rafters in place.
6. To provide a framework for the overhanging roof slats, fabricate short, sloped rafter extensions from pieces of 2×10. Locate them 24 inches on center along each side of the main roof frame. Nail through the perimeter rafters into the extensions (you can also toenail through the extensions into the main rafters for extra holding power).
7. If the sunroof is immediately adjacent to the house, the slats should parallel it. The top slats are 16 feet long. Center a slat lengthwise over the perimeter rafters that parallel the house, as well as over each interior rafter that parallels the house.
8. Fill up each empty bay between rafters with 17 equally spaced slats. The approximate space between the slats is ¾ inch. Lay out all the slats in each bay to check this spacing and make any adjustments before nailing.
9. The overhanging slats mounted on the rafter extensions are butt joined at their ends. These slats are different lengths, becoming longer from top to bottom on the overhang. For the exact required length of each slat piece, measure directly on the rafter extensions.
10. Fasten a thin strip of pressure-treated wood on the underside of each corner below the miter joints, to bring the slats into alignment with each other.
11. Finish the sunroof by applying a penetrating water repellent or water-repellent stain.

244

GARBAGE CAN CORRAL

What are you going to do about those garbage cans? They don't do much for your yard's ambience, though the neighborhood dogs love 'em, out there ripe for the tipping. You could build a little lean-to shelter against the house. But maybe you don't even want that much of a reminder that the cans are there.

Here's a garbage can corral disguised as a section of lattice fence. It's got room for three garbage cans behind two gates. You can't

Shopping List

5 pcs. 4 × 4 × 10' redwood
1 pc. 2 × 4 × 10' redwood
2 pcs. 2 × 3 × 10' redwood
3 pcs. 2 × 3 × 8' redwood
6 pcs. 1 × 4 × 8' redwood
11 pcs. 1 × 1 × 8' redwood
4–4' × 8' panels of ¼" × 1½" redwood lattice
Approx. 350 linear feet of ¼" × 1½" redwood
4 pr. 4" butt hinges
2 sets hook-and-eye latches
12d galvanized nails
8d galvanized nails
6d galvanized nails

see them, and the dogs can't get to them.

The corral and the fence use standard prefab lattice with a minor modification. Extra strips provide more privacy while still allowing air movement.

While the step-by-step that follows doesn't specifically address the construction of this lattice fence, there's enough infor-

mation given to allow you to construct just such a fence. If you can build the corral, you can build the fence to go with it.

Moreover, though this project uses lattice, the corral concept can be adapted easily for use with any kind of screening fence—a board fence, a basket-weave fence, a louver fence.

Cutting List

Number	Piece	Dimensions	Material
5	Posts	3½″ × 3½″ × 108″	redwood
1	Rear top rail	1½″ × 3½″ × 44½″	redwood
1	Rear bottom rail	1½″ × 2½″ × 44½″	redwood
2	Rear vertical nailers	¾″ × ¾″ × 56″	redwood
2	Rear horizontal nailers	¾″ × ¾″ × 43″	redwood
1	Lattice	56″ × 44½″	redwood
2	Rear vertical lattice trim	¼″ × ¾″ × 57½″	redwood
2	Rear horizontal lattice trim	¼″ × ¾″ × 43″	redwood
4	Rear rail fascia	¾″ × 3½″ × 44½″	redwood
1	Rear cap	¾″ × 3½″ × 44½″	redwood
2	Side top rails	1½″ × 3½″ × 23½″*	redwood
2	Side bottom rails	1½″ × 2½″ × 23½″*	redwood
4	Gate rails	1½″ × 2½″ × 29″	redwood
4	Gate stiles	1½″ × 2½″ × 62¼″	redwood
4	Side vertical nailers	¾″ × ¾″ × 56″	redwood
4	Side horizontal nailers	¾″ × ¾″ × 22″*	redwood
2	Side lattice	56″ × 23½″	redwood
4	Side vertical lattice trim	¼″ × ¾″ × 56″	redwood
4	Side horizontal lattice trim	¼″ × ¾″ × 22″*	redwood
8	Side rail fascia	¾″ × 3½″ × 23½″*	redwood
2	Side caps	¾″ × 3½″ × 23½″*	redwood
4	Gate vertical nailers	¾″ × ¾″ × 59¼″	redwood
6	Gate horizontal nailers	¾″ × ¾″ × 27½″	redwood
4	Gate vertical nailers	¾″ × ¾″ × 55¾″	redwood
2	Gate lattice	29″ × 59¼″	redwood
2	Gate top fascia	¾″ × 3½″ × 29″	redwood
2	Gate stops	¾″ × ¾″ × 62¼″	redwood

*The exact length should be determined during construction and these pieces cut to fit.

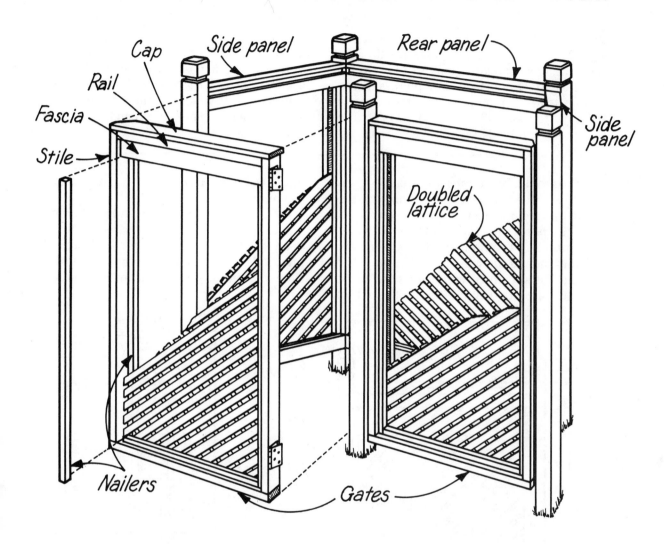

Cap
Side panel
Rear panel
Rail
Fascia
Stile
Side panel
Doubled lattice
Nailers
Gates

1. **Prepare the posts.** The corral has five posts, each extending 6 feet above grade. Because three of them are gate posts, they should be set about 2½ to 3 feet into the ground. Cut the posts accordingly.

Machine the tops next. The edges of the tops are rounded using a ¾-inch rounding-over bit in a router. Then a 1-inch-wide, ¼-inch deep dado is cut around each post, 3 inches from the top edge. Cut the dadoes all at the same time. Clamp the posts together and clamp or tack a straightedge to them to guide the router.

2. **Set the posts.** Lay out the postholes as shown. The three front posts are in line with the fence, so lay them out first. To lay out the two rear posts, stake a point perpendicular to and 24 inches on center from the front center post. The center points for the rear posts will be 24 inches to either side of this point, on a line parallel to the fence line.

Dig the holes, and place a post in each hole. Plumb the posts, and ensure that they are level across their tops. Fill around the center post—to which the gates will be hinged—with concrete. The others can be backfilled with earth.

3. **Frame the back panel.** The lattice panels are set in a framework composed of the posts, top and bottom rails, and nailer strips. With the posts set, start the framework.

Cut a 2 × 4 top rail and a 2 × 3 bottom rail, and toenail them in place. Although the cutting list specifies dimensions for these rails, it is a good idea to measure the actual distance between posts and cut pieces to fit as you build the fence.

Cut the vertical nailers and nail them in place. With stock as slender as the 1 × 1 used for the nailers, it is a good idea to drill pilot holes for the nails to obviate splitting. Then cut and install the horizontal nailers.

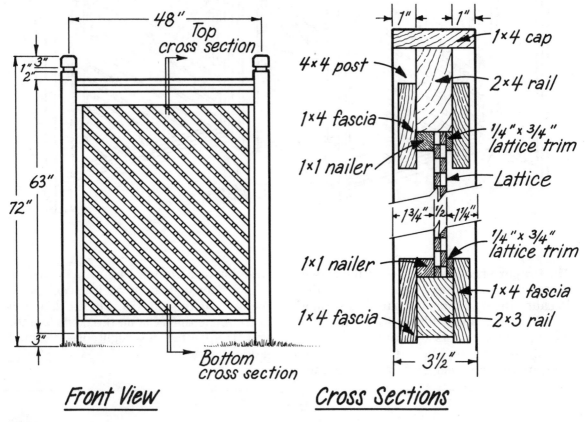

Front View

Cross Sections

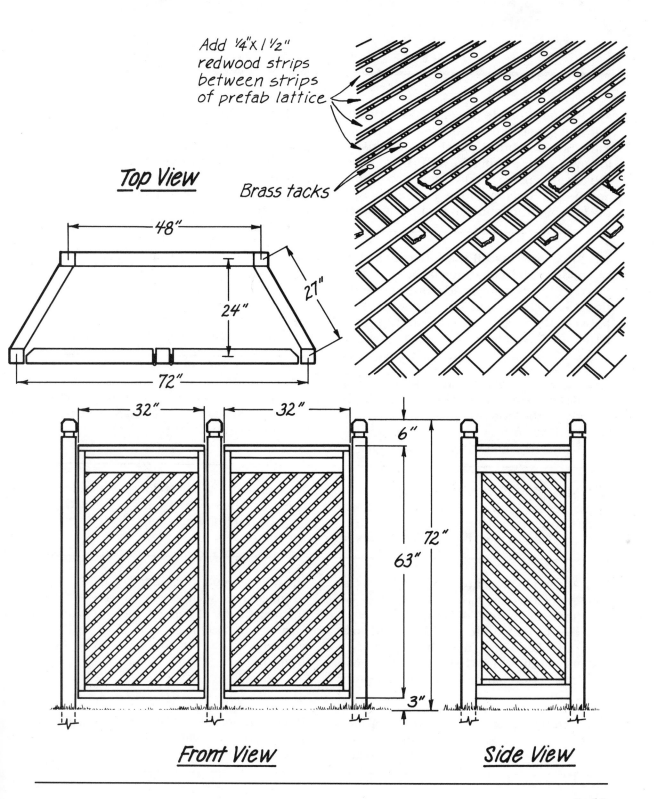

Add ¼"x 1½"
redwood strips
between strips
of prefab lattice

Brass tacks

Top View

48"

27"

24"

72"

32"

32"

6"

72"

63"

3"

Front View

Side View

249

4. **Frame the side panels.** Theoretically, the side panels are at a 60-degree angle to the fence line, but it's best to compensate for any error in setting the posts by scribing the angle in place. To do this, cut both top and bottom rails overlong. Lay one across the tops of a front and rear post. Scribe lines under the piece where it crosses the posts. Cut to these lines. Use the piece as a template to lay out its mate.

Repeat this process for the other side panel.

Toenail the rails in place, then cut and install the nailers.

5. **Make and install the lattice.** The lattice in the corral looks unusual because it is. Start with standard lattice, but add additional ¼-inch by 1½-inch strips of redwood between the strips that make up the prefab lattice. Do this on both sides. Use brass tacks to fasten the new strips in place.

From your new lattice, cut pieces for each frame you've constructed. Fit the lattice in place, and secure it with a nail in each corner.

Cut the trim strips and install them.

6. **Install the fascia and caps.** Cut fascia boards and caps from 1 × 4 stock. The fascia boards for the side panels must be beveled across their ends so they'll fit against the posts properly. Likewise, the cap must be scribed to fit, much as you scribed the rails.

Nail the pieces in place. The top fascia is positioned to create a 1½-inch wide recess between it and the cap.

7. **Make the gate frames.** Cut the rails and stiles for both gates. To provide clearance between the gates and the latch posts, the outside stiles must be chamfered at about 30 degrees; this is best done on a table saw. Next, cut the nailers from 1 × 1 stock.

Assemble the rails and stiles, then install the nailers.

8. **Assemble the gates.** Cut pieces of the modified lattice to fit the gate frames. Also cut the remaining nailers, fascia, and rail caps.

Lay the lattice into the frames, and position the nailers. Drive nails through the face nailers and lattice into the back nailers. Position the fascia and nail it in place. Center the rail caps over the top rails and nail them in place. Use a saber saw to trim the caps flush with the chamfers, and to round the corners at the hinge end (to provide the clearance necessary for the gates to swing freely).

9. **Hang the gates.** Use two pairs of 4-inch butt hinges to hang the gates from the center post. It should not be necessary to mortise the hinges in the gate or post. Install a hook and eye on each gate to latch it.

GATE

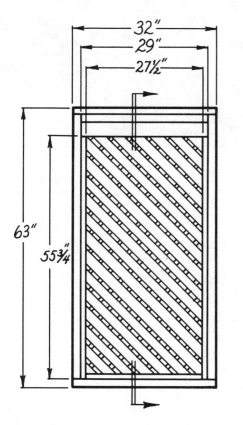

32"
29"
27½"
63"
55¾"

Front View

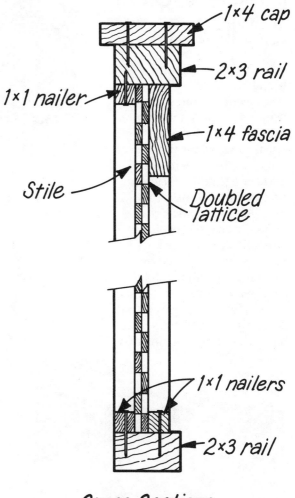

1×4 cap
2×3 rail
1×1 nailer
1×4 fascia
Stile
Doubled lattice
1×1 nailers
2×3 rail

Cross Sections

10. Install stops. Cut two pieces of 1 × 1 stock to 62¼ inches long. Drill pilot holes and screw the pieces to the posts so that the caps cover them and the gates stop on the rails.

251

PROJECT
FIREWOOD SHELTER

If you are building a high privacy fence and you've got a wood stove or fireplace, here's a way to provide cover for up to three cords of wood for the cost of only a little more material and time than you'd spend on the fence alone.

The firewood shelter shown was built as part of a substantial side yard overhaul, which involved erecting a nearly 6-foot-tall fence and laying down an on-grade deck. The fence section that serves as the shelter's back faces the driveway. Because

Shopping List

4 pcs. 4 × 4 × 10′ pressure-treated pine posts w/finials
1 pc. 4 × 4 × 10′ pressure-treated pine
3 pcs. 2 × 6 × 14′ pressure-treated pine
13 pcs. 2 × 4 × 8′ pressure-treated pine
13 pcs. 2 × 4 × 12′ pressure-treated pine
14 pcs. 5/4 × 6 × 14′ pressure-treated pine
4 sheets 1/2″ × 4′ × 8′ exterior-grade plywood
20 pcs. 1 × 6 × 12′ pressure-treated pine
1 pc. 1 × 6 × 8′ pressure-treated pine
5 pcs. aluminum drip edge
6–6″ carriage bolts w/nuts and washers
4 bundles of roofing shingles
1 roll of roofing felt
10d galvanized nails
8d galvanized nails
roofing nails

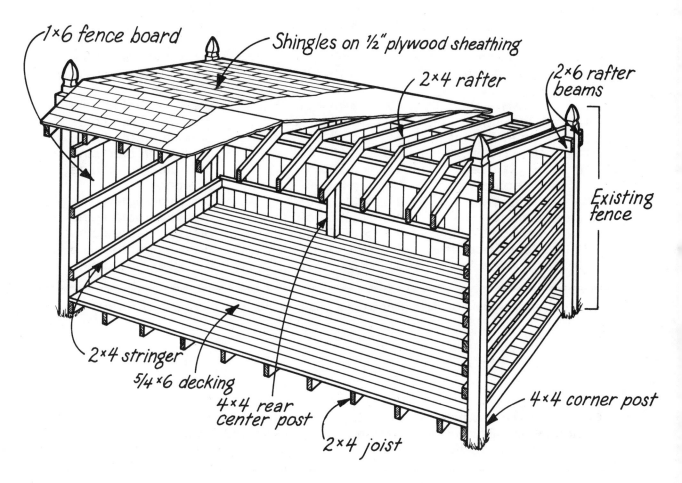

1×6 fence board

Shingles on ½" plywood sheathing

2×4 rafter

2×6 rafter beams

Existing fence

2×4 stringer

5/4×6 decking

4×4 rear center post

2×4 joist

4×4 corner post

it is bolted in place, it is easy to remove, making firewood delivery a snap. Building the shelter into a corner allows the fence to serve as two of the structure's three sides.

The shelter shown is 13 feet wide, a dimension established by the peculiarities of the site. A 12-foot width would be more economical, since the roof could be sheathed with three sheets of plywood instead of four. An 8-foot-wide shelter would use materials even more efficiently, and it would still store two cords of wood.

Likewise, the shelter height was dictated in part by the 5-foot, 9-inch fence height. If your fence is higher, make the shelter higher and give yourself more headroom inside.

The shelter will work with many different styles of fencing, not simply the solid-board style shown.

253

Cutting List

Number	Piece	Dimensions	Material
2	Rear corner posts	3½″ × 3½″ × 111″	pressure-treated pine post w/finial
1	Rear center post	3½″ × 3½″ × 104″	pressure-treated pine
2	Front corner posts	3½″ × 3½″ × 120″	pressure-treated pine post w/finial
10	Joists	1½″ × 3½″ × 71½″	pressure-treated pine
13	Decking	1¹⁄₁₆″ × 5½″ × 156″	pressure-treated pine
3	Rafter beams	1½″ × 5½″ × 159½″	pressure-treated pine
10	Long rafters	1½″ × 3½″ × 96″*	pressure-treated pine
10	Short rafters	1½″ × 3½″ × 36″*	pressure-treated pine
8	Sheathing	½″ × variable × variable*	plywood
3	Stringers	1½″ × 3½″ × 68″	pressure-treated pine
3	Stringers	1½″ × 3½″ × 60″	pressure-treated pine
7	Stringers	1½″ × 3½″ × 63½″	pressure-treated pine
41	Fence boards	¾″ × 5½″ × 69″	pressure-treated pine
3	Stringers	1½″ × 3½″ × 96″	pressure-treated pine

*The exact length should be determined during construction and these pieces cut to fit.

1. **Lay out the posthole locations.** Lay out the locations of the postholes, as shown. The three posts along the back of the shelter are set 3 feet deep, while the two front posts are set only 2 feet deep.

2. **Cut the posts to length and set them.** The posts shown were chosen to harmonize with the Victorian style of the home. Posts with shaped finials are widely available, but you can use whatever post design you like. If you do choose posts with finials, you have to cut them to length and set them carefully. The best approach is to set one post, then stretch level lines from it to help guide the setting of other posts.

The rear corner posts are set at a height of 75 inches (the same as posts in the fence). These posts were cut to 111 inches and set 36 inches deep.

Set at a height of 68 inches, about an inch below the height of the fence boards, the rear center post was cut to 104 inches and set 36 inches deep.

To accommodate the pitch of the roof, the front posts are set at a height of 94 inches. These posts are 120 inches long and are set to a depth of 26 inches. Because of the lateral support they get from the structure of the shed, there is no need to set them any deeper.

Trim the posts to the appropriate length, then set and plumb them. Use a few inches of gravel in the bottoms of the postholes to promote drainage away from the post bottoms. Backfill with earth, tamping firmly.

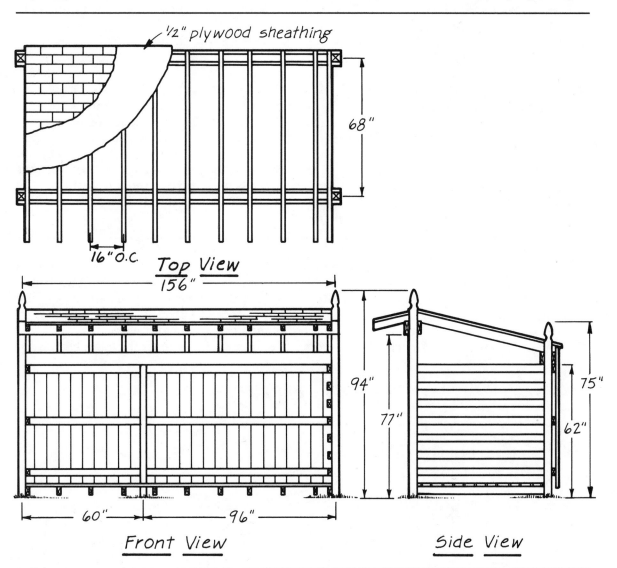

½" plywood sheathing

68"

16" O.C.

Top View
156"

94"

77"

75"

62"

60"

96"

Front View

Side View

3. Install the floor. The shelter shown is incorporated into a ground-level deck, so the flooring is simply an extension of that deck. If you want to support the firewood above the ground, add a floor to your shelter. It is not, however, essential.

To support the decking, cut joists from pressure-treated 2 × 4 stock. At each end of the shelter, nail a joist to the front and rear posts, just at ground level. Level the earth between these end joists and compact it. Then lay the remaining joists on the ground, 16 inches on center.

Lay ⁵/₄ decking on these joists and nail it down.

4. Cut and install the rafter beams. Lay out the locations of the two 2 × 6 rafter beams on the front and back of the two front posts. Drive an 8d nail into the post on each of these lines to rest the 2 × 6 on as you install it.

Repeat the process on the front of the three rear posts.

Cut the three beams. Place one 2 × 6 on the nails across the front posts. Drive a 10d nail through the 2 × 6 and into a post, but don't set it. Move to the other post, check the level of the beam, and if it is okay, nail it to the post. Return to the first post and finish nailing the beam to it. Repeat this process with the two remaining 2 × 6s. Pull the nails you used to hold up the boards.

5. Lay out and cut the main rafter template. Usually when you cut rafters you have no ridge in place, so you have to calculate the angle of the bird's-mouth and ridge cuts. But in this case, it's easy to set an 8-foot 2 × 4 across the beams and mark on it where it touches the 2 × 6s (it will only touch two of the three). While the rafter is on the beams, set a sliding T bevel so you can mark plumb cuts after you take the rafter down and are completing the layout work.

Remove the rafter from the beams and

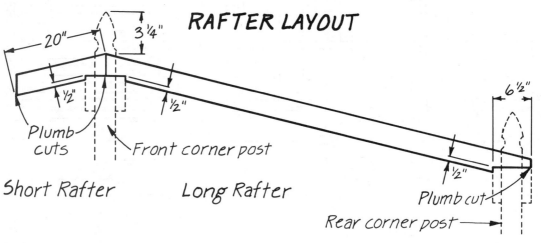

RAFTER LAYOUT

20"   3¼"

½"   ½"

Plumb cuts

Front corner post

Short Rafter   Long Rafter

6½"

½"

Plumb cut

Rear corner post

finish laying it out, as shown. Mark the two bird's-mouths and the front and rear plumb cuts. Set the rafter in position once again to check its fit.

6. **Lay out and cut the short rafter template.** To make a short rafter, start with about 3 feet of 2 × 4. Use the long rafter as a template to lay out a bird's-mouth notch about 1 foot from one end. Cut the notch.

Set both rafters in position. Strike a line on each rafter where it crosses the top of the other. Also scribe along the post's front edge on the short rafter. Take the short rafter down. Measure 20 inches from the post mark and scribe the plumb cut using the sliding T bevel. Cut both rafters on the lines where they cross, and make the plumb cut on the short rafter. Set them in place for a final fitting.

7. **Cut and install the rafters.** If the template rafters fit properly, use them to lay out nine more of each. Cut them out.

Attach sets of rafters at each end of the shelter first. For these end pairs, nail the short rafters to the front posts, then the long rafters to the short.

Assemble the remaining eight pairs of rafters on the ground. Install them on 16-inch centers except for one, which will be less than 16 inches from an end set of rafters.

8. **Sheathe the roof and shingle it.** Measure and cut ½-inch plywood sheathing to fit the roof. After nailing it in place, cover it with roofing felt, then install aluminum drip edge. Cover it with roofing shingles.

9. **Install the fixed sides of the shelter.** The fencing that encloses two sides of the shelter shown consists of 69-inch-long 1 × 6s nailed to three 2 × 4 horizontal stringers. The top and bottom stringers are positioned 4 inches from the ends of the fence boards; the center one is, perhaps obviously, centered between the others. As a decorative element, the top corners of each fence board are trimmed off.

At the closed end of the shelter, the broad faces of the stringers are butted against the inner face of the posts; the posts thus stand proud of the fence boards on the outside. At the back, the stringers are butted against the outside of the posts. The open end has seven horizontal stringers, spaced approximately 6 inches apart, to contain the firewood.

Nail stringers to the appropriate posts, then nail the fence boards in place.

10. **Build and install the removable fence section.** Construct the fence panel, using three horizontal stringers and 1 × 6 fence boards. Attach this section to the appropriate posts with six 6-inch carriage bolts. The bolts go through the fence boards and stringers, as well as the posts.

PROJECT

REDWOOD FENCE, GATE, AND PERGOLA

With its beams and joists projecting on all sides, this pergola evokes the elegance of traditional Japanese architecture. Yet the pergola, as well as the fence and gate, is really quite easy to build. The joints are simple butt joints, for the most part, secured with common nails and bolts.

The fence is built in nominal 8-foot-long, 6-foot-high sections, which are assembled in place between the 4 × 4 posts. In the fence shown, the rails are butted and toenailed between posts set on 8-foot centers.

The gates are shop-made, assembled by building two perimeter frames and sandwiching diagonal slats between them. Galvanized steel L brackets and hinge straps reinforce the gate corners. The latch hardware allows the secondary gate to be locked, with the main

one used for pedestrian passage. Both can be opened to allow passage of a garden tractor or the like.

The fence and gates are attractive and serviceable, and not difficult to build. But the striking element of this project is the pergola. Upon analysis, you'll see that it is little more than a Lincoln Log–style assemblage of massive redwood beams.

Shopping List

Fence

(For one 8-foot section)

2 pcs. 4 × 4 × 8′ clear all-heart redwood

4 pcs. 1 × 6 × 8′ clear all-heart redwood

8 pcs. 1 × 4 × 16′ clear all-heart redwood

1 pc. 2 × 6 × 8′ clear all-heart redwood

1 box #6 × 1¼″ galvanized all-purpose screws

10d galvanized finishing nails

Pergola

4 pcs. 6 × 6 × 10′ clear all-heart redwood

2 pcs. 3 × 8 × 12′ clear all-heart redwood

4 pcs. 3 × 6 × 10′ clear all-heart redwood

5 pcs. 3 × 3 × 14′ clear all-heart redwood

4 pcs. 2 × 5 × 14′ clear all-heart redwood

8 pcs. 2 × 4 × 8′ clear all-heart redwood

8–16½″ × ½″ galvanized hex-head bolts w/nuts and washers

16–11½″ × ½″ galvanized hex-head bolts w/nuts and washers

8–6½″ × ½″ galvanized hex-head bolts w/nuts and washers

4–6″ × 6″ post anchors

10d galvanized finishing nails

8d galvanized finishing nails

Concrete

Gates

13 pcs. 1 × 4 × 16′ clear all-heart redwood

8 pcs. galvanized steel flat corner plates

1 box #6 × 1¼″ galvanized all-purpose screws

2 pr. pin and strap hinges

1 cane bolt

1 gate latch

water repellent or water-repellent stain

The project shown was made of clear all-heart redwood, the top grade. It could be built from pressure-treated wood, but there are strong arguments for using a naturally rot-resistant wood, despite its extra expense. One argument is, of course, that cedar or redwood will look better than pressure-treated wood, especially at first. But more important, the pergola is built of large-dimension lumber. The larger the dimensions, the more prone lumber is to cracking caused by changes in moisture content. Cedar and redwood are much less dense than pressure-treated southern yellow pine, and so will better resist cracking.

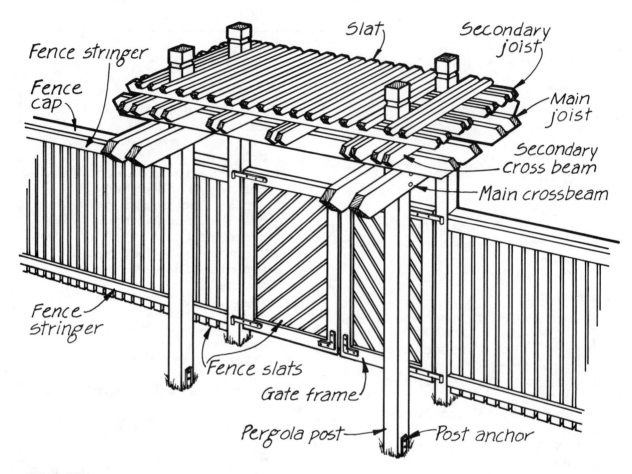

Slat

Secondary joist

Fence stringer

Fence cap

Main joist

Secondary cross beam

Main crossbeam

Fence stringer

Fence slats

Gate frame

Pergola post

Post anchor

The Fence

1. Set the posts. Lay out the locations of the postholes and excavate them to a depth of 2 to 3 feet. Toss 2 or 3 inches of gravel in the bottom of each hole to promote drainage away from the post bottoms.

Set the posts, plumb them, and backfill the holes. After all the posts are set, use a mason's cord with a line level to mark all the posts for trimming. Trim the posts carefully with a circular saw so their tops will be square.

2. Install two of the stringers. Cut the stringers to length. Toenail the top stringer in place, flush with the front edge and the tops of the posts. Use 8d galvanized finishing nails; countersink them. Then toenail the lower stringer in place.

Cutting List

Number	Piece	Dimensions	Material
2	Fence posts	3½″ × 3½″ × 96″	redwood
4	Fence stringers	¾″ × 5½″ × 92½″	redwood
24	Fence slats	¾″ × 3½″ × 64″	redwood
1	Fence cap	1½″ × 5½″ × 96″	redwood
4	Pergola posts	5½″ × 5½″ × 120″	redwood
4	Main crossbeams	2½″ × 7¼″ × 65½″	redwood
4	Main joists	2½″ × 5½″ × 110″	redwood
12	Secondary crossbeams	1½″ × 4½″ × 53½″	redwood
8	Secondary joists	1½″ × 3½″ × 96″	redwood
19	Slats	2½″ × 2½″ × 41½″	redwood
12	Blocks	1½″ × 1½″ × 2″	redwood
8	Blocks	1½″ × 1½″ × 3½″	redwood
4	Gate stiles	¾″ × 3½″ × 65½″	redwood
4	Gate stringers	¾″ × 3½″ × 30″	redwood
32	Gate slats	¾″ × 3½″ × variable*	redwood

*The exact length should be determined during construction and these pieces cut to fit.

3. **Cut and install the fence slats, stringers, and cap.** Cut 24 slats per section. The 1 × 4 slats should be evenly spaced between posts, which means there'll be a gap of just under ⅜ inch between slats. Cutting a few L-shaped spacers to hang on the stringers between slats can expedite the positioning of the slats.

Align the slats flush with the top of the top stringer. Screw them to the stringers using a couple of 1¼-inch galvanized all-purpose screws per slat-stringer joint.

Fit the remaining two stringers (per fence section) in place, concealing the screw heads, and toenail them.

The cap overlaps the tops of the slats and posts. If you will be installing a multi-section fence, use 16-foot lengths of redwood for the cap and, for a quality touch, scarf the joints between cap pieces.

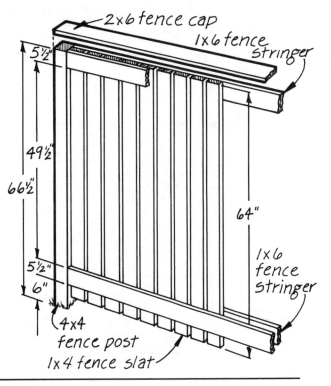

The Pergola

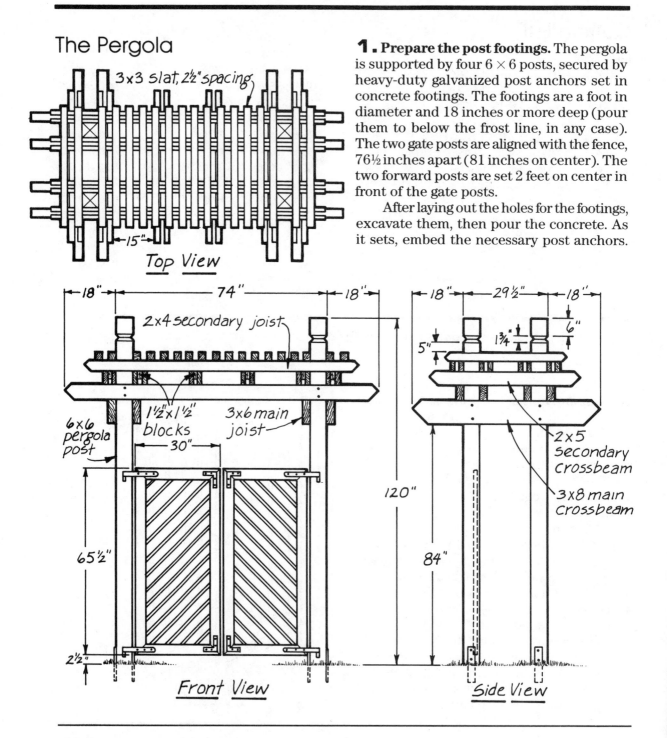

3x3 slat, 2½" spacing

15"

Top View

1. Prepare the post footings. The pergola is supported by four 6 × 6 posts, secured by heavy-duty galvanized post anchors set in concrete footings. The footings are a foot in diameter and 18 inches or more deep (pour them to below the frost line, in any case). The two gate posts are aligned with the fence, 76½ inches apart (81 inches on center). The two forward posts are set 2 feet on center in front of the gate posts.

After laying out the holes for the footings, excavate them, then pour the concrete. As it sets, embed the necessary post anchors.

18"   74"   18"

2x4 secondary joist

6x6 pergola post

1½"x1½" blocks

30"

3x6 main joist

65½"

2½"

120"

Front View

18"   29½"   18"

6"

5"   1¾"

2x5 secondary crossbeam

3x8 main crossbeam

84"

Side View

2. **Cut and notch the posts.** Cut the four 6 × 6 posts to length.

The decorative V-shaped dadoes around the posts near the tops are cut with a circular saw. The dadoes are 1¾ inches wide and positioned 6 inches from the post tops. Lay out the dadoes around all four sides. Set your circular saw to a cutting depth of 1¼ inches, then tilt the blade 45 degrees. Make bevel cuts along each line, forming the V-shaped dadoes. Clean them up with a chisel.

3. **Cut crossbeams, joists, and slats.** Cut the parts composing the pergola's overhead structure to the sizes shown on the Cutting List. Cut the points on each end of each of these elements.

On both sets of crossbeams and the main joists, these points are off center. To lay them out, mark on each end ⅓ down from what will be the top of the board (if any boards are crowned, orient the crowned edge up). Scribe lines on a 45-degree angle from this point to the top and bottom edges. Cut on the lines.

On the secondary joists and the slats, the points are centered. Lay these out and cut them.

4. **Erect the posts.** After the footings have cured for several days, erect the posts. Set the posts in the anchors and mark the locations of the necessary bolt holes. Take them down to drill the ½-inch-diameter holes. Reset the posts, install the 6½-inch-long bolts, plumb the posts carefully, then tighten the bolts.

5. **Assemble the pergola.** This is a matter of layering crisscrossing beams and joists. Whenever the sticks are attached to the posts, use ½-inch-diameter galvanized hex-head bolts, using a washer under both the head and the nut. Where nails are called for, use galvanized finishing nails.

First, align the main crossbeams 84 inches above the ground. Center them above the gateway. Attach them to the posts with 11½-inch bolts.

Next, rest the four main joists on the main crossbeams. Drill ½-inch-diameter holes through the joists and the posts, then install 11½-inch bolts.

The secondary crossbeams are paired into six sets, with two 1½-inch-thick spacers between the beams. Nail the beams and blocks together, then position the paired beams on the main joists, as shown. The pairs adjacent to the posts are bolted in place with a single 16½-inch bolt at each post. The other pairs are toenailed to the joists.

The secondary joists are paired in the same fashion as the secondary crossbeams. After nailing the sets together with the spacers, set them in place, bridging the secondary crossbeams and sandwiching the posts. Bolt them to each post with a single 16½-inch bolt.

Finally, lay the slats out across the secondary joists. Space them about 2½ inches apart. Toenail each slat to each joist.

The Gate

1. **Cut the rails and stiles.** The gate panels are sandwiches, with diagonal slats between two perimeter frames. Cut the rails and stiles forming the frames to length, and miter their ends.

2. **Attach the slats.** The slats are attached diagonally, not only for aesthetics but also to help keep the gates from racking. Notice that direction of the angle is opposite for the two gates.

Lay out two rails and two stiles. Measure and cut slats to rough lengths, then lay them in place on the perimeter frame. Leave about a ½-inch space between slats. Attach them to the frame with 1¼-inch-long galvanized all-purpose screws, two at each end of each slat. Let the slats run a little long, and then trim them flush after the assembly is completed.

Lay a second perimeter frame atop the assembly and screw it to the slats. Attach galvanized flat corner plates to both sides of each gate panel at the latch side's upper and lower corners. On the hinge side, install the hinge straps with carriage bolts.

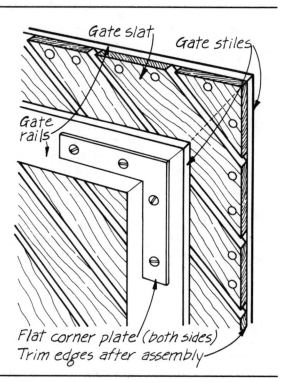

Gate slat
Gate stiles
Gate rails
Flat corner plate (both sides)
Trim edges after assembly

3. **Hang the gate.** Set the gate panels in position. Mark the locations of the pins. Move the gates, and remove the upper hinge straps. Drill pilot holes in the posts for the pins, then turn them into place. To capture the hinge straps, the lower pins must point up, the upper ones down. Fit the gates on the lower pins, then fit the upper hinge straps on the pins, and reinstall them on the gate.

Install the cane bolt on the secondary gate panel, so it keeps that panel closed. Install the latch on the main gate panel.

4. **Apply water repellent.** The entire assembly doesn't need a finish to give it color or character. The redwood used in the project has enough of that. But to weather well, the entire project should be carefully coated with a water repellent or water-repellent stain.

FRAMED STRUCTURES

5

Building decks, gazebos, play structures, and garden sheds is what this chapter is about. While none of these projects is as complicated as framing a house, the techniques, materials, and structural principles are the same. And in many cases, you need the same building permit.

Framing an outdoor structure is one of the most satisfying projects to undertake. You'll get plenty of exercise, but with modern tools and materials, the work is not backbreaking. It's fun: You're outside, the work goes quickly, and unlike interior building, there is no drywall or other finish work that never seems to get quite done. Sure, taking charge of the design and construction process can be quite a challenge. But it's a good way to make sure you build exactly what you want. And the sweat of your own brow has a way of adding special value to any job, no matter how big or small.

It doesn't take an extensive tool collection or years of experience to construct an excellent deck or shed. With some careful planning and a very basic selection of tools, you'll be surprised at what you can achieve over several weekends.

Framing techniques are straightforward,

but it is essential that they be carried out properly. If you paint something wrong it just looks sloppy. If you frame something wrong, it could be dangerous.

Get the Permit

Decks, storage sheds, and other outdoor building projects that involve foundations and framing will usually require a building permit. Before finalizing your design, make sure to consult with your local building inspector or with the municipal building and zoning department. Building and zoning regulations vary from one town to another, so you'll need to comply with the codes that are used in your area.

Your inspector's primary concerns will be setback requirements and sound construction practices. Setback requirements refer to the minimum distance a structure can be from your property lines. These requirements vary from one locality to another, and they can also vary for houses and outbuildings.

As far as sound construction practices are concerned, the basic framing details dis-

265

cussed here will suffice for just about any deck or outbuilding you'll construct. Again, your building inspector can let you know of particular code requirements that apply in your area. For example, extra bracing is required in areas frequently subjected to high winds; and untreated wood shingles may not be approved for use on a roof near an active chimney. It's important to develop a cooperative relationship with your building inspector. More often than not, he'll be able to give you some useful advice about your project.

Once you've satisfied the building inspector, there are still many design factors to consider. Apart from concerns about safety, convenience, and durability, you'll want to build something that will look nice in your yard and enhance the value of your property.

The Tool Chest

Fortunately, you don't need an extensive tool collection to build an excellent deck, shed, or other outdoor structure. The only power tools you'll need are a portable circular saw and an electric drill. Get a carbide-tipped combination blade for your circular saw, and a good selection of drill bits (ranging from ⅛ to ½ inch) for your drill. Complement this power equipment with some basic hand tools: a ten-point crosscut saw and several sharp chisels (½-inch, ¾-inch, and 1-inch blade widths are good).

For general layout work, it's good to have a 2-foot level and a 4-foot level, as well as a framing square and either a combination square or speed square. A 25-foot tape measure is also standard equipment for just about any building project. A line level, designed to be used with strong cord or string, will

enable you to establish a level line around deck posts that have been set in place. Finally, you should equip yourself with a good 16-ounce hammer, a utility knife with extra blades, and a tool belt to hold hammer, nails, knife, and pencil.

To work safely, you'll need protective goggles to wear when using striking tools or power equipment. Ear protection is advisable if you'll be using a circular saw or other power tools for long periods of time. If you'll be handling and cutting pressure-treated lumber, use a good filter mask and follow the safety precautions outlined where this wood is sold. Finally, work with a safe attitude: Take your time, don't take chances, and don't hesitate to ask for help when you need it.

Fasteners and Hardware

Nails. Let's deal with nails first. With their thick shanks and broad, sturdy heads, common nails are designed to provide a strong hold on structural parts. For general framing work, most carpenters use either 8d, 10d, or 12d common nails. The "d" designation stands for "penny," an age-old term denoting nail size (larger numbers mean larger nails). The size, or length, of the nail that you use depends on the thickness of the material you're nailing together. It's important for one-half to two-thirds of the nail's length to penetrate into the base or second piece of stock. Applying this rule, 10d nails are used for most face-nailed connections, where you'll be driving the nail through 1½-inch-thick 2-by stock and into the edge or end of another 2-by. Eight-penny nails

Decks, decks, and more decks: elevated platforms with integral benches and planters, rambling elaborate affairs with curving railings, protected from the summer sun by overhead trellises. There's a design for every style of outdoor living.

267

are commonly used for toenailing, while 12d or 16d nails are meant for fastening beams together.

For nonstructural work, like nailing up trim around a window or door, finishing nails are best. Again, you should apply the one-half to two-thirds penetration rule when choosing nail size. Finishing nails are meant to be "set," so the head of each nail rests below the surface of the wood, creating a depression that is later filled with putty or wood filler. To set nails, you'll need a nail set.

Any nails that will be directly exposed to the weather (like those used to install decking or exterior siding, for example) need extra protection against rust. A special treatment, called galvanizing, gives steel nails a rust-resistant zinc coating. You can recognize galvanized nails by their bumpy, silver-gray coating.

Lag screws. A single hex-head lag screw has the holding power of several nails. For joining large structural members together (on a deck, for example), lag screws are usually better than nails. A screw's threads prevent it from working loose, and screws can be tightened easily and effectively if the wood shrinks over time. The lag screws used in deck construction have shanks with diameters of 3/16 inch, 1/4 inch, or larger. One-half or more of the screw's length should penetrate into the base piece, and a washer should be used beneath the head of the screw. In most cases, screw holes will have to be predrilled.

Lag and carriage bolts. These fasteners have all the advantages of lag screws, but extend all the way through the joined pieces. Instead of a hex head, the carriage bolt has a round head and just beneath, a section of squared shank. Driven into a tight hole with a couple of hammer blows, this

square section of the shank is meant to lock the bolt in place while the nut is tightened. So when installing a carriage bolt, the hole diameter must match the shank diameter.

Framing hardware. Few framed structures are built these days without the assistance of framing hardware. There are many types of framing hardware available, each one designed to improve the strength, speed, and accuracy of connecting structural members. The joist hanger is the most commonly used type of framing hardware. Made from 18-gauge steel and bent to form a square-edged stirrup, this connector is designed to join the end of a joist to the face of another joist, ledger, or beam. Other types of hardware for framing are shown.

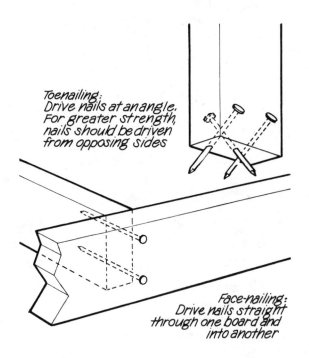

Toenailing:
Drive nails at an angle.
For greater strength,
nails should be driven
from opposing sides

Face-nailing:
Drive nails straight
through one board and
into another

COMMON FRAMING HARDWARE

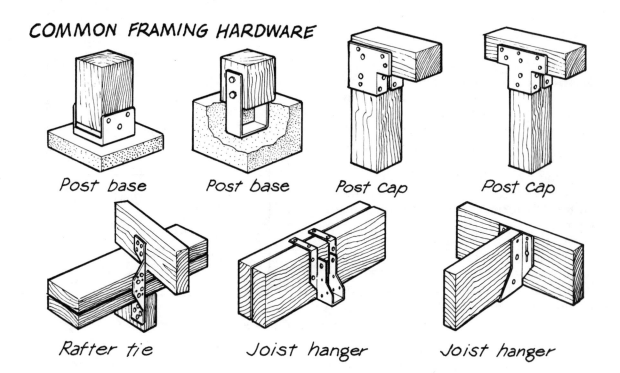

Post base   Post base   Post Cap   Post cap

Rafter tie   Joist hanger   Joist hanger

Deck Design

There are many factors to consider when designing a deck. Before you get into dimensions and construction details, it's important to think in general terms about the way your deck should add convenience, pleasure, and value to your house. The flat, fairly maintenance-free surface of a deck can be a smart alternative to lawn area that needs mowing and other landscaping care. If your property is steep, an elevated deck can provide additional living space adjacent to your house.

In many cases, a deck can be built right against the house, utilizing an existing exterior door for access. In other situations, you may have to add a door to provide deck access, or perhaps convert a window opening into a doorway. French doors or sliding glass doors are popular "deck connections" because they bring in extra light and create less of a barrier between interior and exterior space.

There are plenty of ways to personalize a deck so that it fits your particular needs. For example, you might want to incorporate a privacy screen or fence along one side of the deck. Overhead, a trellis adds privacy and tempers the heat and brightness of long summer days. Hot tubs and decks are natural companions, but require special provisions for wiring, plumbing, and privacy, not to mention structural underpinnings for the tub unit itself.

Depending on the design of your house, your deck might be at or near ground level. Or your needs might call for an elevated deck, perhaps with more than one level. Remember that when you step outside onto the deck or stair landing, you should be stepping down, so that the deck can drain without getting the house wet. If you live in an area where deep snow can accumulate in winter, take this into consideration when determining the level of your deck.

The beauty of deck design is that it can be so varied. Just like houses, decks can be built in all sizes, shapes, and styles. Visiting friends or neighbors with decks can give you some good ideas about your own design. The next step is to start drawing. Using graph paper or an architect's scale, make some scale drawings that show possible plan views and elevations.

After settling on major details such as level, location, and size, you can turn to the fine points, like railings, stairs, decking, built-in benches, and joinery details.

Finally, you can calculate what materials you'll need to do the job. Joist spacing is one of the first things you'll need to consider. The size of your joists will depend on their span. Span tables for structural lumber are available at lumberyards and building supply outlets.

Figure in what material you'll need for railings, stairs, and other elements included in your design. When calculating decking, add 10 percent to the required square footage to make sure you won't run out of material.

Layout. Most decks will contain at least one square corner, so to lay out the location of your deck, it's helpful to know a couple of

CHECKING FOR SQUARE

If A=B, corners are square (90°)

Using the 3-4-5 method

ways to check for square on a large scale. To test for a 90-degree corner, measure 3 feet from the corner along one side and 4 feet along the other. If the 3- and 4-foot points are exactly 5 feet apart (along the hypoteneuse of the triangle), you've got a right-angled corner. Multiples of the 3-4-5 measurements will also work. Comparing the diagonal measurements in a square or rectangle will tell you how close all four corners are to being right angles. Unless the diagonal measurements are equal, at least one corner is "out."

Using wood stakes and string, lay out the perimeter of your deck. Test for square as mentioned above. Once the perimeter is set, you can locate where posts will be and establish center points for post or pier holes. A good way to pinpoint posthole locations is to set up batter boards. Positioned a foot or

Spas and decks are natural mates. A spa requires some sort of housing, both to support the tub and to conceal its mechanicals. It can be a part of the main deck (left) or reside in its own special annex (below).

Decking Patterns

Key aesthetic decisions have to be made during the planning stage of your deck project. A principal consideration is how the decking is to be laid down. Straight, diagonal, herringbone, and parquet patterns are all possible, but the framing must be designed to accommodate the pattern.

Two-by decking installed in the conventional at-right-angles-to-the-joists manner will be supported safely by joists installed on 24-inch centers. Joists must be spaced at a minimum 16 inches on center to support $^5/_4$ decking.

But decking installed at a diagonal to the joists will need more closely spaced support; the span from joist to joist must be measured on the same angle at which the decking will be applied. Thus, if 2-by decking is to be applied at a 45-degree angle, the joists must be at 16 inches on center.

A herringbone pattern dictates the use of doubled joists to support the miter joints.

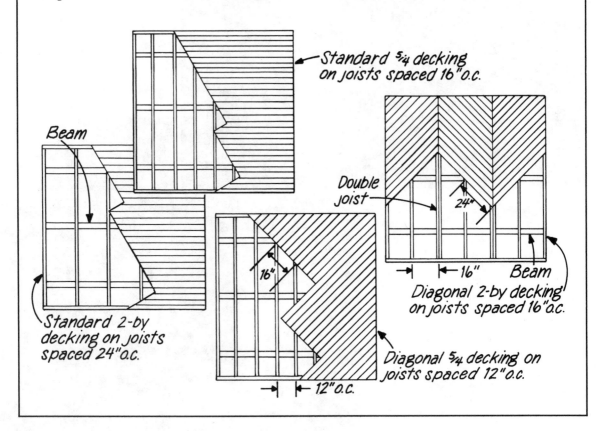

Standard $^5/_4$ decking on joists spaced 16" o.c.

Beam

Double Joist

24"

16"

Beam

Diagonal 2-by decking on joists spaced 16" o.c.

Standard 2-by decking on joists spaced 24" o.c.

16"

12" o.c.

Diagonal $^5/_4$ decking on joists spaced 12" o.c.

so outside the planned deck perimeter, batter boards allow for tight, exact stringed lines, but they don't get in the way when the holes are dug. By dropping a plumb bob where lines intersect at corners, you can make sure that the post or pier is centered exactly. You can even use the plumb bob to position a metal post anchor in the poured concrete pier.

Deck Construction

Regardless of the type of deck you're planning, there are common structural details to consider. Basically, the descriptions given below match the construction sequence you'll use for most deck projects.

Piers and Posts. Unless a deck is built at ground level, it needs a foundation of some sort. Wood posts are used frequently as the vertical members that support the deck and the rest of its framing. The posts—either 4 × 4s or 6 × 6s—can be set on concrete piers, or they can be anchored in the ground, secured in a "jacket" of poured concrete. To calculate how much concrete you'll need, use the following volume formula for each hole or tubular form:

$$0.7854 \times \text{hole or form diameter squared} \times \text{depth of form or hole.}$$

Concrete piers are usually poured in tubular fiber forms, also called Sonotubes. As shown, the forms need to extend at least as deep as the frost line, and they should rest on a 2- to 4-inch bed of gravel. To keep the form plumb, check the inside surface with a level as you're backfilling around it. Poured concrete piers look best when they end at grade level or just above it. At the top

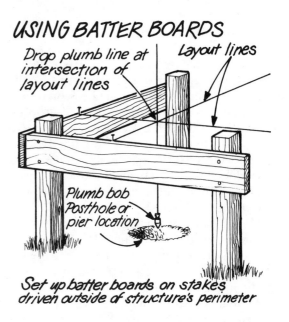

USING BATTER BOARDS

Drop plumb line at intersection of layout lines

Layout lines

Plumb bob
Posthole or pier location

Set up batter boards on stakes driven outside of structure's perimeter

end, either a treated wood pad or a metal post anchor should be cast into the concrete when the form is filled. To encourage good drainage, slope the concrete away from the pad or post anchor.

Posts set directly in the ground also need to extend to the frost line or just below it, resting on a gravel base. At least two diagonal braces, positioned at right angles to each other, should be used to keep the post plumb and square with the deck layout while the concrete is poured around it. The braces can be driven firmly into the ground or nailed to driven wood stakes; the top end of the brace is then nailed to the post.

Again, when the concrete is poured around the post, it's important to slope the top of the concrete away from the post so that water will drain instead of collect. When installing posts, it's easiest to let them run long. Once all the posts are set on their piers or cast in the ground, you can establish a level line and cut each post to its planned elevation.

Beams. In deck construction, beams are usually built up from doubled or tripled 2-by members. Beams can rest on posts, on piers, or even directly on a gravel base at ground level. When doubled 2-by beams are joined to 4 × 4 posts with framing hardware, ½-inch-thick exterior-grade plywood can be sandwiched between beam members to give the built-up beam the same 3½-inch thickness as the 4 × 4 post.

Wherever a beam is used, its purpose is to support a number of smaller-dimension joists. The joists can rest on top of the beam, secured by toenailing and blocking; or they can be installed in line with the beam, using joist hangers. To frame a multilevel deck, both joist positions can be used on the same beam.

Joists. In a deck, the joists provide the direct support for the decking material. Usually cut from 2-by dimension lumber, joists are usually spaced on centers that are 12 inches, 16 inches, or 24 inches apart. Five-quarter deck boards demand 12-inch or 16-inch centers; 2 × 4 or 2 × 6 deck planks can be installed over joists spaced 24 inches on center.

Ledgers. Ledgers perform just like beams, but they're attached to the side of the building along a level line. Joists are fastened to the ledger, either along the ledger's top edge, or along the exposed face of the ledger board.

Ledgers have to be carefully fastened to the house and flashed to promote good drainage. If they're not, water can get trapped behind the ledger board and damage the house as well as the deck structure. In a wood-sided house, it's best to shim the ledger out away from the siding. Lag screws are good for attaching the ledger, as long as they're

Details make the deck. The quality of the design and craftsmanship shows (clockwise from top left) in the way lighting is integrated into the design, the care with which joints are made, the embellishments—such as shaped braces and pegged construction—that are apparent, the special character of railings and benches, even in the novel ways stock materials are used.

275

POST-ON-PIER FOUNDATIONS

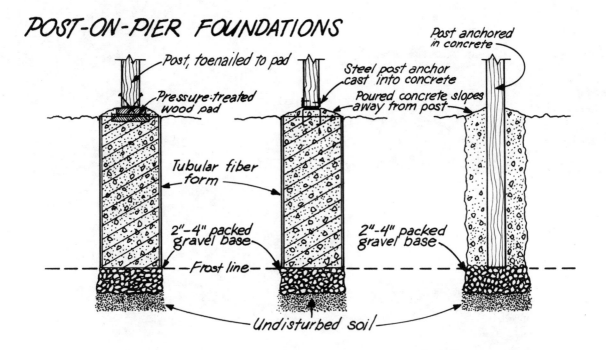

- Post, toenailed to pad
- Pressure-treated wood pad
- Tubular fiber form
- 2"-4" packed gravel base
- Frost line
- Steel post anchor cast into concrete
- Poured concrete slopes away from post
- 2"-4" packed gravel base
- Post anchored in concrete
- Undisturbed soil

driven through siding and sheathing and into solid floor or wall framing. Details for attaching a ledger to masonry walls are also shown in the illustration on page 278.

Bracing. Not every deck needs bracing. Bracing between deck posts is recommended in three situations.

■ Where a freestanding deck is more than 5 feet above the ground.
■ Where the deck—regardless of its height—projects more than 20 feet from a building.
■ Where a deck will be subjected to heavy loads or high winds.

The most common form of bracing for decks that are elevated more than 8 feet is X-bracing. Individual braces extend from the

top of one post to the base of another. Where the braces cross, a scrap of 4×4 is fitted as a spacer, and it and the braces are bolted together. This sort of bracing usually is installed only around the perimeter posts.

If the deck is elevated less than 8 feet, knee bracing may be sufficient. Braces extend from the posts to adjoining joists.

Decking. There are several choices when it comes to decking material. Some builders prefer standard, pressure-treated $5/4$ deck boards with factory-radiused edges. Other builders like to use 2×4, 2×6, or wider planks. If you don't like preservative-treated wood underfoot, consider redwood or cedar decking.

No matter which decking material you use, installation details are important. Each deck board should be installed "bark side up." This means that the growth rings visible in the end grain of the board will show a downward arc or curve when the board is installed. The bark-side-up strategy should prevent individual boards from cupping upward as the wood ages and is exposed to different moisture conditions.

It's also important to have even spacing between deck boards. To promote good drainage, there should be at least a ⅛-inch airspace between adjacent boards. Many carpenters simply use a couple of 16d nails as spacers when positioning decking. The installation pattern of your decking depends on taste, budget, and the configuration of the joists. Decking can cross joists at any angle, but can't run parallel to the joists. Generally, there's less waste when decking runs at 90 degrees to joists.

Instead of precutting deck boards to length before nailing them down, it's usu-ally best to let the boards run long when you install them. When all the decking is installed, it's easy to snap a chalk line and trim the excess all at once with your circular saw, leaving a straight, clean line.

You've got several options when it comes to fasteners for decking. Galvanized nails will do a fairly good job, but there are spiral-shanked nails made especially for decking. These nails also have galvanizing, and the spiral shank provides extra holding power to resist pulling loose as the decking moves over time.

Galvanized all-purpose screws (often called drywall screws, since they were origi-nally developed for drywall work) are an alternative to nails for decking. Screwing down your decking will take more time, and it requires a good "screw-gun" or variable-speed drill with a Phillips bit. You may even

DECK FRAMING: POSTS, BEAMS, AND JOISTS

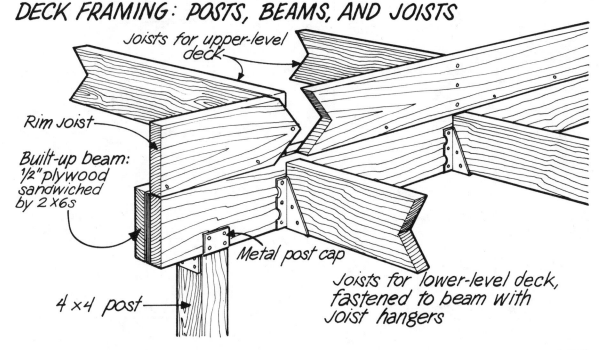

Joists for upper-level deck

Rim Joist

Built-up beam: ½" plywood sandwiched by 2 x 6s

Metal post cap

4 x 4 post

Joists for lower-level deck, fastened to beam with joist hangers

277

LEDGER INSTALLATION

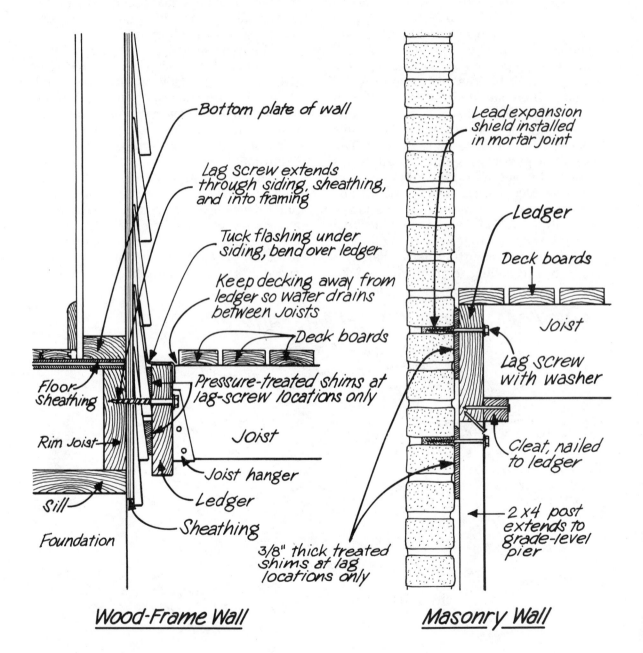

- Bottom plate of wall
- Lag screw extends through siding, sheathing, and into framing
- Tuck flashing under siding, bend over ledger
- Keep decking away from ledger so water drains between joists
- Deck boards
- Pressure-treated shims at lag-screw locations only
- Joist
- Joist hanger
- Ledger
- Sheathing
- Floor Sheathing
- Rim Joist
- Sill
- Foundation
- 3/8" thick treated shims at lag locations only

- Lead expansion shield installed in mortar joint
- Ledger
- Deck boards
- Joist
- Lag screw with washer
- Cleat, nailed to ledger
- 2x4 post extends to grade-level pier

Wood-Frame Wall

Masonry Wall

have to predrill some screw holes if you're fastening 1½-inch-thick planks to the framing. The reward for screwing down the deck is superior holding power. It's also easier to remove a damaged deck board because you can simply unscrew it.

Railings and Balusters. For safety reasons, building codes require perimeter railings on all decks that are 30 inches or more above grade level. The height of the railing should be at least 36 inches. Balusters, or intermediate rails, should be spaced no less than 6 inches apart.

There are many railing designs you can use for a deck. Specially milled cap railings are available from some building supply outlets. Pressure-treated balusters should be available where the cap railings are sold. It's also possible to make your own cap railing if you've got a table saw. Nominal 2×2 balusters can be ripped from 2×4 stock.

The major posts that support the upper and lower rails can be the same posts that extend from ground level to support the deck; or they can be short posts fastened to the joists or beams at the edge of the deck.

Stairs. A stairway needs to be at least 36 inches wide, and open stairways must have a guardrail between 30 and 36 inches high. For comfort and safety, the vertical distance between stair treads (called rise) should be no more than 8¼ inches. Likewise, the depth (or run) of the tread should be at least 9 inches.

Most decks have open-riser stairs, because these stairways drain better and are easier to keep clean than stairways with closed risers. Stair treads are supported by stair carriages, or stringers.

To lay out and cut the stringers for a deck stairway, you have to use the total rise (the vertical distance covered by the stair-
(continued on page 282)

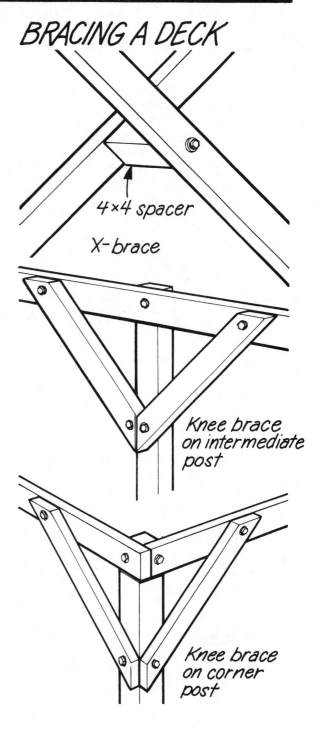

BRACING A DECK

4×4 spacer

X-brace

Knee brace on intermediate post

Knee brace on corner post

279

Nailing It Down

The most exposed part of a deck is the decking. If decking is nailed down incorrectly, the deck's appearance will suffer as the years progress.

First, use spiral-shanked galvanized nails to nail the decking down. A compromise, perhaps, these nails have a reasonable price, the maximum holding power a nail can have, and a coating to maximize their weatherability. Screws will hold better, but they cost more and are more involved to use. Aluminum or stainless steel nails will weather better, but they are expensive.

Orient the decking boards bark side up for the best long-term appearance. If the board should cup, the convex surface will be up, so the board will shed water. The cupping will be less obvious, so the deck will continue to look good.

Drive the nails at an angle, as shown. Drive the nails with a hammer as far as you can without denting the wood, then sink them with a hammer and countersink.

Finally, be prepared to cope with some "spaghetti boards," especially if you will be using 14, 16, or 18 footers. You may have to enlist some muscular help to force these warped pieces into position. Line up one end, and nail it to the first couple of joists. Then force the other end into position, using a pry bar or a chisel as a lever.

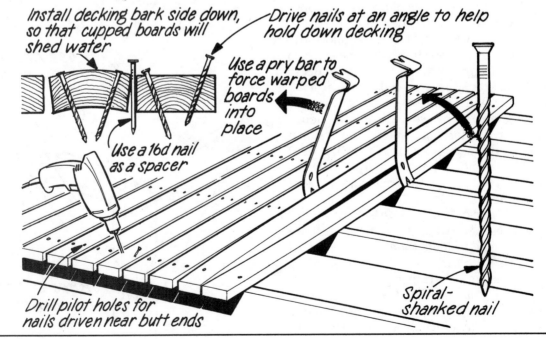

Install decking bark side down, so that cupped boards will shed water

Drive nails at an angle to help hold down decking

Use a pry bar to force warped boards into place

Use a 16d nail as a spacer

Drill pilot holes for nails driven near butt ends

Spiral-shanked nail

POST AND RAIL DETAILS

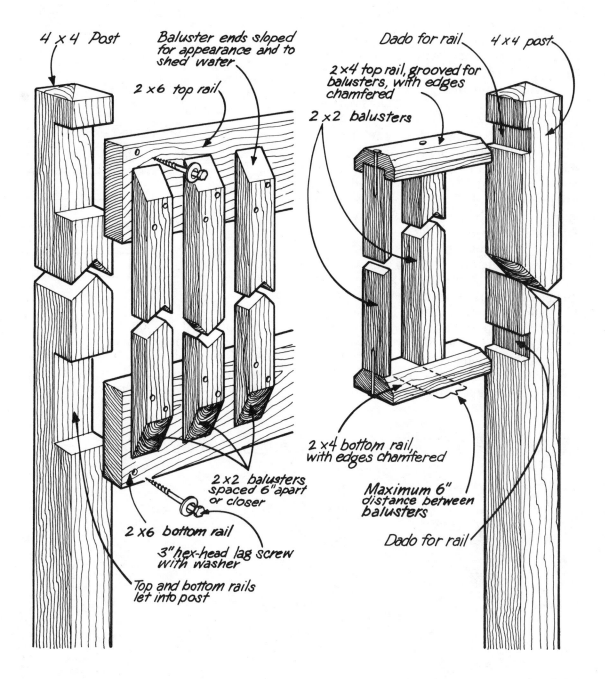

4 x 4 Post

Baluster ends sloped for appearance and to shed water

2 x 6 top rail

Dado for rail

4 x 4 post

2 x 4 top rail, grooved for balusters, with edges chamfered

2 x 2 balusters

2 x 2 balusters spaced 6" apart or closer

2 x 6 bottom rail

3" hex-head lag screw with washer

Top and bottom rails let into post

2 x 4 bottom rail, with edges chamfered

Maximum 6" distance between balusters

Dado for rail

way) and the total run (the horizontal distance) to calculate the rise and run of each step. A good method is to first divide the total rise (45 inches, for example) by an assumed tread rise of 8 inches. This yields 5.62, but since you can't have 5.62 treads, let's assume that there will be 6 treads in your stairway. Dividing 45 by 6 yields a tread rise of 7½ inches.

Once you've determined the rise, it's easy to find the run: Just choose a figure (10 inches, for example) that will yield a sum between 17 and 18 inches when added to the rise of 7½ inches. This shortcut will give your stairway the proper angle of between 30 and 35 degrees.

Use a framing square to lay out cut lines (or lines for cleats or dadoes) on the 2×10 or 2×12 stock that will become your stair stringers. Place the square on the 2-by so that the tread measurement (on the wider blade of the square) and the riser measurement (on the tongue of the square) align over the same edge of the stock. Trace a square layout line on the stock. Extend the tread layout lines if you're planning to use

STAIR DESIGN DETAILS

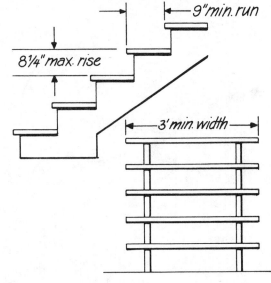

dadoes or cleats to hold the treads.

A pair of stringers will be adequate for short, narrow stairways. For extra-wide or extra-long stairways, add a third cut stringer at the center of the stair. At the top and

STAIR STRINGERS WITH DADOES AND CLEATS

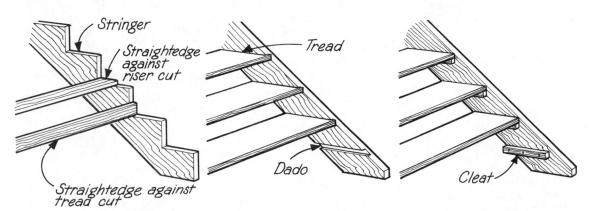

LAYING OUT A STRINGER

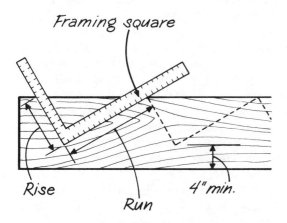

Framing square

Rise

Run

4" min.

bottom of the stairway, install cleats between or across the stringers to reinforce them. Like decking boards, stair treads should be installed bark side up to prevent cupping.

Deck Details

Good details are usually what distinguish a well-crafted deck from its ordinary-looking relatives. There are many simple ways to make your deck look good. Instead of placing nails randomly, try to keep visible nails in a straight line.

Joinery details are important in railings and posts that are visible in the finished deck. Lap joints or miter joints can replace simple butt joints. For example, rim joists that meet near the edge of a deck can join with a miter instead of a butt joint. Take time to smooth handrails, using a hand plane and medium-grit sandpaper or a router with a round-over bit. Posts that support railings shouldn't end with a simple square cutoff. Instead, try a tapered cutoff detail, as shown. In addition to looking good, posts with tapered tops will shed water better than flat-topped posts.

DECK DETAILS

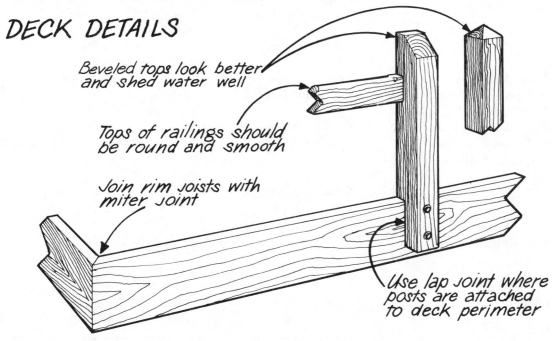

Beveled tops look better and shed water well

Tops of railings should be round and smooth

Join rim joists with miter joint

Use lap joint where posts are attached to deck perimeter

283

Deck Finish Options

How long will your deck last? How will it look years from now? It all depends upon the way you finish and maintain it.

You can paint or stain pressure-treated wood, or you can leave it unfinished to weather to a gray color. If it was dried after treatment it can be painted or stained right away. Otherwise, allow it to air-dry for several weeks before painting or staining it.

Whatever kind of wood you use, treating it with a water repellent will help retard movement of moisture into and out of the wood, cutting down on potential twisting or bending. Water repellent is an economical, easy-to-maintain treatment. If you are not using pressure-treated wood, you may want to consider using a water repellent as a back, end, and edge primer, as well as a face treatment. You can dip, brush, or spray your lumber; follow the manufacturer's directions, and observe all safety precautions.

Paintable water-repellent preservatives contain a mildewcide. For existing decks, begin with a two-coat application. Then apply maintenance coats when the wood no longer seems able to shed water. You can apply paints, stains, or bleaches over paintable water repellents without difficulty, if you decide you want to change the look of your deck later.

The following chart, provided by the Western Wood Products Association, lists deck-finishing options.

Finish	Type	Application Instructions
Paints	Alkyd paints	1 coat alkyd primer, with 2 finish coats
	Oil-based paints	1 coat zinc-free primer, with 2 finish coats
	Latex paints	1 coat zinc-free primer, with 2 finish coats
Heavy Stains (Solid, but somewhat soft color; shows wood texture but little grain	Heavy-bodied oil-based stains	1–2 coats, brushed, dipped, or sprayed
Light Stains (Light coloring with emphasis on wood-grain show-through	Semi-transparent stains	2 coats, brushed on; may be sprayed on, then smoothed with brush
	Semi-transparent resin stains	2 coats, brushed on
Weathering agents	Bleaches	1–2 coats, brushed on; renew in 3–5 years, if needed
Repellents	Water repellents	2 coats; dip before installation, brush afterward

PROJECT THE BASIC DECK

Designed by TECO, a framing hardware manufacturer, this deck is proof that if you can drive a nail without bending it, you have what it takes to build a deck. Building a sound, practical, and even attractive deck is not difficult.

Every deck, no matter how elaborate, has its roots in a basic structure like this. Its elegance lies in its simplicity. Because the main beams are cantilevered beyond the posts that support them, the deck gains a graceful appearance without sacrificing any strength.

The framing is straightforward and, quite naturally, depends upon framing hardware for much of the joinery. An experienced do-it-yourselfer, however, can construct a sound deck without the hardware. The deck rests on 12 posts and is not attached to the house it adjoins. Though the deck shown is 16 × 16 feet, the design is such that the size can be altered simply by increasing or decreasing the

on-center spacing of the joists.

Built of pressure-treated southern pine, this deck has a simple but effective railing, a small stairway, and built-in benches. You can enhance the appearance of even a basic deck by using cedar or redwood for the exposed header and joists, the decking, and the railing. Minor trim embellishments can also greatly enhance the deck's appearance.

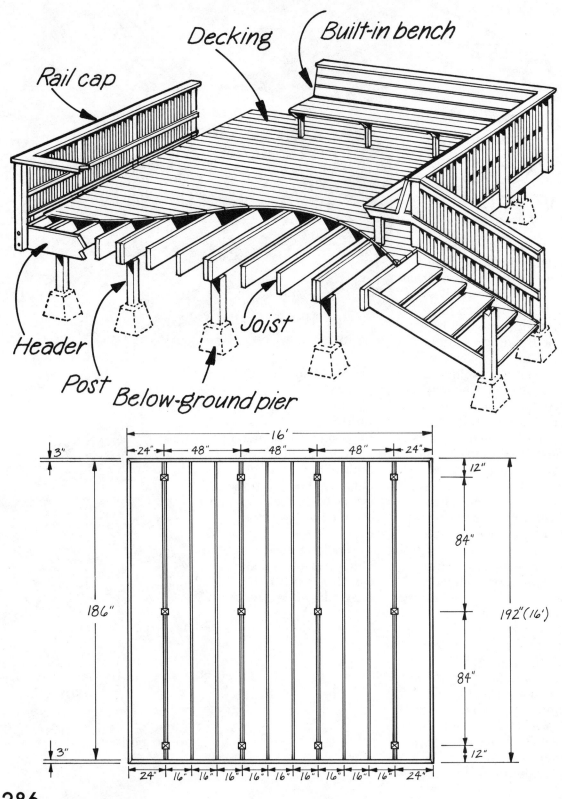

Rail cap

Decking

Built-in bench

Header

Post

Below-ground pier

Joist

16'

24" 48" 48" 48" 24"

3"

3"

12"

84"

192"(16')

84"

12"

186"

24" 16" 16" 16" 16" 16" 16" 16" 16" 16" 24"

286

Shopping List

12 pcs. 4 × 4 × 8′ pressure-treated pine (posts)

9 pcs. 4 × 4 × 8′ pressure-treated pine (railing posts)

3 pcs. 2 × 12 × 8′ pressure-treated pine (stair treads)

2 pcs. 2 × 10 × 12′ pressure-treated pine (rail cap w/benches)

20 pcs. 2 × 8 × 16′ pressure-treated pine (beams and joists)

2 pcs. 2 × 8 × 6′ pressure-treated pine (stair stringers)

34 pcs. 2 × 6 × 16′ pressure-treated pine (decking)

1 pc. 2 × 6 × 16′ pressure-treated pine (rail cap)

12 pcs. 2 × 6 × 12′ pressure-treated pine (seat and back boards)

2 pcs. 2 × 6 × 12′ pressure-treated pine (rail cap)

3 pcs. 2 × 4 × 16′ pressure-treated pine (horizontal rails and nailers)

11 pcs. 2 × 4 × 12′ pressure-treated pine (horizontal rails and nailers)

4 pcs. 2 × 4 × 10′ pressure-treated pine (bench support frames)

1 pc. 2 × 4 × 8′ pressure-treated pine (stair posts)

58 pcs. 2 × 2 × 12′ pressure-treated pine (balusters)

24 post caps or tie-down anchors

4 all-purpose framing anchors

18–5″ × ½″ carriage bolts w/nuts and washers (railing posts)

16–4″ × ½″ carriage bolts w/nuts and washers (railing posts)

4–3½″ × ½″ carriage bolts w/nuts and washers (railing posts)

32 pcs. 3″ angle hardware (bench support frames)

32 pcs. 5″ plate hardware (bench support frames)

8 hangers for 2 × 4s (bench support frames)

10 pcs. step-support hardware w/lag bolts

16d galvanized nails

10d galvanized nails

8d galvanized nails

8 double-width joist hangers

12 joist hangers

1. **Stake out the deck.** Begin by establishing the first corner, then the first side. Drive a stake at the corner and plumb it with a level. Measure from that corner to the second corner, drive a stake there, plumb it, then tautly stretch mason's cord from stake to stake.

Mark the cord 4 feet from one of the stakes. Tie a second line to the outside edge of that stake, and pull it taut toward the third corner of the deck. Mark this line 3 feet from the first stake.

While your helper moves the third stake to the left or right, keeping the line taut all the while, measure the distance between the two marks on the lines. When the distance is exactly 5 feet, the lines are at right angles to each other. Have your helper drive the stake.

Working from the second stake, repeat the procedure to position the fourth and final stake.

2. Locate the post positions. Since the deck is cantilevered, the posts are not on the corners. To locate the posts closest to the corners, use a framing square to measure 24 inches from the end of the deck and 12 inches from the side. Drive a stake at each point. The remaining posts can easily be laid out using these first four as reference points.

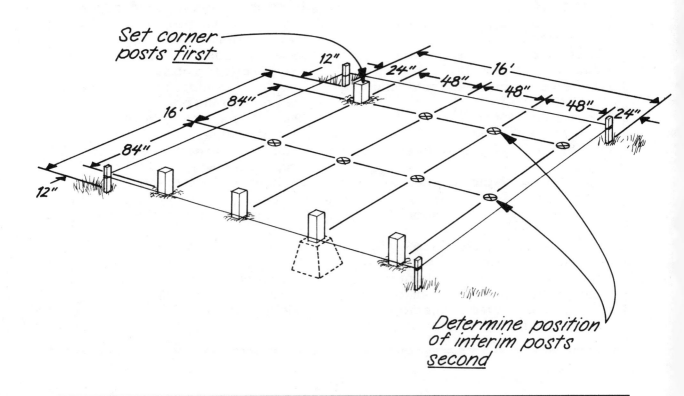

Set corner posts *first*

12"

24"

48"

16'

48"

48"

24"

16'

84"

84"

12"

84"

Determine position of interim posts *second*

3. Set and plumb the posts. Dig holes for posts. Hole depths for posts should be half their height but not less than 2 feet. (Check local building code regulations for frost-line conditions.)

Pour about 2 inches of gravel into the holes and set the posts, checking plumb with a level. When the post is square and plumb, tamp a small amount of loose soil around its base, and temporarily use stakes and braces to hold it in position. When all posts have been squared and plumbed, check the accuracy of their position with a measuring tape and level.

Backfill each posthole with concrete. Let the concrete cure for several days before proceeding with construction.

NOTE: It is all right if posts are too high at this stage, *but be sure they are not too short.*

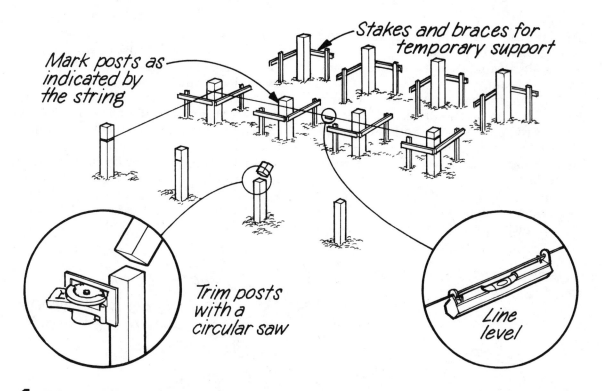

Mark posts as indicated by the string

Stakes and braces for temporary support

Trim posts with a circular saw

Line level

4. Trim the posts to the correct height. To do this, you must first establish where you want the deck surface to be. Then you must select one of the posts as the base, preferably the one set in the lowest spot. All the others will be marked in relation to this post.

The height of the base post is determined by measuring the distance from the eventual deck surface to the ground, then deducting the actual thickness of the decking and the actual depth of the beams.

Mark this point—the baseline—on the base post, and extend it around the four sides of the post with a combination or try square.

Transfer the baseline to the other five posts by stretching a string around the posts. Line it up on the baseline, and attach a line level to it. Adjust the line until it is level. It delineates the cutoff height of all posts. Again, extend this baseline mark around each post with a try square.

Saw the posts off at this line, making sure the cuts are square.

5. Attach the beams to the posts. To create the beams, spike two 10-foot 2 × 8s together with 10d galvanized nails.

Set the beams on top of the cut posts, and attach them using either two tie-down anchors or two post caps. Use 8d galvanized nails.

6. Make the perimeter beams and install them. Spike two 12-foot 2 × 8s together with 10d galvanized nails to create each perimeter beam.

Lay out and fasten two kinds of joist hangers to each perimeter beam. One set of hangers will suspend the perimeter beam on the ends of the beams. The other set will support the joists that you will install between the perimeter beams.

Position double-width joist hangers on the perimeter beam, two with their center-lines 24 inches from the header ends, the other two on 4-foot centers between the first two. Their seats must be *up* and flush with the top edge of the beam. Nail the hangers in place using 16d galvanized nails.

Next, nail hangers for single joists to the perimeter beam with the seat *down*. Locate them on 16-inch centers. Use 8d galvanized nails.

Install the perimeter beam by hanging the seat of the hangers on the ends of the doubled joists. Holding the beam tightly in position, nail the hangers to the sides of the doubled joists, using 16d galvanized nails.

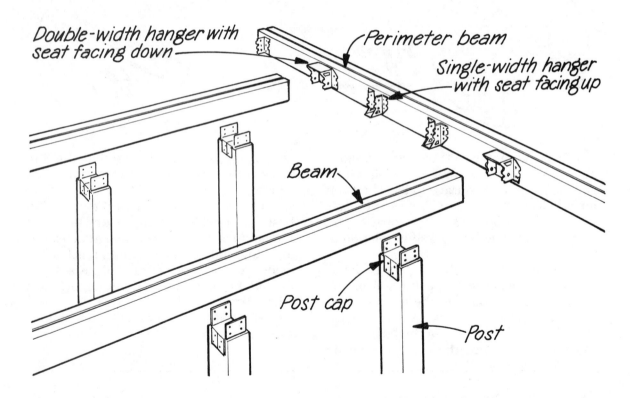

7. Install the joists. Cut the joists to length and drop them into the hangers. Nail through the hangers into the joists with 8d galvanized nails.

8. **Install the end joists.** Using 8d galvanized nails, fasten two all-purpose framing anchors to the end joist, so the right-angle flanges are even with the joist's butt ends. Fit the joist between the perimeter beams and nail it in place.

9. **Lay the decking.** Take particular care when laying the deck boards. This is the job that a contractor will assign to his top craftsman. The deck won't look good unless the decking is put down carefully. It is the most visible part of the deck.

Use galvanized 10d nails. Keep the nails in a straight line. Be patient when putting down deck boards. Take your time.

Lay, square, and fasten the two outside pieces of decking at opposite edges of the deck. If the appearance of the lumber permits, put boards bark side up to minimize cupping. Spread out the rest of the decking on the joists. Start spacing and fastening the deck boards in place from either edge. In most cases, spacing between deck boards is ¼ inch.

Nail down each deck board with at least two nails at each support point for 4-inch boards, three nails for 6-inch boards, and four nails for 8-inch boards. To prevent splitting at the ends of the boards, drill small pilot holes.

When the last deck board has been nailed down, snap a chalk-line against the ends and saw the deck boards off flush with the end joists.

10. **Construct the stairs.** This deck has a short flight of stairs leading from the deck to the ground.

When locating the stairs, ensure that adequate drainage exists at their foot. No one wants to descend from the deck into a muddy sump. This deck clearly doesn't have that problem.

To determine the number of steps needed, divide the total rise (the distance from ground level to deck surface) by 7, the desired rise of individual steps. Decrease the rise if necessary to eliminate fractional steps. The desired tread depth—11 inches if your rise is 7 inches—multiplied by the number of steps will yield the total run of the steps.

With these figures in hand, lay out the stringers. Use the total rise and the total run to determine the length of the stringers. Use a framing square to step off the stair layout.

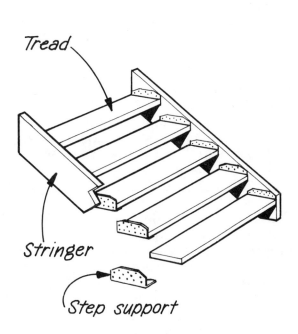

Tread

Stringer

Step support

291

Fasten the stringers to the perimeter beam or end joist. Then install the treads. In the case of the deck shown, the connections were made using framing hardware. Each step consists of one 2×12. Two 2×6s could also be used, which, with a ¼-inch gap between them, yields a tread about 11¼ inches wide.

11. **Build and install a railing.** The simplest railing for a deck features 4×4 posts, two 2×4 horizontal rails, and a 2×6 cap. On the deck shown, this simple installation has been further enhanced through the addition of 2×2 balusters and a 2×4 nailer for the balusters on the decking.

Posts for the railings can be cut to fit against the outside beams with a lap joint and fastened in place with ½-inch carriage bolts long enough to penetrate the post and the perimeter beam. To further stabilize the post, toenail through the post where it rests on the decking. With the 2×6 cap, the posts can be spaced 6 feet apart. (With a 2×4 cap, the posts should be spaced only 4 feet apart.)

Nail or screw the horizontal rails in place against the inner face of the post, one flush with the post top, the other midway between decking and post top. Add the cap, nailing into both the post and the uppermost horizontal rail. To complete the railing shown, cut 2×2 balusters to fit between decking and cap. Nail each baluster to the horizontal rails; use a spare baluster as a spacer to expedite the installation.

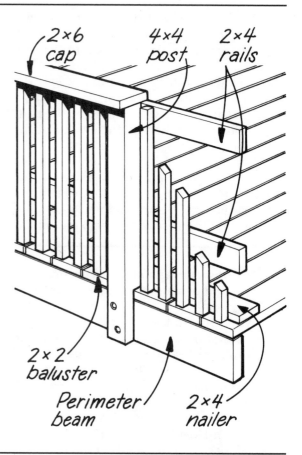

12. **Construct the deck benches.** A common deck feature is built-in seating. This deck has benches built onto the railings. And since it was constructed to demonstrate the myriad uses of framing hardware, the framework of the benches was assembled using various plates and angles.

In sizing the benches, the most important dimensions are the 18-inch seat height and the 20-inch back height. The back should slope for the sake of comfort. Support frames should be spaced about 4 feet apart.

To construct the bench supports, cut the seat posts, seat supports, and back supports from 2×4 stock, as shown. Connect them using galvanized plates on both sides of each assembly.

After the railing is up, but before the cap is installed, mark the locations of the seat supports along the railing. Install a hanger on the lower rail at each mark. Fit the end of the seat support into the hanger, then attach the seat post to the decking and the back support to the top rail with angle plates. Lay 2×6 seat and back boards in place and nail them down.

Capping the railing-bench assembly is the final step. Use a 2×10, ripped on a bevel to an 8-inch width.

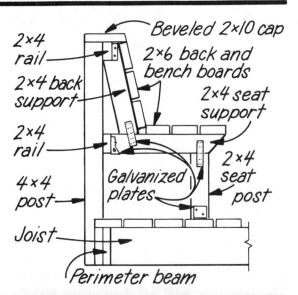

HOW TO PARQUET-PATTERN DECKING

An ordinary deck can be transformed into a very special one in a variety of ways. An easy one is the way in which you apply the decking itself. Even a small deck like the one shown can be embellished with decking that's installed in a parquet pattern.

You have to plan ahead, however. The secret is to use a square framing plan with a single built-up beam and closely spaced joists, as shown in the drawing. It's also important to use clear, all-heart redwood decking boards. This type of decking is dimensionally stable, which is important in a pattern installation with many angled cuts.

1. Install a square piece of 2×6 deck board first, at the very center of the deck, over the built-up beam.
2. Work outward, mitering both ends of each board at 45 degrees. Predrill nail holes at the ends of boards to avoid splitting, and space neighboring boards ⅛ inch apart.
3. Install the decking in concentric fashion, to ensure that all the miter joints of each four-board course line up.

Materials List
55 pcs. $2 \times 6 \times 14'$ redwood decking

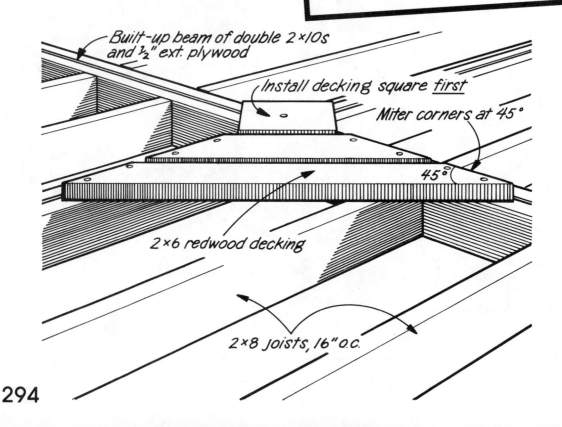

Built-up beam of double 2×10s and ½" ext. plywood

Install decking square _first_

Miter corners at 45°

45°

2×6 redwood decking

2×8 joists, 16" o.c.

RAILING WITH TURNED BALUSTERS

The railing, as much as any other element, defines the deck's character. While most decks have solid-wood railings that reflect the angular, dimension-lumber roots of the structure, this deck features painted, turned balusters.

The white accent relieves the monotony of the natural wood tones. And the shape of the balusters lends a porchlike character to the rambling deck. The balusters are standard items stocked at most home centers and lumberyards. They are sandwiched, top and bottom, between two 1 × 4 redwood stringers. The stringers are attached to posts, and the assembly is capped with a 2 × 6.

1. For each 8-foot section of railing, sand and paint a dozen 3 × 3 turned balusters.

2. While the paint dries, ready the posts. The posts must be notched to receive the 1 × 4 stringers. Using a router or dado cutter, cut two notches 3½ inches wide and ½ inch deep into both the front and back of each post. The lower notches should be positioned so they will be 3 inches above the decking, the upper ones should be flush with the post top.

3. Install the posts on the deck.

4. Lay out the 12 balusters, spacing them evenly apart.

5. Lay the two stringers in place, flush with the tops and bottoms of the balusters. Drive an 8d galvanized nail through each stringer into each baluster.

6. Lift the railing section into place, fitting the stringers into the notches in the posts. Nail the stringers to the posts.

7. Fit the other two stringers into the notches in the backs of the posts and nail them fast. Then drive a nail through each stringer into the back of each baluster.

8. With a router and a ⅜-inch round-over bit, machine a radius along the top edges of the 2 × 6 redwood cap. Then set the cap in place, flush with the front stringer and overhanging the back stringer. Nail the cap to the posts and the stringers.

9. Apply a ⅜ × 1½-inch strip of redwood to the railing, concealing the seam between the cap and the stringer.

10. Apply a finish to the redwood.

Materials List

Number	Piece	Dimensions	Material
2	Posts	3½″ × 3½″ × 36″	redwood
12	Balusters	2½″ × 2½″ × 28″	pressure-treated pine
4	Stringers	¾″ × 3½″ × 96″	redwood
1	Rail cap	1½″ × 5½″ × 96″	redwood
1	Trim molding	⅜″ × 1½″ × 96″	redwood

Hardware
10d galvanized nails
8d galvanized nails

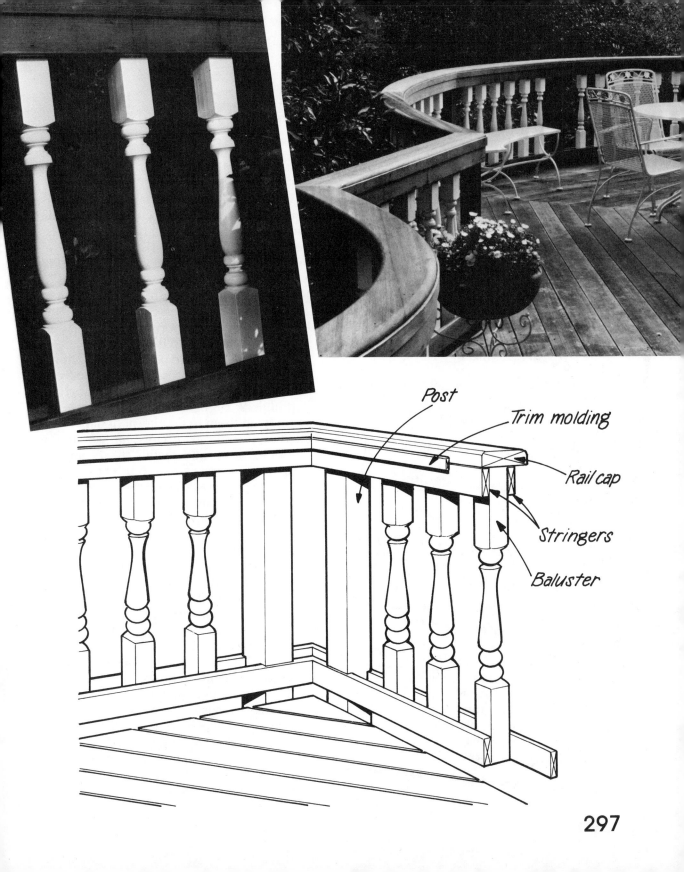

Post

Trim molding

Rail cap

Stringers

Baluster

297

HOW TO DECK WITH TRELLIS

A south-facing deck with no natural shade can benefit greatly from a built-in trellis. Good proportions and subtle structural details are key ingredients in any attractive and effective trellis. Notice here how the structural hierarchy between beams, joists, and trellising is emphasized through the use of overlaps at each level.

The above-grade, 12 × 16-foot deck is built from pressure-treated southern pine and redwood. Used chiefly for the structural parts of the deck, the pine is out of sight in the completed deck, covered by redwood finish materials.

1. Set four 6 × 6 pressure-treated posts in concrete, one at each corner of the deck. These posts act as perimeter supports for the deck and the trellis.
2. Five short posts are positioned as shown in the drawing and also set in concrete. With the corner posts, these support the double 2 × 8 beams. After the posts are set, trim them to a uniform height.
3. Attach double-width joist hangers to the corner posts and install the perimeter beams. Use post caps to connect the beams to the short posts. Hang the center beam from the perimeter beams with double-width joist hangers and connect it to the central post with a post cap.
4. On top of these beams, install pressure-treated 2 × 6 joists on 16-inch centers.
5. Nail redwood 2 × 4 decking to the joists, perpendicular to the house wall.
6. "Skin," or case, the corner posts with redwood boards. Use 1 × 6 boards on two faces and 1 × 8 boards on the other two.
7. To support the trellis, nail a pair of 2 × 10 redwood beams to the two posts farthest from the house. Install a single 2 × 10 across the posts positioned next to the house. It's important for these beams to be perfectly level and parallel.
8. Toenail 2 × 6 joists to the beams, spaced on 16-inch centers.
9. On top of the joists, install 2 × 3s on 12-inch centers.

Shopping List

4 pcs. 6 × 6 × 12' pressure-treated pine (corner posts)
3 pcs. 4 × 4 × 8' pressure-treated pine (foundation posts)
4 pcs. 2 × 8 × 16' pressure-treated pine (beams)
6 pcs. 2 × 8 × 12' pressure-treated pine (beams)
16 pcs. 2 × 6 × 8' pressure-treated pine (joists)
4 pcs. 2 × 10 × 16' redwood (cross beams)
2 pcs. 2 × 6 × 16' redwood (rim joists)
2 pcs. 2 × 6 × 12' redwood (rim joists)
13 pcs. 2 × 6 × 12' redwood (trellis joists)
53 pcs. 2 × 4 × 12' redwood (decking)
13 pcs. 2 × 3 × 16' redwood (trellis members)
8 pcs. 1 × 8 × 8' redwood (post casing)
8 pcs. 1 × 6 × 8' redwood (post casing)
5 post cap connectors
16d galvanized nails
12d galvanized nails
8d galvanized nails
10 double-width joist hangers

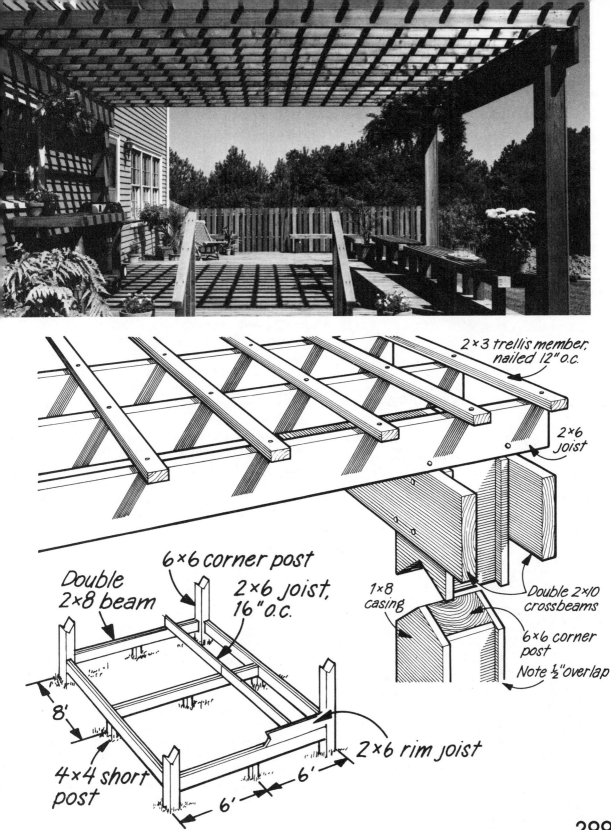

2×3 trellis member, nailed 12" o.c.

2×6 joist

Double 2×10 crossbeams

6×6 corner post

Note ½"overlap

1×8 casing

Double 2×8 beam

6×6 corner post

2×6 joist, 16" o.c.

8'

4×4 short post

6'

6'

2×6 rim joist

Gazebos and Other Outbuildings

Sheds, gazebos, playhouses, and other buildings share quite a few structural details and design elements with decks. Dimension lumber is still the primary structural ingredient. But even though a backyard workshop or gazebo may take up less space than the average deck, it's more complex in terms of materials. Buildings need sheathing for walls and roof, along with windows, doors, and exterior finish materials like shingles or clapboards. Insulation, electricity, and interior finish are options that can upgrade a simple outbuilding into more of a year-round space.

If you're set on building a shed or workshop, design it the same way you'd design a deck—by making scaled drawings that show plan views and elevations. Your elevation drawings will give you window and door locations, wall heights, the number of studs to order, and the surface area you'll need to cover with sheathing and/or siding. The floor plan drawing should give you the size of the foundation, the number of joists and rafters, and the size of the roofing job you'll be undertaking.

Framed structures can be built in a limitless number of sizes and shapes. In spite of this variety, the structural members themselves are basically the same. In most small and medium-size outbuildings, walls are framed with 2 × 4 studs. The studs extend vertically between top and bottom plates, which run horizontally. The bottom plate, also called the sill, rests on the foundation. The top plate—usually a pair of 2 × 4s, or double plate—forms a base for joists, rafters, or both, depending on the design of the building.

Roof structural members can include rafters, purlins, collar ties, and ridgeboard, depending on the design of the roof. It's usually important to incorporate overhangs at eaves and gables. By extending the roof beyond the building's walls, you protect both the walls and the foundation from water damage during rains.

Studs, joists, rafters, and other structural members are usually spaced on centers that are 16 inches or 24 inches apart. This spacing isn't primarily for strength; it has

FRAMED STRUCTURE ANATOMY

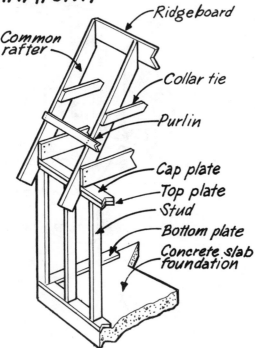

Ridgeboard

Common rafter

Collar tie

Purlin

Cap plate

Top plate

Stud

Bottom plate

Concrete slab foundation

more to do with the 4 × 8 module of plywood and other sheet materials that are used on buildings as sheathing, siding, insulation, and interior wallboard. On-center spacing of 16 inches or 24 inches provides solid backing where one 4 × 8 sheet ends and the next begins.

You can minimize cutting and waste if your building is sized in 2- or 4-foot increments. For example, a shed that's 8 feet high, 10 feet wide, and 12 feet long can be sheathed on all four sides with 11 sheets of plywood. Adding another foot to the shed's width will call for another sheet of plywood, and instead of being able to use standard 10-foot joists and plates, you'll have to order 12-foot-long material and cut it down.

Rafters First

It might seem strange to start a building with the roof framing, but it actually makes a lot of sense. The best time to lay out your rafters is *before* the walls go up. Given the small size of most backyard outbuildings and the simple gable or shed roof designs, it's very easy to lay out the rafters at full scale on the completed foundation or subfloor.

Instead of being given an angle measurement, roof or rafter pitch is most often expressed in terms of rise and run. The run, or horizontal distance, is always 12. The rise is the vertical distance that the rafter spans in 12 inches or 12 feet. So a 12-in-12 (or 12-over-12) pitch is actually quite steep at

RAFTER ANATOMY

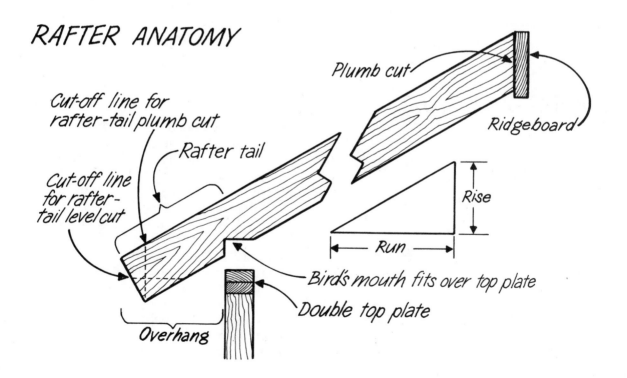

Plumb cut

Ridgeboard

Cut-off line for rafter-tail plumb cut

Rafter tail

Cut-off line for rafter-tail level cut

Rise

Run

Bird's mouth fits over top plate

Double top plate

Overhang

301

FULL-SCALE RAFTER LAYOUT

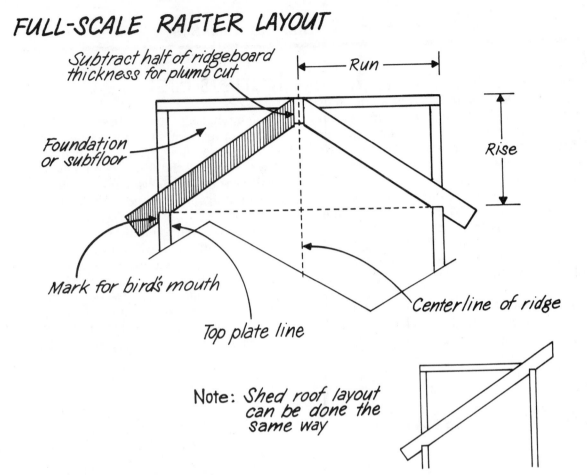

Subtract half of ridgeboard thickness for plumb cut

Foundation or subfloor

Mark for bird's mouth

Top plate line

Run

Rise

Centerline of ridge

Note: *Shed roof layout can be done the same way*

PLATE MARKUP

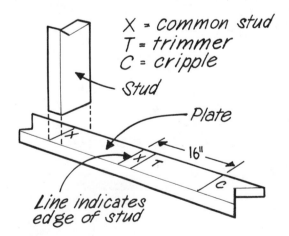

X = common stud
T = trimmer
C = cripple

Stud

Plate

16"

Line indicates edge of stud

45 degrees, while a 6-in-12 pitch describes a roof sloped at 22½ degrees.

The pitch of the rafter determines its length as well as the angles required for plumb and seat cuts. Once you decide on the pitch of your roof, place a 2 × 6 (or whatever stock you'll be using for rafters) flat on the foundation or subfloor of your building. Position the rafter stock over the lines that the eaves and roof peak will follow, giving the rafter the desired pitch from ridge to eaves. In this position, you can mark the rafter for plumb and bird's-mouth cuts; and also determine the overhang and trim detail for the rafter tail. Make a pattern rafter and

Outdoor living can involve a variety of framed structures. Some are utilitarian, housing the paraphernalia of outdoor life (below) or the winter's stockpiles (below right). Others shelter you during your moments of outdoor recreation and relaxation (right).

test its fit against the layout lines on your foundation or subfloor. If it's right, you can go ahead with wall framing. When you get to the roof, all you have to do is make duplicate rafters from your pattern.

Framing the Walls

The construction sequence for a one-story building is fairly simple, regardless of its size. The walls go up first, then the ceiling joists and roof framing are added. Windows and doors are installed after the structure is sheathed. Finally, the roofing, siding, and trim are added.

If possible, frame your walls horizontally, on the completed subfloor or concrete slab. It's much easier to position and nail studs when they're on edge instead of on end. With the top and bottom wall plates held together, lay out your stud locations on these 2 × 4s. Be sure to mark window and door locations, too. Instead of marking the on-center location for each stud, you're better off making a line to show where one edge of the stud should line up, and a large X to denote the "footprint" of the stud. This layout strategy can avoid time-consuming mistakes, especially if you're working with one or more helpers.

Once you've marked up the plates, separate them and "load" the appropriate number of studs between them. Full-length studs can be face-nailed to the plates. Once you've done this, install trimmer studs, cripples, and headers to complete the rough openings for any doors or windows in this wall

FRAMING A WALL

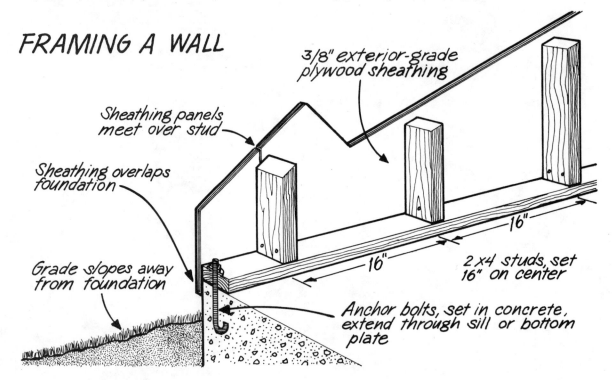

3/8" exterior-grade plywood sheathing

Sheathing panels meet over stud

Sheathing overlaps foundation

Grade slopes away from foundation

16"

16"

2x4 studs, set 16" on center

Anchor bolts, set in concrete, extend through sill or bottom plate

FRAMING ROUGH OPENINGS

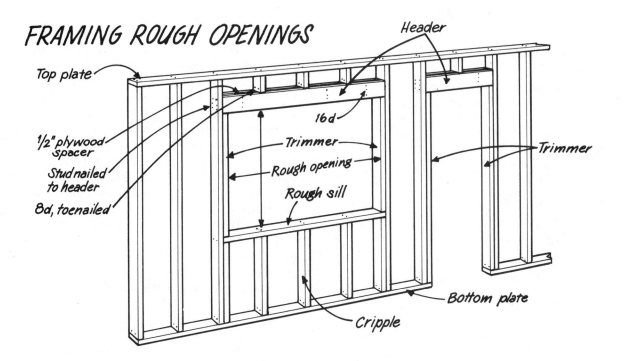

Top plate
Header
1/2" plywood spacer
Stud nailed to header
8d, toenailed
16d
Trimmer
Rough opening
Rough sill
Trimmer
Bottom plate
Cripple

section. Details of rough framing for door and window openings are shown.

Tilt the wall up when you've finished framing it. If you have a concrete foundation, the wall's bottom plate should be anchored to the foundation with anchor bolts or other suitable framing hardware. On a wood subfloor, simply nail the bottom plate in place. Use temporary braces to secure the wall in a plumb position.

Repeat the same procedures for each wall. Overlapping the double top plate at the corners will tie the building's walls together. After checking the walls to make sure they're plumb and square, install the sheathing. Exterior-grade waferboard or CDX plywood (either ⅜-inch or ½-inch thickness) is the least-expensive wall sheathing, but these sheets are meant to be covered by

exterior siding of some sort. In an outbuilding, you might save money by installing your finish siding directly over the wall framing. Hardboard or textured plywood siding, tongue-and-groove boards (installed horizontally, with tongues facing up) and lap-jointed boards are a few exterior wall treatments that eliminate the need for rough sheathing.

Roofing the Structure

Cut and install the ceiling joists and rafters next. If you're using a ridgeboard, it will need to be held in its final position with upright braces until at least a few rafter pairs are installed. Nail each rafter to the ridgeboard at the roof peak, and toenail it to the top of the wall at the seat cut. In a gable

FRAMING A SHED ROOF

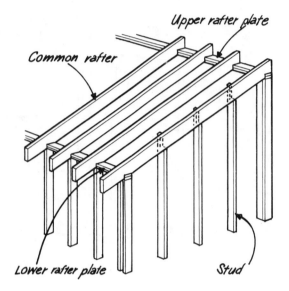

Upper rafter plate

Common rafter

Lower rafter plate

Stud

or shed roof, you can frame an overhang at gable ends by extending purlins as shown.

Sheathe the roof with exterior-grade plywood, waferboard, or tongue-and-groove boards. Houses usually have closed soffits where rafters overhang at the eaves of the roof, but this isn't necessary in a backyard workshop or shed. Likewise, you don't have to worry about insulation or interior wallboard unless you plan to heat your new structure and use it year-round.

For roofing, you can choose asphalt or fiberglass shingles, asphalt-based roll roofing, metal or fiberglass panels, or even wood or slate shingles. Roll roofing is your least-expensive option, and it's also best for low-slope roofs. Shingles of any type shouldn't be used on a roof with a pitch less than 3-in-12.

Roll roofing and asphalt or fiberglass shingles should be installed over solid sheathing that has been covered with a layer of

FRAMING A GABLE OVERHANG

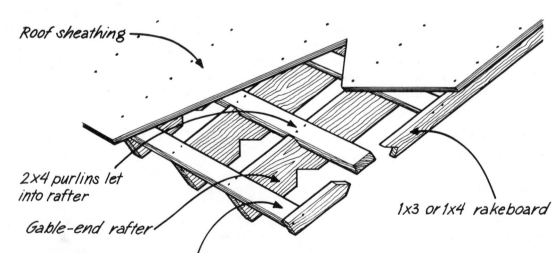

Roof sheathing

2x4 purlins let into rafter

Gable-end rafter

Purlins extend to support gable overhang

1x3 or 1x4 rakeboard

INSTALLING ASPHALT OR FIBERGLASS SHINGLES

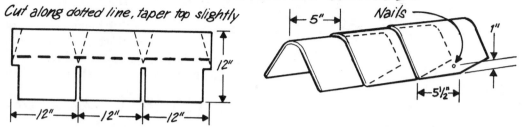

Cut along dotted line, taper top slightly

12"

12" 12" 12"

5" Nails 1"

5½"

To cap the ridge, cut shingles apart and fold individual tabs over ridge

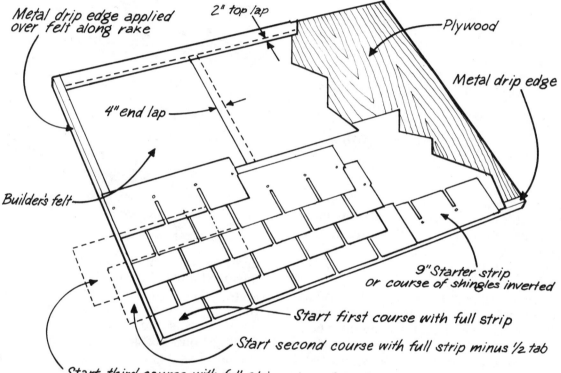

Metal drip edge applied over felt along rake

2" top lap

Plywood

Metal drip edge

4" end lap

Builder's felt

9" Starter strip or course of shingles inverted

Start first course with full strip

Start second course with full strip minus ½ tab

Start third course with full strip minus first tab

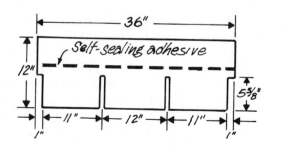

36"

Self-sealing adhesive

12"

5⅝"

11" 12" 11"

1" 1"

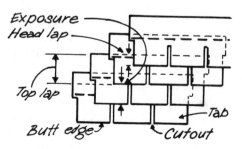

Exposure
Head lap

Top lap

Butt edge

Tab

Cutout

307

APPLYING BUILDER'S FELT

4" side lap

2" top lap

Metal drip edge

Builder's felt

Sheathing

Metal drip edge

messy as roll roofing because you don't need lap cement. The starter course begins at the eaves, and consists of two layers of shingles. The first layer is positioned with the tabs

INSTALLING ROLL ROOFING

Builder's felt

Selvage edge

Nails at edge only

Blind-nail cement

Mineralized surface

Metal drip edge

Blind-nail cement on extra 1/2 lap of roll roofing to start procedure

builder's felt. Along the edges of the roof, metal drip-edge flashing should be installed. This T-profile flashing creates a nice-looking edge trim for the roofing material and also creates a drip edge to keep water away from the edge of the sheathing.

Roll roofing, usually 36 inches wide, is installed in courses, starting at the eaves. The bottom edge and sides of the sheet being applied must be bedded in a generous layer of lap cement. Only the top edge is nailed to the sheathing. This line of nails is covered first with a layer of blind-nail cement; then the bottom edge of the next roll course is bedded over the cement. At the ridge, a "saddle" of roll roofing is cut and applied, covering the top edges of the roofing on both sides of the roof. Here you'll have to use a few roofing nails to anchor the saddle in its cement. Cover all exposed nail heads with a small gob of cement.

Asphalt or fiberglass shingles aren't as

inverted, and the second layer with the tabs in the usual position. The tabs in the second course should then be offset from those in the first course to promote good drainage. This rule holds true for every subsequent course of shingles. For appearance, the tabs in every other course should align vertically. Finish off ridges and hips with an overlapping course of single tabs cut from full-size shingles.

Wood shingles and metal or fiberglass roofing panels don't require solid sheathing. The technique for installing wood shingles is discussed later, as part of several projects. Details for installing metal or fiberglass panels vary, depending on the size and style of the material. Your best bet is to rely on instructions supplied by the particular manufacturer.

PROJECT

GAZEBO

This simple gazebo can be a shady retreat in just about any yard. With the addition of some benches or perhaps a couple of wicker chairs and a small table, this small shelter can convert an empty corner of your yard into a cozy enclave. The materials to build the gazebo are inexpensive, and it's a project that you can finish in a weekend.

Shopping List

4 pcs. 4 × 4 × 10′ pressure-treated pine
2 pcs. 4 × 4 × 12′ construction-grade fir
6 pcs. 2 × 6 × 12′ construction-grade fir
4 pcs. 2 × 6 × 8′ construction-grade fir
8 pcs. 1 × 12 × 8′ #2 pine
100 linear feet of 1 × 2 or 1 × 3 lath strips
32–6″ × ¼″ carriage bolts w/nuts and washers
1 square of red cedar shingles

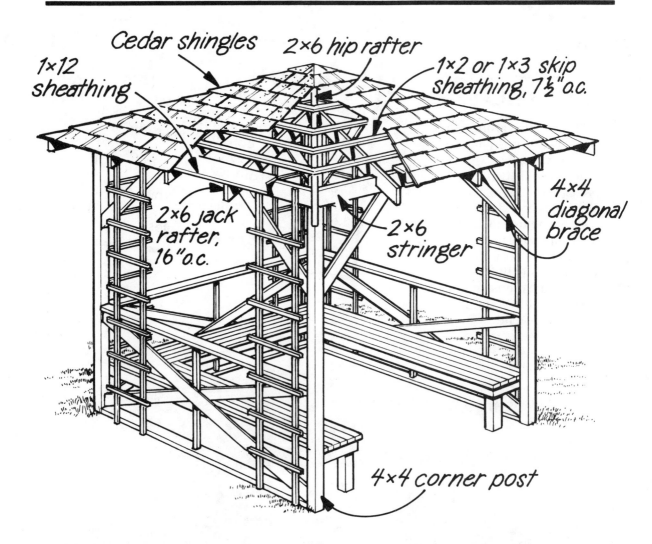

Cedar shingles

1×12 sheathing

2×6 hip rafter

1×2 or 1×3 skip sheathing, 7½" o.c.

2×6 jack rafter, 16" o.c.

4×4 diagonal brace

2×6 stringer

4×4 corner post

Cutting List

Number	Piece	Dimensions	Material
4	Posts	3½″ × 3½″ × 120″	pressure-treated pine
4	Stringers	1½″ × 5½″ × 96″	fir
8	Braces	3½″ × 3½″ × 36″	fir
16	Hip and jack rafters	1½″ × 5½″ × 72″	fir
8	Eaves and hip sheathing	¾″ × 11½″ × 96″	pine
	Skip sheathing strips	¾″ × 1½″ or ¾″ × 2½″	fir

1. Lay out the gazebo. The site you choose for the gazebo should be fairly level and well drained. Using stakes and stringed lines, lay out the locations of your four postholes. This gazebo is a square, and the distance between the outside corners of the posts is 6 feet, 10½ inches.

2. Set, brace, and trim the posts. Make sure you dig holes to a depth below the frost line, and compact 2 to 3 inches of gravel in the bottom of each hole before setting the 4 × 4 posts in place. Use temporary diagonal braces, nailed to the posts and to stakes driven in the ground, to hold each post plumb. Then mark a level line around each post about 8 feet above ground level. Trim the excess from the top of each post with a hand saw.

3. Install the stringers and braces. Instead of plates or beams that rest on top of the posts, this structure is small enough to rely on 2 × 6 stringers to support the roof. Cut the stringers to fit around the outside edges of the posts and flush with their tops; then fasten stringers to posts with 6-inch-long carriage bolts. Next, cut eight 3-foot-long diagonal braces from 4 × 4 stock. Each brace end should be cut at a 45-degree angle. Use carriage bolts to fasten the top end of each brace to its stringer. Where the angled end of the brace meets the post, fasten this joint by driving a 5-inch-long lag screw through the brace and into the post. For appearance as well as strength, counterbore the hex head of the lag screw, and use a washer beneath it.

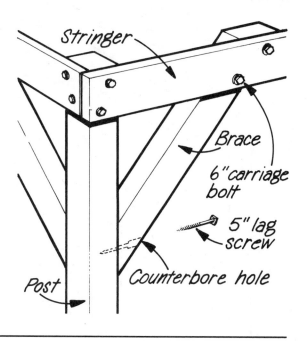

Stringer

Brace

6" carriage bolt

5" lag screw

Counterbore hole

Post

4. Backfill the postholes. As soon as stringers and braces are in place, you should be able to backfill the postholes and remove the temporary braces on the posts. In soft or sandy soil, it might be a good idea to pour concrete around the bases of the posts to help keep them anchored in place.

5. **Frame the roof.** For a hip roof, this one is quite simple to frame. The hip rafters meet at the center of the roof, creating a pyramid shape. To simplify rafter layout, consider opposing hip rafters to be just like opposing common rafters that butt together at the roof peak. The slope of this roof is 4-in-12. Make plumb and seat cuts accordingly, and install first one pair of rafters, then another. Note that the second set of hip rafters will

butt not against each other, but against the already assembled hip pair. So shorten the plumb cut by ¾ inch for each of the second rafters. Rafter tails can be left long and trimmed all at once, after the roof framing is complete. Jack rafters will require a 45-degree-angle cheek cut where they meet the hip rafters. Install them as close to 16 inches on center as possible.

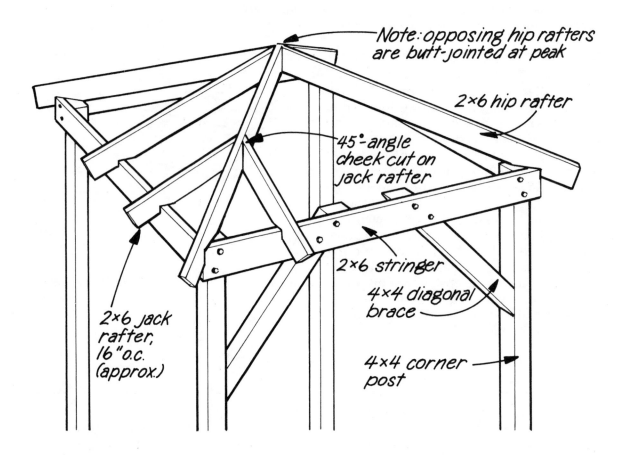

Note: opposing hip rafters are butt-jointed at peak

2×6 hip rafter

45°-angle cheek cut on jack rafter

2×6 stringer

4×4 diagonal brace

4×4 corner post

2×6 jack rafter, 16" o.c. (approx.)

6. Shingle the roof. The cedar shingles on this roof are installed over "skip sheathing," which allows the shingles to "breathe" better than solid sheathing. Skip sheathing is also less expensive. At the eaves, nail down a 1×12 board horizontally across the rafters, its edge overlapping the rafter ends by about 1 inch. Between it and the peak, nail down horizontal 1×2 pine strips on 7½-inch centers.

Shingling a roof is similar to shingling a wall. At the eaves, start with a doubled course that extends about 1 inch past the bottom edge of the 1×12 eaves board. Joints in adjacent courses shouldn't be any closer to each other than 1 inch. At the hips, a cap of "woven" shingles should be installed to guard against water penetration where one roof plane meets another. This detail, shown in the drawing, calls for shingles to overlap alternately where they meet at the hip. A sharp block plane is helpful when "weaving" a hip, because it enables you to trim off just the right amount from the shingles that overlap each other, facilitating a tight fit.

WEAVING CAP SHINGLES AT THE HIP

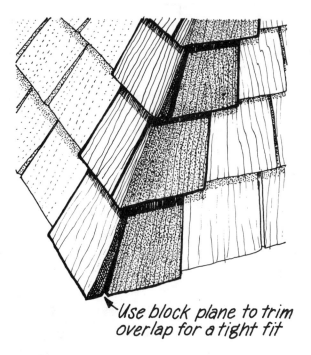

↖ *Use block plane to trim overlap for a tight fit*

7. Finish off the gazebo with personal features. Once the roof is done, you can enjoy the fruits of your labor. For privacy along one or more sides of the gazebo, you can install a lattice screen or combine a screen on the upper half and a railing with balusters below. If grass or bare earth are problems beneath the gazebo, lay a brick or flagstone floor.

PROJECT
SHINGLED GARDEN SHED

Classic detailing sets this shed apart from more plainly finished counterparts that can be bought in kit form at home centers and lumberyards. With its red cedar siding, bay windows, and cross-braced doors, this shed would be right at home on the finest country estate. It can serve as a workshop, as a garden shed, or even as a playhouse. Distinctive features include a hip roof with generous overhangs on all four sides and a pair of bay windows.

And instead of just two doors, this shed has four. The two board-and-batten doors at the center of the shed's front are hinged to a pair of doors that are shingled to masquerade as part of the front wall. This unique design feature gives the shed a versatile personality. It's possible to open just one or two doors; or you can open all four, creating an opening that you can literally drive a tractor through.

It won't take fancy materials or exotic construction techniques to build the shed, but you should recruit the help of a friend for framing and roofing the structure. This is a project to complete over several weekends.

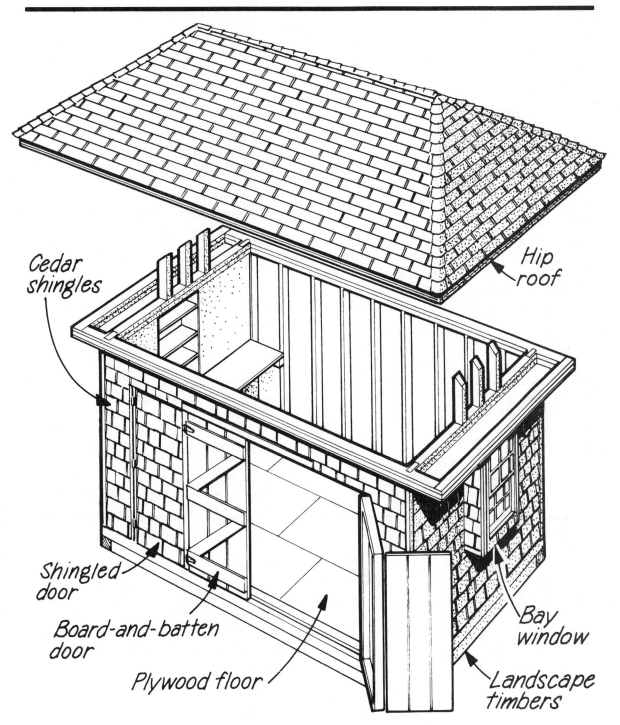

Cedar
shingles

Hip
roof

Shingled
door

Board-and-batten
door

Plywood floor

Bay
window

Landscape
timbers

315

Shopping List

Foundation

4 pcs. 6 × 6 × 12' pressure-treated landscaping ties
4 pcs. 6 × 6 × 10' pressure-treated landscaping ties
12–12" spikes

Floor framing and sheathing

8 pcs. 2 × 6 × 10' pressure-treated
4 sheets ¾" × 4' × 8' exterior-grade plywood
16 joist hangers

Walls and roof

2 pcs. 2 × 12 × 10' (door header)
1 pc. 2 × 8 × 10' (ridgeboard)
4 pcs. 2 × 6 × 10' (hip rafters)
14 pcs. 2 × 6 × 10' (jack rafters)
4 pcs. 2 × 4 × 16' (top plates and extended top plates)
2 pcs. 2 × 4 × 12' (bottom plates)
2 pcs. 2 × 4 × 10' (bottom plates)
4 pcs. 2 × 4 × 10' (soffit plates)
2 pcs. 2 × 4 × 10' (collar ties)
16 pcs. 2 × 4 × 8' (common rafters)

approx. 44 pcs. 2 × 4 × 8' (studs)
60 linear feet of 1 × 3 cedar fascia
21 sheets ½" × 4' × 8' exterior-grade plywood
4 metal tie plates
3½ squares of red cedar shingles
56 feet of metal drip edge
4 squares of roofing felt and asphalt or fiberglass roof shingles

Doors

4 pcs. 2 × 4 × 10' (door stiles and rails)
6 pcs. 1 × 12 × 8' #2 pine
4 pcs. 1 × 6 × 8' #2 pine
3 pcs. 1 × 6 × 6' #2 pine
2 pcs. 1 × 4 × 6' #2 pine
4 pr. 8" tee hinges
6 pr. 4" butt hinges
4 barrel bolt latches
1 thumb latch
2 nylon tack glides

Windows

2–20" × 30" double-hung windows

1 . Construct the foundation. Instead of a conventional sill, this shed rests on a foundation of pressure-treated 6 × 6 landscaping ties. These ties should be placed on a level base. If your local building code permits, a tamped gravel base should be adequate.

Otherwise, you'll have to pour a concrete footing. Depending on how high above grade you want the shed floor to be, lay up 2 to 4 courses of 6 × 6 ties, overlapping the ties at corners and fastening them together with 12-inch spikes.

2. **Frame and sheathe the floor deck.**
Spaced on 16-inch centers, the 2 × 6 joists
are hung inside the uppermost 6 × 6 course,
using joist hangers. Covering the joists and
6 × 6 sill is a floor of ¾-inch exterior-grade
plywood. Once the floor is done, you can use
it as a platform for building the walls.

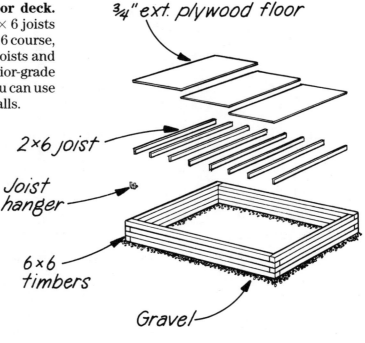

¾" ext. plywood floor

2×6 joist

Joist hanger

6×6 timbers

Gravel

3. **Frame and erect the walls.** The walls
are framed conventionally, except for their
doubled top plates, which extend at the corners of the shed to create an overhang even
with the bay windows (see drawing on page
318).

Working on the floor deck, frame the
back wall first and tilt it up. After nailing its
bottom plate to the floor, brace the framing
plumb and square while you nail up the
plywood sheathing. Follow the same strategy with the two sidewalls. In these walls,
frame only the rough openings for the windows. The window bays are built after the
entire structure is "tight to the weather."

There's not much to the front wall. Use
your straightest studs at the front corners,
and reinforce these two parts of the frame
with blocking. The corners have to be strong
because the weight of the doors will swing
from them. Nail together the built-up header
on the floor, sandwiching a layer of ½-inch
plywood between two 2 × 12s. Assemble
the wall unit, stand it up, and nail it in place.

The final step is to double the top plate
all around the walls. The plates for the front
and back walls extend beyond the sidewalls
to support the soffit plates, which catch the
hip rafters.

FRAMING THE WALLS

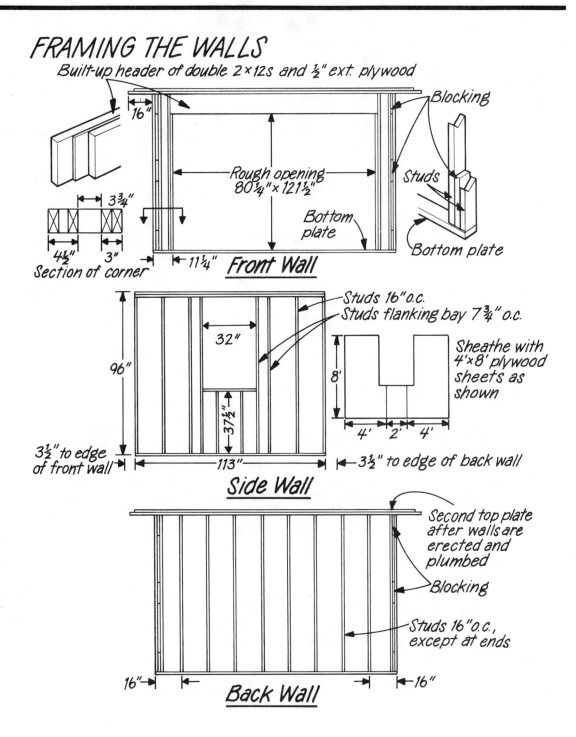

Built-up header of double 2×12s and ½" ext. plywood

16"

Blocking

Rough opening
80¼" × 121½"

Studs

Bottom plate

Bottom plate

3¾"

4½"   3"

Section of corner

11¼"

Front Wall

Studs 16" o.c.
Studs flanking bay 7¾" o.c.

32"

96"

37½"

Sheathe with
4'×8' plywood
sheets as
shown

8'

4'   2'   4'

3½" to edge
of front wall

113"

3½" to edge of back wall

Side Wall

Second top plate
after walls are
erected and
plumbed

Blocking

Studs 16" o.c.,
except at ends

16"

16"

Back Wall

4. **Complete the walls by building the window bays.** Nail a 1 × 2 soffit nailer to the sidewall studs, then nail the ½-inch plywood soffit to it and the underside of the soffit plates.

Frame the two window bays in place using 2 × 4s and ¾-inch plywood. Cut and notch the plywood bay sides, fit them into place in the rough opening, and nail them to the trimmer studs. Cut and nail a frame of 2 × 2 stock to the plywood sill and nail that assembly in place. Using 2 × 4s, frame out the bay to accommodate the double-hung windows you've purchased. Sheathe the end of the bay as necessary. The bays help support the soffits.

Install the double-hung window units and trim them out.

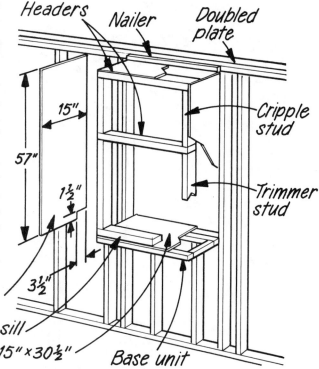

Headers Nailer Doubled plate

15"

57"

1½"

3½"

Cripple stud

Trimmer stud

Plywood bay side, 15" × 57"

Rough sill

Plywood sill, 15" × 30½"

Base unit

5. **Frame the roof.** The hip roof is a little trickier to frame than a simple shed or gable roof. Note in the detail drawings that the common rafters have a 6-in-12 pitch, while the hip rafters have a 12-in-12 pitch. This means that the plumb-cut angle for common rafters will be 22½ degrees, while the plumb-cut angle for hip and jack rafters will be 45 degrees.

Before laying out plumb and seat cuts on your rafters, cut and position the 2 × 6 ridgeboard. With your tape measure, a plumb bob, a level, and some temporary braces, prop up the ridgeboard in its final position: level, exactly centered between all top plates, and 30 inches above them. The diagonal measurement between one bottom corner

of the ridge and the nearest corner of a top plate should be very close to 64 inches. This is the distance to measure between the rafter's plumb cut and seat cut. Cut one common rafter completely, including plumb and seat cuts as well as plumb and level cuts at the rafter tail (overhang is 16 inches, as shown in the detail drawing). Then use this rafter as a pattern to cut the remaining commons.

As soon as a pair of common rafters has been installed at each end of the ridge, you can remove the temporary braces and install the remaining common rafters. Measure, cut, and install the two hip jack rafters next. These are the rafters that line up exactly with the ridge, with their 45-degree plumb

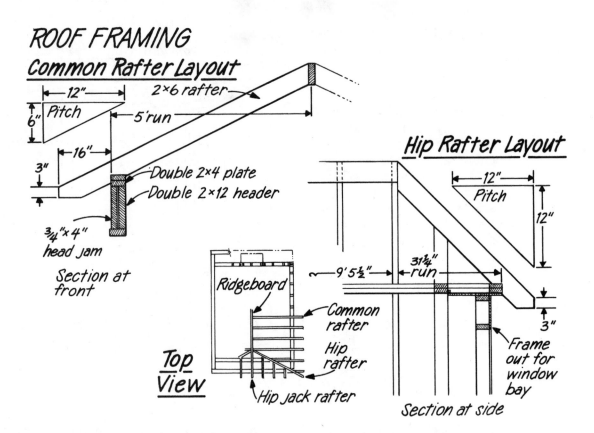

ROOF FRAMING
Common Rafter Layout

12"

Pitch

6"

2×6 rafter

5' run

16"

3"

Double 2×4 plate

Double 2×12 header

¾"×4" head jam

Section at front

Hip Rafter Layout

12"

Pitch

12"

3¼" run

9'5½"

3"

Frame out for window bay

Section at side

Ridgeboard

Common rafter

Hip rafter

__Top__ __View__

Hip jack rafter

cuts butting against the two ends of the ridgeboard. To assure an even overhang along the eaves, it's smart to let the rafter tails of all hip and jack rafters run long. After the roof framing is complete, you can snap a line at the corners and ends of the roof to show the exact cutoff point for each rafter tail.

The hip rafters are installed next. These are the most difficult rafters to cut, because a pair of angled cheek cuts is required to make the hip rafter join snugly against the hip jack rafter and the last common rafter. The jack rafters are installed last, and require only one angled cheek cut where they join hip rafters.

6. Sheathe and shingle the roof. It's good policy to sheathe and shingle the roof as soon as it's framed up. This puts a lid on your structure, and ensures that most of the interior will stay dry in spite of the weather.

Use the same ½-inch exterior plywood to sheathe the roof as was used to sheathe the walls. Nail a 1 × 3 fascia to the rafter ends. Install the metal drip edge, then apply roofing felt to the roof. Finally, shingle the roof with asphalt or fiberglass shingles, following the manufacturer's directions.

7. **Shingle the shed.** After trimming out door and window openings, you can start shingling. The overlap, or "exposure" used in shingling this shed is 5 inches. If you haven't installed shingle siding before, start out on the back of the shed. The first course of shingles is doubled, with shingle butts overlapping the bottom edge of the wall sheathing just slightly (¼ to ½ inch). Subsequent courses can be lined up by snapping a chalk line or tacking up a guide strip. Make sure that joints in adjacent courses aren't any closer to each other than 1 inch.

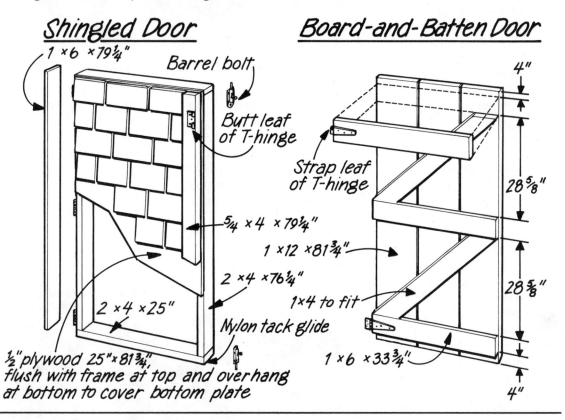

Shingled Door

1 × 6 × 79¼"

Barrel bolt

Butt leaf of T-hinge

⁵⁄₄ × 4 × 79¼"

2 × 4 × 76¼"

2 × 4 × 25"

Nylon tack glide

½"plywood 25" × 81¾", flush with frame at top and overhang at bottom to cover bottom plate

Board-and-Batten Door

4"

Strap leaf of T-hinge

1 × 12 × 81¾"

28⅝"

1 × 4 to fit

28⅝"

1 × 6 × 33¾"

4"

8. **Build and hang the doors.** The secondary doors are actually framed like walls, with 2 × 4s. Attach a 1 × 6 board to the hinge side of each door, and sheathe the doors with ½-inch plywood. The primary doors are simple cross-braced, board-and-batten-style doors made with 1 × 12 boards and 1 × 4 braces.

Give the secondary doors the same shingle treatment as the walls, then hinge them to the side jambs using three 4-inch butt hinges per door. A nylon tack glide, installed at the bottom corner of the door frame, will allow the weight of the door to bear on the floor when the door is closed, instead of on the hinges and wall framing.

PROJECT
GARDEN BRIDGE

The gracefully curved form of this garden bridge not only looks good but it lends greater strength and resilience to the bridge structure. Both the beams and the handrails are laminated from ¾-inch-thick cedar boards.

What is so marvelous about this project is the clever way in which the builders solved the biggest problem in lamination work: the need for a zillion clamps. Using an easily built jig, Fred Matlack and Phil Gehret of Rodale's Design Center substituted fasteners for clamps. They bolted the first ply of the lamination to the jig using tee nuts instead of machine nuts. In the process, the curve was introduced. Subsequent layers were added using galvanized all-purpose screws—designed to be driven without pilot holes using a power screwdriver—to draw each additional ply tightly to the lamination.

The bridge shown is 16 feet long, but you can use the same construction tech-niques discussed here to build a bridge slightly longer or shorter.

It is a fairly large-scale outdoor project that lends itself to winter weekends. Spend one weekend setting up the jig and experimenting with the lamination process, perhaps by building one or both of the handrails. The next weekend, you can build one beam, and so on. By the time spring arrives, you've got the bridge components ready for final assembly outdoors.

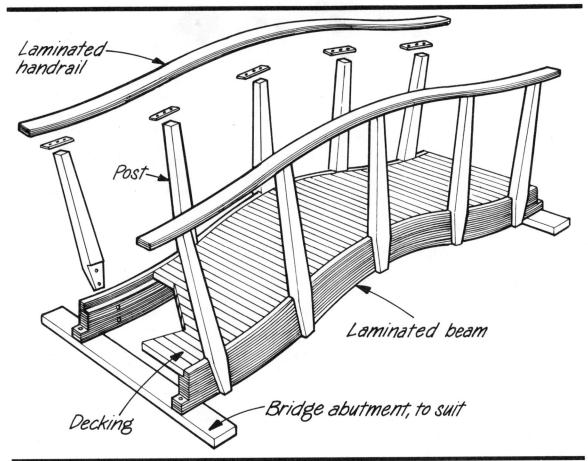

Laminated handrail

Post

Laminated beam

Decking

Bridge abutment, to suit

Cutting List
(For the laminating jig)

Number	Piece	Dimensions	Material
2	Stretchers	1½″ × 3½″ × 192″	fir
3	Plates	¾″ × 6″ × 48″	plywood
13	Blocks	¾″ × 3″ × 6″	plywood

(For the bridge)

Number	Piece	Dimensions	Material
24	Wide plies	¾″ × 3½″ × 192″	clear cedar
4	Narrow plies	¾″ × 1½″ × 192″	clear cedar
8	Handrail plies	¾″ × 5½″ × 192″	clear cedar
10	Posts	3½″ × 3½″ × 36″	cedar
50	Decking boards	1½″ × 5½″ × 40″	cedar

Shopping List

Laminating jig

2 pcs. $2 \times 4 \times 16'$ construction-grade fir
3 pcs. $\frac{3}{4} \times 6 \times 48''$ plywood
assorted blocks
2–$1\frac{1}{2}'' \times \frac{3}{8}''$ hex-head bolts w/washers
8–$\frac{3}{8}''$ tee nuts

Bridge

10 pcs. $4 \times 4 \times 3'$ cedar
50 pcs. $2 \times 4 \times 40''$ cedar decking
8 pcs. $1 \times 6 \times 16'$ clear cedar
24 pcs. $1 \times 4 \times 16'$ clear cedar
4 pcs. $1 \times 2 \times 16'$ clear cedar
10 pcs. steel plate $\frac{1}{8}'' \times 1'' \times 6''$
200–$2\frac{1}{2}''$ galvanized all-purpose
   screws
approx. 1,000 $1\frac{1}{4}''$ galvanized all-
   purpose screws
20–$5'' \times \frac{3}{8}''$ lag bolts w/washers
resorcinol or other waterproof glue

1. Construct the laminating jig. The first step in building the bridge is to make the laminating jig from a pair of straight 16-foot-long 2×4s and several lengths of ¾-inch plywood. Screw three pieces of plywood across the top edges of the 2×4s as shown in the drawing. Then put together enough layers of blocking to achieve the desired height of the curve at the center of the bridge (this bridge curves up about 10 inches). Screw the spacer block to the center piece of plywood.

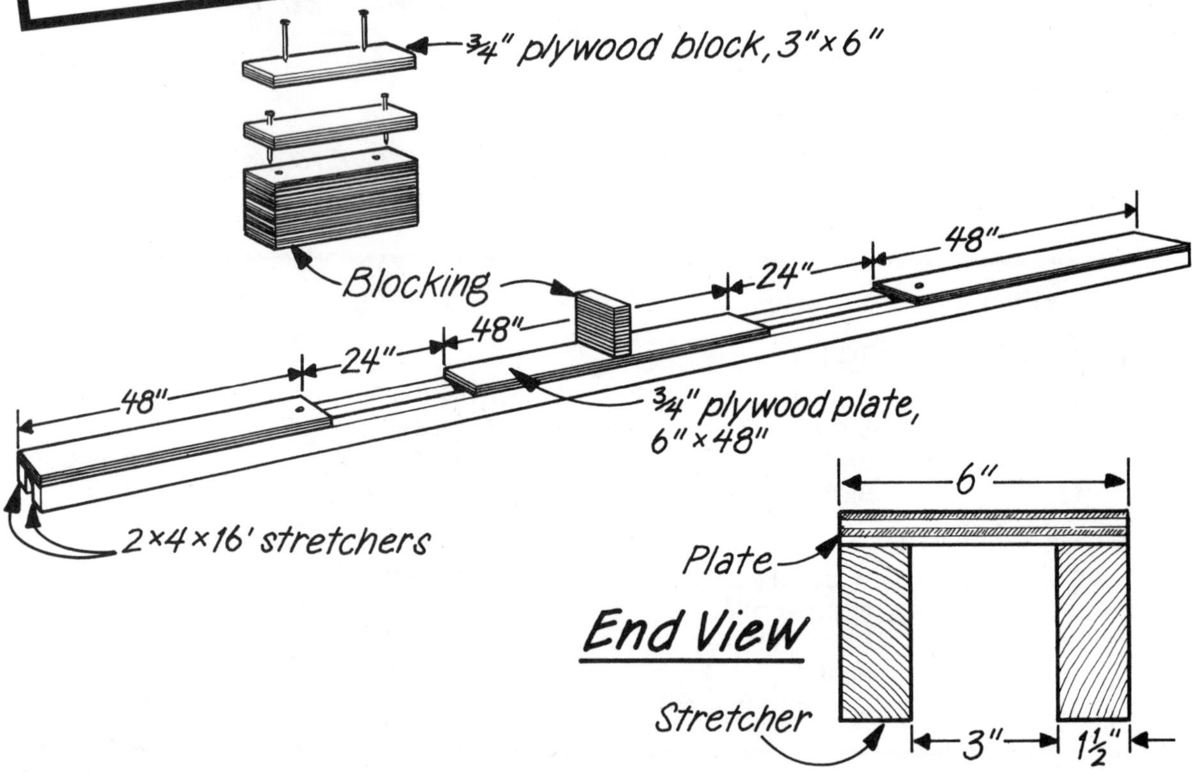

¾" plywood block, 3" × 6"

Blocking

¾" plywood plate, 6" × 48"

48" 24" 48" 24" 48"

2×4×16' stretchers

6"

Plate

End View

Stretcher

3" 1½"

2. **Mount the first ply of the lamination on the jig.** Clamp the bottom 1 × 4 ply of the lamination along the full length of the jig and drill two holes through the 1 × 4 and plywood, about 3 feet from each end of the jig. Now remove the 1 × 4 and use it as a template to drill a pair of holes in the base ply of the second laminated beam, as well as the base plies of the two handrails.

Mount one of the base plies on the jig by installing a tee nut in each hole and screwing into the tee nut from the underside of the plywood.

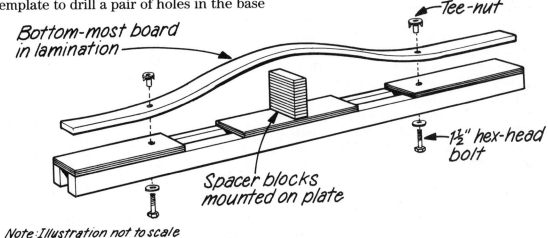

Tee-nut

Bottom-most board in lamination

1½" hex-head bolt

Spacer blocks mounted on plate

Note: Illustration not to scale

3. **Build up the lamination.** Brush the upper face of the 1 × 4 with glue, and screw down the second 1 × 4 lamination with 1¼-inch all-purpose screws. Drive enough screws to pull the 1 × 4 down against its neighboring 1 × 4. Repeat this operation for subsequent plies. To reduce the need for sanding the finished beam, keep the 1 × 4s flush on at least one side, and wipe off glue squeeze-out with a damp rag.

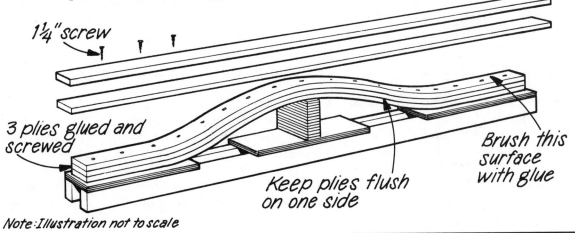

1¼" screw

3 plies glued and screwed

Keep plies flush on one side

Brush this surface with glue

Note: Illustration not to scale

325

4. Finish the lamination. After 12 plies of 1 × 4 have been built up, attach two layers of 1 × 2 cedar to create a ledge for installing the 2 × 6 decking. Give the glue a chance to dry thoroughly before unbolting the beam.

Repeat this technique to make the second beam and the two handrails. Use a belt sander and medium-grit sanding belt to smooth all the laminations. With a router and ¾-inch round-over bit, round over the edges of both rails and the outer edges of the beams.

5. Make the posts. To make the posts, start with 36-inch-long 4 × 4s. Taper each post at both ends, as shown, then mark a half-lap where the post will join the bridge.

After laying out the tapers and the half-lap, cut the tapers on a band saw.

Cut the lower end of the post first, then the upper end. Finally, cut a lap joint where the post will be lag-bolted to the beam.

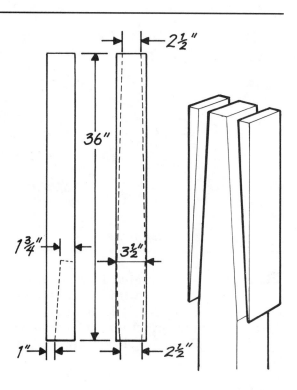

6. Prepare the bridge abutments. Prepare suitable abutments on both sides of the stream where the bridge will be anchored. Landscaping ties or concrete piers will work, as long as they are securely in place. For maximum stability, avoid positioning abutments directly at the edge of the stream bank, where they can be exposed to erosion during heavy water flow. For appearance as well as strength, abutments are best when they're out of sight, nearly buried in firm ground well away from the water's edge.

7. **Assemble the bridge in place.** Mount the two bridge beams on the abutments, then fasten the decking in place. Each 2 × 4 decking board is screwed to the beams using four 2½-inch galvanized all-purpose screws, driven in pilot holes. Allow for a ¼-inch space between boards. (The decking can be installed before anchoring the bridge to its abutments, but this makes it much heavier and unwieldy.)

When the decking is down, install the posts and railings. Instead of screwing through the top of the railing and into the post, screw a steel plate to each post top; then fasten the plate to the railing from underneath. For a really first-rate job, the plates can be mortised into the railings.

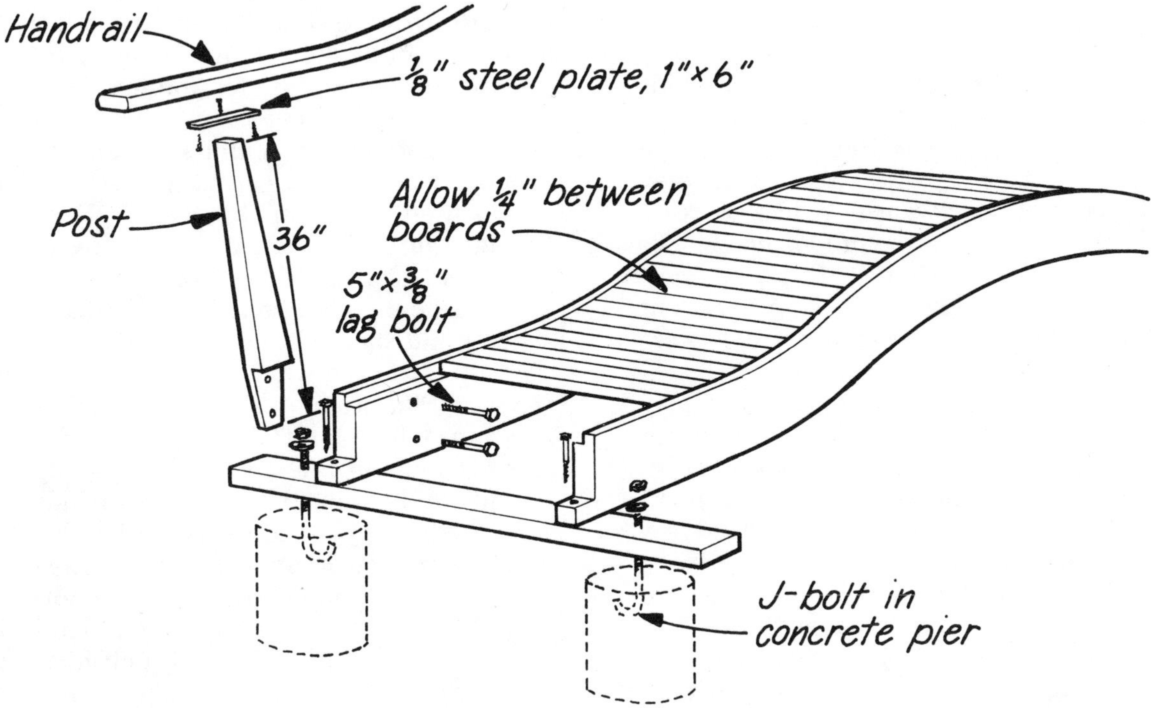

Handrail

⅛" steel plate, 1"× 6"

Post

36"

Allow ¼" between boards

5"× ⅜" lag bolt

J-bolt in concrete pier

Play Structures

It's hard to decide who gets the most fun from a play structure, the builder or the kids. Here's a great chance to get the creative design juices flowing. You'll want to follow the design safety guidelines listed here and your own common sense, but beyond that, there are no rules for what a play structure should be.

Of course, to a large extent, a play structure should be what your kids want, so they'll use it. A good way to begin designing in your head is to take the kids to a park and see what they like. You may want to read a book on the subject—*Home Playgrounds, The Harrowsmith Guide to Building Backyard Play Structures* is an excellent one. Playground equipment catalogs are another good source of ideas.

But there's no reason your play structure can't have some flourish just to make it nice for *you* to look at, especially if your plans include a playhouse. Maybe you've always thought houses with scalloped fascia boards at the eaves look really neat. You may never get to build a full-scale house with that feature, but on a playhouse it's just a few cuts on a few boards. It won't matter to the kids whether you do it or not; they'll fantasize whatever you build into the rustic log fort they wanted. So indulge your own fantasy a bit, and make those scalloped fascia.

• Swings should be at least 30 inches away from other swings and support members.

• Slides should be about 4 feet high for toddlers; about 7 feet high for school-age children. Slides should slope no more than about 30 degrees, and they should level out at the bottom. The bottom of the slide should be about 9 inches from the ground for primary-grade children, less for younger kids, more for older kids.

• Ladder rungs and steps should be at least 9 inches apart so kids can't get their heads stuck between them. Make sure adults can get to any area of the play structure in case of emergency. Rungs should be ¾ to 1½ inches in diameter and should be pinned in place so they can't turn when grasped.

• Platforms should be no higher than 4 feet for toddlers, 5 feet for preschoolers, 8 feet for primary-grade kids, and 10 feet for adolescents. If kids of various ages will be using the play structure, make high platforms accessible only to older kids by using knotted ropes or some other more difficult climbing method. Use 30-inch-high guardrails for platforms more than 2 feet high.

• Countersink bolts and smooth all wooden surfaces children will be in contact with.

PROJECT

PLAY STRUCTURE

For the true backyard adventure, you need more than just swings and slides. When Rodale craftsmen Fred Matlack and Phil Gehret set out to design a play structure, they were asked to come up with something a little bit out of the ordinary. And they did.

Instead of a straight slide, this one has a roller-coaster slide with humps and slumps to make the ride more fun. A two-level enclosure (a fort to the kids) is topped off with a bright fabric roof and a sliding pole. Of course, there's a sandbox. And a yellow nylon climbing net is a feature that's both fun and challenging.

Apart from the fun, the best thing about this play structure is that you can build it yourself, either all at once or in sections. The central tower and slide form the play structure's core, and they need to be built first. (You don't *have* to include the slide when you erect the tower, but it will be difficult to add the slide later.) Once the core is up,

you can add the swing extension, the ladder and chinning-bar extension, or both.

The structure is built primarily of pressure-treated wood, which is economical and decay and insect resistant. Unfortunately, pressure-treated pine is fairly prone to "throw splinters" as it

(continued on page 332)

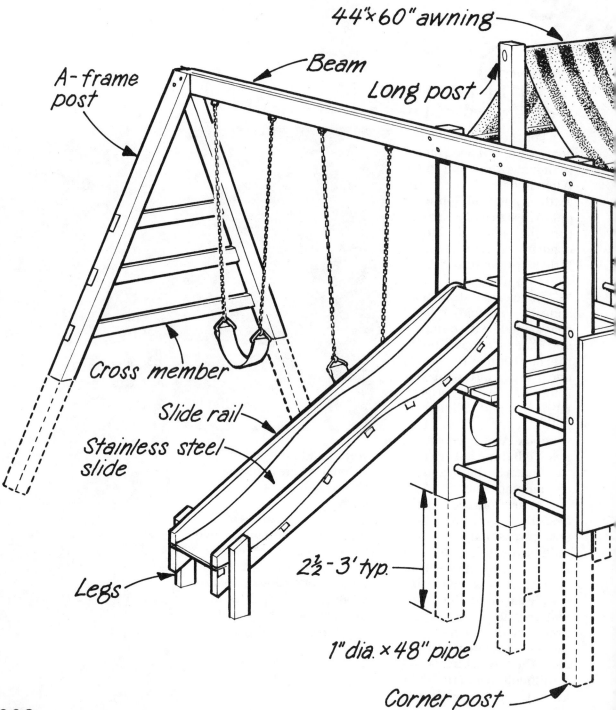

44"x 60" awning

Beam

Long post

A-frame post

Cross member

Slide rail

Stainless steel slide

Legs

2½ - 3' typ.

1" dia. x 48" pipe

Corner post

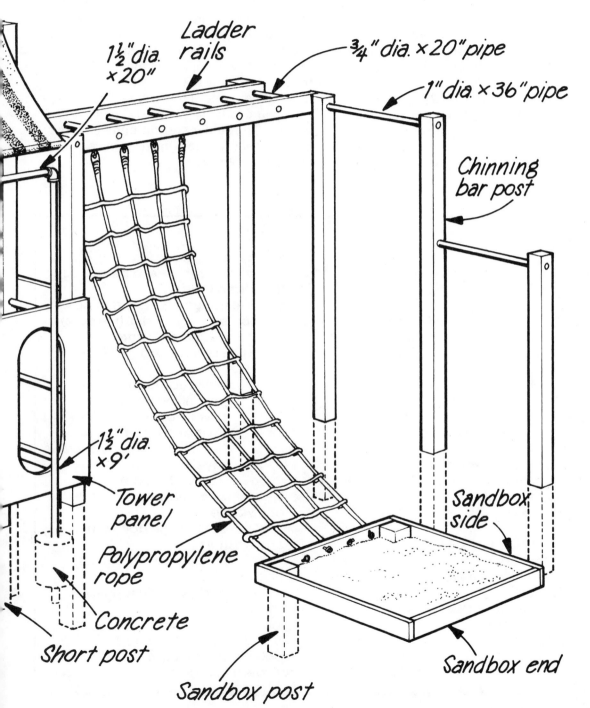

Ladder rails

1½" dia. ×20"

¾" dia. ×20" pipe

1" dia. ×36" pipe

Chinning bar post

1½" dia. ×9'

Tower panel

Polypropylene rope

Concrete

Short post

Sandbox side

Sandbox end

Sandbox post

weathers, and the chemicals used in the treatments can cause infections. The surfaces children will touch, therefore, are made of redwood. The redwood is less likely to splinter with weathering. This is particularly important for areas such as the slide, where little hands will slide along the wood. For further protection against splinters, round over the edges of all the lumber with a router or a block plane and coat the slide rails with exterior, spar, or marine spar varnish.

The design's right-angle configuration and the plywood panels on the tower combine to provide ample racking resistance, so it isn't absolutely necessary to set the tower posts in concrete. The swing's A-brace legs are meant to be set at least 2 feet into the ground. The ladder and chinning-bar posts, because they lack racking resistance, should be set in concrete.

Shopping List

2 pcs. 4 × 4 × 12' pressure-treated pine
8 pcs. 4 × 4 × 10' pressure-treated pine
3 pcs. 4 × 4 × 6' pressure-treated pine
2 pcs. 2 × 6 × 16' pressure-treated pine
1 pc. 2 × 2 × 10' pressure-treated pine
1 pc. 2 × 2 × 8' pressure-treated pine
1 pc. 1 × 10 × 4' pine
approx. 18' of ¼ × ¾" pine
4 pcs. 2 × 10 × 8' redwood
4 pcs. 2 × 6 × 8' redwood
1 pc. 2 × 4 × 10' redwood
3 pcs. 2 × 4 × 8' redwood
2 pcs. 1 × 6 × 10' redwood
2 sheets ¾" × 4' × 8' exterior-grade plywood
1 sheet ¼" × 4' × 4' exterior-grade plywood
1 pc. galvanized steel pipe 1½" dia. × 20" (fire pole)
1 pc. galvanized steel pipe 1½" dia. × 9' (fire pole)
11 pcs. galvanized steel pipe 1" dia. × 48" (tower)
2 pcs. galvanized steel pipe 1" dia. × 24" (tower)
2 pcs. galvanized steel pipe 1" dia. × 36" (chinning bar)
7 pcs. galvanized steel pipe ¾" dia. × 20" (hand ladder)
1 pc. pipe flange 1½" dia. (fire pole)
1 pc. pipe elbow 1½" dia. (fire pole)
2 pcs. swings and hardware
1 pc. stainless steel .018" × 18" × 96" (slide)
#8 × 3" galvanized wood screws
#8 × 2½" galvanized wood screws
#8 × 1¼" galvanized wood screws
#8 × ¾" galvanized wood screws
#8 × ¾" roundhead brass wood screws
5-3" × 5/16" eyebolts
8-9" × 5/16" lag bolts (slide)
6-6½" × 5/16" carriage bolts w/nuts and washers
4-3½" × 5/16" carriage bolts w/nuts and washers
17-3" × 5/16" carriage bolts w/nuts and washers
9 pcs. heavy-duty chain repair link
1 pc. of canvas 50" × 10'
concrete
100 feet of ½" dia. braided polypropylene rope
activated fiberglass resin

333

Tower and Slide

Cutting List

Number	Piece	Dimensions	Material
2	Long posts	3½″ × 3½″ × 144″	pressure-treated pine
4	Corner posts	3½″ × 3½″ × 120″	pressure-treated pine
2	Short posts	3½″ × 3½″ × 72″	pressure-treated pine
2	Slide rails	1½″ × 9¼″ × 96″	redwood
1	Slide deck	¼″ × 18″ × 96″	plywood
9	Slide supports	1½″ × 1½″ × 19½″	pressure-treated pine
2	Legs	1½″ × 3½″ × 10″	redwood
2	Deck boards	1½″ × 3½″ × 51½″	redwood
4	Deck boards	1½″ × 9¼″ × 51½″	redwood
4	Deck battens	1½″ × 3½″ × 19″	redwood
3	Panels	¾″ × 48″ × 48″	plywood

1. **Lay out and dig postholes.** Lay out eight holes on 2-foot centers, forming a 4-foot square. Dig six of the postholes 30 inches deep. Should you hit an obstruction, one or two of the holes could be shallower, so long as the footing is good. The holes for the two short posts need only be dug 20 inches deep. This allows the use of 6-foot posts.

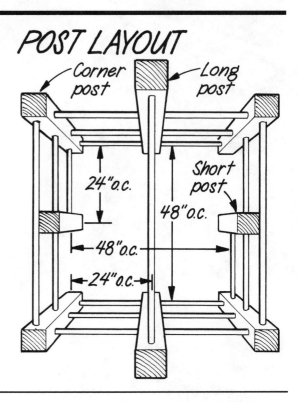

POST LAYOUT

Corner post

Long post

Short post

24″o.c.

48″o.c.

48″o.c.

24″o.c.

2. **Lay out and drill the pipe holes in the posts.** The tower is an assembly of posts and galvanized steel pipes. Most of the pipes must be driven through holes drilled in three posts, so the holes must be very carefully lined up. If a single hole is low or high, the tower may not go together.

To lay out the holes, assign a post to each hole; 10-footers in the corners and the 6-footers and 12-footers opposite each other. Put each post in its hole, plumb it up, and temporarily brace it in place. Lay out the lowest set of holes. While you want the lowest steel bars to be about 5½ inches above grade, it's more important that the bars be level. Select one of the eight posts as the base, preferably the one set in the lowest spot. All the others will be marked in relation to this post. Transfer the hole location to the other seven posts by stretching a string around the eight posts. Line it up on the centerpoint for the hole, and attach a line level to it. Adjust the line until it is level. It delineates the height of the lowest hole in each post. The remaining holes in each post are laid out from this point, as shown.

Remove the posts from the postholes to drill the holes. A drill press is the ideal tool for drilling the holes, since it will ensure that the holes are square.

Trim off each post 2 inches above its top hole.

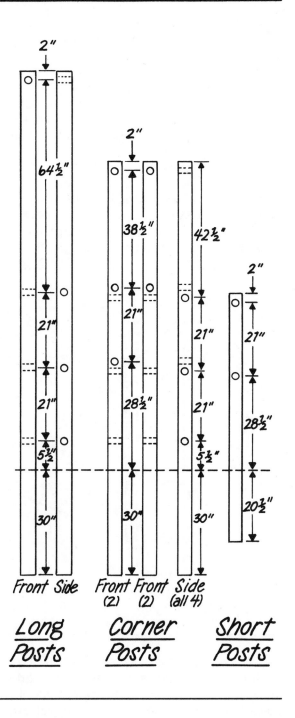

Long Posts — Front, Side

Corner Posts — Front (2), Front (2), Side (all 4)

Short Posts

3. **Cut and shape the slide rails.** If you plan to include the slide with the tower, it must be built next so it can be installed as you assemble the posts and pipes.

Select the redwood boards for the rails. With the pieces clamped together, drill holes for the pipe that will attach the slide to the tower.

On the ends of the rails that attach to the tower, scribe 2-inch radii on the corners. With a pencil and working freehand, lay out the contour of the slide on the side of one rail. Don't let the line come closer than 2 inches from the top or bottom edge of the

board. And make sure the curve levels out at what will be the bottom. When you like the contour, cut along the line with a saber saw. Cut off the two corners you marked, too. Using one of the resulting pieces as a template, scribe the curve onto the other board, and cut that board in two.

Finally, use a piloted rabbeting bit to cut a ¼-inch wide, ¾-inch deep rabbet along the contour of what will be the top segment of the rails. The router should bear on the inside face of the rail, and you should make several passes, cutting slightly deeper with each pass.

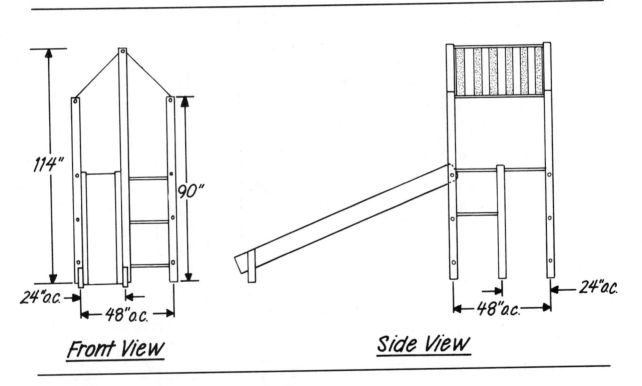

Front View

Side View

4. **Make and install the slide deck.** Use stainless steel for the surface of the slide deck. Don't substitute aluminum, for example, because it is much softer than the steel and

will get nicked, scratched, and dented quickly. Worse, it will leave black smudges on hands and legs and clothing.

Have the steel cut to size where you

SLIDE RAIL LAYOUT

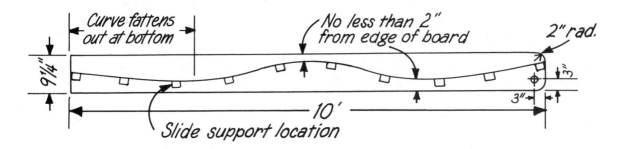

Curve fattens out at bottom

No less than 2" from edge of board

2" rad.

9¼"

Slide support location

10'

3"

3"

buy it. Make sure it is a couple of inches longer than the plywood so you can fold it over on both ends.

Cut the plywood and apply the stainless steel. Install the deck, sandwiching the steel between the plywood and the rabbets. Drive 1¼-inch galvanized screws into pilot holes drilled through the plywood and steel

and into the rails.

The slide deck is pretty stiff. The easiest way to accomplish the assembly job is to set the rails on the edge, lay the deck into place, then stand on it as you work. Screw down one end, then work your way toward the other end. Your weight will force the deck into the rabbets.

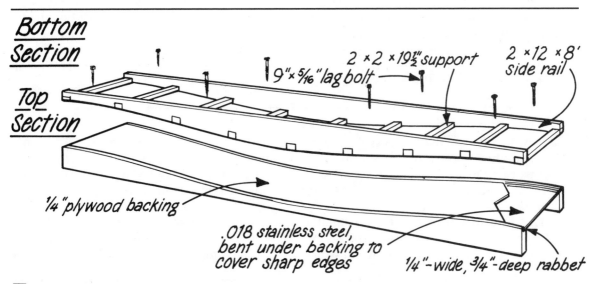

Bottom Section

Top Section

2 × 2 × 19½"support

9" × ⁵⁄₁₆" lag bolt

2 × 12 × 8' side rail

¼"plywood backing

.018 stainless steel, bent under backing to cover sharp edges

¼"-wide, ¾"-deep rabbet

**5.** **Assemble and install the slide bottom.** There are nine supports for the slide deck.

Cut them from 2 × 2 stock.

On one of the rail bottom segments, lay

out notches for the 2×2 supports. The exact locations of the supports are not critical, but there should be one at each end and they should be evenly spaced. Trace around a 2×2 scrap to lay out the notches. Cut them with a saber saw, then use that rail as a template to lay out the second one. After the second rail is notched, install the supports with 2½-inch galvanized screws.

Set the slide bottom assembly in place on the slide deck. Use 9-inch-long, 5/16-inch lag bolts, four in each rail, to fasten them together. Locate the bolts where they will get sufficient penetration into the top rail segment. Drill pilot holes and drive the bolts.

6. **Cut the pipe and assemble the tower.** You need 11 pieces of galvanized pipe, each 48 inches long. Cut the pipe, then begin the assembly process. As you mate the pipes and posts, you will set the posts and erect the tower.

Begin with one of the long posts on the ground. Slide pipes through the lower three holes in it, until the post is centered on the pipes. Next, fit the slide onto the appropriate pipe. Be sure it is aligned so it will be right side up when the posts are erected. With the post still on the ground, slide the pipes about halfway through the corresponding holes in the corner posts. Finally, erect the side, setting the posts in their holes and backfilling enough dirt to hold them up.

If for any reason, the pipes and holes don't quite line up, you may have to use force. If you can flex the pipe a bit and get it aligned with its hole, you can use a sledgehammer to drive it through the hole. Don't hit the end of the pipe directly. Protect it with a scrap of wood. Have one or two helpers stand on the post to immobilize it as a third worker wields the sledgehammer.

Repeat the process to assemble and set up the second side.

Slide a pipe through each short post, stand the short posts in their holes, and fit the pipes into their holes in the corner posts. Now slide pipes into the top holes in the posts. Slide the two short posts into place last.

After all the pipes are in place, plumb the posts and level the pipe rails. Backfill the remaining dirt.

7. **Pin the pipes with screws.** The pipes must be pinned to prevent them from turning or working loose. Use 3-inch galvanized wood screws driven through the posts into the pipes.

This is a little tricky, since too small a pilot hole in the pipe will break the screw and too large a pilot hole in the wood won't allow the screw any purchase. Experiment with a scrap of pipe to find a hole size that will allow the screw to engage the pipe without breaking. Drill through each post and pipe but stop as soon as you feel the bit go through both sides of the pipe. Now when you insert the screw it will penetrate the pipe, then self-tap into the wood on the other side.

8. **Cut and attach the slide's bottom legs.** Cut the legs, position them at the bottom of the slide, and raise the bottom until the lip of the slide surface is 11 inches from the ground. Tack the legs in place to hold the end of the slide at that height. Then drill through the legs and the slide bottom for two carriage bolts on each side. Install the bolts. There is no need to anchor the legs in the ground because the slide is so securely fastened to the tower. This will allow you to lift the end of the slide to mow under it.

9. **Build the two tower decks.** Cut the six deck boards. Place three in position across the bars, with a narrow board between two wide ones, and a ⅛-inch gap between boards. Cut the battens and clamp them under the boards, snug against the bars. Screw up through the battens into the boards. Constructed this way, the deck will be stable, but kids can move it to a different position in the tower.

Repeat the process to construct the second deck.

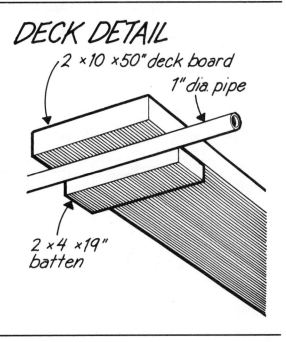

DECK DETAIL
2 × 10 × 50" deck board
1" dia. pipe
2 × 4 × 19" batten

10. **Cut and attach the panels.** Cut the three panels from ¾-inch exterior plywood. Attach one panel opposite the slide using 1¼-inch galvanized screws.

The panels on the ends have peek holes. One has two 16-inch-diameter circular holes, the other an oval-like hole that's 16 inches wide and 36 inches long. Lay out these holes, then cut them out with a saber saw. Attach the panels with screws.

11. **Cut the awning to fit and install it.** Drape the canvas over the bars and cut it to fit. Be sure you allow enough excess to wrap around the bars at either end. Install snaps or sew hook-and-loop tape to the ends of the canvas, so the awning can be removed seasonally or for cleaning.

Swing Extension

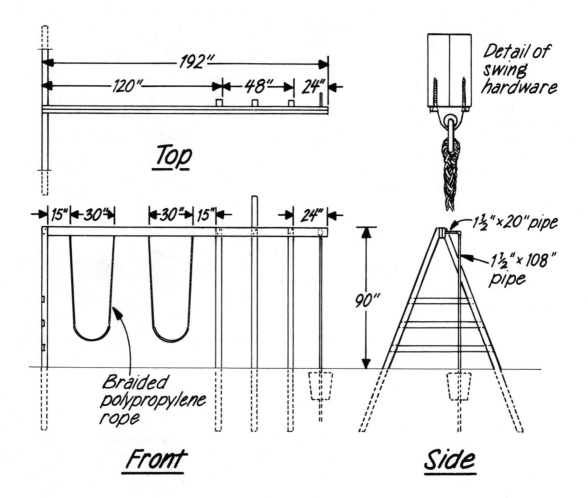

Top

Detail of swing hardware

15" 30" 30" 15" 24"

90"

1½" × 20" pipe

1½" × 108" pipe

Braided polypropylene rope

Front

Side

Cutting List

Number	Piece	Dimensions	Material
2	Beam	1½ × 5½ × 192"	pressure-treated pine
2	A-frame posts	3½" × 3½" × 120"	pressure-treated pine
3	Cross members	1½" × 3½" × variable	redwood

1. Assemble the beam. With the crowns in the same direction, tack the two 2 × 6s together with a few nails. Drill ½-inch holes through both pieces at intervals of one foot, alternating between high and low holes. Counterbore one side so you can countersink the nut when you assemble the beam with 3-inch carriage bolts. After bolting the assembly together, saw the bolts flush with the nuts to prevent injuries.

2. Install the beam. Hoist the beam into place across three posts, as shown, leaving a 24-inch cantilever for the fireman's pole. Drive a nail through it into one post, then level it, using the nail as a pivot point. When it is level, drive a second nail into a second post.

At each post, drill two holes through the beam and the post. Drill counterbores for the nuts in the beam. Fasten the beam to the posts with 6½-inch carriage bolts. Again, saw the bolts flush with the nuts.

3. Dig A-frame postholes. Ordinarily, a swing set should be set in concrete. But this swing set has one end attached to the tower, which is so firmly fixed and rack resistant that there is no need to set the A-frame posts in concrete. Set the posts into the ground, but backfill with soil.

Drop a plumb line from the end of the beam. Your posthole locations will be 36 inches to either side of where the plumb line meets the ground. The holes will be about 2 feet deep. You can try to dig them at the angle the posts will enter, but most likely you'll just have to dig a wider hole.

4. Build and install the A-frame. Set the 10-foot A-frame posts in the holes and scribe notches where they meet the beam. Cut the notches and fasten the posts to the beam with carriage bolts. Drill counterbores for the nuts and saw the bolts flush with the nuts after assembly.

Backfill the postholes, tamping each layer of dirt firmly.

Install the cross braces next. While the A-frame doesn't need three—one would do structurally—using three makes another place for kids to climb. The cross braces are positioned about 1 foot apart, and are let into the A-frame posts. Use a board and a level to mark the positions, then scribe around a scrap of the cross brace stock to mark the notches. With a circular saw set to cut 1½ inches deep, rough out the notches, cleaning them up with a chisel. If you let the braces run a little long, you can trim them flush with the posts after they are screwed in place.

5. Install the swings. The swing seats are commercial models. They are suspended on lengths of braided polypropylene rope attached to swing hangers bolted to the beam. Dangling from each hanger is a heavy-duty chain repair link. The link has a threaded fitting that allows you to open and close the link.

At each end, the rope is threaded through the hardware—a ring on the swing seat or chain repair link–then back-spliced. Back-splicing uses the same principle as Chinese handcuff toys. The braid of the rope is opened up so the free end can be forced into the rope, surrounded by the braided strands. When the rope is pulled, the braid closes back up, tightening around the end. Like the handcuff toy, the more you pull, the tighter the braiding grips the cord it surrounds. (Note that this will only work with braided rope, not twisted rope.)

To make the splice, fashion a tool from a scrap of aluminum flashing. Working several inches from the end of the rope, push the braided strands together so you can insert your tool, as shown. Thread the free end of the rope into the tool and pull it and the rope on through. Pull on the rope and the loop thus formed, and the splice is complete.

Depending upon the swing seats you buy, you may need to loop the rope through the ring on the seat before you splice it.

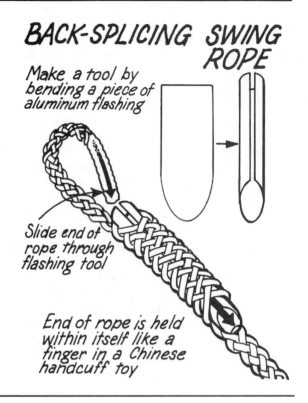

BACK-SPLICING SWING ROPE

Make a tool by bending a piece of aluminum flashing

Slide end of rope through flashing tool

End of rope is held within itself like a finger in a Chinese handcuff toy

6. Assemble and install the fireman's pole. The fireman's pole is assembled from standard plumbing pipe and fittings. Into a 90-degree elbow, turn a 9-foot length and a 20-inch length of 1½-inch-diameter galvanized pipe. Turn a flange onto the other end of the 20-inch pipe. Attach the flange to the beam with carriage bolts, countersinking the nuts. Cut the bolts flush with the nuts after assembly. Anchor the pipe in the ground in about 2 feet of concrete.

Ladder and Chinning Bar Extension

Cutting List

Number	Piece	Dimensions	Material
3	Posts	3½″ × 3½″ × 120″	pressure-treated pine
1	Post	3½″ × 3½″ × 72″	pressure-treated pine
2	Rails	1½″ × 5½″ × 96″	redwood

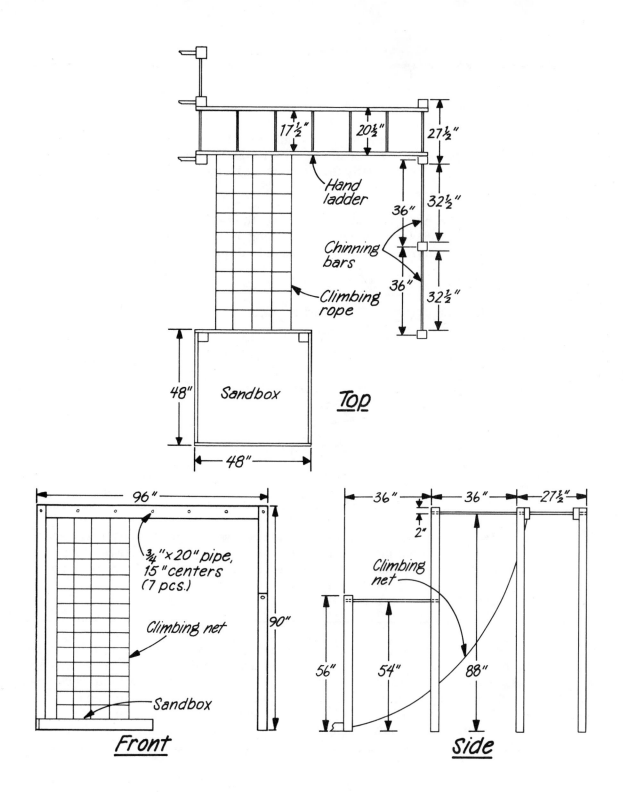

Top

17½" 20½" 27½"

Hand
ladder

32½"

36"

Chinning
bars

Climbing
rope

36"

32½"

48" Sandbox

48"

Front

96"

¾"×20" pipe,
15" centers
(7 pcs.)

Climbing net

Sandbox

90"

Side

36" 36" 27½"

2"

Climbing
net

56" 54" 88"

343

1. **Cut and drill the ladder rails.** The ladder is just that, a ladder made of redwood 2 × 6s and ¾-inch-diameter pipe. It is mounted horizontally between two of the tower posts and two additional posts set specifically to support the ladder.

Start the ladder by clamping the 2 × 6 rails together and drilling holes for seven pipe rungs. The holes are on 15½-inch centers, starting 1¾ inches from either end.

2. **Cut and install the pipe.** Cut seven 20-inch pieces of ¾-inch-diameter galvanized steel pipe. Drive the pipes into one rail, then drive the second rail over the free ends, forming the ladder. Pin the pipes with screws, as in building the tower.

LADDER ASSEMBLY

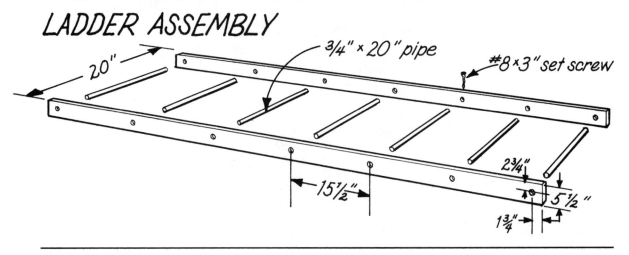

3. **Set the posts.** The post holes are centered 92½ inches from the parallel tower posts and 24 inches from each other. Dig the holes 30 inches deep. Plumb the posts and set them in concrete. The concrete is impor-tant because these posts aren't braced against the racking stresses created when kids swing back and forth on the ladder, on the chinning bars, and on the climbing net.

4. **Install the ladder.** After the concrete sets, cut the posts so their tops are level with the tower corner posts. Drill a 1-inch-diameter hole 2 inches from the top of one post to receive the chinning bar.

Raise the ladder between the tower posts and the new posts, get it level, and hold it in place with clamps. Drill counterbores and pilot holes for lag bolts, two into each post. Install the bolts, making sure the heads are flush with or below the surface of the rails.

5. **Install the chinning bars.** The ladder extension has two chinning bars, one about 7½ feet above the ground, the other about 4½ feet above the ground.

To support the higher bar, place another 10-foot post in a 30-inch hole centered 36 inches from the nearest ladder post. Temporarily brace the post, and, using a 4-foot level or a string and line level, locate the position of the hole for the chinning bar. Drill the hole, cut the bar, and drive it into the post. Reset the post, driving the free end of the bar into the hole previously drilled in the ladder post. Level the bar, plumb the post, then backfill the posthole with concrete.

Follow the same procedure to erect the lower chinning bar, but this time use a 6-foot post and a 16-inch-deep hole.

Sandbox and Cover

Cutting List

Number	Piece	Dimensions	Material
2	Sides	1½″ × 5½″ × 48″	redwood
2	Ends	1½″ × 5½″ × 45″	redwood
2	Posts	3½″ × 3½″ × 3′	pressure-treated pine
2	Sides	as illustrated	plywood
2	Sides	¾″ × 5½″ × 49½″	redwood
4	Tack strips	¼″ × ¾″ × variable	pine
1	Peak board	¾″ × 9¼″ × 48″	pine
4	Braces	¾″ × 5½″ × variable	redwood

1. **Build the sandbox.** The sandbox is simply four pieces of 2 × 6 fastened together with lag bolts, forming a 4-foot-square frame.

To support the climbing net, the sandbox must be anchored to two posts. These posts, positioned inside the sandbox, are 3-foot lengths of 4 × 4, set with about 5 inches above grade. The board that will anchor the ropes should be fastened to the posts with carriage bolts. Drill holes in this board to anchor knotted ends of the climbing net. The five holes are on 9-inch centers, starting 6 inches from either end.

2. **Cut the frame parts for the sandbox cover.** You can make gable ends of the cover frame from the half sheet of plywood left from the tower. Cut them as shown. The sides are cut from redwood stock. Determine the pitch of the gables, and rip a matching bevel along one edge of each side.

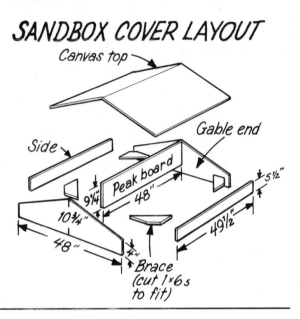

SANDBOX COVER LAYOUT

Canvas top

Gable end

Side

Peak board

5½"

9¼"

48"

10¾"

49½"

48"

4"

Brace
(cut 1×6 s
to fit)

3. **Cut the canvas top and the tack strips.** Cut canvas to extend ¾ inch over each side of the cover. Cut ¼ × ¾-inch tack strips to fit around the top edge of the frame.

Beginning with the gable ends, tack and fold the cover in place on each side of the cover as illustrated before assembling the frame.

4. **Assemble the frame.** Fasten the ends of the frame together with 1½-inch galvanized wood screws. Cut the four corner braces from 1 × 6, as shown, and fasten them in place by driving screws through the frame into their ends. To ensure the canvas doesn't rip out, drive roundhead brass screws through the canvas and the tack strip into the frame edges.

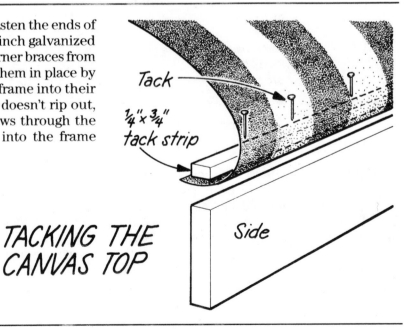

Tack

¼" × ¾"
tack strip

Side

TACKING THE
CANVAS TOP

Climbing Net

1. Cut lengths of rope. The climbing net is made of braided polypropylene rope. Cut five lengths that will give you a good climbing slope between the sandbox and the ladder.

In the play structure shown, the sandbox is 68 inches from the base of the ladder and the ropes are 10 feet long. The horizontal pieces are 3 feet long and 9 inches apart.

2. Make the net. The net is formed of 9-inch squares. Where the vertical and horizontal cords cross, bind them with nylon mason's cord. Apply activated fiberglass resin to each knot using an eyedropper. This will bond the ropes together. Snip loose ends of cord after the resin has cured.

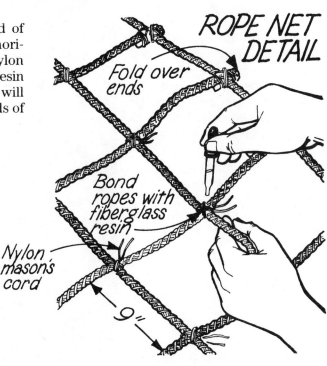

ROPE NET DETAIL

Fold over ends

Bond ropes with fiberglass resin

Nylon mason's cord

9"

3. Attach the net. The net is attached to the ladder the same way the swing ropes are attached to the beam: Loops back-spliced into the rope are connected to eyebolts by chain repair links. The 3-inch eyebolts are screwed into the underside of the ladder rail at 9-inch intervals.

To form the loops, work several inches from the end of the rope. Push the braided strands together so you can insert your tool

made of aluminum flashing. Thread the end of the rope into the flashing and pull the flashing on through. Loop the rope through the repair links, hook the links on the eyebolts, and close the links.

Thread the bottom ends of the rope through the holes in the sandbox and knot the ends. If your play structure doesn't include a sandbox, you can just use two posts and a board to anchor the net.

PROJECT
FREE-STANDING DECK WITH GAZEBO

With its built-in gazebo and brick patio, this free-standing deck answers many needs. Not every backyard is blessed with mature trees. Without the benefit of these shady sentinels, a deck or patio needs some artificial means of tempering the sun's brightness. In the design shown, the deck/gazebo combination is a pleasant oasis in a backyard devoid of trees.

The gazebo's gable roof echoes the style and orientation of the house roof. Pressure-treated lattice panels, installed over the gazebo rafters, provide a generous amount of shade. The railing adds privacy and lends a porchlike character to the structure.

Though the deck isn't connected directly to the house, a small brick patio ties the two structures together while relieving the broad, uniform texture and color of a large lawn.

348

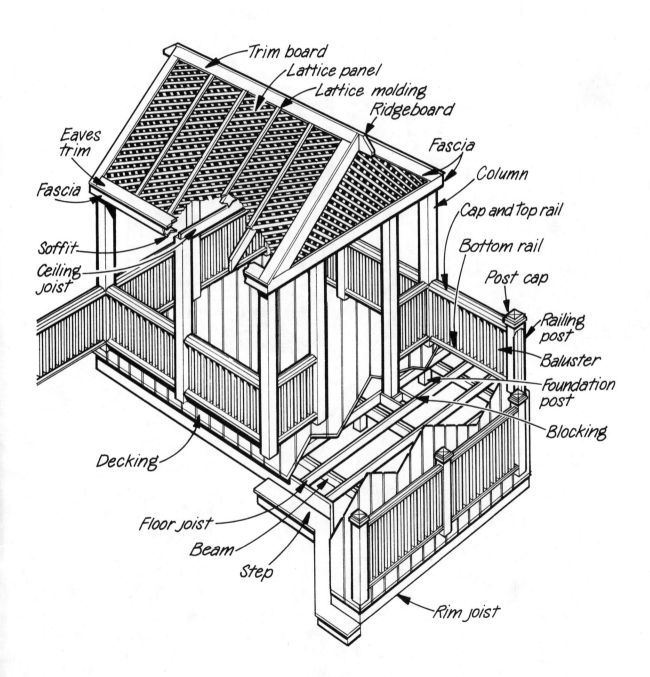

Trim board
Lattice panel
Lattice molding
Ridgeboard
Eaves trim
Fascia
Column
Fascia
Cap and top rail
Soffit
Bottom rail
Ceiling joist
Post cap
Railing post
Baluster
Foundation post
Blocking
Decking
Floor joist
Beam
Step
Rim joist

349

Shopping List

2 pcs. 6 × 6 × 10' pressure-treated pine (gateposts)

9 pcs. 6 × 6 × 8' pressure-treated pine (columns)

2 pcs. 6 × 6 × 8' pressure-treated pine (railing posts)

1 pc. 6 × 6 × 8' pressure-treated pine (fence posts)

3 pcs. 4 × 4 × 10' pressure-treated pine (foundation post)

1 pc. 4 × 4 × 4' pressure-treated pine (foundation post)

1 pc. 2 × 10 × 8' pressure-treated pine (stair treads)

3 pcs. 2 × 8 × 12' pressure-treated pine (joists)

3 pcs. 2 × 8 × 10' pressure-treated pine (beams)

16 pcs. 2 × 8 × 10' pressure-treated pine (joists and rim joists)

3 pcs. 2 × 8 × 8' pressure-treated pine (beams)

400 linear feet of 2 × 6 pressure-treated pine (decking)

6 pcs. 2 × 6 × 12' pressure-treated pine (rafters)

1 pc. 2 × 6 × 12' pressure-treated pine (ridgeboard)

6 pcs. 2 × 6 × 10' pressure-treated pine (railing cap)

5 pcs. 2 × 6 × 10' pressure-treated pine (joists and eaves)

3 pcs. 2 × 6 × 8' pressure-treated pine (fence cap)

11 pcs. 2 × 4 × 10' pressure-treated pine (rails)

4 pcs. 2 × 4 × 8' pressure-treated pine (fence rails)

57 pcs. 2 × 2 × 8' pressure-treated pine (balusters)

15 pcs. 2 × 2 × 8' pressure-treated pine (fence balusters)

5 pcs. 2 × 2 × 8' pressure-treated pine (gate balusters and brace)

2 pcs. 1 × 10 × 12' pressure-treated pine (trim)

6 pcs. 1 × 6 × 10' pressure-treated pine (trim boards)

4 pcs. 1 × 4 × 10' pressure-treated pine (soffit and fascia)

4 pcs. ½ × 1½ × 12' pressure-treated pine (lattice molding)

7 sheets 4' × 8' lattice panels

10 steel post cap connectors

22–6" × ⅜" carriage bolts w/nuts and washers

2 pr. strap-type exterior gate hinges

1 gate latch

16d galvanized nails

12d galvanized spiral-shank nails

8d galvanized nails

semi-transparent stain

1. **Excavate for the deck and patio.** Lay out the postholes according to the framing and foundation plan. In addition to digging out the postholes, now is the time to dig out a base for your brick patio. If you want your bricks to be at grade level, dig down about 5 inches and prepare a bed of level tamped earth. On top of this, 2 to 4 inches of stone dust should be compacted in preparation for laying the bricks.

2. **Set the posts.** Brace all 10 of the 4 × 4 foundation posts plumb while pouring concrete around their bases. Wait about 24 hours before trimming the tops off the posts so that they're all level with each other. Final post height depends on the slope of your yard, and on how high you want the deck surface to be.

3. **Frame the floor platform.** Install the double 2 × 8 beams first. Since 18-foot 2 × 8s are rare, construct the beam by nailing together two 10-footers and two 8-footers; nail an 8-footer to each 10-footer, then lap the elements, forming the full-length beam.

Use post cap connectors to join beams to posts. On top of these beams, 2 × 6 joists are installed on 16-inch centers. Install the rim joists around the deck perimeter as you nail down the joists. Finally, cut stringers for the steps and nail them in place.

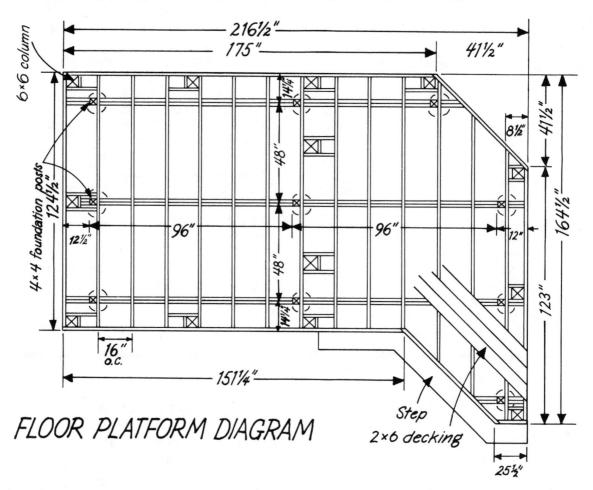

FLOOR PLATFORM DIAGRAM

4. **Fasten the columns to the deck framing.** The 8-foot 6×6s are heavy, so it's important for them to be securely anchored to the deck structure.

Nail 2×6 blocking between floor joists to surround each column with framing. Hold the column in place by driving two or three 10d nails; then drill out for a pair of carriage bolts. These fasteners should extend through the joist or blocking, all the way through the column, and preferably through another adjacent framing member (joist or blocking).

5. **Lay the decking.** The decking is 2×6 lumber, laid on a diagonal. The angle of the decking is established by the skew of the framing at the open end of the deck. Cut the decking to fit around each post.

Nail the treads and risers of the steps.

6. **Nail the gazebo joists in place.** When all the columns are up and the decking is down, nail a single 2×6 ceiling joist across the width of the gazebo, joining the center post of each sidewall. Notch the ends of the joist so it can sit atop the columns, its top edge flush with the top edges of the header joists. This joist will act as a tie-beam, preventing the posts from leaning outward.

Now the 2×6 joists and header joists can be attached to the tops of the columns. Spike them in place with 16d galvanized nails.

ROOF FRAMING

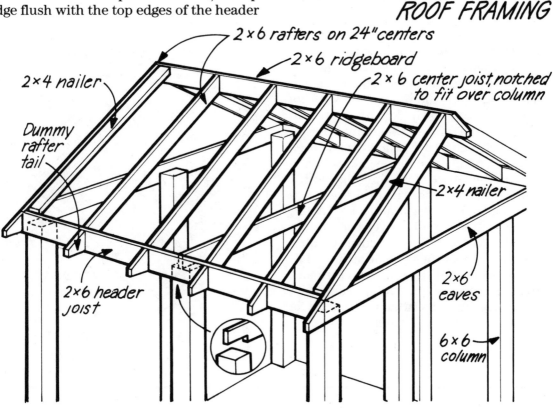

2×6 rafters on 24" centers

2×6 ridgeboard

2×6 center joist, notched to fit over column

2×4 nailer

Dummy rafter tail

2×4 nailer

2×6 header joist

2×6 eaves

6×6 column

7. **Install the rafters.** Start by cutting the 2×6 ridgeboard to length, trimming its ends as shown on the previous page. Then prop it in its final location, using temporary braces. Install the rafter pairs at both gable ends. This will secure the ridge, and you can remove the temporary braces. Note that the rafter pairs on the gable ends are mitered to set atop the joists. The other rafters for this gazebo are slightly different because they're attached *inside* the joists. To cut them, you just need to make 2 identical plumb cuts at each end of the 2×6.

At the gable ends, the rafters are supplemented with 2×4 nailers to support the lattice panels applied to the roof. The ends of the nailers are mitered to fit against the ridge and the header joists.

8. **Frame the eaves.** The eaves overhang is framed using "dummy rafter tails," so named because they're not actually connected to the rafters. Instead, these angled blocks are nailed to the sidewall stringers to serve as supports for the 1×6 eaves trim and 1×4 fascia. Cut the tapered rafter tails from 2×6 scraps and toenail to the header joist opposite the rafters.

An alternate installation technique is to nail through plywood scraps into the butt ends of the rafter tails, then face-nail the plywood to the header joist.

9. **Install the lattice and trim.** Before installing the eaves and facia trim, cut and install the lattice panels that take the place of roofing and provide the gazebo with its pleasantly patterned shade. Nail the lattice to the tops of the rafters, taking care to locate all joints between lattice panels over a rafter. In addition, nail lattice to the gable ends.

Cover the lattice along the ridge with a pair of 1×10 trim boards. Add the 1×6 eaves trim, the 1×4 fascia, and a 1×4 soffit. Then nail lattice molding over each rafter. In addition to protecting the edges of adjacent lattice panels, these single strips of lattice molding accent the roof structure and contribute to its well-crafted appearance.

On the gable ends, attach a 1×6 fascia over the joists, then the rafters.

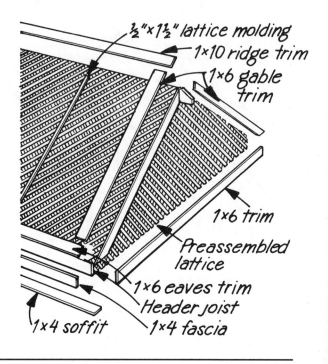

½"×1½" lattice molding
1×10 ridge trim
1×6 gable trim
1×6 trim
Preassembled lattice
1×6 eaves trim
Header joist
1×4 fascia
1×4 soffit

10. **Install the railing.** The railing consists of a beveled 2 × 4 bottom rail, 2 × 2 balusters, a grooved 2 × 4 top rail, and a beveled 2 × 6 cap.

Prefab the pieces in the shop. Bevel the bottom rail and the cap on a table saw. Using a dado cutter mounted in a table saw, plow a 1½-inch-wide, ⅜-inch-deep groove the length of each top rail. Crosscut the balusters to length.

The easiest way to install the railing is to assemble each section of railing (to fit between 2 posts) on the ground. Cut the bottom and top rails to their finished length and then nail them to the balusters. This assembly can then be fastened to its posts by toenailing through the rail ends. Finally, cut and install the cap.

Complete the railing installation by installing the post caps. Each cap consists of a square of 2 × 8 topped by a square of 2 × 6 that has been beveled into a four-sided pyramid.

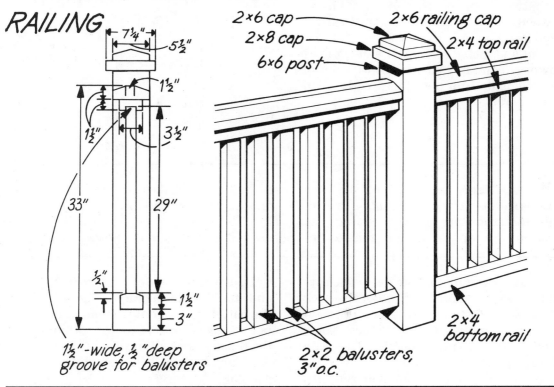

RAILING

7¼"
5½"
1½"
1½"
3½"
33"
29"
½"
1½"
3"
1½"-wide, ½"deep groove for balusters

2×6 cap
2×8 cap
6×6 post
2×6 railing cap
2×4 top rail
2×4 bottom rail
2×2 balusters, 3" o.c.

11. **Set the gate posts (and any fence posts).** The deck shown is supplemented by a section of fence extending from the corner of the house to the back of the gazebo.

Lay out and excavate holes for the 6 × 6 posts. Set the posts, brace them in a plumb position, then backfill the postholes with concrete. Using a string and line level, mark the tops of the fence posts (not the gate posts) and trim them.

12. **Build the gateway pediment.** The pediment is framed with 2 × 6s, lattice is applied, then trimmed with 1 × 6 fascia boards.

Establish the height of the gateposts and trim them on 45-degree angles so they can support the top frame members. Cut the top frame members, bevel crosscutting them at 45 degrees. Nail them together in a miter joint, then nail the assembly to the top of the gateposts. Cut and install a cross member between the posts, and filler blocks between the posts and the ends of the top frame members.

Cut and install an inner framework, as shown. Cut and nail lattice to both sides of the pediment. Trim both faces with 1 × 6 fascia boards.

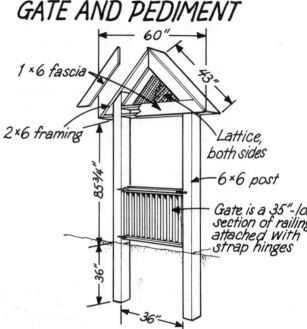

GATE AND PEDIMENT

1 × 6 fascia

2 × 6 framing

60"

43"

85¾"

36"

36"

Lattice, both sides

6 × 6 post

Gate is a 35"-long section of railing, attached with strap hinges

13. **Install fence sections.** Build the fence sections as you did the deck railing. Prefabricate the rails, cap, and balusters in the shop. Cut the top and bottom rails to finished length, nail the balusters between them and install the section between the posts. Nail the cap in place. Then nail the two-layered post caps to the posts.

14. **Build and install the gate.** The gate is nothing more than a section of the deck railing/fencing fitted with a compression brace and hung with strap hinges. Allow about ½-inch clearance between the gate and each gatepost.

Cut and assemble the rails and balusters. Cut a diagonal brace of 2 × 2 stock. Miter the ends to fit. Nail the brace to the rails and to the balusters. It should extend from the top rail on the latch side to the bottom rail on the hinge side. Nail the cap in place.

Hang the gate using strap hinges. Install a latch.

15. **Lay the brick patio.** Start at one corner and work out, setting the bricks in the pattern you've picked. Each brick should be tamped into place and leveled. If you've chosen to have a joint between bricks, dump fine sand or sand-and-cement mix on the bricks, and sweep it into the joints. Then wet the bricks. You'll need to repeat this process two or three times to completely fill the joints.

POOLS, HOT TUBS, AND SPAS

6

More and more these days, with two-worker families and unavoidably tight schedules, we want our homes to be self-contained systems for living—places not only for eating and sleeping but also for recreation, exercise, and entertainment. For those of us who enjoy taking a few laps in a pool or just relaxing in a spa or hot tub, the best place for those facilities is at the house.

Owning a pool isn't inexpensive, but it doesn't cost a fortune. Aboveground pools and vinyl-lined in-ground pools are quite affordable—no more than a good used car. Even an in-ground concrete pool with a built-in spa costs no more, in the long run, than a medium-size pleasure boat or a lifetime family membership in a swim club. And a permanent in-ground pool should appreciate in value along with your house and property.

There is some type of pool or spa available for just about everybody who wants one. Whether you just need something for the kids to splash around in or you're serious about competitive swimming and diving, there are design, siting, and equipment options to consider. If you're thinking about a spa or hot tub for recreation and relaxation, many of the same decisions apply.

Aboveground Pools

An aboveground pool is a good alternative for anyone who wants a pool but doesn't want the expense of installing one in-ground. The difference in cost is significant: An aboveground pool can be installed for a tenth the cost—a few thousand dollars as opposed to tens of thousands. Nearly 60 percent of the swimming pools installed each year are aboveground pools.

Aboveground pools have distinct advantages and disadvantages. One of the advantages is that this type of pool can be installed by a homeowner with only modest do-it-yourself skills. The pools are sold as complete kits, with sidewalls, a vinyl liner, and basic filtration equipment. And because most municipalities consider aboveground pools

357

to be temporary structures, these pools seldom require building permits or are taxed as real property. Check with local authorities, however.

A main disadvantage of an aboveground pool is its limited life—about 15 years on the average. During those years, you can count on emptying the pool and storing the accessories every winter, and replacing the vinyl liner several times. Other disadvantages include limits on shapes, sizes, and depths. Aboveground pools are round or oval; few are more than 4 feet deep. Sizes range from 15- to 28-foot-diameter circles, and from 12×24- to 21×41-foot ovals. If you want a pool for diving or lap swimming, an aboveground pool isn't for you.

Integrating an aboveground pool into the surrounding landscape can be tricky. If you have a small, level backyard, the pool will dominate its surroundings. And with the pool standing as high as most fences, you'll be on display every time you use it. It's possible to install a deck with privacy screening, but that would make the pool even more dominating.

If, on the other hand, you have a large, sloping backyard, an aboveground pool can be worked nicely into the landscape. Depending on the slope of your yard, just a little excavation might make it possible for you to have an aboveground pool surrounded by a handsome deck, all accessible from the natural grade of your yard.

Siting

Your yard's soil type and slope will dictate whether or not you can install an aboveground pool. Generally, there are only two soil conditions that present significant problems; thin, sandy soil and loose, pebbly soil.

Thin, sandy soil can be a problem, because the water in a 16-foot-diameter pool will exert pressure of 250 pounds per square foot on the soil. If the soil's sandy and loose—poorly compacted or impossible to compact—the pool liner could slide and rupture, possibly pulling the sidewalls out of line and causing the structure to collapse.

Loose, pebbly soil could make the sidewall supports unstable; they could roll on the soil. It's possible to circumvent the problem by pouring a concrete footing under the vertical frame members.

Too steep a slope? Manufacturers generally recommend against installing an aboveground pool on a site where the gradient is more than 6 percent. If you have any doubts about your site, talk to an excavator or a structural engineer.

Installation

Installing an aboveground pool can be a do-it-yourself job. Typically, it requires two or three people. The most important thing is to read and understand the manufacturer's directions and to follow them closely. Don't improvise. If you get stuck, get advice on how to continue from the manufacturer or the dealer who sold you the pool.

Begin by leveling the soil for the pool. Remove any sticks or stones that might puncture the liner, then compact the earth with a hand or mechanical tamper. Spread a layer of builder's sand, then, once again, check the surface for level. It's better to cut the high spots than to fill the low ones. Filled spots tend to settle over time.

Once the sand base is leveled and smoothed, set up the pool wall. Though the

Lazing on a summer afternoon (or morning or evening) is so much more rewarding when it's done by your own pool. The kids can frolic; you can float or just hang your feet in the water. A soak in a spa is equally relaxing.

configuration varies among manufacturers, a wall usually consists of a steel or aluminum frame supporting a 4-foot-high corrugated metal or fiberglass panel. After the wall is erected, the base cove is installed around the outside to reinforce the bottom.

The vinyl liner is installed next. The main component in an aboveground pool, a good liner is virgin vinyl at least 20 mils thick, with an embossed surface to help prevent slipping. Typically, the liner is a little oversized to compensate for slight errors in grading. The liner is opened inside the pool structure, then carefully fitted into place as the pool is slowly filled to a 2-foot depth. To ensure the liner goes down smoothly and evenly, this task definitely requires three or four people. Once the liner is properly in

place, the top edge of the pool is finished off with coping, and the skimmer and inlets are installed through the wall.

The plumbing, mechanical, and electrical systems for an aboveground pool are simple and straightforward. At its most complex, the plumbing need only consist of a single pipe—it can be a garden hose—to the inlet of the pool. Aboveground pools don't have floor drains; no plumbing there.

The only electricity required for an aboveground pool is a circuit for the filtration system pump. Most pumps require a 30-amp dedicated circuit (that is, a circuit with nothing else connected to it) with a waterproof outlet. Depending on the pool design, you might need to provide another circuit for outdoor lighting or outlets.

ABOVEGROUND POOL ASSEMBLY

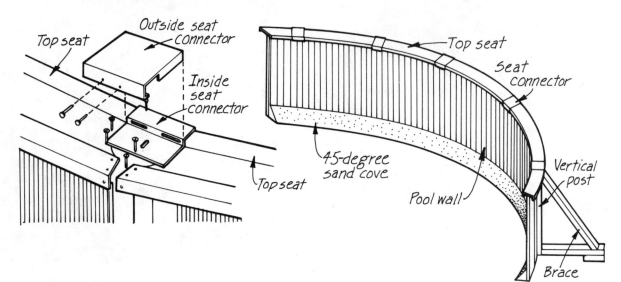

In-Ground Pools

In-ground pools offer an almost limitless range of options, from a small vinyl-lined pool for the kids' splashing and frolicking, all the way to a permanent free-form concrete pool complete with a diving board and a slide, all surrounded by a brick, stone, or concrete patio.

Because of the great number of options available, costs for in-ground pools vary widely. A simple vinyl-lined pool can be installed for a few thousand dollars. At the other end of the spectrum, a custom-designed concrete pool with intricate tilework and fancy landscaping will cost plenty. In the middle ranges, costs between concrete and vinyl-lined pools narrow, and can even overlap. In the South and Southwest, where the climate allows for simpler and lighter construction, a simple concrete pool doesn't cost a lot more than a good vinyl-lined pool. In colder parts of the country, where the construction season is shorter, and concrete pools must be built to withstand heavy frost pressure, the difference in cost between a vinyl-lined and a concrete pool can be significant.

Most folks have a contractor do most, if not all, of the installation work on an in-ground pool. Nevertheless, quite a few people have built their own in-ground pools, subbing out only the excavation work. Though you can rent a backhoe, chances are a good excavator will do the job for less than the cost of a day's rental.

Design Considerations

Many people use a pool more for splashing and playing than for swimming. For this, you need a pool with a large shallow area; figure a minimum depth of 33 inches, increasing to 4 or 5 feet. Such a "play" pool could be any size or shape.

If you want serious exercise swimming laps, you need a straight, long pool with parallel ends and a minimum depth of 3½ to 4 feet, so you won't touch bottom while swimming and turning. Training for competitive swimming? Make the length an even divisor of 75 feet—for instance, 25 or 37½ feet.

Of course, if you want to use your pool for diving, you have to have a large deep area. Diving from a height of 20 inches above the water requires a pool at least 28 feet long, 15 feet wide, and 7½ feet deep at the deep end.

If you want your pool to accommodate swimmers, divers, and frolickers, you'll need at least a 16 × 32-foot pool—that's 512 square feet. One rule of thumb for sizing your pool: Allow 36 square feet for each swimmer and 100 square feet for each diver. If you figure that 10 people—seven swimmers and three divers—might use your pool on its busiest day, you need a pool with an area of 552 square feet, or 16 × 35 feet.

When thinking about the shape of your pool, remember that simple forms—derived from squares, rectangles, circles, and ovals—work best. They're not only easier to design, build, and maintain, they blend more easily into the landscape.

You'll need a generous terrace or patio around the pool to accommodate poolside activities and to keep mud and dirt out of the pool. (The exceptions would be naturalistic pools, which are usually bounded by rock or wood outcroppings carefully positioned to mimic nature.) The paved area should be no less than 3 feet wide on all sides of the pool. Loungers and sunbathers need at least a 3 × 6-foot space all to themselves, as well as a 3-foot space between each person. A poolside table and four chairs need at least a 10 × 10-foot area.

A rule of thumb: The area of the patio should be no smaller than the area of the pool. If, for example, you plan to build a pool that's 20 × 40 feet, you'll want a patio area of at least 800 square feet. If this theoretical pool were surrounded by a 3-foot-wide terrace on three sides, it would need a 12-foot-wide patio along one of the sides.

Divers have special poolside requirements. A diving board can extend over as much as 10 feet of the patio, and divers will need a 2-foot-wide path to the end of the board. A slide can take up as much as 15 feet of patio space.

Concrete Pools

The two most common types of in-ground pools are concrete (in various forms) and

GUNITE POOL CONSTRUCTION

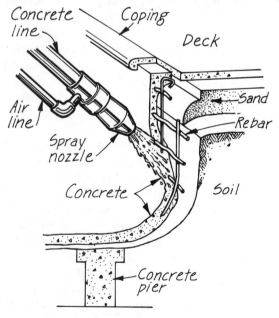

vinyl-lined. One-piece fiberglass pools are also available; relatively new, they're increasingly popular.

Though opinions of pool builders and pool owners vary, most experts agree that concrete is the all-around best material for building a pool. No other material is more adaptable, durable, or repairable. And wouldn't you know it, concrete pools are the most expensive and, for the do-it-yourselfer, the most difficult to build.

Concrete pools are site-built. Nothing is prefab; every job is a custom job. That means concrete pools can be adapted to peculiar curves and slopes and can be modified slightly to accommodate slight variations in grading.

Construction of concrete pools varies regionally, but there are three main construction approaches: Gunite, poured, and block. The interior of a concrete pool can be finished with a cement plaster, applied in a wide range of textures and colors. Pool interiors can be painted any color, during construction or later. White is most popular, but many owners choose other colors. Concrete pool interiors can also be finished—either wholly or partially—in ceramic tile. Tile is by any definition expensive; many owners install only a band of ceramic tile along the water line.

Gunite. Try not to get confused when talking about Gunite. Gunite is a noun, a verb, and an adjective—workers Gunite the Gunite into place, thus building a Gunite pool. Gunite (the noun) is a mixture of hydrated cement and sand; it is sprayed through a hose onto a grid of steel reinforcing bars—called rebar—that is formed in place against the earthen walls of the excavation. The Gunite mixture must be directed carefully so it flows completely under and over the rebar during application. If properly applied, the result is an extremely strong, continuous shell.

Gunite construction allows a pool to be built to any size, shape, and contour. All surfaces, including steps and ledges, are formed at once, providing seamless integration. There are no joints to fail.

Most adaptable of pool-building materials, Gunite can be applied more thickly or reinforced more strongly where unusual soil or frost pressure is a problem. It can be applied over a honeycomb of concrete piers in unstable soil.

The problem with Gunite is that it is hardly a D-I-Y approach. Equipment costs make getting into the Gunite business expensive. If you want the best, it is a Gunite pool, and it will have to be contractor-built.

Poured concrete. Pouring concrete requires more labor than Gunite, but less specialized equipment. Forms for the walls must be set up, lined with rebar, then filled with concrete. After the forms are removed, a steel-reinforced concrete floor is poured and troweled smooth. Sturdy and long-lasting, the only real drawback to poured concrete construction is that it yields only rectangular, circular, and oval shapes.

Concrete block. Block construction is a favorite of small contractors; equipment cost is next to nothing, and labor is relatively low. A block pool is similar in form and construction to a poured pool. The blocks are laid up, and their cores are filled with rebar and mortar. Then, as with poured-concrete construction, the pool floor is poured and troweled smooth. The drawback to this type of construction is that concrete blocks are not waterproof; they must be plastered with mortar to seal them. Differential settlement *will* occur over time, causing slight cracks to open up in the mortar joints. These cracks will eventually "telegraph" through the plaster, causing leaks.

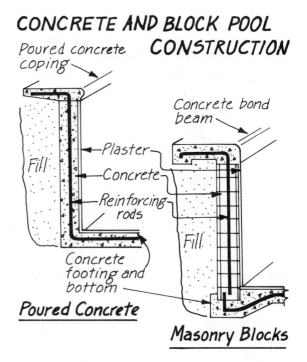

Fiberglass Pools

Once upon a time, fiberglass pools did not have a good reputation. Early models were prone to buckle, crack, leak, and deteriorate quickly because of reactions with chemicals in the soil. Fiberglass pools are stronger and sturdier now; buckling and cracking are no longer problems. Deterioration has been dramatically slowed.

The advantages of fiberglass pools include a wide range of colors and patterns, a generous number of sizes and shapes, and integral steps and ledges. A prime disadvantage is the high transportation cost for these one-piece units.

If you choose a fiberglass pool, the installation job is relatively simple. The hole is dug, the bottom covered with sand, a truck with a crane delivers the pool and places it in the hole, the plumbing is hooked up, the hole is backfilled, and the edge trim is installed. It doesn't take long. But it isn't really a D-I-Y project.

In-Ground Vinyl-Lined Pools

The development of vinyl-lined pools in recent years has brought pool ownership within the means of do-it-yourselfers. The in-ground vinyl-lined pool is very similar to the aboveground pool. It simply requires an excavation. If you can erect an aboveground pool, you can build a vinyl-lined in-ground pool.

Vinyl-lined pools are often sold as complete prepackaged systems. All the manufacturer needs to know is the size and shape of the pool you want. He can provide a kit: sidewalls, liner, pump, filter, accessories.

Sidewall systems. Vinyl-pool sidewall systems typically are modular and made of aluminum, steel, or fiberglass-reinforced plastic. Elaborate sidewall configurations include wood and concrete block. Sidewall systems for aboveground pools are self-supporting; an in-ground pool built with these systems can be filled with water and checked for leaks before the excavation is backfilled. Though configurations differ, all sidewall systems require stable soil—maybe even a concrete footing. All provide continuous support for the pool's vinyl liner.

FIBERGLASS AND METAL SIDEWALLS

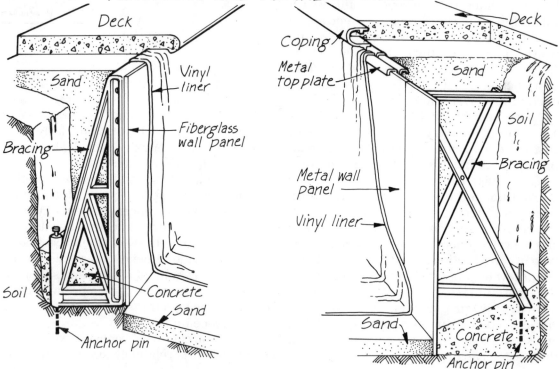

The vinyl liner. The vinyl liner used with all these wall systems is like an extra-large, extra-thick garbage bag. Good liners are at least 20 mils thick and are embossed to prevent frolickers from slipping on the pool bottom. A wide range of colors and patterns is available. The liner is spread over a bed of sand or a special pool-base concrete that uses vermiculite as the aggregate, and the top is secured under coping that surrounds the edge of the pool. Decorative as well as functional, the coping serves as trim around the pool's edge.

Vinyl liners won't take as much abuse as concrete. Chemical imbalances in the pool water can cause a liner to wear out quickly. A chlorine tablet resting directly on the liner will at least discolor it. Ultraviolet light from the sun takes its toll, too, causing fading and cracking. Some liners are treated with stain inhibitors and UV inhibitors to deterioration. Of course, vinyl liners are prey to impact damage; throw a rock against the pool, and it will make a hole.

On the plus side, vinyl liners are easily repaired with manufacturer-supplied patching kits. They clean easily and don't harbor fungus or algae.

Spas and Hot Tubs

What's the difference between an outdoor hot tub and a spa? Mainly, it's that a hot tub is a wooden barrel that sits above the ground, while a spa is an in-ground (or in-deck) concrete or fiberglass mini-pool. Both hot tubs and spas can hold from two to eight people for a hot-water soak. Either can be fitted with hydromassage jets. Both hot tubs and spas require filtration and heating systems similar to—but smaller than—those used with swimming pools. The costs of a hot tub

and spa of similar size are comparable—a few thousand dollars (about the same as a good-quality aboveground swimming pool).

Hot Tubs

The original California-style hot tub was fashioned from a salvaged wine or water barrel. In this primordial model, the water was heated with an open flame. Modern hot tubs, available either finished or in kit form, are specially-designed wooden-staved tubs that use metal hoops to hold the vertical staves in place. Hot tubs are typically from 2½ to 7 feet in diameter and about 4 feet deep.

The main attraction of a hot tub is the wood construction. If your outdoor life calls for hot soaking on a wooden deck, a hot tub is the logical, most aesthetically pleasing choice. The most popular wood for hot tub construction is vertical-grained clear redwood. Maintained properly, a redwood tub should last 10 to 15 years. Even more durable is teak, used for centuries to build high-quality boat decks. Teak is very expensive. Other woods used in hot tubs include cedar, oak, and cypress.

Spas

The spa is the choice when you want to be close to the earth, rather than up on a deck. If you're building an in-ground concrete swimming pool, you can integrate a spa with relatively little added expense. The construction options for a concrete spa are the same as those for a swimming pool—Gunite, poured concrete, or block.

Spas are also available in fiberglass; options include an almost endless variety of sizes, shapes, colors, and patterns. Fiberglass spas are relatively easy to install; they are simply lowered into a hole, onto a sand

MECHANICAL SYSTEM

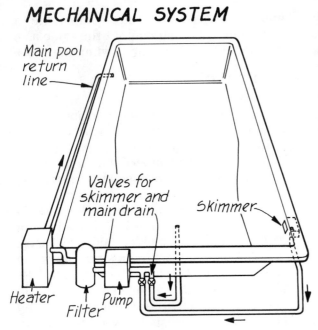

Main pool return line

Valves for skimmer and main drain

Skimmer

Heater

Filter

Pump

provide a locking cover for your tub or spa or to isolate it from unsupervised bathers with a fence.

A hot tub placed on a wood deck is usually reached by way of a ladder, or broad, gradual changes in the level of the deck. Such level changes are pretty good insurance against somebody mistakenly wandering into the tub. It's a good idea to use similar broad level changes around an in-ground spa that's integrated into a patio or terrace.

The support system for a hot tub or spa is very much the same as for a swimming pool. Water must be recirculated, filtered, and heated. The differences are that the equipment used for tubs and spas is much smaller, and the water is heated to between 100° and 104°F and propelled by hydromassage jets.

The Mechanicals

If swimming is going to be fun, then the water in the pool has to be clean. Keeping

bed. Fiberglass spas are available with acrylic or gelcoat lining. Acrylic is more durable and resistant to chemicals and abrasions. But when it is damaged, it is more difficult and more expensive to repair than gelcoat.

Installation

The best spot for a tub or spa is a level part of your yard, away from large rocks or trees, roots, underground utilities, and overhead power lines. Proper siting makes installation and maintenance easier and adds to your enjoyment of the spa. Choose an area with good privacy, protected from prevailing winds that could chill bathers.

Installing a spa requires a building permit in most municipalities. In some areas, codes require spas and tubs to have thermostats to maintain water temperature at a safe limit. It's required by law in many places, and good sense everywhere else, to

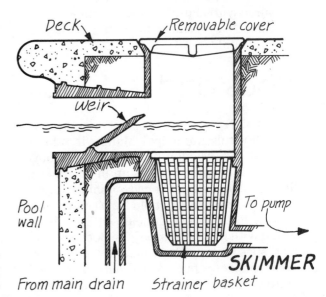

Deck

Removable cover

Weir

Pool wall

To pump

From main drain

Strainer basket

SKIMMER

the pool clean is the job of the pool's mechanical system—its filter and pump. It removes foreign particles from the water as it adds and distributes the necessary chemicals. It also allows you to operate the pool with the initial water supply; you only add water to backwash the filter and to compensate for evaporation and splash-out.

A filtration system is made up of four parts.

■ A surface skimmer, which is the system's inlet; located at the waterline, it traps floating oils or debris before it reaches the filter.
■ The plumbing that carries the water through the filtration loop—from skimmer to pump to filter and back to the pool.
■ A pump that circulates the water through the filtration system.
■ The filter.

Pumps

In operation, a pool pump is simple: An electric motor turns an impeller blade, which pulls water from the pool, runs it through the filter, and returns the water to the pool. Pumps are typically made of bronze or plastic. Bronze is best.

Make sure you get a self-priming pump. They are less apt to break down. Also, don't buy horsepower. Pump horsepower is all but meaningless. What matters is the gallons per minute the pump will move. Make sure, too, that the pump, filter, and pipe diameters are properly matched. The pump will need its own dedicated circuit.

Filters

There are three types of filters for residential pools: high-rate sand, pressure diatomaceous earth (D.E.), and cartridge. Local codes often require a particular type of filter—check before you buy.

Filters come in a variety of sizes. Size is dictated by the amount of water in the pool and the turnover time, which is the number of hours it takes the system to filter all the water. Turnover time varies from 8 to 12 hours; the more people using the pool, the faster the turnover time must be.

High-rate sand filter. The most popular type, the high-rate sand filter is a pressure vessel containing a special sand. Incoming particles are *driven* into the filtering sand at a high flow rate and pressure to make the best use of the filtering media.

The filter must be backflushed from time to time to wash the foreign particles out. A pressure gauge on the filter canister lets you know when it's time to backflush; as debris builds up, so does the pressure inside the filter. When you backflush, between 50 and 200 gallons of graywater are generated. Some municipalities allow this water to be dumped into storm sewers or a residential sewer line, others don't. If yours is one that will not, you'll have to make a dry well for discharge of the backflush water.

Pressure diatomaceous earth filter. Diatomaceous earth filters are smaller and filter out smaller particles than high-rate filters. They also consume less water during backflushing.

The filter medium, diatomaceous earth, is a sedimentary rock that is made up of the fossil skeletons of diatoms, tiny water animals. Inside the filter, the diatomaceous earth is used as a coating around tubes that circulate the pool water.

A diatomaceous earth filter isn't recommended where a dry well has to accept the backflush, because the diatomaceous earth clogs dry wells. Some designs circumvent

FILTERS

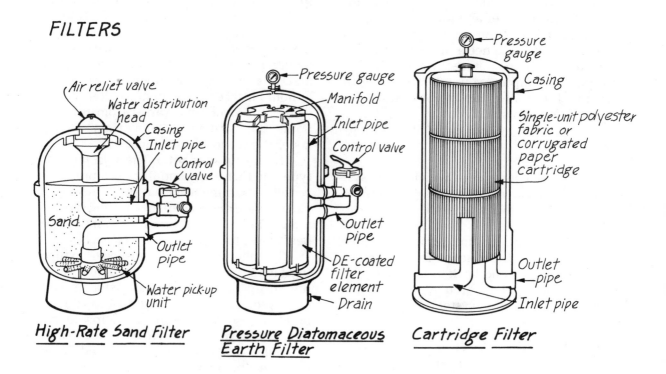

High-Rate Sand Filter

Pressure Diatomaceous Earth Filter

Cartridge Filter

this problem with separation tanks that allow the diatomaceous earth to settle out of the backflush water.

Cartridge filter. Currently third in popularity, cartridge filters are rapidly gaining acceptance. The operation is simple: Insert a cartridge, use it until it's spent, throw it away, then put in a new cartridge. Cartridges are relatively inexpensive. What you gain in convenience, however, you lose in performance: Cartridges don't consistently filter out small particles.

Heaters

Fuel choices for pool and spa heaters are the same as for home furnaces: natural gas, oil, and electric. There are also solar heating systems for pools.

Open-flame heaters burn oil or natural gas. Generally, natural gas is less expensive and more efficient, so gas heaters are decidedly more popular. Oil heaters do a good job and are less expensive to operate than electric heaters.

There are three types of open-flame heaters: coil, tank, and convection. The *coil heater* runs a small, fast-moving volume of water over a large flame. Recovery time is very fast; a coil heater can be used with any size pool. A *tank heater* closely resembles a home hot-water heater; it holds a large, slow-moving volume of water over a small flame. A tank heater costs less than a coil heater.

Recovery time is relatively slow, and this heater doesn't work particularly well in cold climates. In any climate, it is best suited to a small pool or spa. The *convection heater* is a hybrid using a large flame to heat slow-moving water. It is relatively inexpensive and is best suited to a small pool or spa.

An electric heater works much like a home electric water heater, and it has the same drawbacks. Recovery time is very slow, operating cost is very high. An electric heater only makes sense for a very small pool or spa in a warm climate where gas and oil are very expensive or unavailable.

Solar heating is more a matter of design and maintenance than of hardware. Any pool bathed in sunlight is a solar collector. The more hours the pool is in sunlight, the more heat it collects.

Solar heating hardware typically takes the form of a collector that preheats the pool water before it goes to a conventional heater.

A pool equipped with a cover will lose its heat more slowly than an uncovered pool. A cover can keep a pool 10 to 15 degrees warmer than if it were uncovered. A cover is also good for keeping unsupervised swimmers and debris out of the pool.

Pool Landscaping

Many homeowners consider a beautiful poolside setting to be as important as swimming, diving, and playing in the pool. A good design will integrate a generous deck or terrace around the pool, poolside plantings, lighting, and storage space for pool equipment.

Materials for a poolside deck or patio are the same as those used for *any* backyard deck or patio: brick, stone, tile, or concrete, even wood. Attractive designs can be achieved with a combination of materials.

Masonry decking. For the area immediately beside the pool—the 3-foot-wide strip—masonry may be the best choice. The paving could take any of several forms. Popular and easy to install is concrete, finished with a suitable texture—one that would give good purchase for wet feet without being too rough. Similar in function, but different in appearance and texture, is exposed-aggregate concrete. Other high-quality and durable paving materials include brick, stone, paving blocks, or ceramic tile.

Whatever material you choose, make sure you grade the area around the pool carefully, and install the paving material carefully, so the water is shed *away* from the pool's coping.

Wooden decking. Wood is an excellent material for decking just about anywhere. Especially for a deck surrounding an above-ground pool, wood is the material of choice.

Fences. Some special considerations apply to poolside fencing. The most important of these is safety: In most localities it's the law—and everywhere it's good sense—that you enclose your pool with a fence, to keep unsupervised children, pets, and non-swimmers out of the pool. Check locally for specific poolside fencing requirements. In any case, it's a good idea to install self-closing and self-latching gates to keep the pool area secure. Privacy is another consideration. A fence can be designed specifically to keep pool users from being on display.

Poolside lighting. Consider safety as well as aesthetics when lighting your pool. The aesthetic is largely a matter of personal taste, safety is not. Take special care to see that the pool is well and equally lighted for nighttime use. Poolside is not the place for

Pool landscaping integrates the setting with the use. A brick patio and gazebo are appropriate to a wooded setting (below), while a deck furnished with loungers suits an open setting (bottom). Privacy and access to the home are vital for a spa (right).

Water Level

A water level is used to determine whether two points that are separated by distance or obstruction are in the same plane. It is an ideal—and easily contrived—tool to use to lay out posts for a fence or deck, or as here, for a large swimming pool and deck.

To make a water level, fit short lengths of transparent plastic tube at each end of an ordinary garden hose. Buy a set of garden hose fittings (one male, one female) and two 1-foot lengths of clear plastic tubing with the same inner diameter as your garden hose. Fit the tubing on the fittings, screw the fittings onto the hose. You have a water level.

Use the water level to mark an elevation on stakes or posts. Mark the elevation on a stake and tie or tape one end of the level to that stake. Fill the hose with water so that it's visible in the plastic tubing at both ends. Align the level's free end at a stake you want to mark with the same elevation.

Fill the level to near the mark and measure the distance between the mark and the water level. Then you can add or subtract this distance from the level shown on the other stake. This approach works best for marking elevations that are close to existing ground level because the level works best if

Clear vinyl tubing

At least 30"

Hose end-fitting threaded onto hose

the ends are at least 30 inches from the ground. So fill to this level and measure down from there.

The versatility of a water level lies in the fact that it doesn't matter what path the hose takes between the two points. It can be laid on bumpy ground, go around corners, or be piled in loops. One word of caution, though; if part of the hose is in shade and part in the sun, the reading will be inaccurate because the warmer water is less dense.

falls caused by poor lighting.

Poolside structures. You'll need at least one poolside "house" to make your installation complete. It can be as simple as a lean-to to shelter your pump and filter from the elements and provide storage space for maintenance equipment—a net, a vacuum, and such. But you can build an elaborate pool house that not only houses equipment but provides changing facilities for guests.

PROJECT
VINYL-LINED IN-GROUND POOL

Pool building is not a traditional do-it-yourself project. But thanks to two technological developments, the skills needed to build an in-ground swimming pool are not much different from those needed to build a fence. Those developments are tough, tear-resistant vinyl and pressure-treated wood.

Realizing this, several companies are marketing kits containing all the pool components D-I-Yers can't build: liner, fittings, filter, surface skimmer, and pump, along with plans for complete pool construction. After a hole is dug, a wall system is constructed of wood that is pressure-treated to the point that it won't rot, even when buried in the ground (the same material is used to construct building foundations). The vinyl liner is installed, and you've got an in-ground pool for a lot less money than a contractor-built model.

You *can* do it yourself.

Shopping List

6 pcs. 4 × 4 × 12' pressure-treated
construction fir

1 pc. 4 × 4 × 8' pressure-treated
construction fir

4 pcs. 2 × 6 × 10' pressure-treated
construction fir

53 pcs. 2 × 6 × 8' pressure-treated
construction fir

8 pcs. 2 × 4 × 8' pressure-treated
construction fir

12 sheets ¾" × 4' × 8' pressure-
treated ACX plywood

1" × ³⁄₁₆" flathead stove bolts

2 pounds of 4d galvanized box nails

10 pounds of 16d galvanized box nails

4d galvanized nails

12 cubic feet of portland cement

18–60-pound bags of ready-mix
concrete

96 cubic feet of pool-base aggregate

panel adhesive

water putty or Bondo

Components supplied in pool kit

1 horsepower pump

filter

surface skimmer

16' × 32' vinyl liner

96 feet of molded liner track

96-foot roll of insulation foam

wall fittings

Note: All lumber is CCA pressure-treated to 0.6 pounds per square inch for in-ground use.

Built with a kit and plan from Sunland Pool Systems of Del Mar, California, the pool shown is 32 feet long, nearly 16 feet wide, and 7 feet deep at one end. The walls supporting the vinyl liner are 39 inches high—the depth of the shallow end.

Since the pool walls are strong enough to contain the water without backfilling, the pool doesn't have to be completely below grade, making the design easily adaptable to any site. For example, if the site slopes, the pool can be below grade on the high side and above grade on the low side. Since the depth of excavation will vary with the site, all excavation depths cited are measured from the lip of the pool.

Most of the work can be handled by two people, although you'll need to call in a couple of extra hands when it comes time to spread the liner.

It's important to note that the wood required for the pool walls is not commonly stocked by lumberyards, though most will order it. What's required is wood that has been pressure-treated with CCA to a level of 0.6 pounds per cubic foot. (Most lumberyards stock wood that has been pressure-treated to 0.4 pounds per cubic foot, a level suitable for ground contact, but not for in-ground use.) It is essential to use galvanized nails.

Because the pool has a wooden cap rail, it's easy to integrate a wooden deck into the plan. If you'll be building a deck, be sure to draw up plans before building the pool. Your deck framing plan will affect the pool lip elevation.

Construction of the pool is involved, so an overview is helpful in keeping all the steps in perspective. After laying out the

373

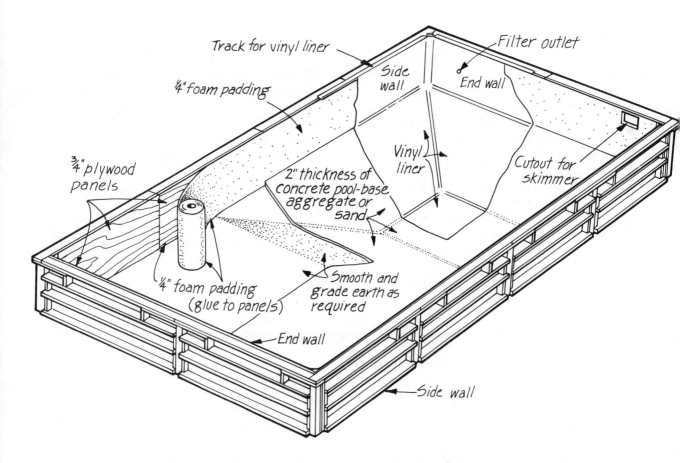

Track for vinyl liner

¼" foam padding

Side wall

Filter outlet

End wall

¾" plywood panels

2" thickness of concrete pool-base aggregate or sand

Vinyl liner

Cutout for skimmer

¼" foam padding (glue to panels)

Smooth and grade earth as required

End wall

Side wall

pool, hire a backhoe operator to excavate the hole. Then set posts at 8-foot intervals around the perimeter to support plywood panels. The panels are backed with horizontal braces and covered with foam padding to protect the liner. Next, set up the plumbing.

Then refine the excavation with a pick and shovel, and cover the bottom with a special concrete using vermiculite as the aggregate. Install a plastic liner track along the lip of the pool, then the liner.

1. Lay out the pool. Start by digging a test hole at your selected site. Make the hole as deep as the planned excavation. If you hit bedrock or water, build the pool elsewhere (or get professional assistance).

If you are satisfied with the site, use string and stakes to roughly define an 18 × 34-foot perimeter. This is about a foot larger on each side than the finished pool, giving you room to set the posts. Roughly square the

374

Cutting List

Number	Piece	Dimensions	Material
12	Posts	3½″ × 3½″ × 72″	fir
12	Panels	¾″ × 39″ × 96″	plywood
12	Horizontal braces	1½″ × 5½″ × 92½″	fir
12	Horizontal braces	1½″ × 5½″ × 95″	fir
12	Horizontal braces	1½″ × 5½″ × 90¾″	fir
48	Vertical spacers	1½″ × 3½″ × 11¼″	fir
8	Cap rail joiners	1½″ × 5½″ × 48″	fir
4	Cap rail joiners	1½″ × 5½″ × 24″	fir
20	Blocking	1½″ × 5½″ × 9″	fir
4	Cap rail	1½″ × 5½″ × 96″	fir
4	Cap rail	1½″ × 5½″ × 102¼″	fir
4	Cap rail	1½″ × 5½″ × 92½″	fir
4	Side wall nailers	1½″ × 3½″ × 37½″	fir
4	Corner blocks	3½″ × 3½″ × 39″*	fir

*4 × 4 ripped diagonally

perimeter with a framing square. When the stakes are in proper position, remove the strings.

Next, set up batter boards at each corner, about a foot outside the stakes. Run strings from corner to corner, adjusting them until they intersect at the stakes.

Remove the first stakes. Now you can more accurately square the layout by moving the strings along the horizontal pieces of the batter boards. The rectangle will be square when the short sides measure 18 feet, the long sides measure 34 feet, and the distance between both diagonals is 38 feet, 5⅝ inches. Mark the ground directly under the strings with lime or dry cement as a guide for the backhoe operator.

In the unlikely event that your site is perfectly flat, you don't need further layout. But your site almost certainly has some slope, so you'll need stakes to define the leveled height of the pool lip. Drive a stake into the ground at each corner of the layout (at the intersections of the strings), just outside

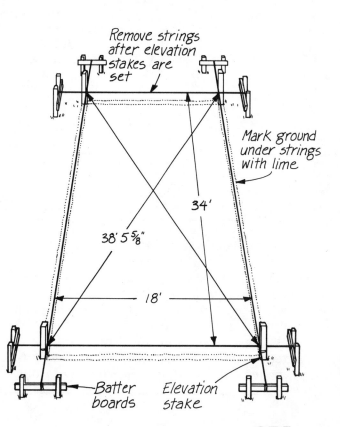

Remove strings after elevation stakes are set

Mark ground under strings with lime

34′

38′ 5⅝″

18′

Batter boards

Elevation stake

the rectangle. Set these stakes firmly, so they won't be disturbed during the excavation and construction work to follow; you'll need to reference them in a number of subsequent steps. With the elevation stakes set, you can remove the strings from the batter boards.

Mark the lip height on the elevation stake at the site's highest point, then use a water level to transfer it to the other three stakes. Now run a string around the perimeter at this height.

2. Dig the hole. Now it's time to call the backhoe operator. First have him dig the entire pool to a 41-inch depth, using a story pole to monitor depth. Then he can dig the deep end, but have him leave a 2-foot-wide ledge to stand on as you construct the deep-end walls. Follow the diagram for the pool liner dimensions, adding 2 inches in depth for the base. Essentially, he'll dig to the shallowest depth, then move to a spot 22 feet from one end and 10 feet from the other, where he'll excavate to 84 inches. Then he'll shape the slope between the deep end and the shallow end.

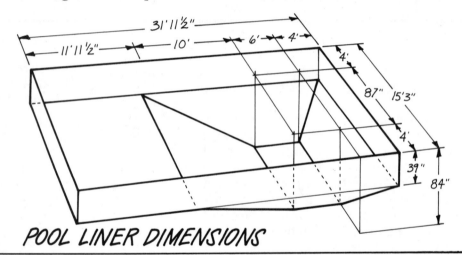

POOL LINER DIMENSIONS

3. Lay out and set the posts. The posts must extend either 2 feet below the bottoms of the plywood walls or below the frost line, whichever is deeper. Eventually, each post will be trimmed to 3 inches below the pool lip, but let them run long for now.

Reset strings on the batter boards to reflect these inside dimensions: 15 feet, 5 inches × 32 feet, 1½ inches. When the layout is square, the diagonals will measure 35 feet, 7⁹⁄₁₆ inches.

Set the posts outside the strings, positioning them as shown. Do the corner posts first. Dig the holes about 1 foot in diameter and as deep as necessary. Spread several inches of gravel in the bottom of each hole, then drop in the posts. Partially backfill with soil, and use temporary braces to support

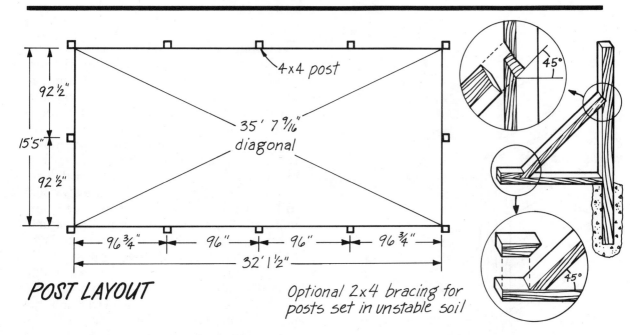

POST LAYOUT

Optional 2x4 bracing for posts set in unstable soil

the posts while you plumb them. Take your time; the posts must be absolutely plumb if the rest of the job is to come out right. When a post is plumb, backfill its posthole with concrete. Check for plumb again. Allow the concrete to cure for a week before beginning wall construction.

If your soil is unstable, brace the posts with struts constructed of 2 × 4s, as shown.

4. Trim the posts. Use your water level to transfer the pool lip elevation from an elevation stake to a post. On the post, measure 3 inches down from the pool lip height, and mark it there for trimming. Using the water level, transfer that elevation to every other post. To double-check the marks, drive a nail into each corner post at the mark, then stretch a string from nail to nail, around the pool's perimeter. The string should hit the mark on each post.

When you are satisfied your marks are level and at the proper elevation, extend the marks around the posts and cut them off. Wear a face mask when cutting this wood; it's heavily treated.

5. Cut the wall panels. Rip the 12 sheets of plywood to 39 inches wide. Then, measuring from the factory edge, draw parallel lines on the good side of the plywood at 13½ inches and 26¼ inches. These are nailing lines for the horizontal braces, which are installed later.

Treat the cut edges with brush-on wood preservative.

377

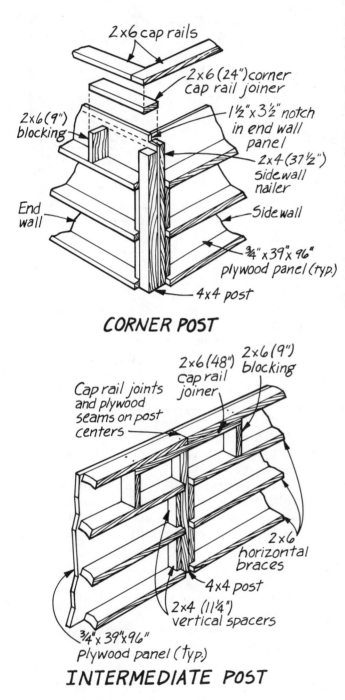

2x6 cap rails

2x6 (24") corner
cap rail joiner

2x6 (9")
blocking

1½"x3½" notch
in end wall
panel

2x4 (37½")
side wall
nailer

End
wall

Side wall

¾" x 39" x 96"
plywood panel (typ.)

4x4 post

CORNER POST

2x6 (48")
cap rail
joiner

2x6 (9")
blocking

Cap rail joints
and plywood
seams on post
centers

2x6
horizontal
braces

4x4 post

2x4 (11¼")
vertical spacers

¾" x 39" x 96"
plywood panel (typ.)

INTERMEDIATE POST

6. **Construct the end walls.** The plywood panels are installed good side out, the top edges 3 inches above the post tops. It's important to orient the factory edge to the bottom of the wall, where the protection of its pressure treatment is most needed.

Starting at one end of the pool, attach the first panel. Line up the end of the panel on the middle post's centerline, and allow it to overlap the corner post. Nail the plywood to the posts with 3½-inch galvanized box nails, spacing them every 6 inches. Attach another panel, completing the end wall. Butt the panels tightly at the center post.

Measure and cut two 2 × 6 horizontal braces to fit between the posts. Toenail them to the posts at the bottom. Nail through the plywood into the braces; use a digging bar to back up the braces as you nail.

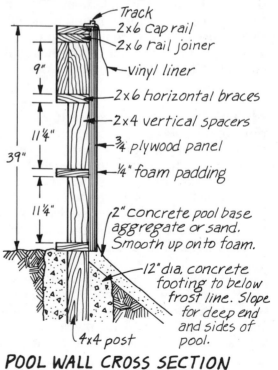

Track

2x6 Cap rail

2x6 rail joiner

Vinyl liner

9"

2x6 horizontal braces

2x4 vertical spacers

11¼"

¾ plywood panel

39"

¼" foam padding

11¼"

2" concrete pool base
aggregate or sand.
Smooth up on to foam.

12" dia. concrete
footing to below
frost line. Slope
for deep end
and sides of
pool.

4x4 post

POOL WALL CROSS SECTION

378

Cut four 11¼-inch vertical spacers from 2 × 4 stock. Stand them on the bottom braces and nail them to the posts. Nail the panels to the spacers.

Measure and cut two more horizontal braces and nail them to the tops of the spacers. Nail the panels to the braces (this is where the nailing lines on the plywood become useful). Make a second set of spacers and a third set of braces and attach them in the same way.

From 2 × 6 stock, cut one 48-inch and two 24-inch cap rail joiners. The long joiner is centered across the top of the center post and nailed in place. The short ones are positioned atop the corner posts, as shown, and nailed in place. Cut 2 × 6 vertical blocks to fit between the free ends of the joiners and the upper braces. Nail them in place.

Cut two 2 × 6 cap rails. These rails butt together over the center post, and end shy of the corner posts. This allows the cap rails of the sides to overlap the corner posts, tying the sides and ends of the pool together. Drive nails through the rails into the joiners and through the plywood into the rails. To allow the side cap rails to overlap the corner posts, the plywood must be notched. Cut the notches, as shown.

Finally, cut two 2 × 4 sidewall nailers. Nail through them into the plywood and the post.

After the first end wall is completed, repeat the process to construct the other end wall.

7. **Assemble the side walls.** The side walls are built in the same sequence as the end walls. The only difference is that there are no joiners (and their accompanying vertical blocks) at the corners. Try to butt all panels tightly together. If, however, there are gaps of more than ⅛ inch, fill them with water putty or with polyester resin auto body putty.

8. **Install the filter/pump unit.** With the walls constructed, it is time to install all the "mechanicals"—plumbing, wiring, pump, and filter. The first thing you must do is decide where the pump and filter unit will be located. While you'll want an inconspicuous location, remember that the farther the pump has to move the water and the more circuitous the plumbing, the less efficiently the system will work.

The unit could be supported on a platform of concrete block or tamped earth, but a small concrete slab is better. Lay out, excavate, and pour the slab. While the concrete cures, excavate trenches for the plumbing and wiring. In brief, the pump pulls the water from the pool through the skimmer. It pushes the filtered water back into the pool through the filter outlet. These two fittings are installed in the pool wall next.

9. **Install the skimmer and filter outlet.** The skimmer, which collects floating debris as it takes in water for filtering, is located at least 24 inches from a corner, about ½ inch below the cap rail.

Start by scribing the outline of the skimmer and its flange on the plywood. Cut a hole that will allow the skimmer, but not the flange, to pass through. For the skimmer to be flush with the foam that will be applied to the plywood, the flange must be recessed ¼ inch into the back of the panel. Scribe around the flange with a utility knife to score the plywood, then excavate the recess with a chisel.

The skimmer is mounted with ³⁄₁₆ × 1-inch flathead stove bolts. Mark the mounting holes, and drill and countersink them so the bolts will lie flush with the panel surface.

The filter outlet should be on the same wall as the skimmer, about 2 feet from the other corner and about 21 inches below the cap rail. To mount the fitting, mark a 2⅝- to 2¾-inch-diameter hole. Drill a starter hole and cut the full hole with a saber saw. Mount the outlet.

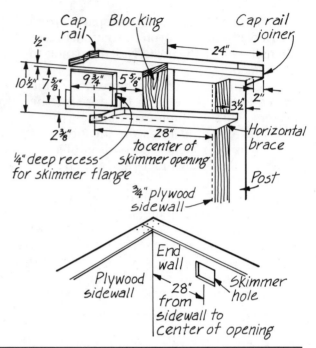

10. **Make plumbing and wiring connections.** If the pump and filter unit will be 10 feet or less from the pool, use 1½-inch Schedule 40 PVC pipe to connect the skimmer to the pump and the filter to the outlet. If the unit will be more than 10 feet from the pool, install 2-inch pipe between the skimmer and the pump.

Cut the PVC pipe with a hacksaw. Do a dry run, fitting the pipe, ells, and tees together before permanently attaching them. In mak-

ing your permanent connections, it's easiest to start from both ends, working toward the longest pipe sections in the middle. Wrap all the male threads with teflon joint tape and turn them into the female threads until they are hand tight; don't use a wrench. Many pool pumps will run on either 220 or 110 volts; 220 volts is more economical to run. To provide 220-volt service, you'll have to set up a separate circuit. Run the cable for this circuit before you backfill around the pool.

11. **Make inside corner pieces.** Rip two 8-foot 4 × 4s in half diagonally. This is most easily done on a table saw. But it can be done with a circular saw set to cut a 45-degree bevel; make two passes with the saw, then finish the cut with a hand saw. Smooth the

sawed surfaces with a Surform tool, a plane, or a belt sander.

Cut two 39-inch pieces from each 8-foot piece. Fit one into each corner with the sawed surface facing into the pool. Nail the wedges into the panels at the edges.

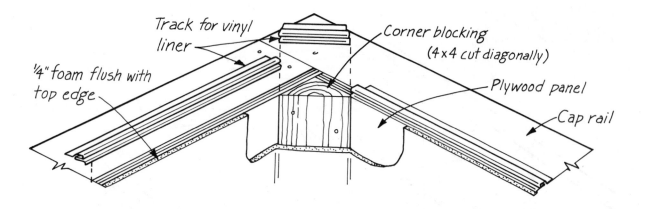

Track for vinyl liner

Corner blocking (4 x 4 cut diagonally)

¼" foam flush with top edge

Plywood panel

Cap rail

12. **Attach liner track.** Lay the liner track on the cap rails, flush with the inside of the pool walls, as shown. Use 4d galvanized box nails to fasten the track to the rails. Space the nails about 6 inches apart. Cut short lengths of track to fit over the corners.

13. **Attach the roll foam.** The foam can be attached to the panels with hot-melt glue, mastic, or construction adhesive. Apply the glue to the wood panels, covering about 4 feet at a time. Apply the foam as you unroll it, smoothing it out as you go. When you come to a corner wedge, run a bead of glue along its joint with the panel. Roll foam edges tend to be a little uneven, so align the low spots along the top of the wall. Later, you can trim the top with a sharp utility knife.

14. **Shape the bottom of the pool.** To refine the shape of the deep end, set up an arrangement of strings to define the flat bottom, as shown. To keep them from blowing around, tie a small weight—a nut or bolt is fine—to each of the four vertical strings that delineate the corners of the deep end's roughly 6 × 7-foot flat bottom.

Excavate the area delineated to a depth of 86 inches (2 inches deeper than the finished pool to allow for the special concrete base). Then cut away the ledge the backhoe left, sloping the sides from the bottom of the walls to the perimeter of the flat bottom. Move and remove dirt as necessary with a flat shovel. As the work nears completion, smooth the bottom with a 2 × 4. Check the flat bottom with a 4-foot level to be sure it really is level. Then use the 2 × 4 to smooth the sloping sides of the deep end.

If the excavation was done properly, you won't need strings for the shallow end. Use the flat shovel, level, and 2 × 4 to flatten and level the bottom, 2 inches lower than the bottoms of the wall panels.

SHAPING THE POOL BOTTOM

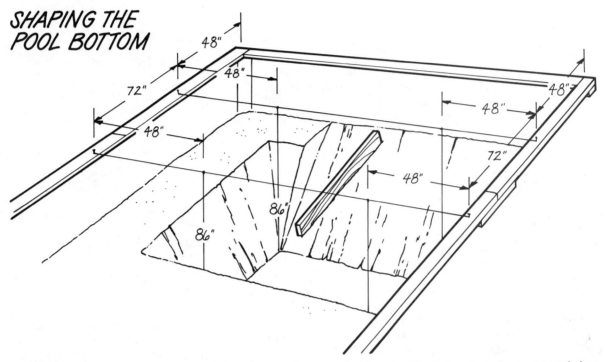

48"
48"
72"
48"
48"
48"
72"
48"
86"
86"
86"

15. Surface the pool bottom. The bottom of the pool must be covered with a 2-inch layer of a surfacing material. Some pool builders use washed mason's sand, others a cement mixed with a special type of vermiculite, called pool-base aggregate. This mixture produces a light, spongy base that cushions the liner. Regardless of the material used, the surface must be smooth and free of stones and sharp ridges, for these can weaken and even puncture the liner.

If you use the special concrete mix, read and follow the mixing instructions on the bags of aggregate. These are useful primarily as a starting point, since workable proportions vary with temperature and humidity. Start with small batches until you get a mixture that spreads easily but holds its shape on the sloped areas. Use a watch to time the mixing of each batch; you want the ingredients thoroughly blended, but overmixing will make the concrete runny and increase the curing time.

Because you don't want joints in the bottom, it's important to complete the surfacing in one day. Rent a 5-cubic-foot electric cement mixer, and ready all your tools in advance. You'll need a spade, a shovel, wooden floats (those with round ends work well), gloves, two buckets, a hose with a shut-off nozzle. And some willing helpers.

Start at the deep end. Moisten the soil to keep it from sucking the water out of the concrete, weakening it. Work as a team: Have one person place buckets of concrete along the pool's edge, while another dumps them and spreads the mix. The concrete must overlap the foam. Work in the sequence shown. The concrete will spread easiest if you jiggle it as you go. Once you get a uniform layer in an area, smooth the mixture down with hard, fast swipes of the float. Work your way to a corner of the shallow end so you can hop out and lean over to finish the job.

The pool's bottom can have gentle waves in its contours and still look good. But nicks and scratches or small pebbles or leaves dropped in will cast a noticeable shadow in some light. If you find any flaws the day after the concrete is spread, you can drop gently to the bottom in bare feet, walk gingerly to a spot where a correction is needed, and use a metal trowel to smooth ridges or dents.

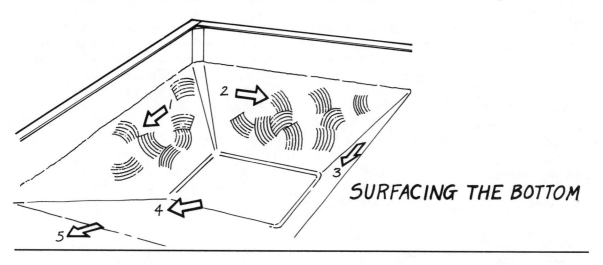

SURFACING THE BOTTOM

16. **Install the liner.** To prevent debris from collecting in the pool, install the liner the day after the bottom is surfaced. The liner will slow evaporation, allowing the bottom to cure exceptionally well.

Though the liner is stretchable and forgiving, you can make it even more so by keeping it in a warm room overnight, then spreading it in the sun while you make a final inspection and cleaning of the pool bottom. Make sure you set all nails in the cap rail, and make sure the slot in the liner track is clear of concrete or dirt.

You need a crew of at least four people. The liner is marked "shallow" and "deep." Spread out the shallow end and have two people hold the corners in place while two others spread out the deep end. Be careful not to snag the liner.

Now locate and position the corner seams of the liner. Have each person clip the liner into both tracks at their corner. Then work toward the center of each side and each end, clipping the liner into the tracks. Pull the liner sideways in the track to adjust for tight spots and slack along the rim. Clip the liner into the four short corner tracks. At both sides of each corner wedge, drive a 4d galvanized box nail through the liner and track into the wall. Be careful not to drive the nails so far that the heads rip through the liner.

Make any final adjustments to the liner lip position to eliminate wrinkles, and you are ready to fill the pool.

17. **Begin the fill.** The trick is to work with the weight of the water to position the liner as the pool fills. At first, the water's weight will create wrinkles in the sides. Don't worry about these now; most will disappear as the water rises. Your first concern must be to center the liner on the pool bottom. You can still hop in the pool and slide the liner around. Pushing on the sides with a push broom can help center the bottom (though you must be sure the broom has no sharp edges or corners).

18. **Attach the wall fittings.** When the water is within 4 inches of the filter outlet, the liner will be fully seated, so you can attach the inside wall fitting. Rub a little dirt around the outlet opening, making the screw holes visible through the lining. Twist a Phillips screwdriver into the holes until it pops through the liner. Install the front ring. Use a sharp utility knife to slice out the liner material inside the fitting's opening.

When the water is within 4 inches of the skimmer, puncture the liner for the skimmer frame's mounting screws, as you did for the filter outlet. Cut across the skimmer opening, as shown, and smear a heavy grease on the front of the skimmer and on the gasket. Slip the gasket through the cut in the liner and press it in place on the skimmer. Position the other gasket and the frame on the outside of the liner and fasten them with the screws. Cut away the liner material remaining in the skimmer opening. Now you can fill the pool until it is halfway up the skimmer front.

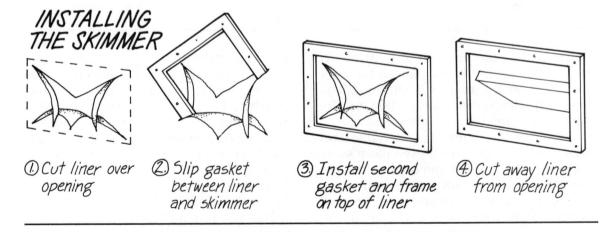

INSTALLING THE SKIMMER

① Cut liner over opening

② Slip gasket between liner and skimmer

③ Install second gasket and frame on top of liner

④ Cut away liner from opening

19. **Make final adjustments.** Sometimes, as the water's weight tightens the liner, it may pop out of the track at spots. Usually you can fix this by running your hand up the side to create a little slack and then tucking the lip back into the track. If the liner pops out again, you can cure the problem permanently by sticking it back in and securing it with a piece of ⅛-inch vinyl tubing or a window screen mounting molding stuck between the track and the liner lip.

PROJECT
POOL
DECK

The parquet pattern of this deck is especially well-suited for poolside. For one thing, the alternating squares of 2-foot boards look better than long runs of decking. Long boards, all running in the same direction, would accentuate the fact that the deck area beside the pool is only a few feet wide. Patterned decking downplays this narrowness, and adds texture and visual interest to the deck as well.

On a more practical level, short boards are less prone to warp. This is important because a poolside deck is subject to many more cycles of wetting and drying

than any other deck. Another minor advantage is the ease with which access hatches can be concealed in the decking. You need access to the pool's skimmer, if not other mechanicals, and hatches provide that access easily.

385

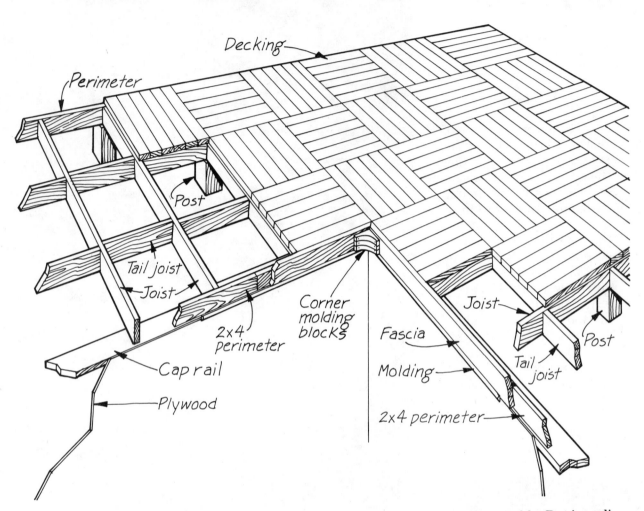

Decking

Perimeter

Post

Tail joist

Joist

2x4 perimeter

Corner molding blocks

Cap rail

Plywood

Fascia

Molding

2x4 perimeter

Joist

Post

Tail joist

The following plan assumes that the entire pool is at grade and that the entire deck will likewise be at grade. It uses a grid of 2 × 4 joists set on 2-foot centers to support the ends of the 2-foot decking boards. The joists are supported by the pool's cap rail and by precast concrete piers located on 4-foot centers and simply set on tamped earth.

The footing *you* provide for *your* deck will depend on your site and your climate. In a frost-free climate, the configuration presented here is entirely suitable. But in a climate where the ground freezes annually, you need to establish footing below the frost line.

An inexpensive way to do this is to use 4-inch-diameter nonperforated PVC drainpipe as a form for concrete piers. Dig a posthole to below the frost line. Set a pipe in the hole, plumb it, backfill, then cut off the pipe at the desired elevation. Fill the pipe with concrete. The smooth PVC offers extra frost-heave protection; moving earth will slide on it instead of heaving it.

The footing question gets even more complicated if your pool is built into a significant slope. You may need to use piers on the side at grade, then go to a system of posts and beams on the elevated side. And if you face this situation, it may save labor to increase the girth of the joists so you can cut back the number of posts necessary.

Clearly, you must plan your particular deck thoughtfully. The construction is a much simpler matter.

Shopping List

2 pcs. 2 × 6 × 16' redwood
6 pcs. 2 × 6 × 12' redwood
2 pcs. 2 × 4 × 16' redwood
2 pcs. 2 × 4 × 14' redwood
22 pcs. 2 × 4 × 12' redwood
22 pcs. 2 × 4 × 10' redwood
220 pcs. 2 × 4 × 8' redwood
20 lbs. 16d galvanized finishing nails
1 box 1" paneling nails
48 precast concrete piers
12 pcs. 1" × 8' plastic molding
resorcinol glue
water repellent

1. Lay out your deck on paper. Every deck tends to be site specific, and a pool deck is particularly so. A major benefit of the modular design of this deck is the ease with which it can be modified to accommodate varying situations.

The layout shown provides a 2-foot-wide walkway along one side of the pool and a 6-foot one along the other, 4 feet at one end and twice that at the other. Adding to the width along any side can be done easily in 2-foot increments.

If your deck will deviate from the plan shown, lay it out on paper. Establish your pier placements and framing needs, including the placement of tail joists. To establish the latter, you must mark the orientation of the decking for each 2-foot-square module.

2. Stake out the piers. You've got a head start on most deck projects because your ledger board already is in place in the form of the pool cap rail.

Set up batter boards about a foot beyond each corner of the deck. Using a water level, set the tops of the batter-board crosspieces at the same elevation as the pool's cap rail. Tie strings to the batter boards and square up the perimeter by measuring from the inside of the deck wall to the strings. You can double-check for square with the 3-4-5 method.

The string must delineate the centerline of the perimeter joists, which is the center point for the piers. The joists around the pool's edge are set back 1½ inches from the edge to accommodate the eventual installation of a fascia. Therefore, the string should be ¾ inch (half the thickness of the fascia) closer to the pool than the planned width of the deck. Where the deck is 4 feet wide, for example, the string should be 48¾ inches from the inner edge of the pool's cap rail.

When the strings are set, drop a plumb line at each string intersection and every 4 feet along the perimeter, to mark the pier locations with small stakes.

Stake out any additional piers next. If your deck is no more than 4 feet wide, you don't need any more piers. Otherwise it's a simple matter to measure 4-foot intervals along the pool cap rail to run strings perpendicular to the outside perimeter piers.

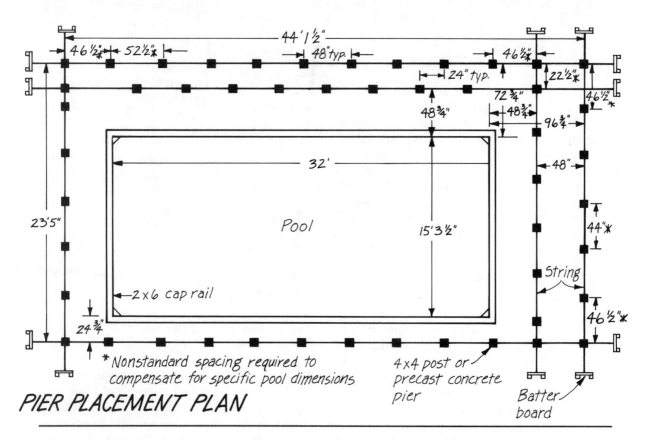

PIER PLACEMENT PLAN

Labels in the plan: 44' 1½", 46½"*, 52½"*, 48" typ., 46½"*, 24" typ., 22½"*, 72¾", 48¾", 48¾", 96¾", 46½"*, 48¾", 48", 32', Pool, 15'3½", 44"*, 23'5", String, 46½"*, 2×6 cap rail, 24¾"

* Nonstandard spacing required to compensate for specific pool dimensions

4×4 post or precast concrete pier

Batter board

3. Frame the deck. The basic plan is to construct a perimeter frame for the deck using 2 × 4s. Then the perimeter frame ringing the pool is installed. This rests on the cap rail. The side framing members extend beyond the pool to the perimeter frame.

The size of the deck—24 feet, 6½ inches by 44 feet, 3 inches—dictates that some framing members will have to be made by joining pieces end-to-end. To make these joints, scab an 18-inch length of 2 × 4 to the sides of the adjoining pieces, across the joint, as shown on the framing plan.

Next, the intervening spaces are filled in with joists set on 2-foot centers. Again, because of the deck's size, which stems from the pool's dimensions, several nonstandard joist placements are required. These are indicated on the framing plan.

DECK CROSS SECTION

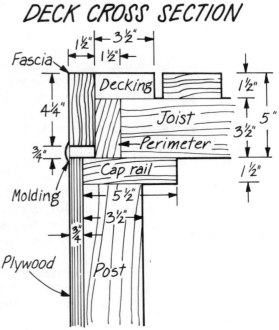

Labels: Fascia, 1½", 3½", 1½", Decking, 4¼", Joist, 1½", 5", Perimeter, 3½", ¾", Cap rail, Molding, 5½", 1½", 3½", ¾", Plywood, Post

388

FRAMING PLAN

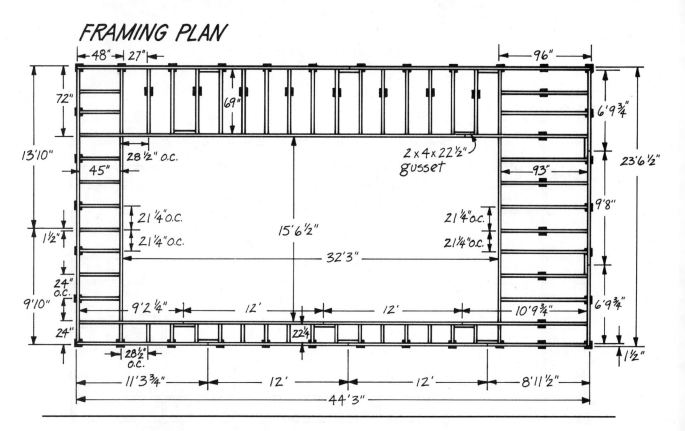

4. Cut and install the tail joists. The tail joists are necessary, in the parquet decking scheme, to support the decking in those modules oriented parallel to the "regular" joists. It's tedious but essential work. Happily, the positioning of the tail joists is staggered, which means they can be face-nailed between joists,

saving a bit of work.

All the tail joists are 22½ inches long. Because there are so many of them—79 in the plan shown—it's worthwhile to set up a radial arm or cutoff saw to knock them out assembly-line fashion. Clamp a stop block to the saw's fence, 22½ inches from the blade.

INSTALLING TAIL JOISTS

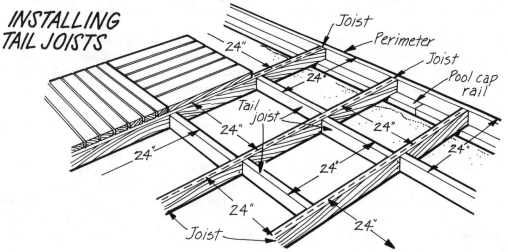

DECKING PLAN

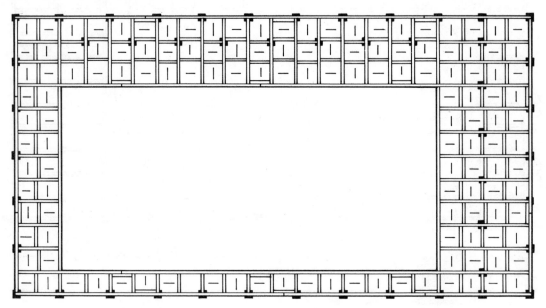

Butt the stock against the stop and cut; no need to measure each piece.

After the pieces are cut, nail them in place.

Position tail joists in relation to the perimeter framing member that they parallel.

Hook your tape measure on the perimeter frame and mark the joists every 24 inches. The tail joists are positioned on one side of the 24-inch line or the other, depending upon what orientation the decking will be.

Consult your decking plan.

5. Frame around the skimmer. The location and configuration of the skimmer will dictate exactly how you frame around it. In no case should it involve more than a few extra pieces fitted around the square skimmer top. Later, when installing the decking, make a hatch by nailing battens across the backs of the 2×4s composing the module that's to cover the skimmer. Lay the module in position, but, obviously, don't nail it down.

6. Cut and install the deck boards. The amount of cutting involved in a parquet deck is its major drawback. Use the stop-block set-up on a radial arm or cutoff saw for this chore.

Because the kerf consumes ⅛ inch or so, you can't get full 24-inch lengths from stock-length 2×4s without generating a lot of undersized scraps. So plan to cut almost all the decking to $23^{15}/_{16}$ inches.

The deck shown has some nonstandard modules, necessitated by the specific dimensions of the pool. Custom rip and/or crosscut the decking for them after all the standard modules are in place.

Use a 24-inch long scrap of ½-inch plywood as a spacer as you nail down the decking, six boards to a square. Make sure you keep the decking square to the framing.

7. Make and install the fascia. The best material for the fascia is clear redwood or cedar 2 × 6. Rip the stock to a 4¼-inch width. Make sure the exposed face and edge are smooth and splinter-free. You may want to round the exposed edge with a router and round-over bit.

Install the fascia flush with the deck surface, using 16d galvanized finishing nails. Scarf end-to-end joints between lengths of fascia for the best appearance.

8. Install the corner trim. To conceal the pool's corner blocks, make special trim pieces. On a piece of heavy cardboard, lay out a template, as shown. Cut out the template, and use it to lay out 12 trim pieces on scraps from the fascia. Cut the trim pieces using a saber saw.

Glue and clamp the pieces in sets of three with resorcinol glue, and let the glue set overnight before sanding each block smooth. Drill pilot holes, then nail the blocks to the fascia with 16d galvanized finishing nails. Since the blocks are 4½ inches thick, position them ¾ inch shy of the deck surface.

The final trim to install is a molding to cover the gap between the fascia and the liner, a space housing the liner track. Because of the constant moisture, a thin wooden molding is unsuitable for this application. Use a 1-inch-wide (imitation wood) plastic molding. Nail it to the fascia, using 1-inch ribbed paneling nails of a matching color, spacing the nails about a foot apart.

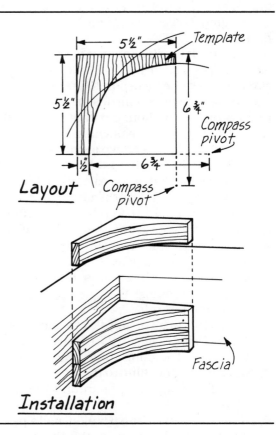

9. Finish the deck. As with all other decks, an application of a water repellent is a good idea. The deck shown was treated with a wood bleach to bring out the wood's golden hues, then coated with a clear wood preservative.

HOW TO DECK FOR A HOT TUB

Decks combine well with hot tubs, but there are special design and construction details to consider. Privacy is important, so your deck will probably need to incorporate some kind of fence or screen on at least one side. The hot tub needs its own support, independent of the deck framing. Also, the tub's pump, heater, and water lines have to be accessible.

The deck pavilion shown is simple but elegant. The roughly 9 × 9 structure can stand alone, or be incorporated into a larger deck or terrace plan. The design is meant to provide privacy without creating a confined feeling for bathers. The pavilion is enclosed with redwood lattice above a simple railing of 2 × 2 balusters. Lattice is also used below the perimeter joists to conceal plumbing and hot-tub equipment. Overhead, open 2 × 6 rafters, joined to a 4 × 6 ridge beam, heighten the sense of enclosure without blocking a star-studded view for nighttime bathers.

1. Set the eight 4 × 4 posts that support the deck. The hot tub requires its own concrete pad for support.
2. Set up the hot tub.
3. Frame the deck using 2 × 6 stock, as shown. Using diagonal 2 × 6 braces, frame an octagonal opening around the hot tub.
4. Nail the 2 × 6 decking to the joists, fitting it as closely as possible around the hot tub.
5. Along each side of the pavilion, nail a pair of 2 × 6 tie-beams across the three side posts. These tie-beams should be cantilevered 8 inches and trimmed at a 45-degree angle at each end.

Shopping List

1 pc. 4 × 6 × 10' redwood (ridge beam)
2 pcs. 4 × 4 × 14' redwood (ridge posts)
6 pcs. 4 × 4 × 12' redwood (posts)
1 pc. 4 × 4 × 12' redwood (stair posts)
2 pcs. 4 × 4 × 10' redwood (rafter beams)
1 pc. 2 × 12 × 12' redwood (stair stringers)
5 pcs. 2 × 6 × 12' redwood (rafters)
1 pc. 2 × 6 × 12' redwood (joists)
3 pcs. 2 × 6 × 12' redwood (decking)
9 pcs. 2 × 6 × 10' redwood (joists)
8 pcs. 2 × 6 × 10' redwood (decking)
4 pcs. 2 × 6 × 10' redwood (tie beam)
3 pcs. 2 × 6 × 10' redwood (stair treads)
1 pc. 2 × 6 × 10' redwood (stair rail)
4 pcs. 2 × 6 × 8' redwood (decking)
4 pcs. 2 × 4 × 8' redwood (top rail)
4 pcs. 2 × 3 × 8' redwood (bottom rail)
4 pcs. 2 × 2 × 8' redwood (balusters)
14 pcs. 2 × 2 × 8' redwood (fascia)
3 pcs. 1 × 6 × 8' redwood (railing fascia)
3 pcs. 1 × 4 × 10' redwood (railing fascia)
1 pc. 1 × 4 × 8' redwood (railing fascia)
24 pcs. 1 × 1 × 8' redwood (nailers)
5 pcs. 4' × 8' redwood lattice
12-6" galvanized spikes
16d galvanized nails

Note: All redwood is construction heart grade.

6. Along the front and back of the structure, rest 4 × 4 rafter beams on the ends of the tie-beams and spike them to the top ends of the posts, using 6-inch-long galvanized spikes driven in drilled pilot holes. For appearance, let the 4 × 4 plates extend 12 inches beyond the corner posts, and trim a 45-degree angle off the underside of each cantilevered end.

7. The center side posts extend to support the 4 × 6 ridge beam, which in turn supports the 2 × 6 rafters. Cut the ridge beam to cantilever 12 to 14 inches beyond the

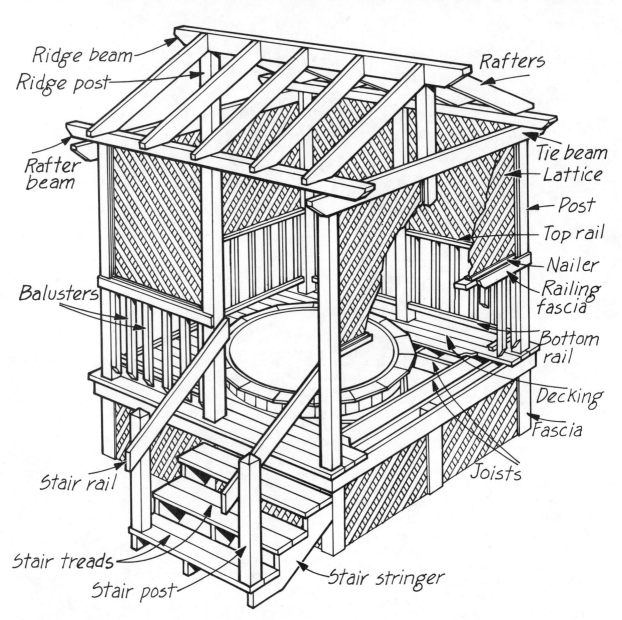

Ridge beam
Ridge post
Rafter beam
Balusters
Stair rail
Stair treads
Stair post
Rafters
Tie beam
Lattice
Post
Top rail
Nailer
Railing fascia
Bottom rail
Decking
Fascia
Joists
Stair stringer

posts, then trim the ends at a 45-degree angle. Toenail the ridge beam to the posts.

8. Cut the rafters and toenail them to the ridge and the plates.

9. The railing for the pavilion uses 2 × 2

balusters. Nail them to a bottom rail made of a 2 × 3 ripped to a 2-inch width. Nail through the 2 × 4 top rail into the baluster tops. The balusters are beveled at their bottom ends.

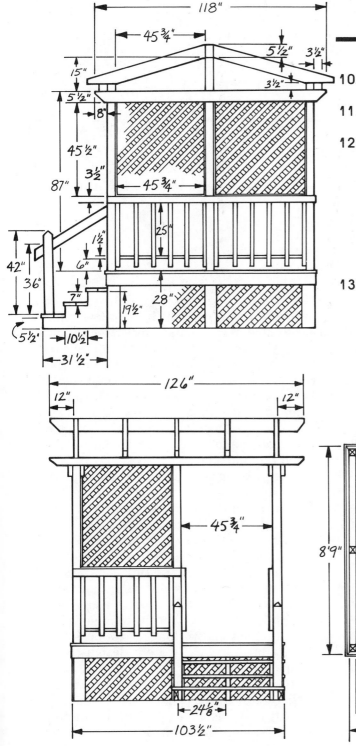

10. Trim out the railing with 1×4 fascia boards.
11. Lattice panels can be framed into the upper openings, between 1×1 nailers.
12. Install the lower lattice panels the same way, using 1×1 nailers as stops behind the lattice, and securing it with 1×6 fascia boards applied over the posts. Instead of nailing the fascia to the deck framing, fasten them with galvanized screws. This way, it's easier to remove and reinstall the lattice, should you or the plumber need to get below the deck.
13. Build and install the steps. Lay out and cut three stair stringers. Set them in position, toenail them to the perimeter joist and nail down two 2×6 stair treads per step.

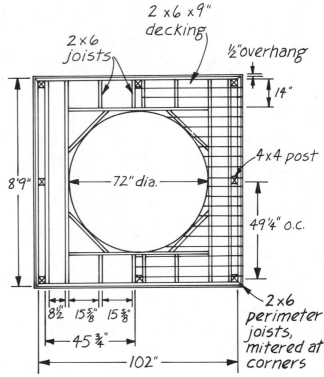

OUTDOOR FURNITURE

7

Sitting on the ground under a tree, lying in the grass—these are natural parts of outdoor living. But would you seriously consider being served exclusively by such seating arrangements? Do you want to have to sit directly on that new deck?

Outdoor furniture is clearly an essential part of outdoor living. The issue here is whether you are going to buy your outdoor furniture or build it. If you've got the skills and gumption to take on some other outdoor project, you've surely got what it takes to tackle an outdoor furniture project.

The art of making outdoor furniture is different from any other type of woodworking. The methods and techniques are a blend of cabinetry and carpentry—a finished outdoor furniture project looks like a piece of furniture, but it's built like a deck.

The reason is the weather. Out of doors, your project has to survive extreme changes in temperature and humidity. You have to plan ahead for the distortion and decay that result when wood gets hot, cold, or wet. Just as important, you have to prevent as much of that distortion and decay as possible by providing a way for the wood to shed the rain and dry quickly.

Water tends to collect wherever two pieces of wood join together. Consequently, outdoor furniture should have as few joints as possible. What joints it does have should be very simple—butt joints, lap joints, maybe an open mortise-and-tenon. Outdoor furniture joints usually are loosely fitted—more loosely than acceptable cabinet or furniture joints. A good outdoor joint might be $1/16$ to $1/8$ inch oversized to allow the wood to swell in wet weather and to allow it to dry out quickly when the rain stops.

One reason you can use sparse, loosely fitted joinery in outdoor furniture is that the parts are rarely glued together. Out in the weather, wood expands and contracts enough to break even waterproof glue bonds. Larger parts must be held together with hardware—nails, screws, and bolts. As in carpentry, it is the hardware, rather than the joinery, that holds the project together.

Building outdoor furniture is not necessarily fine woodworking. It *can* be, but it doesn't have to be. Create a design that's compatible with your skills. Select materials that you can afford, that you can work with, that fit the design.

All it takes is some thoughtful planning, a little sweat, and a lot of care. Don't be intimidated. You *can* do it.

Most outdoor furniture accommodates your natural desire to "take a load off." What can be more relaxing than sitting in the shade of a spreading lawn tree? Or stretching out in the sun? Whether it's a simple bench or an ensemble for the deck, furniture designed and crafted for the outdoors is an essential part of outdoor living.

Construction Techniques

Before tackling any outdoor furniture-making project, you need to have basic woodworking skills. You need to learn how to lay out the parts on your stock (planning how to make the best use of the wood), how to cut them out accurately, and how to join them securely.

The sturdiness and weather-resistance of outdoor furniture projects will depend to a large extent on how the projects are put together. You may use strong, weather-resistant wood, but the furniture you build won't hold up unless you employ the proper techniques for fastening the pieces of wood to each other. You should use construction techniques that will enable the finished projects to stand up to heavy use and to moisture and temperature extremes.

So learn what the suitable joints are. Then learn the techniques used to fabricate and bond these joints.

Joints

The type of joints used in making your furniture will affect its final appearance and durability. There are hundreds of joints in woodworking, but a few basic joints are all you need for outdoor furniture projects.

Fundamental principles apply to all joinery: Use the simplest joint that will assure the strength needed in the construction. Consider your skills and available tools when planning what joints to use. But the primary rule in outdoor furniture construction is to remember that each joint should be either shielded from the weather or oriented so that it sheds water. If a joint must be left

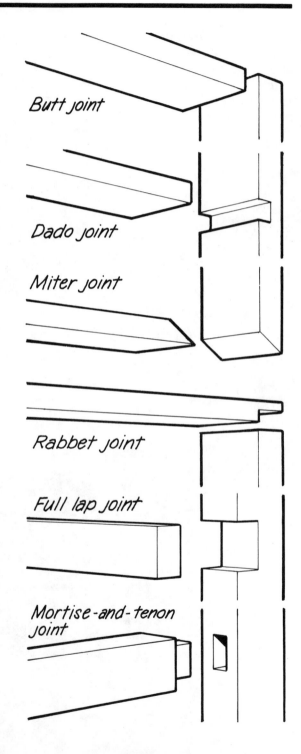

Butt joint

Dado joint

Miter joint

Rabbet joint

Full lap joint

Mortise-and-tenon joint

exposed to the weather, seal it with a high-quality caulking compound.

Butt joint. This is the simplest joint, formed by butting two squared-off pieces of lumber together. Though inherently weak, it can be reinforced with dowels or a spline. In outdoor projects, the butt joint usually derives its strength from the hardware—nails, screws, bolts—used to fasten it together.

Rabbet joint. Here, an L-shaped groove (called a rabbet) is cut into the end or edge of a piece of wood. The joint is formed by fitting a second piece into the rabbet. The width of the rabbet should match the thickness of the adjoining piece, and the depth should be one-half to two-thirds the thickness of the board being rabbeted. A variation is to rabbet both pieces.

Dado joint. A dado is a groove cut across the grain. It is commonly used to provide support for a member that fits into the groove.

Lap joint. In this joint, large dadoes or rabbets cut in one or both pieces allow them to be interlocked (lapped) with their faces flush. In a full-lap joint, only one piece is notched. In any of the half-lap joints, both members are notched, usually with half the total material to be removed coming from each piece. Within these broad categories, there are many variations.

Miter joint. Usually used to join pieces at right angles, this joint hides the end grain of both pieces being joined. It is used primarily for decorative effect. Pure miter joints are not strong, and should be reinforced with fasteners, dowels, a spline, or a key.

Mortise-and-tenon joint. This joint is commonly found in leg and rail construction. The basic elements are the mortise, which is a hole—round, square, or rectangular—and the tenon, which is a tongue cut on the end of the joining member to fit the mortise. It takes time and care to make a mortise-and-tenon joint, but it will pay off in strength and neat appearance.

In general, the mortise should be at least $5/16$ inch from the outside face of the work, and at least $1/8$ inch deeper than the length of the tenon. The tenon should be about half the thickness of the stock. A slight taper on the tenon will allow it to fit easily yet snugly into the mortise.

Layout

The first stage in any project is planning exactly how you will cut the pieces from the stock you bought at the lumberyard. This involves marking locations of saw cuts, holes to be drilled, rabbets, dadoes, and grooves.

This is a critical process. It's going to be tough to get the project built right if you lay it out wrong. Shop teachers tell their pupils to "measure twice and cut once," and that's

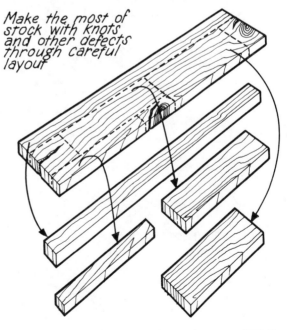

Make the most of stock with knots and other defects through careful layout

good advice. A hole drilled in the wrong place can be plugged with a piece of dowel, perhaps, and a mispositioned groove can sometimes be patched with a strip of wood. But a board can't be stretched to the proper size if you cut it too short.

So measure twice and cut once.

As you lay out a project, look for defects in the wood that will affect the use of each board. Warped, twisted, or cupped boards may be totally unusable. Some defects like checking, knots, or other blemishes can be either cut off as scrap, or located where they won't be seen in the finished project.

Laying out a whole project at one time may not be the best approach. Sometimes you'll want to cut pieces as you go, cutting them to fit rather than to a size specified on paper. You'll have to judge individual situations.

In doing the layouts, remember that your saw will consume some of the wood, turning it into sawdust. Generally, a power saw will create a wider kerf than a hand saw; about ⅛ inch for carbide-tipped circular saw blades.

The key tools for layout work are a rule, a square, and a scriber. The rule can be a tape measure, folding rule, or yardstick, the square a try square or framing square, the scriber a pencil, knife, or awl. For rough work a pencil line is okay, but for fine work, use a knife to score the line, making it more precise. For some jobs, you may need a compass or dividers, for others a marking gauge.

USING A COMBINATION SQUARE

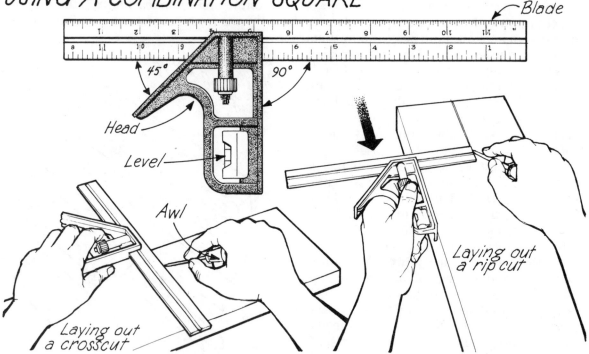

Blade

45°   90°

Head

Level

Awl

Laying out a rip cut

Laying out a crosscut

Safety

Most cabinetmakers can tell some pretty grisly tales of fingers consumed by the tools of their trade. We take it as a given fact that safety is a primary concern around a wood shop. Yet everyone has lapses of attention that can lead to disaster.

Safety isn't simply a matter of using the blade guards and wearing goggles. It's working thoughtfully and staying alert. It's keeping tools in good repair and using the correct tool for each job. It's routinely cleaning up after yourself. It's having a helper around when you need extra hands, and not having distractions when you need to concentrate.

Here are some general safety guidelines:

• Be ready mentally for the work. Don't drag yourself into the shop if you are tired, irritable, distracted, or preoccupied.

• Dress the part. Leave the jewelry, including your wedding ring and watch, on the dresser. Wear fairly close-fitting clothes, and roll up your sleeves. Wear goggles and ear mufflers or earplugs when appropriate. Use a dust mask when making many repetitive cuts with power tools—especially when working with pressure-treated wood. Wear a respirator when applying finishes with volatile solvents in a confined space.

• Maintain a well-ordered workplace. Get yourself a big waste barrel, use it, and empty it regularly. Sweep up when you finish work, picking up scraps of wood. Keep tools and materials stored neatly, accessibly, and out of the way. Give yourself enough room to work around each shop tool you have.

• Know your tools. Read tool manuals or books, or take a course to learn how to adjust, maintain, and operate power tools correctly and safely. Take time to set up for a task, using firm work supports and whatever clamps, jigs, guides, or guards are necessary and appropriate.

Finally, be prepared for accidents. Get a first aid kit and keep it handy. Know how to use it.

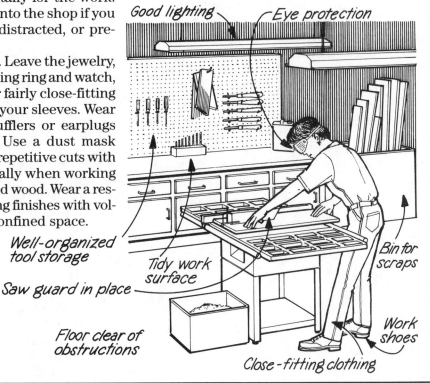

Good lighting

Eye protection

Well-organized tool storage

Tidy work surface

Saw guard in place

Floor clear of obstructions

Bin for scraps

Work shoes

Close-fitting clothing

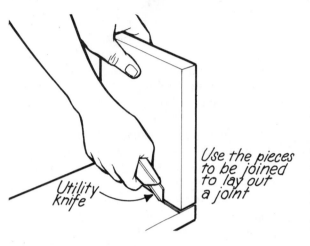

Use the pieces to be joined to lay out a joint

Utility knife

For laying out long cuts on plywood, you may find a chalk line useful.

If you have shop tools, such as a radial arm saw or a table saw, some of your layout work will be cutting work. That's because you can set up a variety of cutting guides on these power saws that help you to cut the size of piece you want. It takes some time and care to set up the guides, but once they're set, they'll allow you to produce as many uniform pieces as you need.

Marking pieces to be cut from larger boards or panels isn't the only layout work

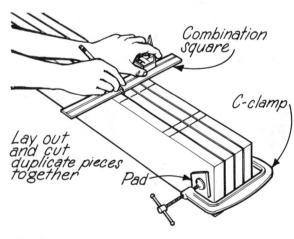

Combination square

C-clamp

Lay out and cut duplicate pieces together

Pad

you'll have in making outdoor furniture. There may be dadoes and grooves to be laid out, or holes to be drilled. When you do this kind of layout work, make your measurements from a common point. And remember where that point is so that it remains your single point of reference.

Keep the process in mind as you do your layout, so you make marks that are pertinent. No need to mark more than the center point of a hole to be drilled, for example. If you are plowing a groove with a router, a single position line will suffice; the router's setting and bit will determine the width and depth.

A trick used by skilled woodworkers is to use the parts being joined as measuring devices. In other words, if you are joining two pieces of 2-inch stock with a lap joint, lay one piece on top of the other and mark off the width of the laps, instead of measuring the desired width with a rule.

If you have duplicate pieces to make, lay them out at the same time. Clamp the pieces together and measure, mark, and cut them as a single unit.

Finally, but of primary importance, identify the pieces. This is vital in a complicated project. Don't be shy; lightly write "top" or "bottom" or "part A" on the wood. And if orientation may be a significant problem, mark an edge as the top, or one side as the front and the other as the back. Mark parts for joining, so that you glue each tenon into its custom-fitted mortise.

Cutting

The cutting picks up where layout leaves off. Crosscutting is cutting across the grain of the wood. Ripping is cutting with the grain.

There are combination blades for circular saws that can rip and crosscut, and for most work such a blade is okay. But finer cuts are achieved using rip blades for ripping, crosscut blades for crosscutting, and plywood blades for cutting plywood, hardboard, or particleboard.

Crosscutting

We'll assume you have a working familiarity with hand saws and power circular saws for crosscutting. For greater accuracy than freehand cutting, you can clamp a guide —any straight scrap of wood will do—to the wood being cut.

Very fine and accurate crosscuts, including those made on an angle, can be made with a backsaw and miter box. In the last few years, motorized miter boxes—also called "chop saws"—have become so common that even do-it-yourselfers are using them. They're

THE BASIC CUTS

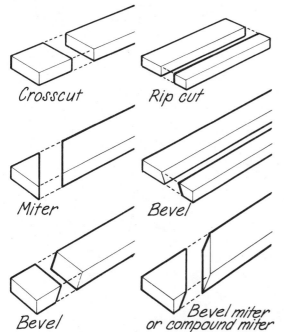

Crosscut

Rip cut

Miter

Bevel

Bevel

Bevel miter
or compound miter

CROSSCUTTING WITH A RADIAL ARM SAW

To cut several pieces to a given length, tack a stop to an extension table

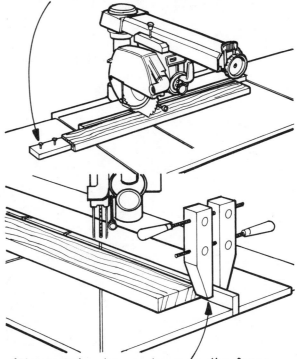

Alternately, place a clamp on the fence

most useful for cutting moldings and trim and crosscutting boards up to about 6 inches wide.

A radial arm saw is a natural for crosscutting. Miters, which are cuts made at an angle across the board's face, and bevels, which are cuts made at an angle through the board's thickness, are easily made. The work remains stationary while the blade is moved. If auxiliary tables are set up on either side of the saw itself, extremely long workpieces can be cut easily.

A table saw will also crosscut, miter,

403

and bevel. But in using a table saw, the workpiece is moved, while the blade remains in a fixed position. An accessory called a miter gauge is always used to guide the work in crosscutting and mitering with a table saw. Freehand cuts should *never* be made.

Ripping

A rip cut is made to establish the width or thickness of a board. The table saw is equipped with a fence, parallel to the blade, that is designed specifically to produce rip cuts. A portable circular saw is faster and easier to operate than a hand saw, but it's difficult to cut a perfectly straight line without a guide. You can also rip boards on a radial arm saw but it's usually awkward and considered to be unsafe.

Cutting Panels

For many projects, you'll find plywood to be indispensable. But it comes in unwieldy

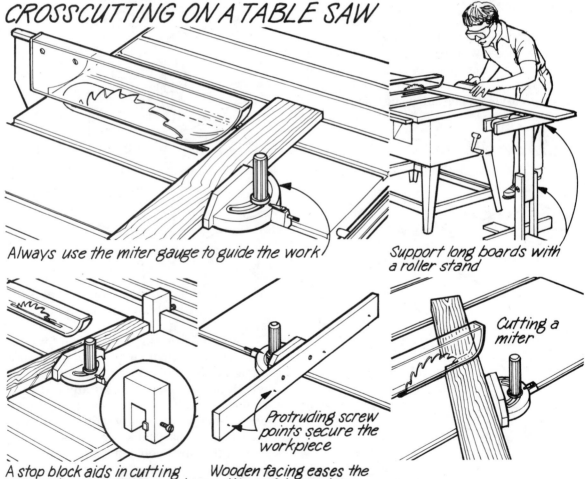

CROSSCUTTING ON A TABLE SAW

Always use the miter gauge to guide the work!

Support long boards with a roller stand

A stop block aids in cutting many pieces to the same size

Protruding screw points secure the workpiece

Wooden facing eases the cutting of long pieces

Cutting a miter

RIPPING WITH A TABLE SAW

Use the fence to guide rip cuts

Measure from the fence to the closest point on the blade

Use push sticks to guide the work safely

4×8-foot sheets that are tough to cut accurately. And because of the glues used in creating these and other man-made building materials like particleboard and hardboard, saws quickly become dulled.

Here's how to deal with this special cutting problem.

First, use the tools you'd use to crosscut,

unless you feel the extent of your project merits further investment. Remember that man-made panels will dull the blades quickly, so invest in a carbide-tipped blade for your power saw.

Finally, build a couple of sturdy sawhorses and use them, together with several expendable 8-foot 2×4s, to support the

A Fingerboard

A fingerboard can be made from an 18-inch length of 1×6. Cut off one end at a 60-degree angle. Make a series of stopped rip cuts into the mitered end, leaving a ¼-inch kerf. The longest finger should be about 8 inches.

To use the fingerboard, clamp it with a C-clamp to the left side of the saw table so that its fingers will hold the board to be cut in contact with the fence. Then you can feed the board into the blade without fear of kickback.

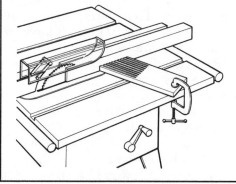

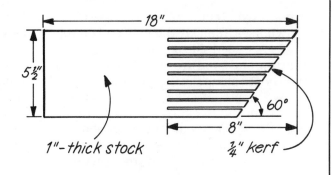

1"-thick stock

18"

5½"

60°

8"

¼" kerf

Circular Saw Rip Guide

You can easily build a circular saw guide. Use it for cutting panels and for ripping. A 4-foot guide can be made by cutting a 4-inch-wide strip and a 12-inch-wide strip from the 4-foot dimension of a plywood or particleboard panel. Be sure the narrow strip has the factory edge, which will be true. Glue and screw the narrow strip atop the wide strip, with the true edge facing in. The face of the saw's shoe will ride on the broad strip, while the edge of the shoe glides against the edge of the narrow strip. The first cut you make will trim the broad strip.

To use the guide, clamp or tack it to the plywood, lining up the sawed edge of the guide with the cutting line. Then slide the circular saw along the guide, cutting as you go.

Further, it's a good idea to measure your saw before making the guide, so you can make the narrow strip sufficiently wide so that clamps you use to secure the guide will be cleared by the motor housing.

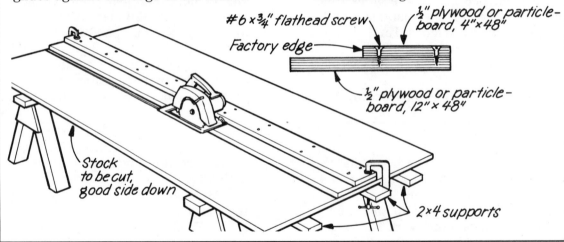

#6 x ¾" flathead screw

Factory edge

½" plywood or particle-board, 4" x 48"

½" plywood or particle-board, 12" x 48"

Stock to be cut, good side down

2x4 supports

plywood as you cut. Lay the 2 × 4s across the sawhorses, then lay the plywood on top of the 2 × 4s, good side down. After scribing the cutting lines, you are ready to cut. Clamp a guide board along the first cutting line. Set the saw's depth of cut just 1/16 to 1/8 inch greater than the thickness of the plywood, plug in the saw and cut. You'll cut shallow kerfs through the 2 × 4s, but as long as you set the depth of cut carefully, you won't seriously erode their strength.

Plywood panels can be cut using a table saw or a radial arm saw, but their large size makes them difficult to deal with on these shop tools. A good compromise is to halve or quarter the sheet with a circular saw, then make any further cuts using one of the shop saws. In the interests of safety, and to avoid botching an expensive piece of plywood, you should have someone help you maneuver any piece larger than 4 × 4.

When cutting plywood, you will want to

Groove

Dado

Rabbet

minimize splintering damage to the best face. You can do this by cutting with the good face up with a hand saw, table saw, or radial

arm saw, and with the good face down with a circular saw. The splintering occurs when the teeth leave the cut. The differences in approach reflect the different directions in which the various power saws turn.

Grooving, Dadoing, and Rabbeting

In woodworking terms, a groove is a channel cut into a board running with the grain. When a channel cuts across the grain, it is a dado. When it is cut at the edge of a board, so that it has only one side, it is a rabbet, whether it runs with or across the grain. When cut in making a lap joint, rabbets and dadoes are usually called laps. A blind or stopped groove or dado means

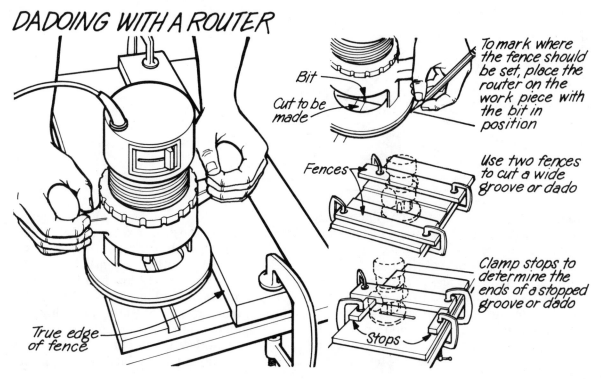

DADOING WITH A ROUTER

Bit

Cut to be made

To mark where the fence should be set, place the router on the work piece with the bit in position

Fences

Use two fences to cut a wide groove or dado

Clamp stops to determine the ends of a stopped groove or dado

Stops

True edge of fence

407

T-Square Router Guide

A router can machine grooves and dadoes almost anywhere on a board or panel—unlike a table saw with a dado cutter. The one thing you must do is clamp a straightedge to the workpiece to guide the router. Setting up that straightedge, making sure it is properly aligned, can be a trial.

This T-square router guide simplifies things. From 3-inch-wide hardwood stock—maple or birch are good choices for this—cut 14-inch and 30-inch pieces. Using glue and screws, attach the 30-inch guide bar to the 14-inch crosspiece, forming a T-square. Be very sure the guide bar is perfectly perpendicular to the crosspiece.

To set up the guide, butt the crosspiece against the edge of the panel to be routed, and the guide bar will be at a perfect right angle. Apply a clamp to the free end, and you are ready to rout.

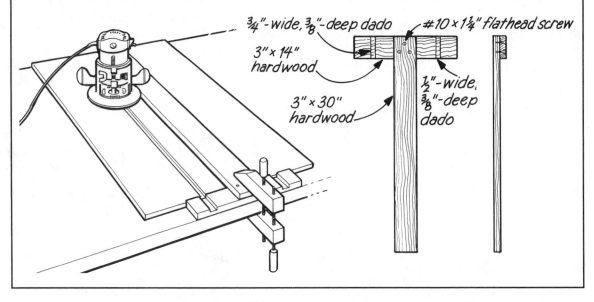

¾"-wide, ⅜"-deep dado   #10 x 1¼" flathead screw

3" x 14" hardwood

3" x 30" hardwood

½"-wide, ⅜"-deep dado

that the channel does not extend completely from edge to edge, it ends shy of either or both edges.

The router is one of the best tools for cutting grooves, dadoes, and rabbets. With a router, you usually need to lay out only the position of one edge of the groove. Clamp a straightedge to the workpiece to guide the movement of the router. If the groove is unusually wide, as would be a lap, then you may need to use two fences delineating the two edges of the groove. The diameter of the bit and the depth setting of the router will determine its width and depth.

There are literally dozens and dozens of different bits made for routers. Of interest at this point are straight and rabbeting bits. Straight bits are most commonly used for grooving and dadoing. The straight bit cuts a clean groove with a flat bottom and perpendicular sides. The diameter of the bit determines the width of the groove, and unless the channel to be cut is unusually wide, it's far wiser to cut a groove with a single pass of the proper-size bit than to make repeated passes with a too-small bit. Special rabbeting bits have a shank that extends below the cutters, forming a pilot that rides along the edge of the board, controlling the width of the cut. With such bits, the bit itself is the guide.

If you have a table or radial arm saw, you can cut grooves, dadoes, and rabbets with repeated cuts, or you can buy a dado cutter, which will cut various-size grooves with a single pass.

Dado cutters come in several varieties. The best design is the traditional multi-bladed assembly, which consists of two circular blades and several chippers of different thicknesses. The chippers are sandwiched between the circular blades. The number and thicknesses of chippers used determine the width of the groove. Most dado assemblies will cut grooves ranging from ¼ to ¾ inch in width, but the variety of groove widths possible within that range is limited. The depth of cut is adjusted by the saw mechanism.

Mounted in a power saw, the dado cutter plows grooves and some rabbets as it would rip, and cuts dadoes and other rabbets as it would crosscut. To lay out a cut simply delineate the position of the channel; its width and depth are established by the tool.

For most such work, the process is as simple as that. For some specialized joinery, the use of special jigs, fences, guides, and stops is advisable, partly so that the work is done properly and partly so that it is done safely. This situation occurs more frequently with the table saw than with the radial arm saw, because the blade settings are less flex-

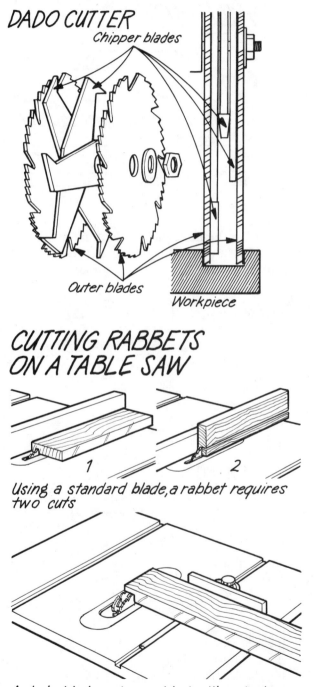

DADO CUTTER

Chipper blades

Outer blades

Workpiece

CUTTING RABBETS ON A TABLE SAW

Using a standard blade, a rabbet requires two cuts

A dado blade cuts a rabbet with a single pass

409

DRILL BITS

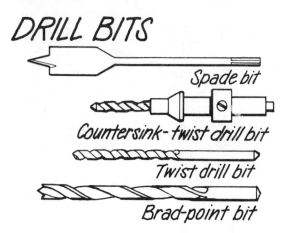

Spade bit

Countersink-twist drill bit

Twist drill bit

Brad-point bit

ible on the table saw. The radial arm saw's blade can be adjusted in degrees from a plumb vertical to a level horizontal, while

CUTTING A MORTISE

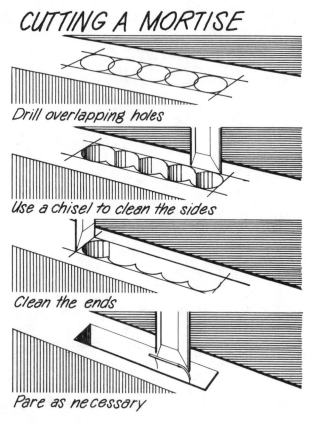

Drill overlapping holes

Use a chisel to clean the sides

Clean the ends

Pare as necessary

the table saw's blade will only adjust from a plumb vertical to a 45-degree angle. Thus most cuts can be made with the radial arm saw while the work lies flat and secure on the table, while to make some of the same cuts with the table saw will require the work to be stood on end or on edge. In all cases, the work is moved on the table saw while it usually is stationary on the radial arm saw. Moreover, the blade on the radial arm saw is always above the work, right where you can see it, while on the table saw, the work oftentimes obstructs your view of the blade.

Drilling Holes

In traditional joinery, drilling accurate holes is an important skill to master. There are many different uses for drilled holes and many types of drill bits and tools to make them.

Ordinary twist drill bits are probably the most common. They work well for making rough holes such as pilot holes for nails in hardwood. A step up are special brad-point wood bits. These have a sharp center point to keep them from wandering off center when beginning to cut, and two outer spurs which make a smoother surface on the walls of the hole. Spade bits, which need to be driven at high speeds in an electric drill, are good for making quick crude holes up to 1½ inches.

A pilot hole for a screw can be drilled with a separate drill bit and countersinking bit, but a better approach is to use a combination countersink-twist drill bit. These bits are commonly available for number 6 through 12 screws. The countersink sleeve adjusts with a set-screw to accommodate different screw lengths. These bits can also make counterbores for inserting dowel plugs over screw heads for a neat appearance.

PIPE CLAMP

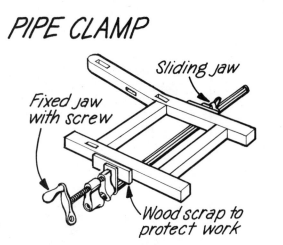

Sliding jaw

Fixed jaw with screw

Wood scrap to protect work

Cutting Mortises

Cutting a mortise-and-tenon joint is traditionally done with a mallet and chisel. The work goes faster if you remove the bulk of the waste for the mortise by drilling a series of holes, then square up the sides with a chisel.

The easiest way to cut mortises is with a mortising attachment on a drill press. This

HAND SCREW

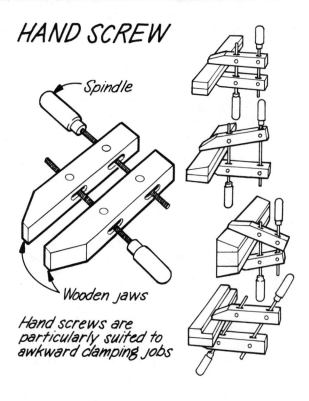

Spindle

Wooden jaws

Hand screws are particularly suited to awkward clamping jobs

combination drill-and-chisel tool actually "drills" a square hole. By making a series of

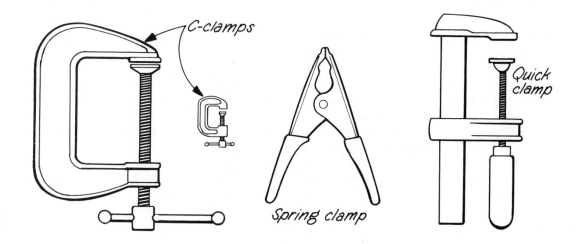

C-clamps

Spring clamp

Quick clamp

GLUING

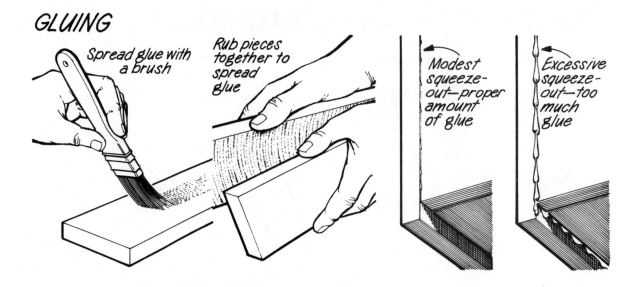

Spread glue with a brush

Rub pieces together to spread glue

Modest squeeze-out—proper amount of glue

Excessive squeeze-out—too much glue

these square holes, you can create almost any size mortise you want. The attachment is expensive, however, and setting it up takes a lot of time. For cutting only a few mortises, use the traditional approach. (A tenon, the other element of the mortise-and-tenon joint, is formed by cutting a rabbet into each face of the workpiece.)

Assembly

After the deliberation of layout and fabrication, assembly requires a faster pace. Glue must be applied, pieces joined together, and nails or screws driven or clamps applied, all before the glue dries. The process should be preplanned and well rehearsed.

The first thing to do is dry fit each assembly. This is like a dress rehearsal without glue to determine whether all the joints fit properly: snug but not so tight that they must be hammered together. You'll learn what clamps you'll need and just where and how to set them.

Clamps

After the glue is spread and the parts joined, clamps are used to compress the joint and hold the parts in position until the glue dries.

Bar or pipe clamps. These clamps are good for jobs in which the jaws must span long distances. Bar clamps are stronger, but they are expensive. Less-costly pipe clamps are bought in a kit of two separate jaws that are mounted on a length of ordinary black or galvanized steel pipe.

Hand screws. These wooden-jawed clamps are good for routine clamping jobs, because the jaws won't mar the work surfaces. They come in sizes ranging from those with 4-inch-long jaws that open 2 inches to those with 24-inch-long jaws that open a maximum of 17 inches.

C-clamps. These all-metal clamps have a C-shaped frame, with a threaded rod on one end that clamps the workpiece against the other end of the frame. Many sizes and styles of C-clamps are available, ranging from little ones with a maximum opening of only an inch through giants that open to a foot or more. Deep-throated clamps allow you to clamp the work farther in from the edge.

Spring clamps. These clamps are like jumbo-sized clothespins with heavy springs to keep the jaws tightly closed. They are available in many sizes, but none can exert the pressure of other types of clamps. They are good for keeping small parts in place and filling in between other larger clamps.

Quick clamps. These are a hybrid, combining the qualities of C-clamps and bar clamps, adding versatility to a clamp collection.

Fasteners

Nails, screws, and bolts are the mechanical fasteners you are likely to use in constructing outdoor furniture. As emphasized repeatedly throughout this book, fasteners used outdoors should be galvanized. For some outdoor furniture projects, you may want to use brass fasteners for aesthetic reasons.

Nails. For most projects, you'll use galvanized finishing nails. Each has a small head that can be driven below the surface of the wood with a countersink. The small depression is concealed with exterior wood filler.

To increase holding power, drive nails at a slight angle. Try to avoid positioning two nails along a line in the grain, for this will likely split the wood. For hardwoods, you may have to drill a small pilot hole to sink nails without bending their shanks. A general guide for length is to choose a nail so at least half its shank will penetrate the second of the two pieces being joined.

Screws. Until recently the slotted flathead wood screw was the most common screw fastener.

<table>
<tr><td>

Finishing Tips

• Seal the bottom ends of legs with melted paraffin or spar varnish to keep them from soaking up water.

• If you intend to apply a preservative stain or paint to a project, apply the first coat *before* you assemble the parts. This ensures that *all* surfaces will be coated.

• You can paint or stain pressure-treated lumber, but it's wise to wait a month or so to give the wood a chance to dry out. There's no need to keep it in your shop while it dries; the lumber will dry well enough for painting out in the sun.

• Avoid finishing outdoor furniture will polyurethane. Most brands of polyurethane dry too hard to expand and contract with the wood when it's placed out of doors. After a year or so, the finish will peel off. Use spar varnish or a 1:1 mixture of spar varnish and tung oil instead.

</td></tr>
</table>

Now the Phillips head "all-purpose screws," derived from screws used for hanging drywall, have all but replaced flathead wood screws. The all-purpose screws, with their tuliped heads and coarse threads, are easily driven with power screwdrivers or drills equipped with Phillips bits. These screws can be neatly self-countersunk by adjusting the driving torque of the drill. For outdoor use, galvanized all-purpose screws are available.

For a neater appearance, and regardless of the kind of screw you use, you can drill counterbores so the screws can be concealed beneath wood plugs. You can buy plugs, or make them with a plug cutter, a tool that is driven by a drill. Use plugs whose thickness matches their diameter.

You should try to use a screw long enough to get at least an inch of bite into the second piece.

Glue

Despite manufacturers' claims, few glues are able to withstand the havoc wrought by weather. Until recently, in fact, it was almost unthinkable to use glue in an outdoor project. Today, the situation is a little better. A few glues are now available that provide significant aid for the carpenter who is building objects that will be used outdoors.

Yellow glue. Also known as carpenter's wood glue, yellow glue is usually sold in squeeze bottles. An aliphatic resin, it dries quickly, is easy to sand, and is quite strong. It can be used in a wide range of temperatures. However, it offers only slight to moderate water resistance, so it should only be used on those parts of a project that will be protected from water.

Resorcinol resin glue. The adhesive of choice for outdoor wood projects, resorcinol is very strong and totally waterproof. It originally was intended for use on the hulls of wooden boats. Resorcinol glue has lengthy assembly and clamping times. It must be used at temperatures at or above 70°F. The higher the temperature, the faster the glue will set. It has good gap-filling qualities, good heat resistance. Its main drawback is that it dries to a dark film, so the glue lines might show in light-colored wood. A minor drawback is that two ingredients, a syrupy liquid and a powder, must be mixed just before use.

Epoxy resin glue. Epoxy is strong, fills gaps well, cures quickly, and is completely waterproof. It is also somewhat brittle. A specialized glue, it is useful for bonding metal, glass, or plastic to wood. Like resorcinol glue, you mix two ingredients together to prepare epoxy for application.

Using Glue

Make sure the mating surfaces are clean and smooth. Then spread glue on both. If spreading from a squeeze bottle, apply a zigzag bead of glue. If you are using a mixed glue, use a glue brush or a stick. When possible, rub together the two pieces to be joined to even the spread. End grain sucks up a lot of glue, so spread a second coat there after the first has had a chance to soak in.

Press the pieces together and clamp or fasten with nails or screws. A tiny amount of glue squeezed out of the joint line means you've used the right amount of glue; rivulets mean you've used too much. This squeeze-out should be cleaned up as quickly and completely as possible. Stains and other finishes won't adhere to dried glue left behind. Wipe up water-soluble glue with a wet sponge before it dries. Excess dried glue can be removed with a sharp knife, chisel, or scraper.

Finishing

Surface preparation is an important step before applying any finish. Preparing the surface means sanding. Sometimes it's easier to sand the individual pieces than it is to sand the assembled project. If you do finish sand the pieces before assembly, take precautions during gluing to avoid dried glue on the surface.

There are several types of sandpaper to choose from, but aluminum oxide, a man-made material that's harder than either flint or garnet, may be the best. It's readily available, long lasting, and can be used with a power sander or by hand.

Very coarse paper has a grit size ranging from 16 to 30; coarse ranges from 36 to 50 grit; medium is 60 to 100 grit, fine 120 to 180 grit, and very fine is 220 to 400 grit. If the wood is rough with lots of tool marks, start with a fairly coarse paper, say a 50 grit. Otherwise, a medium or fine paper is suitable for the initial sanding.

Use a belt sander for rough-sanding large surfaces or individual pieces before assembly. The sander should be kept moving and should be kept flat on the surface. It is very easy to gouge the surface with a belt sander.

Intermediate sanding is best done with a finishing sander, which uses regular sandpaper mounted on a pad. Finishing sanders with straight-line action are best because they won't leave cross-grain scratches. You should always sand with the grain, whether using a belt sander, finishing sander, or your own hand labor.

For hand sanding, use a commercial sanding block, or simply wrap a piece of sandpaper around a scrap of wood. For odd shapes, use odd-shaped scraps, like a piece of dowel.

After all your sanding is done, but before applying a finish, use a vacuum cleaner to remove the dust from the wood. Then wipe it with a clean rag dampened with mineral spirits.

Materials and Tools

You are getting serious about building your own outdoor furniture when you start to think about the materials you'd use, about the tools you'd need. You can't think about process without interrelating the materials and the tools involved.

By now you should have a good idea of the principles and techniques involved. You know what woodworking operations you need to perform to build the kind of outdoor furniture you desire. Along the way, you may have picked up fundamental information about materials and tools.

Lumber

Most of what you need to know about the lumber you use for outdoor furniture is in the Appendix. But here are a few tips to bear in mind when buying lumber. They can help ensure that you get exactly the lumber you need for the minimum expenditure possible.

■ Long boards are usually cheaper than short ones. For example, if you need two 8-foot-long 2×10s, you'll save money if you buy a 16-foot-long 2×10 and cut it in half yourself, rather than buy two 8-footers.

■ If you need a short length of a particular size board, see if the local lumberyard has a "cut-offs bin." Lumberyards often accumulate short—4 feet and under—boards that are of little use to their commercial customers. You can often get high-quality wood at low prices, and you can avoid building up a "cut-offs bin" of your own.

■ Before buying lumber of any particular grade, take a look at the next lower grade. For example, you may decide that you want #2 pine. Before buying it, look over the lumberyard's #3 pine. Sometimes the differences in quality are insignificant. If you are lucky, the quality difference won't matter for your project, but the wood will be less costly.

■ If possible, buy lumber that has edge grain rather than flat grain. Such wood is relatively rare, but looking for it can be worthwhile, especially for any wide boards you intend to use. Edge-grain boards will swell, shrink, and twist much less than flat-grain boards.

■ As a general rule, always buy about 10 percent more wood than you think you'll need. There's always a certain amount of waste, due to splits at the ends of some boards, knots that show up at exactly the wrong place, and so forth. The extra 10 percent should compensate for these problems.

Plywood

For many projects, you'll find plywood to be indispensable. You can get plywood made of either softwood or hardwood, but you will be most likely to use a softwood plywood for your outdoor furniture projects.

Traditionally, plywood has been sold in exterior and interior grades. Exterior plywood is put together with waterproof glue; interior plywood isn't. Recently, interior plywood has all but disappeared. Still, you should check to be sure that any plywood you buy for outdoor projects is intended for outdoor use.

Tools

Most accomplished craftsmen love their tools. And for good reason. Tools are personal. They are the conduit through which your skill shapes a project. Working with them often generates a familiarity and respect that's a joy to experience. Good tools work better, stay sharp longer, and are easier to maintain than the cheaper alternatives. For these reasons, buy the best you can afford.

Consider which projects you've chosen to build. Look over the cutting, fabrication, and assembly operations. What joints are used? What materials? What skills do you have? The answers to these questions will help you select the tools you will need.

Hand Tools

Hand tools are the backbone of your shop. You'll be using them for all the fundamental building techniques discussed above. A basic collection should include tools from the following categories:

Layout tools. For layout work, you need a tape or folding rule, a combination square or try square, a pencil, and a utility knife. At the next level you might also have a framing square, a level, a yard-long straightedge, a sliding T bevel, a marking gauge, and a pencil compass.

Cutting tools. Start with a basic crosscut hand saw. Buy one with 10 teeth per inch, which is a compromise between speed and smoothness of cutting.

The backsaw and miter box are very useful if you're doing handwork, but not too important if you are using power saws. Power miter boxes have replaced the old miter boxes for serious woodworkers.

You'll want to have an assortment of wood chisels. A set of four—¼-, ½-, ¾-, and 1-inch widths—with plastic handles will work for most jobs.

Hand planes are tricky to set up and use properly, but they're worth learning how to use. For most work you need only a block plane and a smoothing plane.

Drills. An eggbeater-style hand drill is handy but optional. You should have a collection of drill bits, including brad-point bits and combination countersink-twist drill bits for pilot holes for screws.

Hammers. A 16-ounce claw hammer will serve well for general duty, but driving 4d nails may require the lighter touch of a 10- or 12-ounce hammer. A wooden mallet is useful for striking chisels and for tapping the pieces of an assembly into alignment.

Garden benches come in plain and fancy. The elaborate bench at left is a project for an experienced woodworker, but the simple construction above is within the ability of most backyard builders.

Screwdrivers. A set of flat-bladed and Phillips screwdrivers is fine.

Clamps. Details on the various clamps available are found under the heading Clamps, earlier in this chapter. There's an old woodworking adage: "You can never have too many clamps." Include bar or pipe clamps, hand screws, C clamps, spring clamps, and band clamps in a complete collection.

Don't overlook a bench-mounted vise as a vital clamping device.

Portable Power Tools

Portable power tools, once the province of the professional, have steadily become more popular with the do-it-yourself woodworker. There is a greater variety of serviceable, reasonably priced power tools available than ever before. If you're planning to spend much time at woodworking, these tools will pay for themselves in added convenience and quality results.

Circular saw. With a circular saw you'll be able to make crosscuts and rip cuts with ease. A guide, either bought or homemade, will extend the versatility of a circular saw, enabling you to make long rips and to cut plywood panels.

A combination blade, which comes with most saws, is okay for general work, but it's better to get a set of blades: one for ripping, one for crosscutting, one for plywood cutting. Carbide-tipped blades will produce smoother cuts and will outlast conventional blades many times over.

Power drill. The basic tool kit should include a ⅜-inch electric drill with variable speed and reversing features. Cordless drills are great for ultimate portability, but lack the power of a good medium-duty corded model.

You'll need a selection of drill bits, including the aforementioned brad-point bits, twist drill bits, and countersink-twist drill bits. For large-diameter holes, you can use spade bits. And don't forget a Phillips bit to drive screws.

Router. Routers are said to be one of the fastest-selling new tools—no doubt because they are so versatile. You can cut dadoes, grooves, and rabbets with a router, the proper bit, and a homemade jig or two. These basic cuts will allow you to craft strong, attractive joints, and with a few other bits you can put finished edges on projects.

Be sure you get a router with easy-to-grip handles, a positive depth-adjustment system, and a ¾ or more horsepower motor. Initially, buy only those bits you are sure to use. A ¾-inch straight bit, a ⅜-inch rabbeting bit, and a ¼-inch round-over bit will get a lot of use in building outdoor furniture. In time, your collection of bits will grow.

Saber saw. This multipurpose portable saw may be best known for its ability to cut curves, and particularly inside circles. But it is a versatile saw and can substitute for a circular saw on the job.

The cutting edge on this tool is an interchangeable straight blade. All sorts of blades are available, including ones that cut metal. The blade reciprocates up and down, like the needle on a sewing machine. Because it is only connected to the saw at one end, the blade can be inserted in a hole drilled through a board and then make an interior cut. The narrowness of the blade allows it to saw tight curves. But the flexibility of the blade doesn't lend itself to making square cuts in thick stock; if you rush the cut the blade can flex, and the resulting cut will be irregular and out of square with the face of the board.

Sanders. The belt sander is a relatively coarse tool, designed primarily to remove a lot of material quickly. The width and circumference of the belt determine the sander's size.

The finish sander will put a very smooth finish on wood, but isn't very good for rough sanding. Ordinary sandpaper—usually a quarter of a standard sheet—is mounted on the pad. Orbital sanders move the pad in a circular path, thus always cutting with and across the grain. Straight-line sanders only move the pad back and forth, putting you in control over sanding with or across the grain.

Shop Tools

Shop tools are the permanent, heavy-duty counterparts of the portable power tools above. You don't need these stationary tools to build outdoor furniture, but they certainly expand your woodworking horizons. Many of the projects that follow do, in fact, involve operations that can only be performed on stationary power tools.

Table saw. This saw is the heart of most workshops. It is a cast-iron table with a circular saw blade projecting through its center. The blade can be raised or lowered to adjust the depth of cut, and tilted to make bevel cuts. An adjustable fence, parallel to the blade, guides rip cuts. The table saw excels at handling rip cuts and producing very accurate crosscuts, miters, and bevels. Dado blades and molding cutters can be used.

The size of the table saw is given in terms of the blade diameter. Ten-inch models are fairly standard for home shops. A 1-horsepower motor is a minimum requirement, though more power is better. Look for a fence that moves and locks easily, and extension tables to support large workpieces.

Band saw. This is the power saw that cuts curves. But it does a whole lot more than that. It cuts faster and deeper than any other shop tool. A saber saw can do some of the chores of a band saw, but lacks the speed and capacity of this shop tool.

The blade is a thin steel band, ranging from ⅛ to ¾ inch wide, welded into a loop. It is looped around two or three wheels mounted in a housing and powered by a ½- to 2-horsepower motor. The blade passes through the center of a 12- to 14-inch-square metal worktable.

The size of the saw is determined by its throat depth, that is, the distance between the blade and the saw frame. The throat depth dictates the widest cut that can be made. The depth of cut is dictated by the adjustability of the upper guide assembly that surrounds the blade above the worktable, and ranges from 3 inches up to 7½ inches on large models. The width of the blade dictates the radius of cut that can be made; the more narrow the blade, the tighter the radius of curve that can be cut.

The typical home shop band saw is a 14-inch model with a ½- or ¾-horsepower motor.

Radial arm saw. This is essentially a circular saw mounted in a yoke in which it can swivel and swing. The yoke is in turn mounted on an overhead arm that can be raised and lowered and swung from side to side. Because of all these pivot points, it's a saw that's hard to keep aligned and adjusted. The radial arm saw excels at making crosscuts, though it can handle rip cuts, miters, bevels, and combination cuts, too.

The diameter of the blade determines the saw's size. A 10-inch saw is typical for the home shop. Look for ball-, roller-, or needle-bearing construction, easy-to-use controls, and a 1- to 2-horsepower motor.

Drill press. The drill press is a versatile shop tool that can rout, sand, and cut mortises, as well as drill holes. It is available in bench-top or floor models. A standard size is the 15-inch drill press, which means it can drill a hole in the center of a 15-inch-wide board.

419

HOW TO GARDEN BENCH

How often have you longed for a shady bench to rest those weary bones after a morning's weeding, or regretted not having a flat, steady surface for some impromptu potting work, or just wished for a seat on which to "set a spell" and delight in the fruits of your labor? Here's a simple, rugged model that will enhance the appearance of any garden.

1. A piece of 2×12 rough-cut spruce is used for the top and legs. Out of an 8-foot plank, cut one 64-inch piece for the top and two 16-inch pieces for the legs. Sand all pieces lightly, especially edges and corners.

2. On the bottom of the seat plank, 8 inches from each end, cut a ½-inch-deep channel the thickness of the legs. This can be done either with repeated cuts of the table saw or with a hand saw and a hammer and chisel.

3. Cut a small V notch on the bottoms of the 16-inch legs. Cut a hole large enough to insert a 2×4 in the middle of each leg. (Mark the hole, drill out the bulk of the material with a brace and bit, then clean up the edges with a hammer and a chisel.)

4. Cut a 53-inch length of 2×4. Cut corners on 45-degree angles, as shown.

5. Insert legs into the channels. Glue and nail from the top with 16d nails. Insert the 2×4 into the holes in the legs. Drill ½-inch holes in the 2×4 on each side of each leg and insert 3-inch-long ½-inch dowels. (You can fashion your own from a piece of scrap wood.) Two coats of linseed oil will help weatherproof the wood.

Materials List

Number	Piece	Dimensions	Material
1	Top	1½″ × 11¼″ × 64″	spruce
2	Legs	1½″ × 11¼″ × 16″	spruce
1	Stretcher	1½″ × 3½″ × 53″	spruce
4	Dowels	3″ × ½″ dia.	

Hardware
16d galvanized nails
waterproof glue

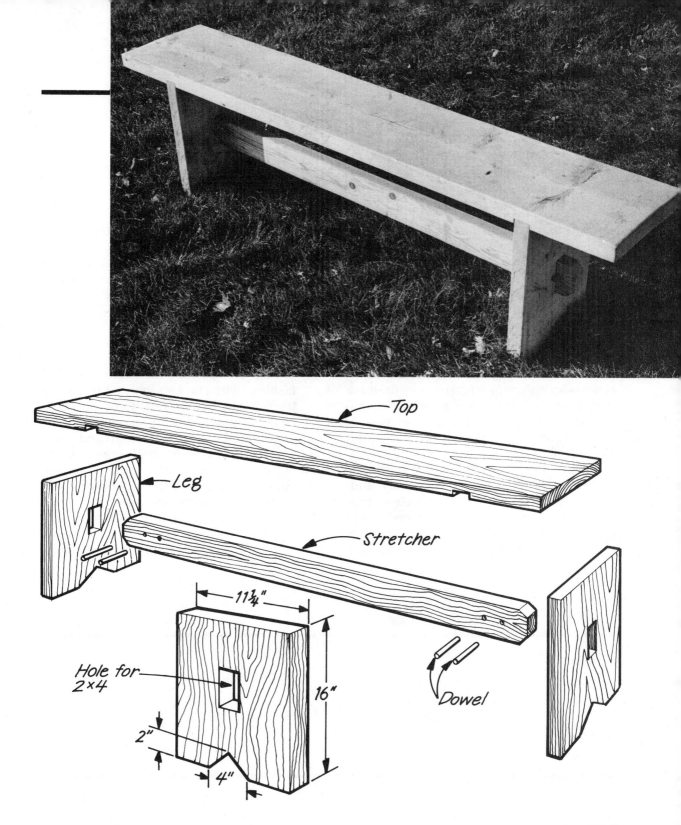

Top

Leg

Stretcher

Hole for
2×4

Dowel

11¾"

16"

2"

4"

HOW TO BACK-DOOR MUD CATCHER

The usual doormat is okay for brushing the dust off your loafers, but dirt is one of the big drawbacks to outdoor living. A load of mud on the gardening boots requires a mat with some starch. And that's what this distinctive wooden doormat has.

The grid is stiff and sturdy, just the ticket for scraping the dirt off shoes. The big gaps won't clog after only a scrape or two. And the mud-catcher is cleaned as easily as it cleans shoes. Just pick it up, sweep under it, then hose it off. It's easy to make, not bad to look at, and you'll probably never wear it out. It'll stand up to years of heavy (and dirty) feet.

Because it will spend its life outdoors, resting on the damp (and occasionally muddy) doorstep, it's wise to use a rot-resistant wood for this project. Redwood, cedar, and cypress are all reasonable choices, as is pressure-treated wood. We chose a durable hardwood, oak, to make the mud-catcher shown.

1. Cut 1 × 2s to length. You'll need seven rails 32¾ inches long and nine cross members 25¼ inches long.
2. Measure and mark the dadoes on two rails and two cross members, as shown. Measure carefully to guarantee tight-fitting joints.
3. Clamp the rails together, butcher-block fashion, with the two marked pieces on the outside. Use a straightedge and pencil to extend the layout marks across the edges of all the pieces. Clamp and mark seven cross members in the same way.
4. Set a circular saw for a ¾-inch depth of cut. Clamp a scrap board across the 1 × 2s to serve as a guide for the saw, and cut dadoes. Position and reposition the guide to cut the cheeks of each dado, then saw freehand to remove the wood between

Materials List

Number	Piece	Dimensions	Material
7	Rails	¾″ × 1½″ × 32¾″	oak
9	Cross members	¾″ × 1½″ × 25¼″	oak

Hardware
8 #8 × 2½″ brass flathead wood screws

the cuts. Clean up the bottoms of the dadoes with a ¾-inch chisel. Repeat the entire process to dado seven of the cross members.

5. Assemble the pieces without glue to check the fit, and trim the dadoes with the chisel, if necessary. Apply glue when everything fits. A finishing nail or a screw through the underside of every other joint eliminates the need for clamps.

6. The two undadoed cross members are the scrapers. Fasten them from the underside of the assembly with 2½-inch brass flathead wood screws. Drill pilot holes for the screws or you'll split the wood.

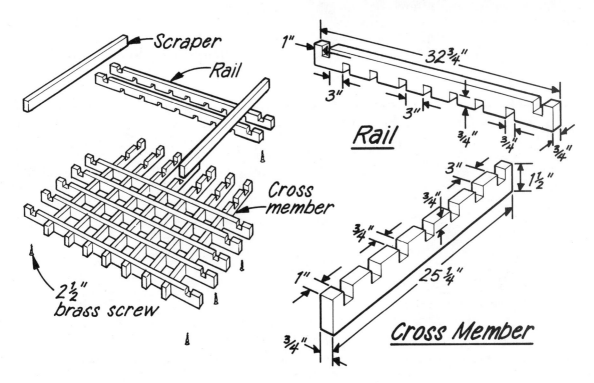

Scraper

Rail

Cross member

2½" brass screw

Rail 1" 32¾" 3" 3" ¾" ¾" ¾"

Cross Member 3" 1½" ¾" ¾" 1" 25¼" ¾"

HOW TO TUB PLANTER

Whether you're growing tomatoes with alyssum on your rooftop or a compact Key lime on your sun deck, this tub planter makes a durable and attractive base for your contained garden. Because wood is porous, it is one of the best materials for planters, insulating plant roots and soil from excessive heat.

Several design features make this 8-cubic-foot box especially sturdy. The platform bottom is of double thickness and includes narrow gaps between boards to provide for expansion and contraction, as well as drainage. The top edge of the box is held firmly together with a braced band and mitered cap.

The galvanized wood screws add strength and allow you to disassemble the box so that you can root-prune dwarf fruit trees or large shrubs when necessary.

Finally, casters on the bottom of the planter allow you to move it from the porch, patio, or deck in summer to a bright kitchen or sun space in winter.

1. The 22¾-inch-square base has two layers of three boards each. Cut six boards to length. Lay out the base with three boards over three boards, as shown. Drive screws through the top layer into the bottom layer. Attach the casters.
2. Turn the base over, so it rests on the casters. The sides should extend to within 1¼ inches of the ground. Install the side boards individually, driving screws through predrilled holes into the base. Tie the corners together by driving three or four 1⅝-inch #6 screws through one corner board into the edge of the board it overlaps.
3. Miter the ends of the four band pieces, as

Materials List

Number	Piece	Dimensions	Material
6	Bottom boards	¾″ × 7¼″ × 22¾″	redwood
12	Side slats	¾″ × 7¾″ × 23¾″	redwood
4	Bands	¾″ × 1½″ × 25¾″	redwood
4	Caps	¾″ × 2″ × 26¾″	redwood
16	Battens	¾″ × 1½″ × 22¼″	redwood

Hardware
12-16 #6 × 1⅝″ galvanized wood screws
1 box #6 × 1¼″ galvanized wood screws
4–3½″ metal corner braces
4 heavy-duty casters
clear wood finish for exterior wood (or other ultraviolet inhibitor)

424

shown. Chisel $1/16 \times 3\frac{1}{2}$-inch recesses in the ends for metal corner braces. Screw the bands in place, then attach the metal braces.

4. Cut the four cap pieces and miter the ends. Install the cap flush with the inside of the planter, so it conceals the edges of the sides as well as the braced band.

5. Screw the battens to the sides to cover the joints between the side boards. The corner battens are flush with the side edges.

6. To retain the redwood color, paint the outside of the planter with clear wood finish. It's not necessary to paint the inside of the planter.

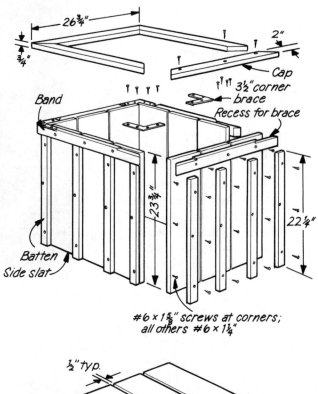

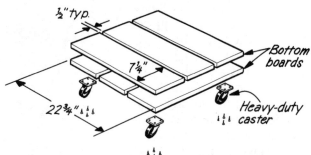

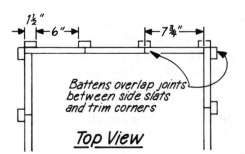

PROJECT

TRESTLE PICNIC TABLE AND BENCHES

Anyone who enjoys the outdoors should have a picnic table. The only thing more satisfying than a picnic in the out-of-doors is a picnic in the out-of-doors on a table you built yourself.

This clean and simple design has been around forever. There's nothing fancy about it but it works, and if you take care of it this table could be around for a couple of generations.

The bolted construction is sturdy and allows you to use very simple tools and joints. You should be able to do a good job on this project with a saber saw, drill, screwdriver, and a couple of wrenches.

Depending on your tastes you can make this table of redwood or cedar. Or you can use construction-grade fir and paint or stain it. Whatever you choose, you'll get a light but sturdy table that will be a favorite outdoor dining spot for years to come.

Shopping List

2 pcs. 2 × 6 × 12' redwood
1 pc. 2 × 6 × 8' redwood
3 pcs. 2 × 4 × 12' redwood
1 pc. 2 × 4 × 8' redwood
2 pcs. 2 × 3 × 12' redwood
2 pcs. 2 × 3 × 8' redwood
1 pc. 1 × 2 × 10' redwood
50 #6 × 2½" galvanized all-purpose screws
44 #6 × 2" galvanized all-purpose screws
4-5½" × ¼" galvanized carriage bolts w/nuts and washers
8-4½" × ¼" galvanized carriage bolts w/nuts and washers
6-4" × ¼" galvanized carriage bolts w/nuts and washers
exterior-grade paint, stain, or wood preservative

426

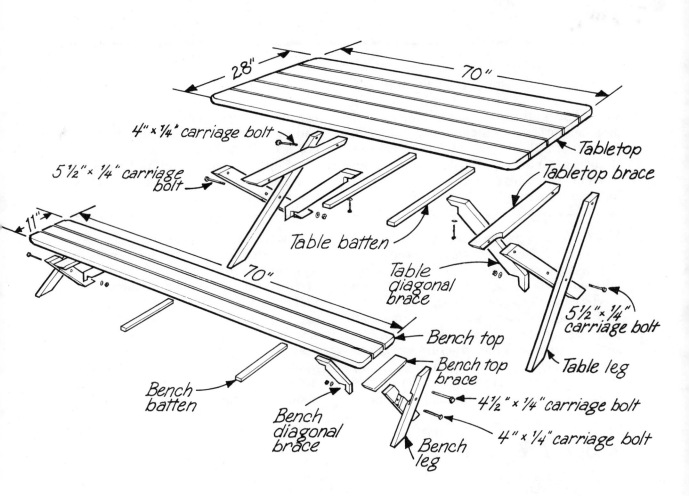

4" x ¼" carriage bolt

5½" x ¼" carriage bolt

Tabletop

Tabletop brace

Table batten

28"

70"

11"

70"

Table diagonal brace

5½" x ¼" carriage bolt

Table leg

Bench top

Bench top brace

Bench batten

Bench diagonal brace

Bench leg

4½" x ¼" carriage bolt

4" x ¼" carriage bolt

Cutting List

Number	Piece	Dimensions	Material
5	Tabletop	1½" × 5½" × 70"	redwood
2	Table battens	¾" × 1½" × 27"	redwood
4	Table legs	1½" × 2½" × 37½"	redwood
2	Table top braces	1½" × 3½" × 27"	redwood
2	Table diagonal braces	1½" × 2½" × 20"	redwood
6	Bench top	1½" × 3½" × 70"	redwood
4	Bench battens	¾" × 1½" × 10"	redwood
8	Bench legs	1½" × 2½" × 18¼"	redwood
4	Bench top braces	1½" × 2½" × 10"	redwood
4	Bench diagonal braces	1½" × 2½" × 12"	redwood

1. **Cut and assemble the tabletop.** The top is composed of five lengths of 2 × 6 stock. After cutting the boards, lay them out on a flat surface, arranging them bark side up so that if they cup, you won't have five troughs as a tabletop. You don't want blemishes or defects exposed, so use your best judgment in arranging the boards.

Mark a 2-inch radius on the outside corners of the two outer boards, and cut the corners off with a saber saw. If you like, you can discreetly bevel or round over the top edges of all the boards.

Flip the boards over. Cut the battens, bevel the ends at 45 degrees, and screw them to the top boards.

2. **Cut the legs, and top and diagonal braces next.** The lengths given in the materials list are total lengths, but the legs are mitered on both ends. If you lay out the pieces carefully you can avoid some waste. With judicious layout work, you can get all four legs out of a 12-foot 2 × 3. Note that the actual geometry of the structure works out to a leg angle of 48 degrees, but if you miter the ends at 45 degrees—a standard angle you can lay out with a combination square—

you won't have any problems.

Notch one end of the top braces so the legs don't have to be lapped. Bevel the ends of the braces to reduce their menace to picnickers' knees.

Cut the diagonal braces and, with a saber saw, notch them. The notches provide flat seats for the fasteners that will hold the assembly together. You should locate the notches so the fasteners extend through about 1½ inches of the brace.

TABLE LEG LAYOUT

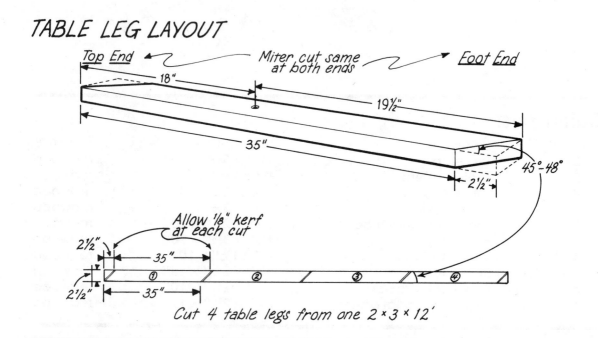

Cut 4 table legs from one 2 × 3 × 12'

3. **Assemble the legs and braces.** First, drill holes for the three bolts that will join the legs and braces. Clamp the top brace near the edge of the tabletop or a workbench. Stand two legs in position, get the alignment set, then clamp them where they cross. While a helper holds the legs against the top brace, drill through the leg and the brace. Since the holes are deep—a minimum of $3\frac{1}{3}$ inches—you may need to drill through the leg and into the brace, then remove the leg and complete the hole in the brace. Get the holes in perfect alignment.

After the first set of legs and braces has been bored, do the second set.

4. **Build the benches.** The benches are built in the same general way as the table, except that the legs are mitered at 60 degrees and paired with half-lap joints. The top brace, consequently, does not need to be notched. When placing the leg and brace assemblies on the seat boards, place them so there is a 54-inch space between the legs. This will allow the benches to fit under the table when not in use.

To lay out the half-laps, cut the legs and miter them. Then lay one leg atop the other, align them, and scribe lines on each leg, using the other as a guide.

To cut the half-laps, set a circular saw to cut half the thickness of the stock ($\frac{3}{4}$ inch). Cut just inside the lines you marked, then make additional cuts between the first two. Chisel out the waste and clean up the bottom of the recess. Test fit the legs together, and

5. **Apply a finish.** Take care to spread the paint or varnish in between all the boards. Apply at least two coats.
NOTE: If the table is to sit directly on the

Now screw the top braces in position on the bottom of the tabletop. Be sure they are oriented properly. Bolt the legs in place with carriage bolts, washers, and nuts, orienting the threaded ends of the bolts toward the center of the table. Have a helper hold a diagonal brace in position. Drill through the legs and the brace; bore the hole in two stages if necessary. Install a carriage bolt, washer, and nut. Repeat the process to install the second diagonal brace.

Finally, change bits and drill pilot holes through the free ends of the diagonal braces. Drive screws through the braces into the tabletop.

BENCH LEG AND BRACE

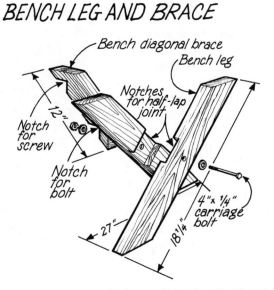

Bench diagonal brace
Bench leg
Notches for half-lap joint
Notch for screw
Notch for bolt
12"
27"
18¼"
4" x ¼" carriage bolt

use a chisel or file to refine the fit if it is too tight.

ground you may want to add an extra coat of paint or other preservative to the ends of the legs, to limit moisture absorption. Renew this application yearly.

PROJECT
2×4 OUTDOOR FURNITURE

Outdoor furniture constructed of 2 × 4s has been popular for years, not only for its appearance, but for its durability and comfort. There are many variations, but generally the furniture is constructed of redwood with galvanized fasteners. In commercial versions, the cushions are often supported by a grid of steel springs and straps.

The outdoor furniture set shown includes a chair, a settee that is no more than a wide chair, a table, and a chaise lounge. It is a swell ensemble for the patio, deck, or a grassy terrace. It's so easy to build. The only power tools you need are a circular saw, a drill, and a router. All the wood is used at stock dimensions. There's no fancy joinery.

Moreover, the pieces don't *have* to be built of expensive wood. Redwood or cedar is nice, but experience demonstrates that a furniture piece built with joints that won't trap mois-

430

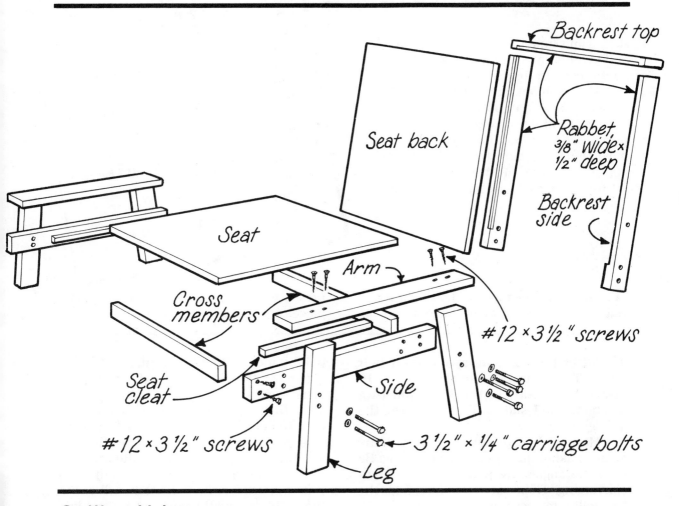

Backrest top

Rabbet, 3/8" wide × 1/2" deep

Backrest side

Seat back

Seat

Arm

Cross members

#12 × 3½" screws

Seat cleat

Side

#12 × 3½" screws

3½" × ¼" carriage bolts

Leg

Cutting List—Chair

Number	Piece	Dimensions	Material
4	Legs	1½" × 3½" × 22"	fir
2	Sides	1½" × 3½" × 29½"	fir
2	Cross members	1½" × 2½" × 20"	fir
2	Arms	1½" × 3½" × 27"	fir
2	Backrest sides	1½" × 3½" × 25½"	fir
1	Backrest top	1½" × 3½" × 20"	fir
2	Seat cleats	1½" × 1½" × 12"	fir
1	Seat	20" × 21"	plywood
1	Seat back	18" × 22"	plywood

ture using fundamentally sound material, and given a modicum of care and maintenance, can last for decades.

The cushions are homemade, though suitable cushions are available wherever such outdoor furniture is sold. If you plan to use purchased cushions, don't build until you have them. Measure the cushions, and if appropriate, alter the dimensions of the furniture so the cushions will fit properly.

Chair

1. **Cut the frame pieces.** Choose the material you want to work with—redwood, fir, pressure-treated pine, cedar—and cut all the pieces at one time.

2. **Miter the legs and lay out their bolt holes.** The basic angle in the chair is 10 degrees. It is easiest to deal with if you use a protractor and sliding T bevel to set the angle.

Mark the legs, top and bottom, with the angle, making the legs 21¼ inches long. Be sure the angles are parallel, rather than converging. Then cut. Thus modified, the legs will intersect the sides at an angle 10 degrees off vertical.

The bottom edges of the sides meet the legs 10¾ inches from the foot, so scribe a line on the legs at that point to aid in the layout. The front legs meet the sides at a point 2 inches from the front, and the rear legs meet the sides ⅛ inch from the rear. Mark these points on the lower edge of the sides, then, using your sliding T bevel, scribe that 10-degree angle across the face of the side, so the front legs lean toward the back and the rear legs lean toward the front.

Lay the legs on the sides and drill two ¼-inch holes for the bolts that will secure them. (In drilling the holes in the rear legs, try to avoid positioning the bolts so they conflict with the rear cross member; we had such a conflict, which was resolved by chiseling an inside corner off the cross member.)

3. **Assemble the basic frame from the sides and cross members.** After drilling appropriate pilot holes and countersinking, drive two 3½-inch #12 screws through the sides into the butt ends of each cross member. The front cross member should be flush with the bottom of the sides, while the rear cross member should be flush with the top of the sides. Bolt the legs to the basic frame.

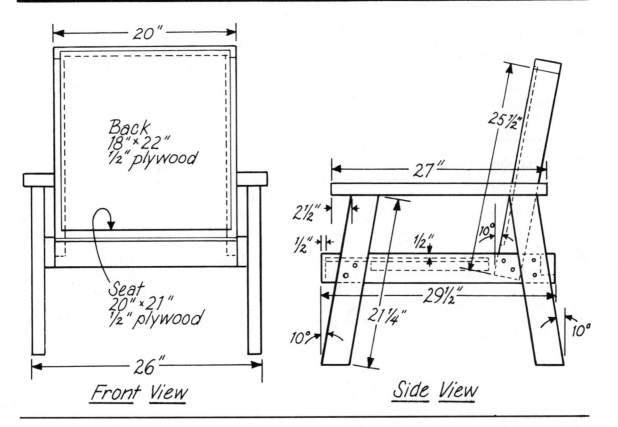

Back
18" × 22"
½" plywood

Seat
20" × 21"
½" plywood

20"

26"

Front View

27"

25½"

2½"

½"

½"

10°

29½"

21¼"

10°

10°

Side View

4. Install the arms. The arms can be given a more finished appearance by cutting a slight bevel around the top edge with a block plane and rasp. Secure the arms to the legs with 3½-inch #12 galvanized screws. The arm overhangs the front leg by 2½ inches, and the inner edge must be in the same plane as the inner edge of the sides. Position the arms, and have someone hold them in place while you drill pilot holes and drive the screws.

5. Assemble the seat back. After drilling pilot holes and countersinking, drive two 3½-inch #12 screws through each end of the backrest top into the butt ends of the backrest sides.

With a router and a rabbeting bit, machine a ⅜-inch-wide, ½-inch-deep rabbet into the backrest assembly for the plywood seat back to set into; the rabbet extends across the lower edge of the backrest top and 21⅝ inches down the inner edge of each side. (If you haven't the tools to cut the rabbet, cut appropriate lengths of 2 × 2 or 1 × 1 for cleats and secure them to the inside of the backrest assembly, ½ inch from the front edge. Then cut the plywood back a bit smaller so it will fit into the assembly and rest against the cleats.)

433

6. **Install the backrest assembly.** This assembly tilts off vertical at the same 10-degree angle as the legs. Have a helper hold the assembly in place and drill one ¼-inch hole through each side and backrest side.

Bolt the assembly in place, make final adjustments and drill a second hole, and finish bolting the back in place. Drill a pilot hole through each backrest side into the arm; countersink and drive a 2½-inch #12 screw.

7. **Install the seat panels.** A cleat is positioned on each inner face of the sides, 1 inch below the top, with two 2½-inch #12 galvanized screws in each.

Cut a 20 × 21-inch piece of ½-inch exterior-grade plywood for the seat, and an 18 × 22-inch piece for the seat back. Install the seat and seat back with the good side down.

8. **Apply a finish.** Paint or varnish the completed chair. Take care to apply the finish evenly, to the bottom as well as the top. Apply at least two coats.
NOTE: If the chair is to sit directly on the ground, you may want to add an extra coat of paint or other preservative to the ends of the legs to limit moisture absorption. Renew this application yearly.

Settee

The settee is constructed in the same manner and sequence as the chair. The only difference is that the backrest top and the cross members, and consequently the seat and the seat back panels, are longer. Cut the pieces as indicated in the Cutting List and assemble them in accordance with the directions for the chair.

Before installing the seat panel, cut and install a 26½-inch 2 × 2 seat brace extending from cross member to cross member, midway between the sides. Drive a 3-inch

Cutting List—Settee

Number	Piece	Dimensions	Material
4	Legs	1½″ × 3½″ × 22″	fir
2	Sides	1½″ × 3½″ × 29½″	fir
2	Cross members	1½″ × 2½″ × 48″	fir
2	Arms	1½″ × 3½″ × 27″	fir
2	Backrest sides	1½″ × 3½″ × 25½″	fir
1	Backrest top	1½″ × 3½″ × 48″	fir
2	Seat cleats	1½″ × 1½″ × 16″	fir
1	Seat brace	1½″ × 1½″ × 26½″	fir
1	Seat	21″ × 48″	plywood
1	Seat back	22″ × 46″	plywood

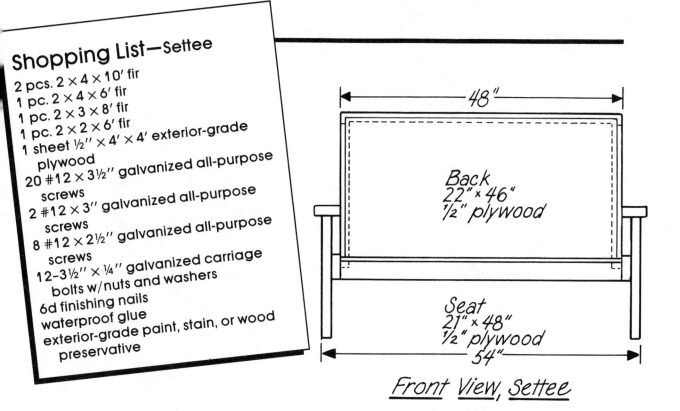

Shopping List—Settee

2 pcs. 2 × 4 × 10' fir
1 pc. 2 × 4 × 6' fir
1 pc. 2 × 3 × 8' fir
1 pc. 2 × 2 × 6' fir
1 sheet ½" × 4' × 4' exterior-grade plywood
20 #12 × 3½" galvanized all-purpose screws
2 #12 × 3" galvanized all-purpose screws
8 #12 × 2½" galvanized all-purpose screws
12–3½" × ¼" galvanized carriage bolts w/nuts and washers
6d finishing nails
waterproof glue
exterior-grade paint, stain, or wood preservative

48"

Back
22" × 46"
½" plywood

Seat
21" × 48"
½" plywood
54"

Front View, Settee

#12 screw through the cross members into each end of the brace. This brace will pre-vent the seat from sagging. You may want to use a seat panel cut from ¾-inch plywood.

Chaise

1. Assemble the basic frame. Cut the sides, front and back ends, and seat cleats.

Using two 3½-inch #12 screws at each joint, fasten the sides to the end pieces, making sure the bottom of the front end is flush with the bottoms of the sides. The seat cleats are secured to the sides with five 2½-inch #12 screws in each. The cleats are located 1 inch below the top edge of the sides and 7½ inches shy of the very front of the assembly.

2. Install the front legs. Cut two 11-inch legs from 2 × 4 and a 21-inch length of ¾-inch dowel for the rung. Drill a ¾-inch hole in the middle of each leg, 4 inches from the foot. Clamp one leg in position, butted against the seat cleat, with the top of the leg flush with the top of the cleat. Drill two ¼-inch holes through the side and the leg. Repeat the process with the other leg.

Drive the rung into the ¾-inch hole in one leg, then force the other leg on the other end of the rung, making sure the legs are parallel. With the chaise frame upside down, slip the leg assembly in position and bolt it in place with four 3½-inch carriage bolts with nuts and washers.

Rabbet 3/8" wide × 1/2" deep

Backrest Top

Backrest side

3 1/2" × 1/4" carriage bolt

Seat back

Backrest support

Backrest support rod

Back end

Armrest

Armrest support

Seat

Rear leg

Hitch-pin clip

Side

Axle

Wheel

Seat cleat

Front end

1/2" flat washers

Front leg

Front leg rung

3. **Install the rear legs and wheels.** Cut the legs, axle, and wheels.

Drill a 1/2-inch hole for the axle in the middle of each leg, 1 inch from the bottom. In succession, clamp each leg in position 7 1/4 inches from the very rear of the chaise frame and 1 inch below the top edge of the sides, and drill two 1/4-inch holes for the mounting bolts. Drill a 1/8-inch hole 2 1/2 inches from each end of the axle for the hitch-pin clip.

Insert a clip in one of the holes, then in succession add a washer, a wheel, another washer, and a leg. Repeat the process at the other end of the axle, then position the assembly on the chaise frame and bolt in place.

4. **Fabricate and assemble the backrest.** Cut the sides, top, supports, and support rod. Fasten the sides and top together, driving two 3 1/2-inch #12 screws through each side into the butt ends of the top.

436

Shopping List—Chaise

1 pc. 1 × 8 × 2' #2 pine
1 pc. 2 × 4 × 14' fir
1 pc. 2 × 4 × 12' fir
1 pc. 2 × 3 × 2' fir
1 pc. 2 × 2 × 12' fir
2 pcs. 36" × 3/4" dia. dowel
1 sheet 1/2" × 4' × 4' exterior-grade plywood
1 pc. 36" × 1/2" dia. steel rod
12 #12 × 3 1/2" galvanized all-purpose screws
18 #12 × 2 1/2" galvanized all-purpose screws
12–3 1/2" × 1/4" galvanized carriage bolts w/ nuts and washers
4–1/2" flat washers
2 hitch-pin clips
6d finishing nails
exterior-grade paint, stain, or wood preservative

Cutting List—Chaise

Number	Piece	Dimensions	Material
2	Sides	1½″ × 3½″ × 63″	fir
1	Back end	1½″ × 3½″ × 21″	fir
1	Front end	1½″ × 2½″ × 21″	fir
2	Seat cleats	1½″ × 1½″ × 34″	fir
2	Front legs	1½″ × 3½″ × 11″	fir
1	Front leg rung	21″ × ¾″	dowel
2	Rear legs	1½″ × 3½″ × 9″	fir
2	Wheels	¾″ × 6″ dia.	pine
2	Backrest sides	1½″ × 3½″ × 29″	fir
1	Backrest top	1½″ × 3½″ × 18″	fir
2	Backrest supports	1½″ × 1½″ × 11½″	fir
1	Backrest support rod	24″ × ¾″	dowel
1	Seat	½″ × 21″ × 42″	plywood
1	Seat back	½″ × 18½″ × 23″	plywood
2	Armrests	1½″ × 3½″ × 14″	fir
4	Armrest supports	1½″ × 1½″ × 8½″	fir

Using a router and a rabbeting bit, machine a ⅜-inch-wide, ½-inch-deep rabbet into the backrest for the plywood seat back to set into; extend the rabbet across the lower edge of the top and 23 inches down the inner edge of the sides. (If you haven't the tools to cut the rabbet, cut appropriate lengths of 2 × 2 or 1 × 1 for cleats and secure them to the inside of the seat back assembly, ½ inch from the front edge. Then cut the plywood seat back a bit smaller so it will fit into the assembly and rest against the cleats.)

In the middle of the backrest sides, 15 inches from the top, drill a ¼-inch-diameter hole. Drill a similar hole 1 inch from the bottom of the sides. In each support, drill a ¼-inch-diameter hole in the middle, ¾ inch from one end, and a ¾-inch hole in a similar spot at the other end.

Force the supports over the ends of the support rod, so that 1½ inches of the rod project through the support. Then bolt the support assembly to the backrest frame with 3½-inch carriage bolts. Finally, bolt the backrest assembly to the chaise frame.

5. **Make the backrest support notches.** Measure from the rear end of the frame and square a line across the top of the sides at 2¼, 5, 8, and 11 inches. These lines are at the centers of the notches, which are made with a half-round rasp.

6. **Cut and install the seat and back panels.** Both can be cut from ½-inch exterior-grade plywood. Secure them with several 6d finishing nails.

7. Cut and install the armrests. Cut the armrests and supports. The supports must be notched half their thickness and the depth of the sides, so that they lap onto the sides. Secure them in place with two 2½-inch #12 screws in each. The rear supports are 20 inches from the rear of the frame, the front ones 32 inches from the front of the frame. Center the armrests on the supports and secure in place with ¼-inch dowel.

8. Apply a finish. Take care to apply the finish to the bottom as well as the top, using at least two coats.

NOTE: If the chaise is to sit directly on the ground, you may want to add an extra coat of paint or other preservative to the ends of the legs and to the wheels to limit moisture absorption.

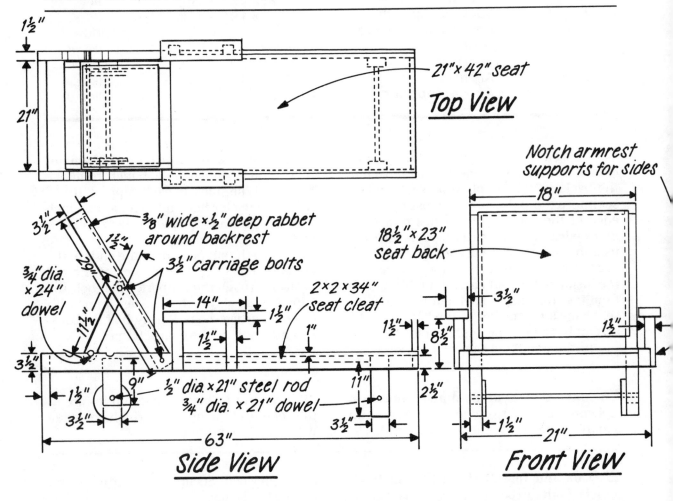

Top

Cleat

Leg

3½'' × ¼'' carriage bolt

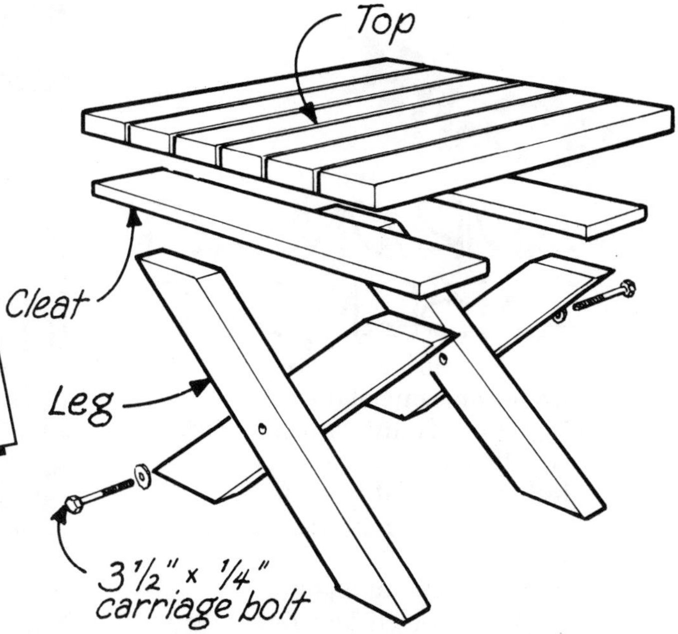

Cutting List—Table

Number	Piece	Dimensions	Material
6	Top	1½'' × 3½'' × 21''	fir
4	Legs	1½'' × 3½'' × 21''	fir
2	Cleats	¾'' × 3½'' × 20''	pine

Table

1. Cut the parts for the table. Mark and cut parallel 55-degree angles on the ends of the legs. For a finished appearance, use a block plane to bevel the top edges of the top pieces.

2. Assemble the legs. Measure 10¼ inches along one edge of each leg from an *acute* angled corner. Using a try square, mark a perpendicular across the face of the leg. Find the center of the face on that line, then drill a ¼-inch hole through the leg.

Using 3½-inch carriage bolts, fasten the pairs of legs together. Set each pair on its feet, lay a cleat across the top, and drive 2-inch #12 screws through the cleat into each leg.

3. Assemble and finish the table. Lay out the top pieces. Set the leg assemblies in place and drive a screw through each cleat into each of the top pieces.

Apply a finish, taking care to get it between all the top boards.

PROJECT

ADIRONDACK ENSEMBLE

The Adirondack chair has become one of the classic pieces of outdoor furniture. Its flat-board, angular design is right at home in the backyard or on the deck or porch.

This popular chair apparently evolved from one called the Westport, which was designed and patented around the turn of the century. It was named for a small town in New York's Adirondack region. The Westport has the same simple, angular planes, but the back and seat are not slatted.

Shopping List

1 pc. 5/4 × 6 × 12' #2 white pine
1 pc. 5/4 × 4 × 10' #2 white pine
1 pc. 1 × 6 × 12' #2 white pine*
5 pcs. 1 × 4 × 10' #2 white pine
2 pcs. 1 × 3 × 10' #2 white pine
1 box #6 × 2'' galvanized all-purpose screws
1 box #6 × 1⅝'' galvanized all-purpose screws
1 box #6 × 1¼'' galvanized all-purpose screws
resorcinol glue
putty
exterior-grade paint

*Try to get one with two 30" clear lengths from which to cut the arms.

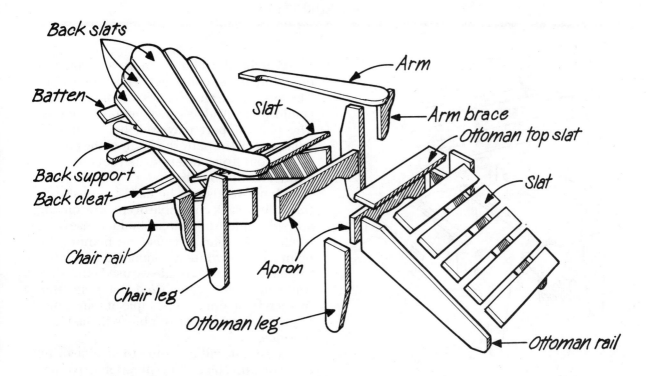

Back slats

Batten

Back support

Back cleat

Chair rail

Chair leg

Ottoman leg

Arm

Arm brace

Ottoman top slat

Slat

Slat

Apron

Ottoman rail

Cutting List—Chair and Ottoman

Number	Piece	Dimensions	Material
2	Chair legs	1 1/16″ × 3 1/2″ × 21 1/2″	pine
2	Ottoman legs	1 1/16″ × 3 1/2″ × 15 1/2″	pine
2	Chair rails	1 1/16″ × 5 1/2″ × 31 1/2″	pine
2	Ottoman rails	1 1/16″ × 5 1/2″ × 24″	pine
2	Aprons	3/4″ × 5 1/2″ × 21 1/2″	pine
1	Back cleat	1 1/16″ × 3 1/2″ × 21 1/2″	pine
1	Back support	1 1/16″ × 3 1/2″ × 28 1/2″	pine
2	Arms	3/4″ × 5 1/2″ × 29″	clear pine*
1	Center back slat	3/4″ × 5 1/2″ × 35 1/2″	pine
2	Back slats	3/4″ × 3 1/2″ × 33″	pine
2	Back slats	3/4″ × 3 1/2″ × 29 1/2″	pine
2	Arm braces	1 1/16″ × 3″ × 10″	pine
1	Batten	3/4″ × 2 1/2″ × 20″	pine
9	Seat slats	3/4″ × 3 1/2″ × 21 1/2″	pine
1	Ottoman top slat	3/4″ × 2 1/2″ × 23 5/8″	pine

*Try to cut two 30-inch clear lengths from #2 white pine.

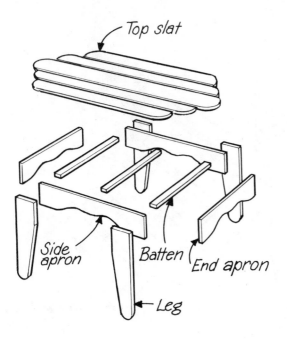

Top slat

Side apron

Batten

End apron

Leg

Comfortable chairs are usually considered difficult to construct. This one is not. The look of the chair belies its comfort. It *is* comfortable. And its construction *is* simple. The hardest part may well be the job of enlarging all the patterns. Many of the pieces are laid out from patterns, then cut out with a saber saw or band saw.

Many woods can be used to construct this Adirondack ensemble of chair, ottoman, and side table. Commercial builders use oak, birch, and cedar. Because we planned to paint the set—white is common, but bright, primary colors are great!—we used pine. Use waterproof glue, galvanized fasteners, and freshen the paint every couple of years, and your Adirondack ensemble will last for decades.

Surely, it will continue to be a favorite outdoor sittin' place for generations to come.

Cutting List—Table

Number	Piece	Dimensions	Material
4	Table legs	$\frac{3}{4}'' \times 3\frac{1}{2}'' \times 17\frac{3}{4}''$	pine
2	Side aprons	$\frac{3}{4}'' \times 3\frac{1}{2}'' \times 18''$	pine
2	End aprons	$\frac{3}{4}'' \times 3\frac{1}{2}'' \times 11\frac{3}{4}''$	pine
3	Battens	$\frac{3}{4}'' \times 1\frac{1}{2}'' \times 10\frac{1}{4}''$	pine
1	Top slat, center	$\frac{3}{4}'' \times 3\frac{1}{2}'' \times 33\frac{1}{2}''$	pine
2	Top slats	$\frac{3}{4}'' \times 2\frac{1}{2}'' \times 30''$	pine
2	Top slats	$\frac{3}{4}'' \times 2\frac{1}{2}'' \times 25''$	pine

1. **Assemble the necessary tools and materials.** This ensemble is built entirely from pine, using a combination of dimension lumber boards and $\frac{5}{4}$ stock, which ordinarily dresses out to a finished thickness of $1\frac{1}{16}$ inch. Stair tread is a commonly stocked lumber that's $\frac{5}{4}$.

Waterproof resorcinol glue and various lengths of galvanized all-purpose screws (much like drywall screws) are specified, though you can use regular slotted flathead wood screws if you prefer. Make sure they are galvanized in any case.

To cut the rounded ends on the slats and the shapes of the aprons and rails, you will need a band saw or saber saw.

2. **Cut and assemble the parts forming the lower frame assemblies.** Start by cutting the legs and rails for both the chair and the ottoman from ⁵⁄₄ pine. Take the dimensions for the legs from the Side View and lay out the pieces on the stock. Enlarge the rail patterns and sketch them on the stock. Use a band saw or saber saw to cut out the parts. Machine a ¼-inch radius on all the exposed edges using a router and ¼-inch round-over bit.

Assemble the legs and rails with glue, then screw through the rails into the legs.

Be sure to make left and right assemblies (mirror images of each other). Line up the rails 1 inch from the front edge of the legs to leave room for the aprons.

Cut the front aprons from 1 × 6 boards. Enlarge the apron pattern, sketch two on the stock, and cut them out using a band saw or saber saw. Attach the aprons to the front ends of the rails with screws. The edges of the legs should be ¼-inch proud of the faces of the aprons. Cut the back cleat and bevel it. Fasten it across the rails, 12 inches from the back end.

3. **Cut and assemble the arms and back support.** Cut the back support from ⁵⁄₄ stock, rounding the ends on a 3½-inch radius. Rip a 35-degree bevel along the front edge. Form 3½-inch-wide notches at each end by trimming away the bevel.

Cut the arms from 1 × 6 stock (try to avoid knots in these pieces), and machine ¼-inch radii all around the edges.

Glue and screw the arms to the back support. Keep the curved ends of the arms flush with the curved ends of the back support and be sure the arms are 20½ inches apart at the front.

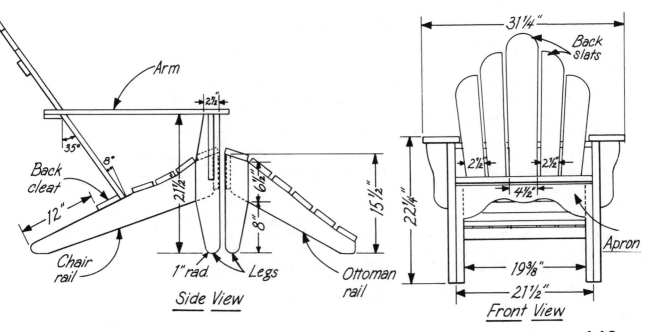

443

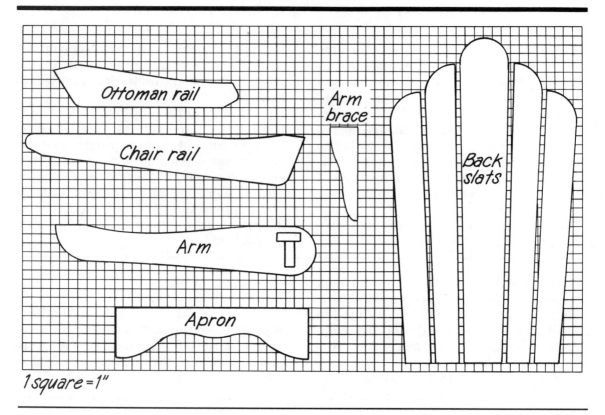

Ottoman rail

Chair rail

Arm brace

Arm

Back slats

Apron

1 square = 1"

4. **Start the back assembly.** Cut the center back slat. Enlarge the pattern and sketch it on the stock, then cut it out with a band saw or saber saw. Radius the edges, then glue and screw it to the back cleat. Be sure that it is lined up on center.

Now fasten the arm-back support assembly to the slat and the tops of the legs. You may want to temporarily clamp it in place and do a little measuring (or just plain eye-balling) to be sure it is where you want it before you actually fasten it. The slat should be centered on the back support, and the arms should be level.

5. **Cut and install the back, seat, and ottoman slats.** The remaining back slats are cut from 1 × 4 stock. Enlarge the patterns and sketch them on the stock, then cut out the slats with a band saw or saber saw. Radius the edges, then glue and screw them to the back cleat and back support.

Enlarge the arm brace pattern and trace two of them on the stock. Cut them out, radius the curved edges, and mount them against the arms and legs.

Cut a batten and 10 seat slats. Radius all exposed edges, and install these pieces to complete the chair and ottoman. Note that one seat slat is 2⅛ inches longer than the others. Use this one at the top of the ottoman to cap the ends of the legs.

444

6. **Cut out and assemble the legs and side aprons for the table.** Lay out the legs using the dimensions shown on the side view. Note that they are tapered along one edge only, and their bottoms are rounded. Enlarge the side apron pattern and sketch it on the stock. Using a band saw or saber saw, cut out these parts. With a router and ¼-inch round-over bit, radius all exposed edges.

Glue and screw the parts together, forming two U-shaped frames. The legs overlay the aprons. Keep the ends of the aprons 1 inch back from the edges of the legs.

7. **Complete the leg-and-apron assembly.** Enlarge the end apron pattern and sketch it on the stock. Cut out the aprons, radius the edges, then glue and screw them to the ends of the side aprons, thus joining the two assemblies made in the previous step.

Cut three battens. Screw one to the inside of each end apron. The third batten is installed in the next step.

8. **Make and install the top.** Cut out the tabletop slats, and round the ends as shown. Arrange them facedown on a flat surface. Apply glue to the top surfaces of the leg-and-apron assembly, turn it upside down, and position it carefully on the slats. Drive screws through the battens and into the slats. Glue and screw the third batten across the middle of the slats.

9. **Apply a finish.** Fill the screw holes with wood putty. Then sand, prime, and paint all three units a color that will go well with your favorite set of tall glasses.

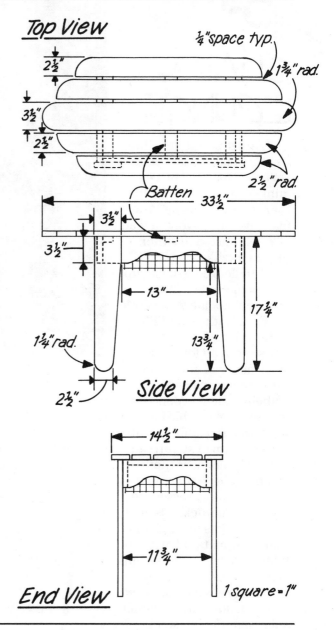

445

PROJECT
CHAISE LOUNGE

An attractive, lean but strong, wooden chaise lounge isn't easy to find. You certainly can't buy one for less than a king's ransom. And plans usually involve a load of 2 × 4s spiked together into a cratelike affair.

Challenged to come up with something a little different, Rodale woodworkers Fred Matlack and Phil Gehret turned to ⁵/₄ mahogany stair tread for their basic material and to the saber saw to execute a few embellishments. Mahogany is a relatively stable hardwood that is readily available —in the form of stair tread— in the ⁵/₄ thickness they desired. The ⁵/₄ thickness— which usually dresses out to an actual thickness of $1^{1}/_{16}$ inch—has more girth than 1-by material, without taking on the excessive bulk of 2-by stock.

For the slats, they used ³/₄-inch mahogany. Although such material is a stock item in many lumberyards, they had to buy flooring, then rip off the tongues and grooves.

The saber saw came into play to cut the scroll-like profiles on the ends of the sides. It also was used to cut odd-shaped notches.

The result is a chaise lounge that is interesting and relatively inexpensive to build, yet has great weatherability, good strength, and a graceful, lean appearance.

Shopping List
2 pcs. ⁵/₄ × 12 × 8′ mahogany stair tread
5 pcs. 1 × 4 × 8′ mahogany flooring
1 pc. 60″ × 1″ dia. hardwood dowel
1 pc. 26½″ × ½″ dia. threaded rod
2—7″ × ½″ wheels
1 pkg. #6 × 2″ galvanized wood screws
2—½″ lock nuts
2—½″ flat washers
2—2″ × 3″ tight-pin hinges
2—1″ × ¼″ roto hinges
semi-gloss urethane finish

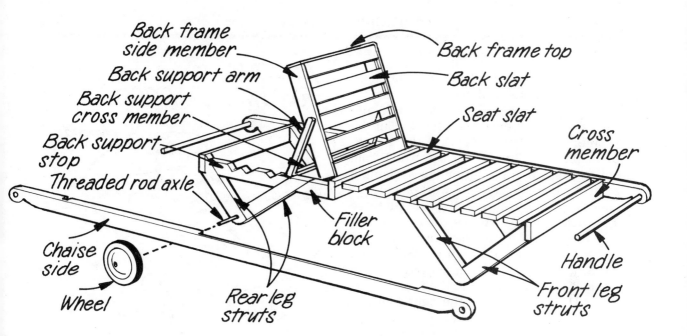

Back frame side member
Back support arm
Back support cross member
Back support stop
Threaded rod axle
Chaise side
Wheel
Rear leg struts
Filler block
Back frame top
Back slat
Seat slat
Cross member
Handle
Front leg struts

Cutting List

Number	Piece	Dimensions	Material
2	Chaise sides	$1\frac{1}{16}'' \times 3\frac{1}{2}'' \times 89''$	mahogany
3	Cross members	$1\frac{1}{16}'' \times 3\frac{1}{2}'' \times 22\frac{3}{4}''$	mahogany
2	Handles	$24\frac{1}{8}'' \times 1''$	dowel
2	Rear leg struts	$1\frac{1}{16}'' \times 2\frac{1}{2}'' \times 14\frac{1}{8}''$	mahogany
2	Rear leg struts	$1\frac{1}{16}'' \times 2\frac{1}{2}'' \times 17''$	mahogany
2	Front leg struts	$1\frac{1}{16}'' \times 2\frac{1}{2}'' \times 17\frac{3}{4}''$	mahogany
2	Front leg struts	$1\frac{1}{16}'' \times 2\frac{1}{2}'' \times 20\frac{1}{4}''$	mahogany
2	Cross braces	$1\frac{1}{16}'' \times 3\frac{9}{16}'' \times 22''$	mahogany
2	Cross braces	$1\frac{1}{16}'' \times 2\frac{1}{2}'' \times 19\frac{7}{8}''$	mahogany
11	Seat slats	$\frac{3}{4}'' \times 2\frac{1}{2}'' \times 22\frac{3}{4}''$	mahogany
2	Back frame side members	$1\frac{1}{16}'' \times 2\frac{1}{2}'' \times 19\frac{3}{4}''$	mahogany
2	Back frame top and bottom	$1\frac{1}{16}'' \times 2\frac{1}{2}'' \times 20''$	mahogany
5	Back slats	$\frac{3}{4}'' \times 2\frac{1}{2}'' \times 18\frac{1}{2}''$	mahogany
2	Back support arms	$\frac{3}{4}'' \times 1\frac{1}{2}'' \times 13''$	mahogany
1	Back support cross member	$\frac{3}{4}'' \times 1\frac{1}{2}'' \times 21\frac{1}{2}''$	mahogany
2	Back support stops	$1\frac{1}{16}'' \times 1\frac{1}{2}'' \times 13\frac{1}{2}''$	mahogany
2	Filler blocks	$1\frac{1}{16}'' \times 2\frac{3}{4}'' \times 5\frac{5}{8}''$	mahogany

1. Cut the sides. Cut the sides to length from the $5/4$ stock. Enlarge the pattern for the scrolled profile and the handle hole, and sketch it on both ends of each side. Cut the profile with a saber saw. Drill the 1-inch-diameter hole. To prevent the wood from splintering when the bit emerges, clamp a scrap back-up block to the workpiece.

With a router and a straight bit, cut three $1^{1}/_{16}$-inch-wide, $3/8$-inch-deep dadoes in each side to accept the cross members. Note the positions of the dadoes on the Side View. Because the largest commonly available straight bit is a $3/4$-inch bit, the trick here is to cut the dadoes to just the right width.

Since you have six dadoes to cut, it is worth the trouble to make the modest router jig shown to help you with this operation.

Complete the joinery cuts on the sides by routing a $3/8$-inch wide, $3/4$-inch deep rabbet along the top edge for the slats. The rabbet should extend from the front dado to the middle dado.

The final operation is to machine a $1/4$-

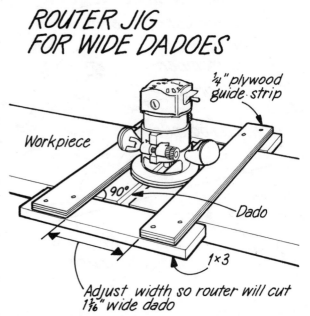

ROUTER JIG
FOR WIDE DADOES

Workpiece

$1/4$" plywood guide strip

90°

Dado

1×3

Adjust width so router will cut $1\frac{1}{16}$" wide dado

inch radius on the inside edges of the handle cutouts. The rest of the frame will be radiused after it is assembled, but the area around the handles will be difficult to reach with the router then.

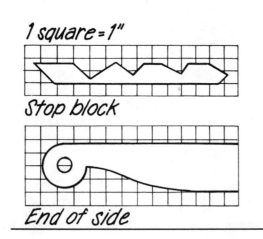

1 square = 1"

Stop block

End of side

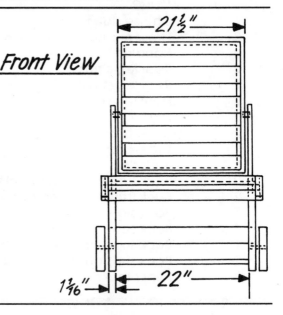

Front View

$21\frac{1}{2}$"

$1\frac{1}{16}$"

22"

2. **Cut the cross members and handles, and assemble the frame.** The cross members are cut from the ⁵/₄ stock, the handles from 1-inch-diameter dowel.

After dry assembling the chaise frame to check the fit of the joints, apply glue and assemble it. Drive two or three 2-inch #6 galvanized all-purpose screws through the side and into the cross member at each joint. Countersink the screw heads and cover them with wood plugs.

After the glue has cured, use a router and a ¼-inch round-over bit to machine a radius on the frame's edges. Doing this after assembly helps produce neat corners. Don't radius the rabbeted edges.

3. **Build the legs.** The front and rear leg assemblies are constructed in the same way, but are slightly different sizes. To make each V-shaped assembly, two leg struts are joined in a half-lap joint. One strut is notched to fit the cross member, while the other is mitered at 45 degrees.

Cut the leg struts to size.

Cut the half-laps on all the leg parts at the same time using a router and straight bit. Line up the pieces edge to edge, with scrap pieces on the outside. Align the butt ends and clamp them tightly together. Nail a straightedge to the scraps to guide the router and control the length of the laps. Since the assembled laps will be trimmed to give them a curved edge, it's okay if they run a trifle long.

Glue up the assemblies. After the glue cures, lay out the miters and notches on the strut ends, scribe the 2½-inch radius curve at the joints, and make the cuts with a saber saw.

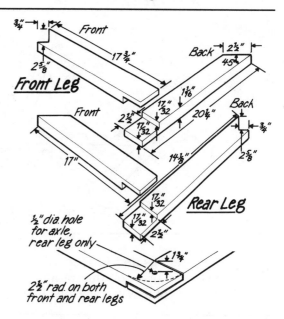

Lay out and drill the ½-inch-diameter axle holes through the rear legs.

Finally, radius the edges of the assemblies with a router and ¼-inch round-over bit.

4. **Cut and assemble the cross braces.** Each cross brace is constructed from two pieces of ⁵/₄ stock. The longer of the two pieces is notched on each end, and the shorter is glued to it, forming a V-shaped brace that fits into the crooks of the leg assemblies and holds them apart.

Cut the pieces to length, then lay out and notch the longer pieces. Glue the second

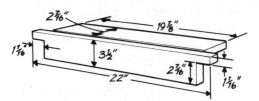

part of each brace in place. Finally, radius the edges of the assemblies with a router and ¼-inch round-over bit.

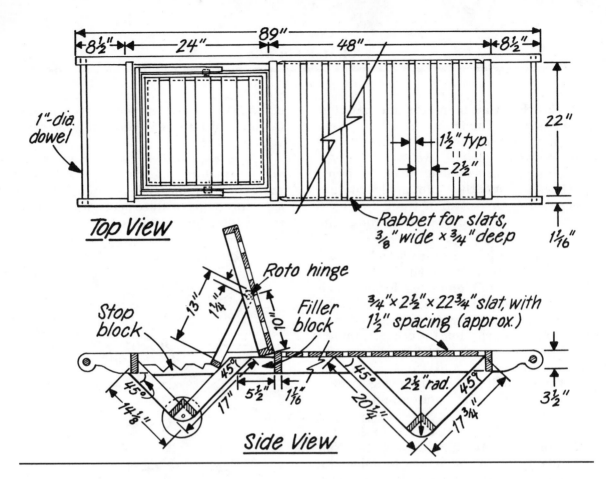

Top View

Side View

1"-dia. dowel

Roto hinge

Stop block

Filler block

Rabbet for slats, ⅜" wide × ¾" deep

¾" × 2½" × 22¾" slat, with 1½" spacing (approx.)

5. **Install the legs and braces.** Glue and screw the legs in place on the frame.

Fit the cross braces in place. Install them with glue and screws, countersinking the screw heads and covering them with wood plugs for a finished appearance.

6. **Cut and install the seat slats.** The slats are cut from 1 × 4 stock. Machine a rounded edge on each slat, then install them, spacing them evenly apart.

7. **Build the back.** The back consists of a ⁵/₄ frame with slats that match the seat slats. It is hinged to the lounge and supported by a U-shaped back support that is attached to the back with roto hinges.

Cut the back frame members from the ⁵/₄ stock. Using a router and rabbet bit, machine a ⅜-inch-wide, ¾-inch-deep rabbet along one edge of each frame member, as shown. Cut a 1¹/₁₆-inch wide, ⅜-inch deep rabbet across the ends of the top and bottom frame members. Since the width of the rabbet exceeds the capacity of rabbeting bits, machine these rabbets the same way you cut the half-laps.

Drill a stopped hole in each side member for the roto hinges. These must be positioned accurately so the support will pivot easily.

NOTE: Roto hinges are wood and steel pivots

450

that glue into holes in the project. They come in a variety of depths and diameters. Be sure you have the hinge in hand before drilling the hole. A Forstner bit is best for this job, but a brad-point bit will work. The important thing is to make a clean, accurate hole without having a center point go clear through the wood.

Assemble the back with glue and screws. Countersink the screw heads and cover them with wood plugs. Round over the edges of the back. Don't round over the rabbeted edge.

Cut the slats and round over their edges. Install the slats.

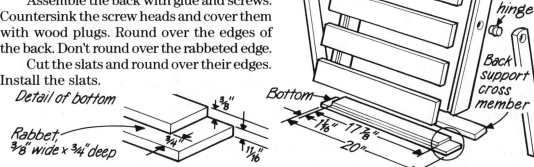

8. Build the back support.
Cut the arms and the cross member. In the arms, drill 1-inch holes for the roto hinges. Glue and screw the pieces together. Remember that the holes on the arms face in. Radius the edges of the assembly with a router and a ¼-inch round-over bit. Finally, install the back support on the back with the roto hinges.

9. Install the back and back support.
Enlarge the pattern for the back support stops and sketch it on ⁵⁄₄ stock. Cut the stops using a saber saw. They should fit snugly between the ends of the leg struts. Screw them to the sides of the chaise.

Next, cut and install two filler blocks. The filler blocks fit between the middle cross member and the leg strut. They keep the back support from falling between the leg and cross member if the back is pulled all the way forward. Screw the blocks to the chaise sides.

Finally, using two tight-pin hinges, install the back assembly.

10. Finish the chaise.
Sand all surfaces. Be sure all exposed edges are radiused. Apply two coats of a urethane finish.

PROJECT
FOLDING SERVING CART

Outdoor living isn't complete without a little something to nibble on. Burgers. Hot dogs. Barbecued chicken. Potato or macaroni salad. Chips. Iced tea or lemonade. Mmmmm. That's real livin'.

This folding cart makes serving the picnic just a little more pleasant. The top surface is just a bit over 16 inches by 24 inches, expansive enough for a substantial cargo of food and drink. Load it with picnic stuff in the kitchen, then wheel it out to the deck or patio and park it next to the grill. If you tile the top or use a big ceramic trivet to protect the wood, you can even use the cart as a base for a small gas grill or hibachi.

Although the cart folds for easy storage, the top is hinged to the legs at the end you'll use to wheel the cart. It won't collapse when you lift the handle opposite the wheels to move it. Moreover, because the legs are joined to each other and to the top with concealed hinges, the cart won't fall into a heap of parts when you attempt to fold it for storage.

We chose to make this cart from mahogany because it is a relatively stable hardwood and is readily available in the dimensions we wanted. The side rails are made of ⁵⁄₄ stock, which we bought as stair tread. The rest of the parts are cut from 1 × 4, which we bought as flooring.

Two unusual bits of hardware are critical to this project. The first is the roto hinge. Available through many mail-order woodworking suppliers, the roto hinge consists of two hardwood disks that sandwich a metal washer slightly larger in diameter than the disks.

Shopping List
1 pc. ⁵⁄₄ × 12 × 4' mahogany stair tread
3 pcs. 1 × 4 × 8' mahogany flooring
1 pc. 48" × 1" dia. hardwood dowel
2-6" × 1 ½" wheels
1 pkg. #6 × 2" galvanized all-purpose screws
2-1⅞" × ½" shoulder bolts
2-⅜" tee nuts
2-⅜" flat washers
4-1" × ¼" roto hinges
waterproof glue
urethane finish

The assembly is riveted together, with the rivet acting as a spindle. These hinges are used to join the two elements of the leg assembly,

452

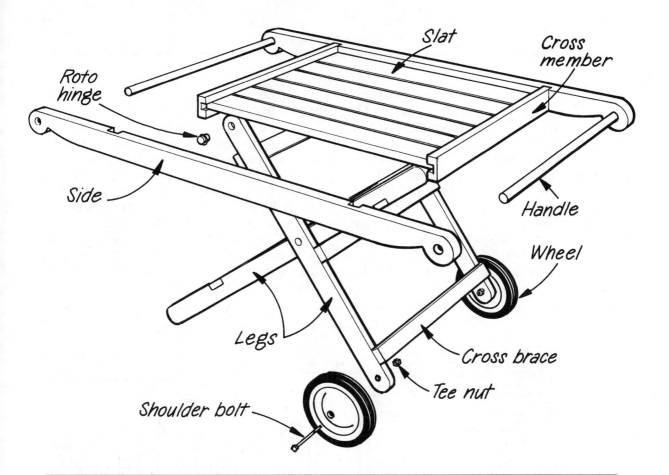

Slat

Cross member

Roto hinge

Side

Handle

Wheel

Legs

Cross brace

Tee nut

Shoulder bolt

Cutting List

Number	Piece	Dimensions	Material
2	Sides	$1\,^{1}/_{16}'' \times 3\,^{1}/_{2}'' \times 44''$	mahogany
2	Cross members	$1\,^{1}/_{16}'' \times 3\,^{1}/_{2}'' \times 17\,^{1}/_{8}''$	mahogany
2	Handles	$18\,^{1}/_{2}'' \times 1''$	dowel
6	Slats	$^{3}/_{4}'' \times 2\,^{1}/_{2}'' \times 25\,^{5}/_{8}''$	mahogany
2	Legs	$^{3}/_{4}'' \times 1\,^{1}/_{2}'' \times 38''$	mahogany
2	Legs	$^{3}/_{4}'' \times 1\,^{1}/_{2}'' \times 36''$	mahogany
3	Cross braces	$^{3}/_{4}'' \times 1\,^{1}/_{2}'' \times 16\,^{1}/_{4}''$	mahogany
2	Cross braces	$^{3}/_{4}'' \times 1\,^{1}/_{2}'' \times 14\,^{3}/_{4}''$	mahogany

as well as to join the top to the legs.

Another bit of hardware you may never have heard of is the shoulder bolt. Sold as a replacement for a lawn mower axle, a shoul-der bolt usually has a ½-inch shank with ⅜-inch threads on the end. Because these bolts come in different lengths, you must match them to the wheels you buy.

453

1. Cut the sides. Cut the sides to length from the 5/4 stock. Enlarge the pattern for the scrolled profile and the handle hole, and sketch it on both ends of each side. Cut the profile with a saber saw. Drill the 1-inch-diameter hole. To prevent the wood from splintering when the bit emerges, clamp a scrap back-up block to the workpiece.

With a router and a straight bit, cut two $1\frac{1}{16}$-inch wide, $\frac{3}{8}$-inch deep dadoes to accept the cross members. Note the positions of the dadoes on the Side View. Because the largest commonly available straight bit is a

$\frac{3}{4}$-inch bit, the trick here is to cut the dadoes to just the right width.

Since you have four dadoes to cut, it is worth the trouble to make the modest router jig shown to help you with this operation.

Next lay out and bore the stopped holes for the roto hinges that join the top assembly to the leg assembly. A Forstner bit is the best tool for the job, but a brad-point bit will work. The important thing is to make a clean, accurate hole that is deep enough to receive the hinge without having a center point go clear through the wood.

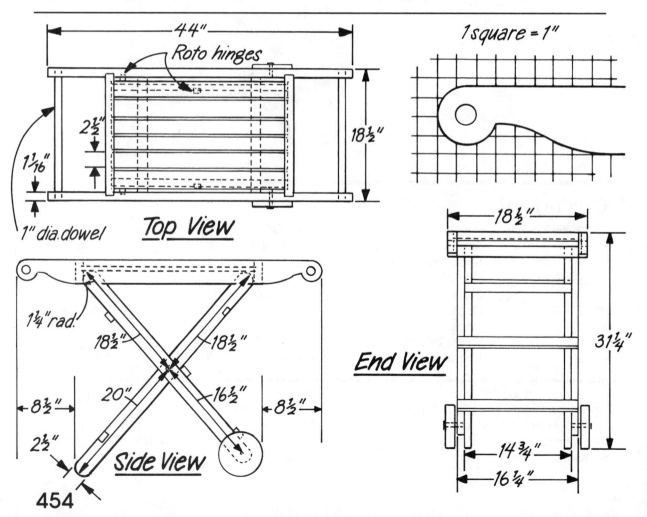

Top View

1 square = 1"

Side View

End View

454

NOTE: Roto hinges are glued in place. They are available in a variety of both depths and diameters, so it's a good idea to get the hinges first, then drill the holes to fit. For this project, we'd recommend a fairly large size. The hinge should be inserted ½ inch into the wood and should require a hole ¾ to 1 inch in diameter.

The final operation is to machine a ¼-inch radius on the inside edges of the handle cutouts. The rest of the frame will be radiused after it is assembled, but the area around the handles will be difficult to reach with the router then.

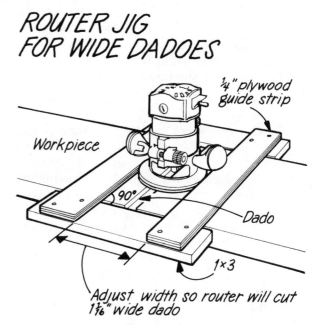

ROUTER JIG FOR WIDE DADOES

¼" plywood guide strip

Workpiece

90°

Dado

1×3

Adjust width so router will cut 1⅟₁₆" wide dado

2. **Cut the cross members, handles, and slats.** The cross members are cut from the ⁵⁄₄ stock, the handles from 1-inch-diameter dowel, the slats from 1 × 4 stock.

A ¾-inch-wide, ⅜-inch-deep groove must be plowed in each cross member to accept the slats, as shown. This can be done using a table-saw-mounted dado cutter or a router equipped with an edge guide and fitted with a ¾-inch straight bit. If you rout the groove, be sure to make several passes, cutting a bit deeper with each pass until the desired depth is achieved.

Using a router and a ¼-inch round-over bit, machine a radius on all the exposed edges of the slats.

TOP JOINERY

8½"

Dado 1⅟₁₆" wide × ⅜" deep

Cross member

1" dia. hole for rotohinge

¾"

5/8"

2"

1⅜"

Handle

Groove ¾" wide × ⅜" deep

Slat

3. **Assemble the cart top.** Dry assemble the top to check the fit of the joints. Check also to ensure that there is sufficient clearance between the top edges and the slats for

your piloted round-over bit. If there's enough clearance, apply glue and assemble the top.

After the glue has cured, use a router and a ¼-inch round-over bit to machine a radius on the frame's edges. Doing this after assembly helps produce neat corners. However, if it appears that the pilot will mar the slats, machine the radius around the inside edges of the top before final assembly. Remove the slats, reclamp the top frame, and machine the radius. Then proceed with assembly.

4. Cut the parts for the leg assemblies. Because one pair of legs has wheels, it is shorter than the other pair. And because the leg assembly without wheels fits inside the assembly with wheels, there are two different lengths of cross braces. As you cut the parts, label them lightly in pencil, so you don't get them mixed up.

Lay out a 1¼-inch radius on both ends of each leg. Cut the radius with a saber saw or on a band saw. Then, using a router and round-over bit, machine a radius on all the edges of the legs only.

Notch the two long legs to accept cross braces. The short legs do not have the cross brace let in.

Lay out and drill the stopped holes in the legs for the roto hinges. As noted before, the holes should have a flat bottom, and you should have the hinges in hand to ensure the holes are properly sized for them. Locate the holes carefully so that the geometry of the leg assembly will be correct. Moreover, be sure you drill the holes for the leg hinges in one face of the short legs, and the holes for the top hinges in the opposite face.

Finally, lay out and drill the holes in the short legs for the tee nuts that secure the shoulder bolt axles. Three-eighths-inch tee nuts require ½-inch-diameter holes.

5. Assemble the legs. Dry assemble the two leg units separately. With a router and round-over bit, machine a radius on the cross braces so their corners blend into the legs. It is easier to do this before the legs and top are finally assembled.

To assemble the legs and top, glue roto hinges into the holes in the outer legs. Then join the legs to the top by gluing the protruding hinge elements into their holes in the top. Next, glue the inner legs in place on their roto hinges. Finally, install the cross braces. Screw the cross braces that fit into the notches first. Then install the braces that go at the top and bottom of the outer legs. The final brace to be installed is the center one, which keeps the legs from collapsing should someone inadvertently lift the wrong end of the top. To establish its proper position, set the cart up, butt the brace against the inner legs and screw it in place.

6. Finish the cart. Sand all surfaces. Be sure all exposed edges are radiused. Apply two coats of a urethane finish.

Finally, install the wheels. Insert the tee nuts from the inside of the leg. Use a ⅜-inch flat washer on the shoulder bolt to "capture" the leg, and tighten the shoulder bolt into the tee nut.

PROJECT
ENGLISH GARDEN FURNITURE SET

Whether you entertain on a meticulously manicured patio or unwind with friends in a lush grotto, this set will fit in. Not only that, it will add to the atmosphere.

The ritzy garden catalogs advertise furniture pieces like these for hundreds of dollars. The furniture's handsome, the prices are garish.

Now you can build your own! The complete ensemble includes a bench, a chair, and a table. Build whichever pieces you want.

The construction of this set involves a considerable amount of mortise-and-tenon joinery. This joint can be made the old way with hammer and chisel, skill and patience. Or you can use a power drill to hasten the completion of the mortises, perhaps even a drill press with a mortising attachment to lessen the handwork further. Either way, you'll experience a real sense of

accomplishment upon the completion of your English garden furniture set.

Though there are a lot of joints involved, the design of the bench and chair isn't complex. As shown in the illustrations, it consists of two identical side assemblies that are joined together by rails and seat slats. The side assemblies are made first by joining the front and rear legs for each assembly with three horizontal pieces: the arm rest, side seat rail, and stretcher.

Once the side assemblies are together, the frame of the piece can be completed by joining the top rail, rear seat rail, and front seat rail. The seat slats are the last parts to be attached.

White oak is an ideal wood for a project of this type, although it could be done in anything from mahogany to teak. The key is that the wood should be hard (though that doesn't necessarily mean it should be a hardwood) and one of the rot-resistant varieties. While this type of furniture is not intended to be left out in the weather year-round, it can be expected to get wet periodically.

You should also use a somewhat weather-resistant finish. This can range from the penetrating stains and oils to the spar varnishes or polyurethanes. Whatever you choose be sure it is classed as exterior finish.

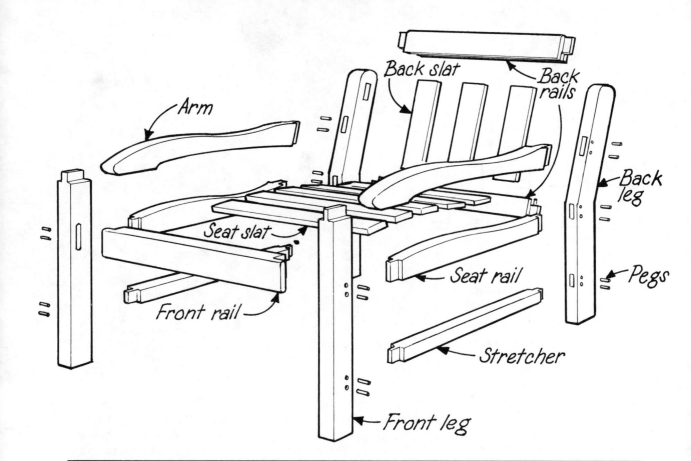

Arm

Back slat

Back rails

Back leg

Seat slat

Pegs

Front rail

Seat rail

Stretcher

Front leg

Materials List—Chair

Number	Piece	Dimensions	Material
2	Front legs	1 7/8″ × 2 1/2″ × 25 1/2″	oak
2	Back legs	1 7/8″ × 4″ × 33″	oak
2	Arms	1 7/8″ × 2 1/2″ × 22″	oak
2	Seat rails	1 7/8″ × 2 1/2″ × 17 1/2″	oak
2	Stretchers	1 7/8″ × 1 7/8″ × 17 1/2″	oak
1	Front rail	1 7/8″ × 3 1/4″ × 22 1/4″	oak
2	Back rails	1 7/8″ × 2 1/2″ × 22 1/4″	oak
3	Back slats	1″ × 3″ × 14″	oak
5	Seat slats	1″ × 2 1/4″ × 24″	oak
28	Pegs	1 1/4″ × 1/4″ dia.	birch dowel

Hardware
20 pcs. 3/8″ × 1/2″ oak plugs
20 #8 × 2″ galvanized all-purpose screws
resorcinol or other waterproof glue
exterior-grade paint, stain, or wood preservative

1. Shop for lumber. If you approach this right, it can be as much fun as building the set. Take the time to check out *all* the lumberyards in your area. Some cater to building contractors and do-it-yourselfers, while others supply cabinetmakers and furniture builders. Find out which species and sizes of woods are stock and which are special order. Better yet, find out if any local sawmills or craftsmen have wood to sell.

When buying wood as thick as that used for this project, you will surely run into variety. Hardwood sizes are unpredictable. The stock we bought came through surfaced to 1⅞ inch, but you may find your supplier handles only 1½ inch, 1¾ inch, or 2 inch. This is not a serious problem so long as you remember to adjust the dimensions to account for the thickness of your stock.

Since lengths and widths are usually not standard either, you can simply go to your supplier with the cutting list and see what is available. Let him help you figure out what sizes he can supply to give you the best yield. There's a cutting list for each unit.

2. Cut out the parts for the side assemblies. The first parts to be cut out are those making up the side assemblies. Cut the legs, stretchers, seat rails, and arms to the sizes shown on the cutting list.

Normally, it is easier to make joinery cuts in a board before you cut it to an irregular shape. The back legs of this project are an exception to the general rule; the shape must be cut before the mortises.

Lay out each back leg, as shown, on a 36-inch-long board. Note the grain direction; the layout shown minimizes the width of board needed. The trick is to locate the bend in the leg first, then methodically to extend the layout from that point. Using a band saw or saber saw, cut out each leg.

Enlarge the patterns for the arms and the seat rails, and sketch them on the stock of these parts. *Don't* cut the curves on the arms or seat rails, though. It will be a lot

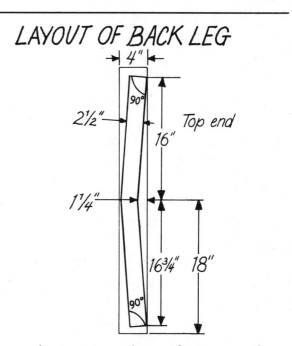

LAYOUT OF BACK LEG

easier to cut mortises and tenons on these pieces while they're straight.

3. Cut the mortises for the side assemblies. Whether you are building the chair or the bench, the general procedure is the same. Lay out the side assembly parts on a flat work surface. Lay out the mortises needed to join these assemblies, as indicated in the Side View and Layout of Leg Mortises.

The mortises are all ½ inch wide and 1⅛

459

LAYOUT OF LEG MORTISES

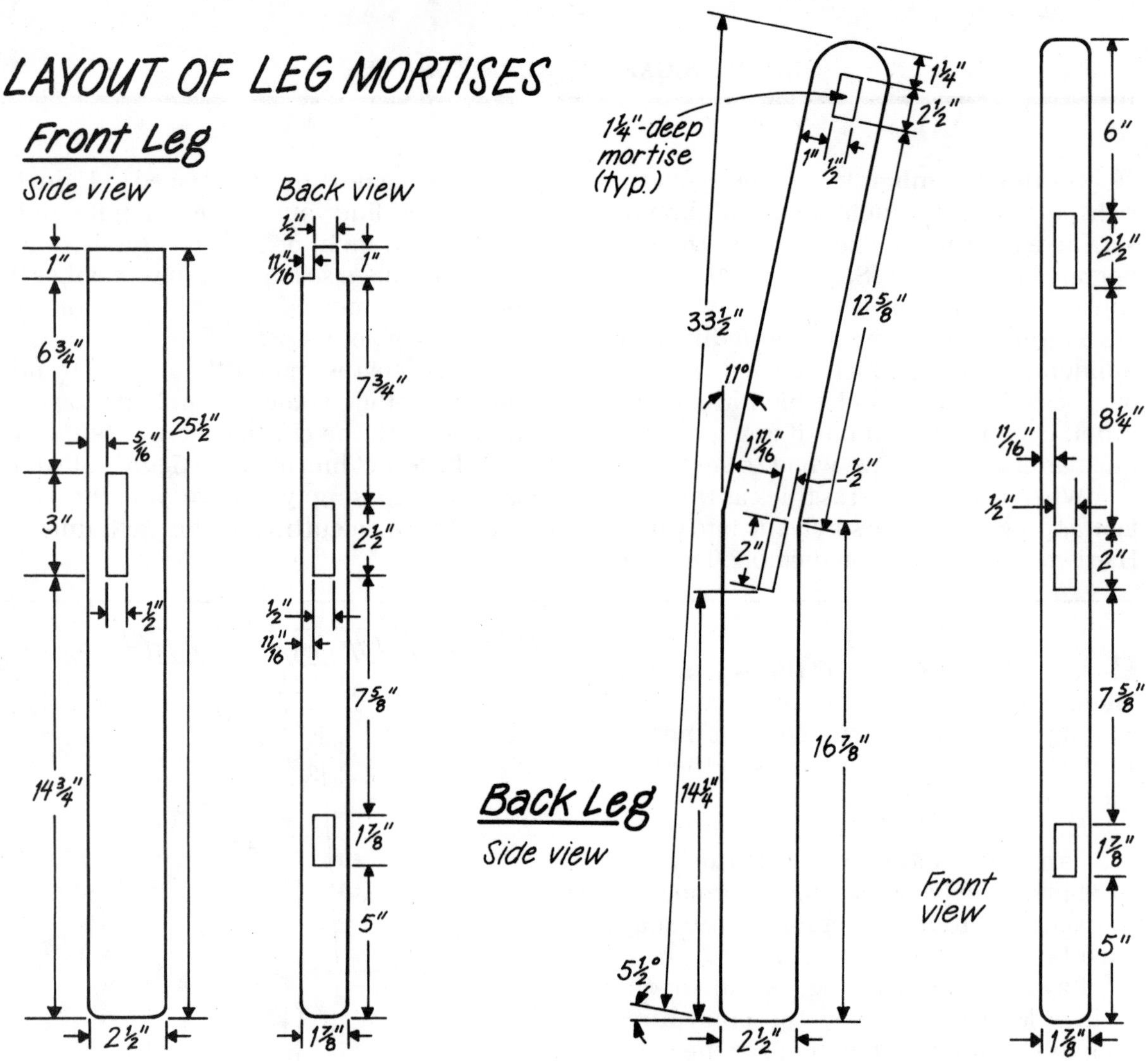

Front Leg
Side view
Back view
1"
6¾"
3"
14¾"
25½"
5/16"
½"
2½"
½"
1"
11/16"
7¾"
2½"
½"
11/16"
7⅝"
1⅞"
5"
1⅞"
Back Leg
Side view
1¼"-deep mortise (typ.)
1¼"
2½"
1"
½"
33½"
12⅝"
11°
1 11/16"
½"
2"
14¼"
16⅞"
5½°
2½"
Front view
6"
2½"
8¼"
11/16"
½"
2"
7⅝"
1⅞"
5"
1⅞"

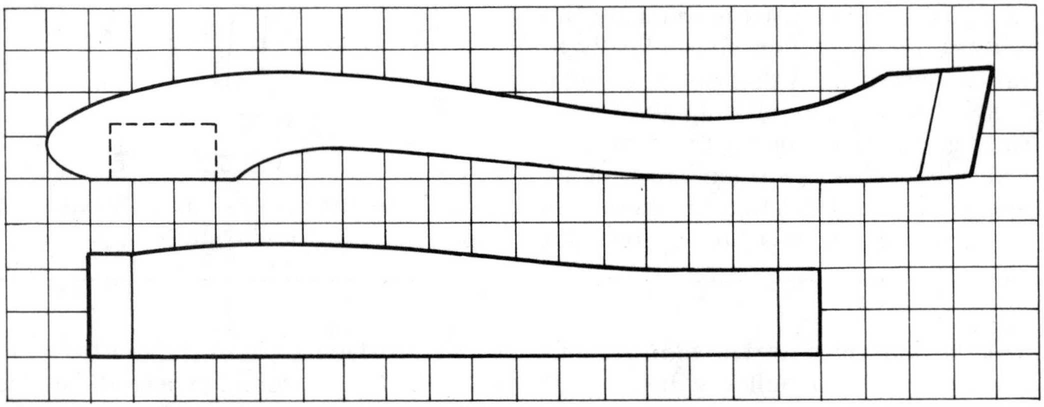

1 square=1"

inches deep. The heights vary; follow the illustrations carefully.

Rough out each mortise with a drill, removing as much of the wood within the layout lines as possible. Clean up the sides of the mortises with chisels. Different chisels are appropriate for different parts of the mortise. Use a broad chisel for the sides, a narrow chisel for the ends.

While most of the mortises are straightforward, those for the arm-to-back leg joints must be at an angle. To rough out this angled mortise in the back leg, support the leg on an angle block, as shown, and drill out the waste on a drill press.

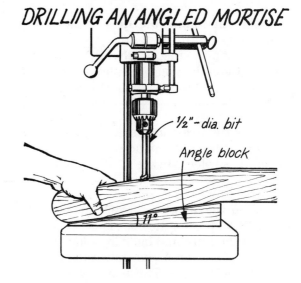

DRILLING AN ANGLED MORTISE

½"-dia. bit

Angle block

11°

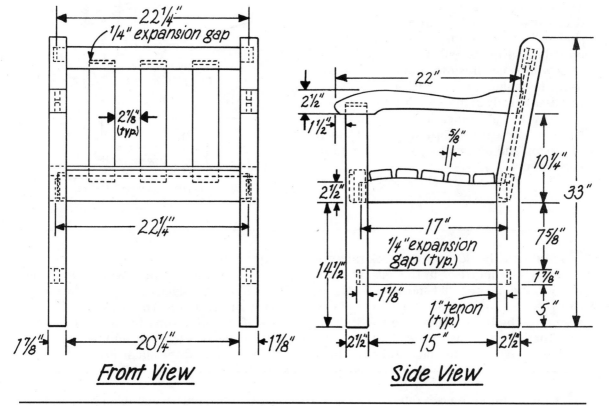

Front View

Side View

4. **Cut the tenons on the side assembly parts.** Lay out the pieces on a work surface and overlap the pieces where they will be joined. Carefully mark the shoulders of the tenons, and cut them ½ inch wide and 1 inch long. Pare away at the tenons until you can dry assemble the frame. Once you get a tenon to fit into its mortise, mark both sides of the joint so you don't get them mixed up.

5. **Cut the arms and seat rails to their final profiles.** Use a band saw or saber saw to cut these pieces to the profiles you traced on them earlier. Then carefully sand the sawed edges, and finish sand all the parts of the side assemblies.

6. **Make the rails.** Cut the rails and machine a ¼-inch radius on the edges.

On the front and back legs, lay out the mortises for the rails, as shown in the Layout of Leg Mortises. These mortises should be ½ inch wide, 2 inches high, and 1⅛ inches deep, but *don't* center them on the legs. Locate them off-center, so they will align with the outside edge of the rail. The tenons on the rails will be cut flush to the outside of the rail. This eliminates interference with the mortises already in the legs. Cut the mortises.

Now cut ½ × 2-inch tenons on the rails. Note that these tenons are shouldered ¼ inch at the top and bottom to get rid of the radiused corner.

MORTISE-AND-TENON DETAILS

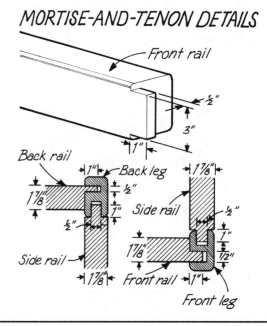

7. **Make the back.** Once the back rails are fitted to their mortises in the legs, you can lay out and cut the slat mortises in them. Cut the slats to fit these mortises, and dry assemble the back. Make sure the rails fit into their mortises with the slats in place. Radius the edges of the slats, and sand them and the rails.

To be sure the rails will fit their mortises in the back legs when the slats are in place, dry assemble the back and the back legs. If the rails won't fit, determine which slat (or slats) is too long and trim it.

Finish sand the slats and rails.

8. **Glue up the side assemblies.** Dry assemble and clamp each side assembly to check for fit (and to practice the clamping routine). If the fit is satisfactory, glue up both units.

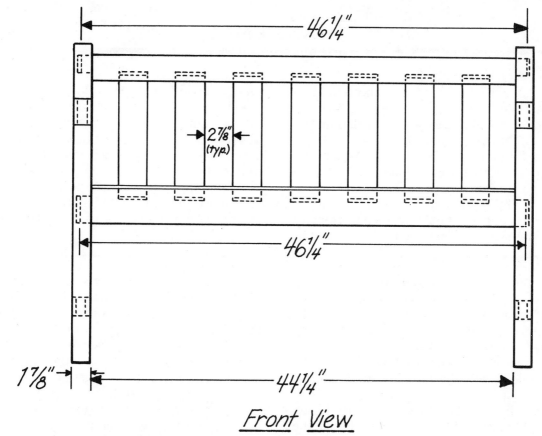

Front View

Materials List—Bench

Number	Piece	Dimensions	Material
2	Front legs	1⅞″ × 2½″ × 25½″	oak
2	Back legs	1⅞″ × 4¼″ × 33″	oak
2	Arms	1⅞″ × 2½″ × 22″	oak
2	Seat rails	1⅞″ × 2½″ × 17½″	oak
2	Stretchers	1⅞″ × 1⅞″ × 17½″	oak
1	Front rail	1⅞″ × 3¼″ × 46¼″	oak
2	Back rails	1⅞″ × 2½″ × 46¼″	oak
7	Back slats	1″ × 3″ × 14″	oak
5	Seat slats	1″ × 2½″ × 48″	oak
28	Pegs	1¼″ × ¼″ dia.	birch dowel

Hardware

20 pcs. ⅜″ × ½″ oak plugs
20 #8 × 2″ galvanized all-purpose screws
resorcinol or other waterproof glue
exterior-grade paint, stain, or wood preservative

After the clamps are set, stand the two assemblies side by side to be sure that one of them does not lean farther back than the other. This simple precaution can save you from building a twisted seat. Adjust the clamps to make the two frames line up before the glue dries.

Drill the peg holes next—two per joint. Each hole should be ¼ inch in diameter and 1¼ inches deep. Coat the pegs with water-proof glue and drive one into each hole. If the mortise-and-tenon joints are accurately fitted and properly glued, they shouldn't fail. The pegs are good insurance, however; should a glue joint fail, the pegs will keep the piece from collapsing.

After the glue has set and the clamps are removed, machine a ¼-inch radius around all of the frame members, then sand them.

9. **Complete the assembly.** Be sure you have a perfectly flat surface on which to set the legs as you clamp the unit together. Make a final dry run; if everything is satisfactory, repeat the process using glue.

Assemble the back rails and slats. The slats don't actually have to be glued into their mortises, since they can't fall out. But these joints are likely to hold moisture. Resorcinol glue will fill any gaps in fit and seal the joint against moisture. If you don't want to glue the slats, use a silicone caulk; this waterproof substance will fill all the gaps and seal the joint.

Lay a side assembly on the floor. Fit the back assembly into its mortises, then install the front rail. Fit the second side assembly in place. Now set the unit on its feet and apply the clamps, using cauls to prevent the steel jaws from marring the wood.

While the glue sets, cut and radius the seat slats. Once the glue has dried in the frame joints, drill countersunk pilot holes and screw the seat slats in place. Cover the screw heads with wooden plugs.

Drill the stopped peg holes for the remaining joints. Coat the pegs with waterproof glue and drive one into each hole.

Sand the unit thoroughly and apply several coats of finish.

Table

1. **Cut the tabletop parts.** The tabletop components are all cut from stock that measures an actual 1¼ inches thick. From this stock, cut the ends, sides, and slats. With a router and a round-over bit, machine a ¼-inch radius on edges that will be exposed.

2. **Cut the joinery for the top.** First, plow a groove ½ inch wide and ⅝ inch deep along the inside edge of the end pieces. This is most easily done with a table-saw-mounted dado cutter or a straight bit in a table-mounted router.

Next, lay out and cut the mortises in the side pieces. Excavate as much of the waste as possible by drilling a series of ½-inch-diameter stopped holes. Use a chisel to clean up the sides of the mortises. The mortises should be ⁹⁄₁₆ to ⅝ inch deep.

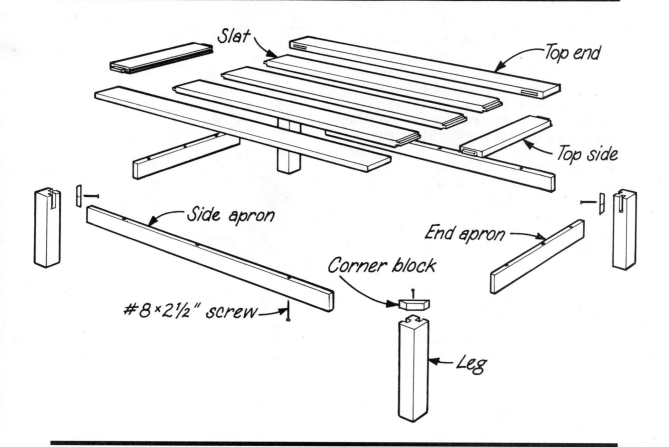

Materials List—Table

Number	Piece	Dimensions	Material
2	Top ends	1¼″ × 3⅜″ × 12″	oak
2	Top sides	1¼″ × 3⅜″ × 36″	oak
3	Slats	1¼″ × 3⅜″ × 30¼″	oak
4	Legs	1⅞″ × 1⅞″ × 12¾″	oak
2	Side aprons	⅞″ × 2½″ × 31½″	oak
2	End aprons	⅞″ × 2½″ × 12¾″	oak
4	Corner blocks	⅞″ × 2″ × 3¾″	oak

Hardware
14 #8 × 2½″ galvanized all-purpose screws
resorcinol or other waterproof glue
exterior-grade paint, stain, or wood preservative

Finally, cut tenons on the ends and the slats. To form each tenon, cut a ½-inch-wide, ⅜-inch-deep rabbet across each face of the board. Do this on a table saw fitted with a dado cutter or with a router and a rabbeting bit. It's a good idea to cut a test tenon on a scrap to ensure that it properly fits the grooves in the end pieces. The tenons on the slats are used in this form, but the tenons on the end pieces must be trimmed to fit their mortises. Since there are only four tenons, use a back saw to trim the shoulders, as shown. Use a chisel to pare the tenon to fit the mortise.

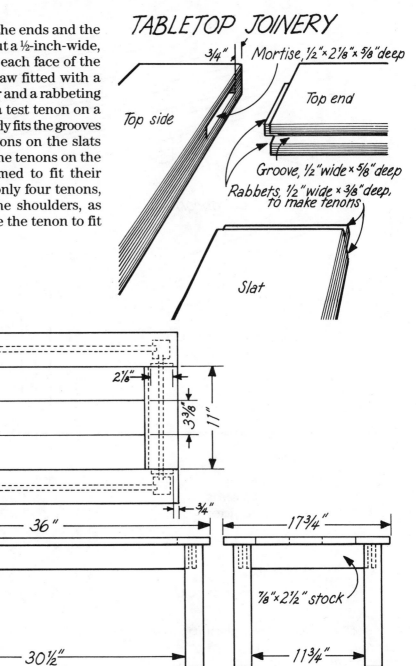

TABLETOP JOINERY

3/4"   Mortise, ½" × 2⅛" × ⅝" deep

Top side   Top end

Groove, ½" wide × ⅝" deep

Rabbets, ½" wide × ⅜" deep, to make tenons

Slat

TABLE

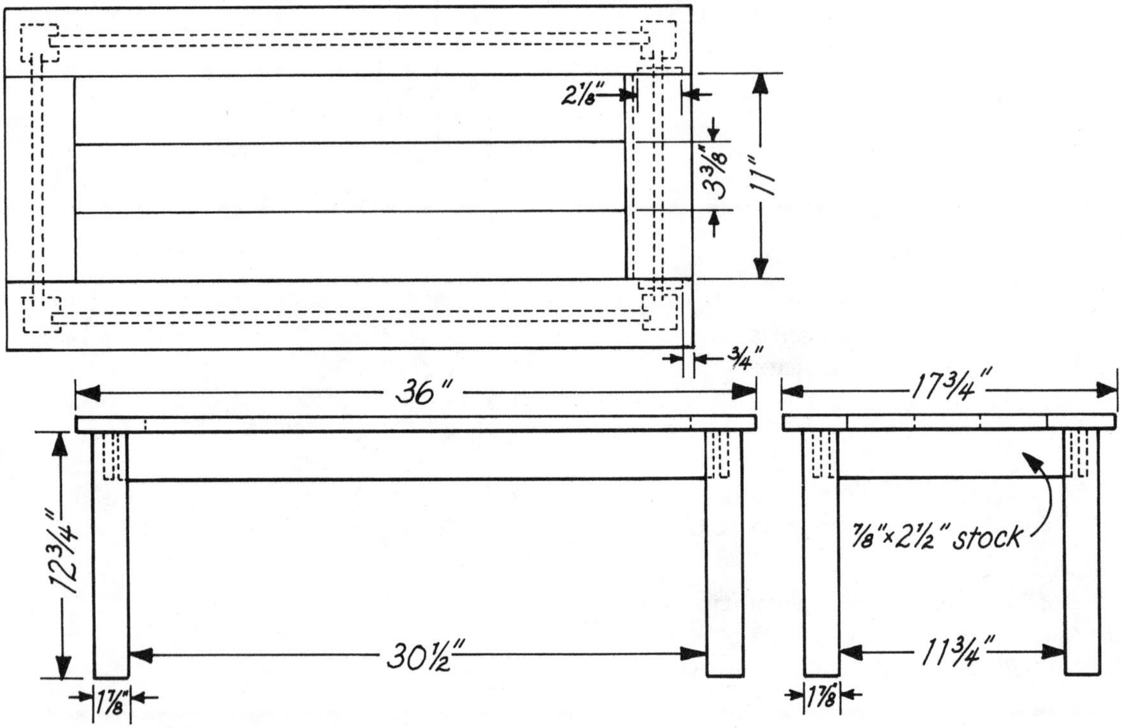

2⅛"

3⅜"

11"

¾"

36"

17¾"

12¾"

⅞" × 2½" stock

30½"

11¾"

1⅞"

1⅞"

3. **Glue up the top.** After finish sanding all the tabletop parts, dry assemble the top to check the fit of each joint and to rehearse the final assembly routine. Then glue up the top.

Apply glue only to the mortise-and-tenon joints between the ends and sides. The slat tenons should not be glued into the grooves in the end pieces; these pieces should be free to expand and contract with changes in temperature and humidity. To seal moisture out of the joints, you may want to seal them with silicone caulk; apply caulk in the groove, fit the tenons in place, then wipe up any squeeze-out.

4. **Cut the joinery in the legs and aprons.** First, cut the legs from 1⅞-inch stock and the aprons from ⅞-inch stock. Machine a radius on edges that will be exposed. The legs and aprons are joined with slot mortises and tenons.

Cut the mortises with either a straight bit in a table-mounted router or with a dado cutter. Because the slots are offset from the outside edge of the legs, you need two set-ups. First, set up to cut a ½-inch-wide, ½-inch-deep slot, ⁹⁄₁₆ inch from the edge of the leg. Clamp a scrap block to the outfeed end of the fence to stop the cut when it is 2½ inches long. Cut a slot in each leg. Change the setup so the slot will be cut ¹³⁄₁₆ inch from the edge of the leg. Cut another slot in each leg. Square the ends of the slots with a chisel.

Now cut the tenons on the aprons the same way you did those on the tabletop parts. The tenons are centered on the stock, and are ½ inch thick and ½ inch long.

LEG-TO-APRON JOINERY

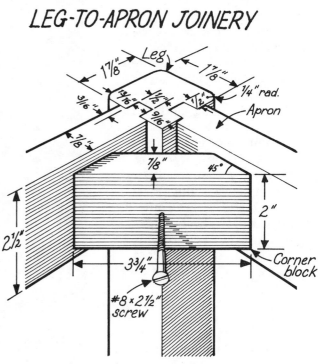

5. **Assemble the base.** After finish sanding all the legs and aprons, dry assemble the base to check the fit of each joint and to rehearse the final assembly routine. Then glue and clamp the aprons to the legs. While the glue cures, cut corner blocks as shown. After the clamps are removed, glue and screw a block to each inside corner.

6. **Mount the top on the base.** Lay the tabletop upside down on a workbench. Set the base assembly in place. Drill pilot holes through the aprons into the tabletop, then drive screws to fasten the parts together.

Sand and finish the entire table.

467

PROJECT

GARDEN SWING

Swinging in the garden is pure nostalgia. Who didn't experience *some* sort of back-yard swing as a child—a fancy double-seated garden swing, a porch glider, even an old tire hung from a tree branch. Rocking gently with Grandma or Grandpa. Roughhousin' with friends.

So no outdoor setting in which you can really *live* is complete without a swing.

This swing is an out-growth of the English garden furniture set presented previously. In a manner of speaking, it's the bench with the legs cut off.

The process of building the swing does duplicate that of building the chair or the bench, except for the initial layout of the side assemblies. On the bench, the back leg bends just *above* the seat level; the seat rail mortise is cut per-pendicular to the edge of the leg. On the swing, the seat rail mortise—like the arm mortise—must be cut into the back post at an angle. The layout process is a little bit different.

The completed swing can be suspended from an arbor or a gazebo, on a porch or deck.

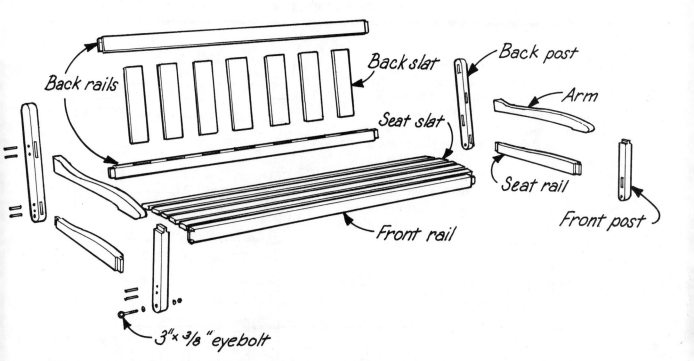

Back rails

Back slat

Back post

Arm

Seat slat

Seat rail

Front post

Front rail

3" × ⅜" eyebolt

Materials List

Number	Piece	Dimensions	Material
2	Back posts	1⅞″ × 2½″ × 21″	oak
2	Front posts	1⅞″ × 2½″ × 13½″	oak
2	Seat rails	1⅞″ × 2½″ × 17½″	oak
2	Arms	1⅞″ × 2½″ × 22″	oak
1	Front rail	1⅞″ × 3¼″ × 46¼″	oak
2	Back rails	1⅞″ × 2½″ × 46¼″	oak
7	Back slats	1″ × 3″ × 14″	oak
5	Seat slats	1″ × 2½″ × 48″	oak
20	Pegs	1¼″ × ¼″ dia.	birch dowel

Hardware
20 pcs. ⅜″ × ½″ oak plugs
20 #8 × 2″ galvanized all-purpose screws
4–3″ × ⅜″ eyebolts w/2 washers and 1 nut each
chain
resorcinol or other waterproof glue
exterior-grade paint, stain, or wood preservative

1. **Cut out the parts for the side assemblies.** The first parts to be cut out are those making up the side assemblies. Cut the posts, seat rails, and arms to the sizes shown on the cutting list.

Enlarge the patterns for the arms and the seat rails, and sketch them on the stock of these parts. Lay out the radiuses on the top and bottom of the back post and the bottom of the front post. *Don't* cut the curves, though. It's easier to cut mortises and tenons on these pieces while they're straight.

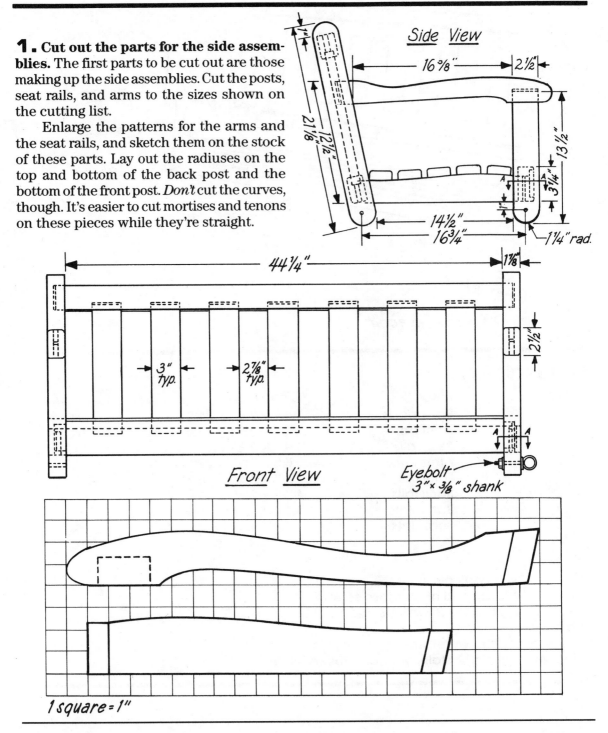

Side View

Front View

Eyebolt
3" × 3/8" shank

1 square = 1"

2. Cut the mortises for the side assemblies. Lay out the mortises, as indicated in the Side View and Post Layouts. All are ½ inch wide and 1⅛ inches deep. The heights vary; follow the illustrations carefully.

The mortises in the back post are cut at a 10-degree angle, as indicated on the Side View. Set a sliding T bevel to the angle using a protractor. Mark the angle across the post at each mortise to help line it up.

Rough out each mortise with a drill, removing as much of the wood within the layout lines as possible. Clean up the sides of the mortises with a chisel. To rough out the angled mortises, support the post on an angle block, as shown in the previous project, English Garden Furniture Set, and drill out the waste on a drill press.

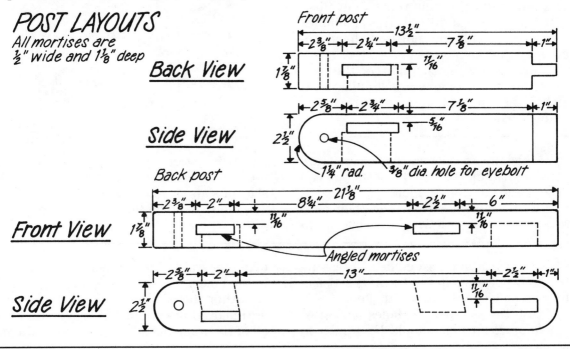

POST LAYOUTS
All mortises are ½" wide and 1⅛" deep

3. Cut the tenons on the side assembly parts. Lay out the pieces on a work surface and overlap the pieces where they will be joined. Carefully mark the shoulders of the tenons, and cut the tenons ½ inch thick and 1 inch long. Pare away at the tenons until you can dry assemble the frame. Once you get a tenon to fit into its mortise, mark both sides of the joint so you don't get them mixed up.

4. Cut the parts to their final profiles. Use a band saw or saber saw to cut these pieces to the profiles you traced on them earlier. Drill the ⅜-inch-diameter holes in the posts for the eyebolts. Then carefully sand all the parts.

5. Make the rails. Cut the rails and machine a ¼-inch radius on the edges.

On the front and back posts, lay out the mortises for the rails, as shown in the mortise layouts. These mortises should be ½ inch wide, 2 inches high, and 1⅛ inches deep, but *don't* center them on the posts at seat level. Locate them off-center, so they will align with the outside edge of the rail. The tenons on the rails will be cut flush with the outside of the rail. This eliminates interference with the mortises already in the legs. Cut the mortises.

Now cut ½ × 2-inch tenons on the rails. Note that these tenons are shouldered ¼ inch at the top and bottom to get rid of the radiused corner.

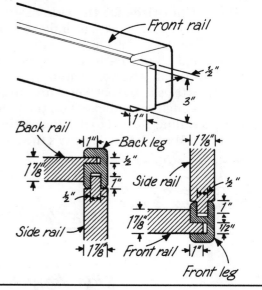

MORTISE-AND-TENON DETAILS

6. Make the back. Once the back rails are fitted to their mortises in the posts, you can lay out and cut the slat mortises.

To be sure the rails will fit their mortises in the back legs when the slats are in place, dry assemble the back and the back posts. If the rails won't fit, determine which slat (or slats) is too long and trim it.

Finish sand all the slats and the rails.

7. Glue up the side assemblies. Dry assemble each side assembly. If the fit is satisfactory, assemble both units with glue.

Drill the stopped peg holes next—two per joint. Each hole should be ¼ inch in diameter and 1¼ inches deep. Glue the pegs in the holes.

After the glue has set and the clamps are removed, machine a ¼-inch radius around all of the frame members, then sand them.

8. Complete the assembly. Dry assemble the swing a final time. If everything is satisfactory, repeat the process using glue.

Assemble the back rails and slats.

Lay a side assembly on the floor. Fit the back assembly into its mortises, then install the front rail. Fit the second side assembly in place.

Cut and radius the seat slats. Drill countersunk pilot holes and screw the seat slats in place. Cover the screw heads with wooden plugs.

Drill peg holes in the remaining joints, and glue pegs in them.

Sand the unit thoroughly and apply several coats of finish.

Finally, install the four eyebolts using two washers with each. Install the chain on the eyebolts, and hang your swing.

PROJECT
PATIO CHAIR AND OTTOMAN

After working hard in the yard and garden, or playing hard on the court, you deserve a break—and a comfortable place to sit while enjoying the fresh air. This patio chair fills the bill perfectly. It offers the cushiness of a living-room-bound Barcalounger, as well as the clean lines and distinctive design of custom-made patio furniture.

The band saw is a key tool in the construction of this chair. It is used to cut the legs and arms.

We chose to make the chair of western red cedar for its natural beauty and resistance to decay, although it's not really the sort of piece you'd thoughtlessly leave out in the rain. A protected patio or porch is an appropriate setting for it. You can use a clear penetrating-oil finish. If more outdoor protection is desired, either a clear water repellent or exterior semi-transparent stain is a good choice.

Shopping List—Chair
1 pc. 4 × 4 × 10' clear western red cedar
1 pc. 4 × 4 × 8' clear western red cedar
4 #6 × 2½'' galvanized flathead wood screws
resorcinol glue
finish material of your choice

Fitted with your plump, soft cushions, and supplemented with its matching ottoman, this chair will be the most popular of your outdoor furnishings. Imagine yourself . . . nestled in the chair . . . feet up . . . the Sunday paper and a tumbler of chilled orange juice at your side. . . .

Get the picture? Build the chair!

473

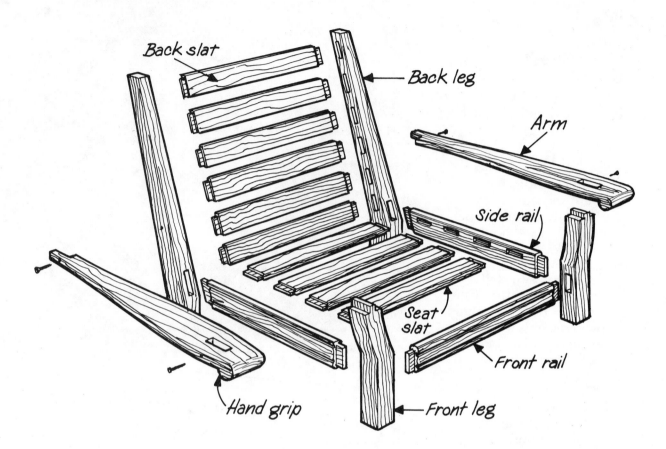

Back slat · Back leg · Arm · Side rail · Seat slat · Front rail · Front leg · Hand grip

Cutting List—Chair

Number	Piece	Dimensions	Material
2	Back legs	2½″ × 3″ × 36″*	cedar
2	Arms	1″ × 3½″ × 31″*	cedar
2	Hand grips	1″ × 3½″ × ¾″	cedar
2	Front legs	3½″ × 3½″ × 18″*	cedar
2	Side rails	1½″ × 3½″ × 24″	cedar
1	Front rail	1½″ × 3½″ × 26½″	cedar
6	Back slats	1″ × 3¼″ × 26½″	cedar
4	Seat slats	1″ × 3¼″ × 28″	cedar

*Dimensions of piece before tapers or shapes are cut.

1. **Make the back legs and arms.** Lay out the two back legs and arms as shown. If you lay out the piece judiciously and cut carefully, you can get one arm and one leg from a single 36-inch length of $3\frac{1}{2} \times 3\frac{1}{2}$-inch stock.

The leg tapers from bottom to top in both its width and thickness. The exact dimensions of the curves and tapers are not critical. Keep in mind that the two arms are mirror images of each other, as are the inner tapers of the legs. (References to left and right in the text and illustrations are from the point of view of being seated in the chair.)

Cut out the back legs and arms with a band saw. While a saber saw can be used, the blade will tend to wander because of the deep cuts necessary. Smooth the surfaces of the legs and arms; the soft cedar will cut fast, so be careful.

Lay out the locations for the mortises on the back legs and arms but don't cut them yet.

CUTTING PLAN

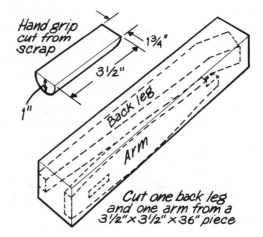

Hand grip cut from scrap

$1\frac{3}{4}"$

$3\frac{1}{2}"$

$1"$

Back leg

Arm

Cut one back leg and one arm from a $3\frac{1}{2}" \times 3\frac{1}{2}" \times 36"$ piece

Cut out two $1 \times 1\frac{3}{4} \times 3\frac{1}{2}$-inch hand grips from scrap. Glue the grips to the underside of the front edge of the arms. Round the tips of the arms and grips.

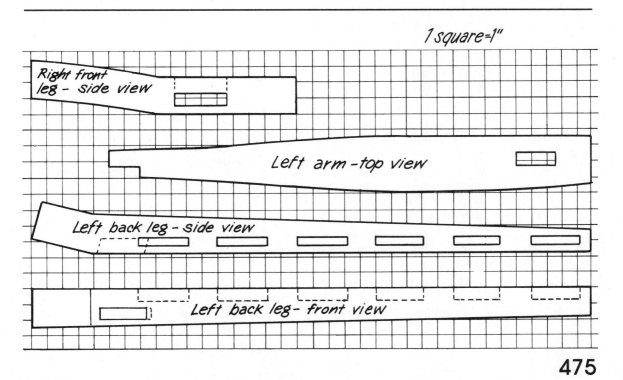

1 square=1"

Right front leg - side view

Left arm - top view

Left back leg - side view

Left back leg - front view

475

2. **Make the front legs.** Lay out the front legs, then cut them out on a band saw. Cut two opposing sides first—sides 1 and 2 in the illustration. Reattach the waste pieces temporarily with double-sided tape, and cut the other sides—sides 3 and 4 in the illustration. Remove the waste.

Lay out a tenon for the arm on the top of each front leg. As shown, the tenon is located ½ inch from the outside face of the legs. The legs will be mirror images of each other; once the tenons are cut the legs will *not* be interchangeable.

Lay out the locations on the front legs for the mortises that accept the rails, but don't cut them yet.

FRONT LEG DETAIL

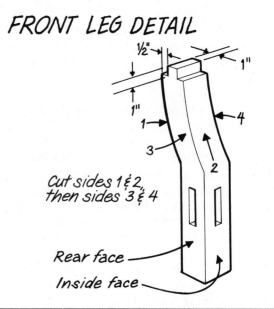

Cut sides 1 & 2, then sides 3 & 4

Rear face

Inside face

3. **Make the rails.** Cut out two side rails and a front rail. The rails can be ripped from 3½ × 3½-inch stock. If your table saw's blade won't cut completely through the stock, flip the piece end for end and make another pass, finishing the cut.

Shape the rails with a ½-inch beading bit in a router, preferably using a router table. See the rail cross section detail for the location of the beading cuts. Make a trial cut on scrap first. Machine a ¼-inch radius on the other two edges.

Machine a cove on the rails with a table saw. To do this, remove the saw's rip fence, and clamp a straight 2 × 4 to the table as shown. Feed the beaded side of the rails into the blade along the fence to cut the cove.

It's best to take several light cuts, increasing the blade height each time until the cove is complete, instead of trying to cut the cove in one pass. Size the cove so there is about ⅛ inch of flat surface between the

SHAPING THE RAILS

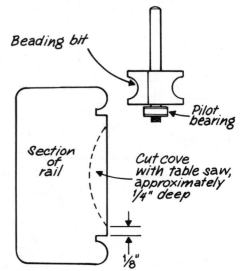

Beading bit

Pilot bearing

Section of rail

Cut cove with table saw, approximately ¼" deep

⅛"

cove and the bead; the depth of the cove is not critical.

You can adjust the shape of the cove by

COVE CUTS SETUP

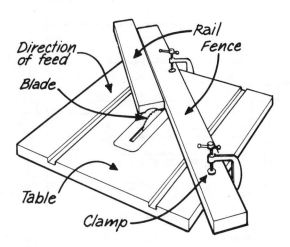

RAIL TENON DETAIL

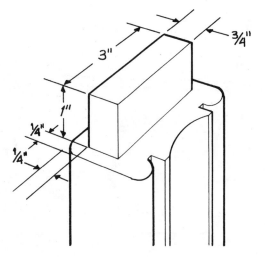

changing the angle of the auxiliary fence. Moving the fence more parallel to the blade will give a narrower cove at a given blade height, while moving the fence more perpendicular to the blade will give a wider cove at the same blade height.

NOTE: Raising the blade on some table saws moves it backward or forward at the same time, so there's no guarantee the center of the cut will remain in the same place. The best approach is to make trial cuts on scrap to discover the correct relationship of fence angle and location, and final blade height to get the finished cove you want. Make tem-

porary reference marks on the table to indicate the section of blade exposed when the final height is correct. Then, keeping the fence in position, lower the blade and make the successively deeper cuts in the rails. Don't raise the blade beyond the temporary marks.

Lay out and cut a ¾-inch-thick tenon on the ends of each rail, 1 inch deep and 3 inches wide, with ¼-inch shoulders on each end and on the side opposite the cove. The rear tenons on the side rails will have shoulders at a 76-degree angle to the rail, to match the angle of the rear legs.

---

4. Make the slats. Cut six back slats (26½ inches long) and four seat slats (28 inches long). Lay out and cut a ½-inch-thick tenon on each end of each slat, one inch long and

3¼ inches wide (the same width as the slat itself—there are no shoulders on the narrow ends of the tenons).

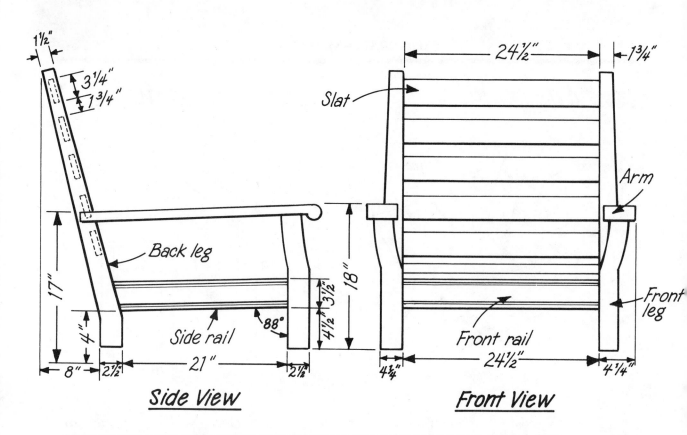

Side View

Front View

5. Cut all the mortises. By waiting until now to cut the mortises, you can set up a more efficient "production line" to finish them all at once. Also, since the slats are completed you can test the fit of their tenons in the mortises.

Cut out the blind mortises in the front and back legs to accept the rails. Rough out the mortises with a drill bit slightly smaller than the finished size, and then cut to the layout lines with a chisel. Alternatively, you can use a drill press with a mortising attachment. The mortises should be about $1/16$ inch deeper than the length of the tenons.

Also cut the through mortises in the arms to accept the front leg tenons, and the blind mortises in the side rails and back legs to accept the slats.

6. Assemble the side frames. First dry assemble the pieces (front and back legs, side rails, and arms). Adjust the fit of the joints by paring the shoulders of tenons if necesary. Make sure everything fits before proceeding. Disassemble the side frames.

Glue together each side frame individually using resorcinol glue. Glue the arms over the front leg tenons. Drive galvanized screws through the arms into the legs.

7. Assemble the entire chair. First dry fit the chair to check the fit of the joints, and make any necessary adjustments. When you're satisfied that everything fits, glue the whole chair together.

Sand all surfaces and apply a finish.

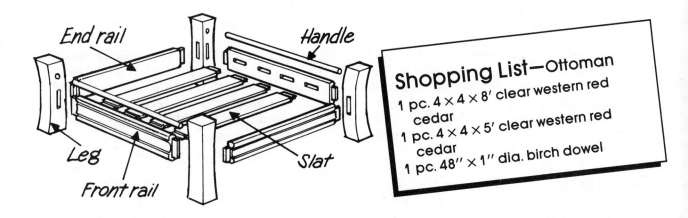

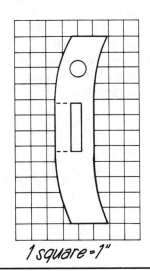

Shopping List—Ottoman

1 pc. 4 × 4 × 8' clear western red cedar

1 pc. 4 × 4 × 5' clear western red cedar

1 pc. 48" × 1" dia. birch dowel

Cutting List—Ottoman

Number	Piece	Dimensions	Material
4	Legs	3½" × 3½" × 12"*	cedar
2	Front and back rails	1½" × 3½" × 26"	cedar
2	End rails	1½" × 3½" × 21½"	cedar
4	Slats	1" × 3¼" × 27½"	cedar
2	Handles	22" × 1"	dowel

*Dimensions of piece before tapers or shapes are cut.

Ottoman

1. **Make the legs.** Lay out the four legs as shown, using the gridded lines. Cut out the legs using a band saw. Use the same technique as for the front legs of the patio chair —cut two opposing sides first, reattach the waste pieces temporarily with double-sided tape, and then cut the other sides.

Lay out the locations for the two blind mortises on each leg that accept the rails, but don't cut them yet.

Lay out and drill a 1-inch-diameter, 1-inch-deep hole in each leg for the handles.

1 square = 1"

2. Make the rails. Cut out front and back rails, and two end rails. The rails can be ripped from nominal 4 × 4 stock. If your table saw's blade won't cut completely through the stock in one pass, flip the piece end for end after the first pass and make a second cut.

Shape two edges of the rails with a ½-inch beading bit in a router, then machine a ¼-inch radius on the other two edges.

Machine a cove on the rails with a table saw, as you did the chair rails.

Lay out and cut a ¾-inch-thick tenon on the ends of each rail, 1 inch deep and 3 inches wide, with ¼-inch shoulders on each end and on the side opposite the cove.

Lay out the four blind mortises in each end rail to accept the slats.

---

3. Make the slats. Cut four 1 × 3¼ × 27½-inch slats. Lay out and cut a ½-inch-thick tenon on each end of each slat, 1 inch long and 3¼ inches wide.

---

4. Cut all the mortises. You can save setup time by cutting the blind mortises in the legs and the end rails at one time. Rough out the mortises by using a drill bit slightly smaller than the finished size, then cutting to the layout line with a chisel. The mortises should be about $1/16$ inch deeper than the length of the tenons.

---

5. Make the handles. If you choose to buy standard 1-inch birch dowel for the handles, it can be cut to length and stained to match the color of the red cedar.

---

6. Assemble the ottoman. Dry fit the parts together to check the fit of the joints, and make any adjustments before proceeding. When you're sure everything fits well, assemble the ottoman with resorcinol glue, and clamp overnight to dry. Sand all surfaces and apply the finish of your choice.

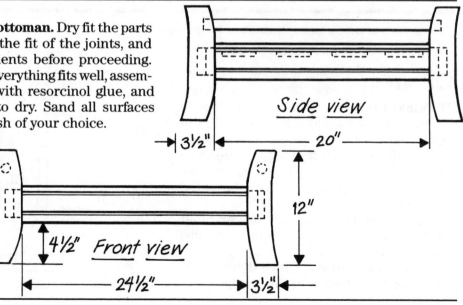

Side view

3½"   20"

12"

4½" Front view

24½"   3½"

Cushions

If you're handy with a sewing machine, making these cushions for the patio chair and matching ottoman will be a snap. If sewing is new to you, this is a good project to get you started. All the seams are straight and simple. Get a friend to show you how to thread the sewing machine's bobbin and needle, and how to stitch a straight line—that's all there is to it.

Buy upholstery fabric that will be heavy enough to wear well, and that is pleasing to your eye. You may want to buy a heavy-gauge needle for the sewing machine, and heavy upholstery thread, too—check with the clerk at the fabric store for guidance.

Shopping List—Cushions
2 pcs. 31″ × 58¾″ upholstery fabric (chair cushion covers)
1 pc. 31″ × 52¾″ upholstery fabric (ottoman cushion cover)
3 pcs. 23″ × ¾″ hook-and-loop tape
upholstery thread
heavy gauge sewing needle
2 pcs. 2″ × 20″ × 22″ foam rubber (chair cushions)
1 pc. 2″ × 18″ × 22″ foam rubber (ottoman cushion)
polyester or cotton batting

1. **Prepare the fabric.** Cut two pieces of fabric 31 × 58¾ inches. Each piece will make one chair cushion. Cut one piece of fabric 31 × 52¾ inches for the ottoman cushion.

Take one of the 31-inch edges and make a ½-inch-wide fold along the edge, bringing the face side (the outside surface of the upholstery) over the back side (the side that will end up inside the finished cushion). Make another ½-inch fold in the same way over the first fold. Sew a line of hem stitches over the fold about ¼ inch in from the edge. Repeat this folding and hem stitching on each 31-inch edge of each piece of fabric. The 58¾-inch pieces will become 56¾ inches long and the 52¾-inch piece will be 50¾ inches long after hemming.

Cut three 23-inch lengths of hook-and-loop tape (each length has a hook strip and a loop strip). Separate the hook strips from the loop strips. Sew a hook strip on the back side of the fabric, centered on the 31-inch

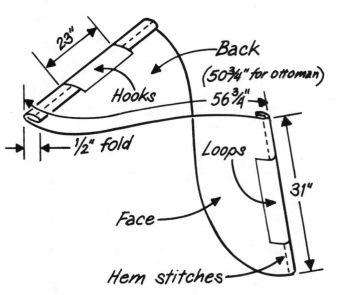

edge. Sew a loop strip on the face side of the fabric, also centered on the 31-inch edge, as shown. Sew hook and loop strips on the other fabric.

2. **Sew the fabric into the shape of a cushion.** The side seams of the cushion are sewn with the fabric inside out–that is, with the back side exposed. That way, when you turn the fabric face side out after sewing, the seams will be hidden inside the cushion.

Turn the fabric face to face and mate the hook-and-loop strips. Sew a line of stitches along the sides, about ½ inch in from the edge, to close in the perimeter of the fabric.

To give the cushion a full shape, sew in short vertical seams at each corner. To do this, take one corner at a time, grasp the fabric on both sides near the corner and pull

CROSS-SEWING CORNERS

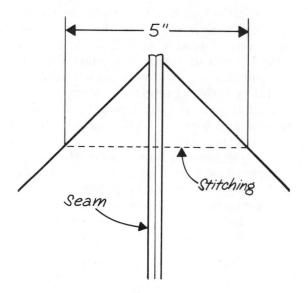

outward. Still pulling outward, fold the fabric flat and sew a line of stitches 5 inches long across the corner, as shown. Repeat for each corner of each cushion. Open the hook-and-loop strip and turn the fabric right side (face side) out.

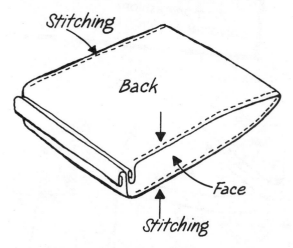

3. **Stuff the cushions.** Cut two blocks of foam rubber $2 \times 20 \times 22$ inches for the chair cushions and one block of foam $2 \times 18 \times 22$ inches for the ottoman cushion. Wrap the foam blocks in polyester or cotton batting to soften their shape. Stuff the foam and batting into the covers, and close the hook-and-loop strips.

PROJECT

PATIO CHAISE AND CHAIR

A true chaise is a two-wheeled, horse-drawn carriage. While neither this chaise nor its matching chair is horse-drawn, they do have wheels. And the wheels sure do make it easy to move them from one spot to another on the deck or patio. Following the sun (or the shade) is easy, for anyone can lift the back of either the chaise or the chair and wheel it to a new spot.

The fenderlike arch of the armrests is the focal point of the design, lending a unique Art Deco appearance to the pieces.

Making these curved armrests may seem like a challenge, but it is really quite easy. If you've got a saber saw and can use it, you can cut out and assemble the jig needed to laminate the arms. Three winter weekends should be all it takes to complete either the chaise or the chair.

Made from pine lumber, these pieces of outdoor furniture are painted. Pick out the cushion fabric before you buy the lumber, then buy a can of paint to complement it when you stop at the lumberyard. If your neighborhood is overstocked with redwood patio furniture, then this set of colorful outdoor seats is the perfect backyard spruce-up.

Shopping List—Chaise

- 1 pc. 2 × 3 × 12' clear pine
- 1 pc. 5/4 × 6 × 4' #2 pine
- 2 pcs. 5/4 × 4 × 8' #2 pine
- 4 pcs. 5/4 × 3 × 8' #2 pine
- 2 pcs. 1 × 6 × 10' #2 pine
- 1 pc. 1/2" × 4' × 8' plywood
- 1 pc. 49" × 1/2" dia. steel rod
- 2–12" × 2" wheels
- 2 #8 × 3" galvanized all-purpose screws
- 1 box #8 × 2" galvanized all-purpose screws
- 2–1/2" push nuts
- 4–1/2" flat washers
- 1" underlayment nails
- carpenter's glue
- resorcinol glue
- oil-based primer
- exterior-grade enamel top-coat paint
- 2 pcs. 47" × 50" upholstery fabric (cushion covers)
- 2 pcs. 3" × 22" × 22" foam rubber (seat cushions)
- 2 pcs. 3" × 22" × 26" foam rubber (back cushions)

Cutting List—Chaise

Number	Piece	Dimensions	Material
5	Jig layers	½″ × 21″ × 46″	plywood
12	Clamping blocks	½″ × 2½″ × 2½″	plywood
8	Arm plies	¼″ × 2½″ × 72″	clear pine
2	Rails	1¹⁄₁₆″ × 3½″ × 44″	pine
2	Back supports	1¹⁄₁₆″ × 3½″ × 15″	pine
2	Seat sides	1¹⁄₁₆″ × 2½″ × 22″	pine
1	Seat front	1¹⁄₁₆″ × 2½″ × 42″	pine
1	Seat back	1¹⁄₁₆″ × 2½″ × 42″	pine
4	Seat slats	¾″ × 2½″ × 37¾″	pine
2	Back sides	1¹⁄₁₆″ × 2½″ × 34″	pine
1	Back bottom	1¹⁄₁₆″ × 2½″ × 37¾″	pine
1	Back top	1¹⁄₁₆″ × 5½″ × 42″	pine
5	Back slats	¾″ × 2½″ × 37¾″	pine
1	Seat support	1¹⁄₁₆″ × 2½″ × 47″	pine
1	Cross member	1¹⁄₁₆″ × 3½″ × 42″	pine
2	Seat fillers	1¹⁄₁₆″ × 2½″ × 21″	pine

Cutting List—Chair

Number	Piece	Dimensions	Material
5	Jig layers	½″ × 21″ × 46″	plywood
12	Clamping blocks	½″ × 2½″ × 2½″	plywood
8	Arm plies	¼″ × 2½″ × 72″	clear pine
2	Rails	1¹⁄₁₆″ × 3½″ × 44″	pine
2	Back supports	1¹⁄₁₆″ × 3½″ × 15″	pine
2	Seat sides	1¹⁄₁₆″ × 2½″ × 22″	pine
1	Seat front	1¹⁄₁₆″ × 2½″ × 22″	pine
1	Seat back	1¹⁄₁₆″ × 2½″ × 22″	pine
4	Seat slats	¾″ × 2½″ × 17¾″	pine
2	Back sides	1¹⁄₁₆″ × 2½″ × 34″	pine
1	Back bottom	1¹⁄₁₆″ × 2½″ × 17¾″	pine
1	Back top	1¹⁄₁₆″ × 5½″ × 22″	pine
5	Back slats	¾″ × 2½″ × 17¾″	pine
1	Seat support	1¹⁄₁₆″ × 2½″ × 27″	pine
1	Cross member	1¹⁄₁₆″ × 3½″ × 42″	pine
2	Seat fillers	1¹⁄₁₆″ × 2½″ × 21″	pine

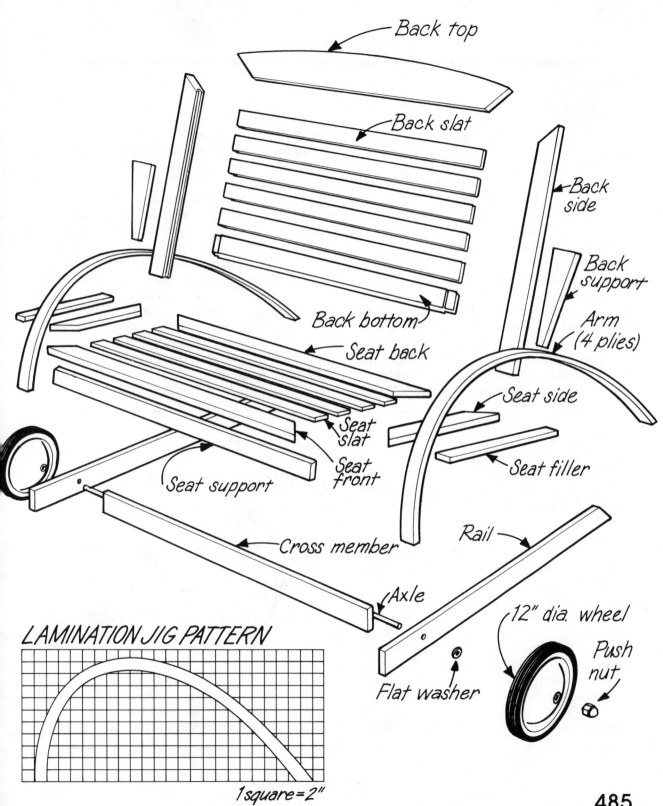

Back top

Back slat

Back side

Back support

Arm (4 plies)

Back bottom

Seat back

Seat side

Seat slat

Seat filler

Seat front

Seat support

Cross member

Rail

Axle

12" dia. wheel

Push nut

Flat washer

LAMINATION JIG PATTERN

1 square = 2"

485

1. Assemble the necessary tools and materials. The chaise and the chair are identical but for the lengths of the various horizontal pieces—the front and back of the seat frame, the top and bottom of the back, the slats, the seat support, and the cross member. The chaise is 20 inches wider than the chair. It takes two cushions; the chair takes one. By following the step-by-step instructions that follow, you can make either the chair or the chaise. Refer to the cutting list for the specific dimensions of the various parts.

Both pieces are built entirely from pine, using a combination of dimension lumber boards and 5/4 stock, which ordinarily dresses out to a finished thickness of $1\frac{1}{16}$ inch.

Resorcinol glue and various lengths of galvanized all-purpose screws are specified, though you can use regular slotted flathead wood screws if you prefer. Make sure they are galvanized in any case. Throughout the project, it's a good idea to countersink the screw heads. That way later application of wood filler and paint will make for a seamless appearance.

The only essential tools are a table saw (or a radial arm saw), a saber saw (or band saw), and a dozen or so clamps. You need the saber saw to cut the top of the back and the bending jig used to make the arms. Forming the arms requires a lot of clamps, a dozen or more. Our furniture builder used quick clamps, but C-clamps or large hand screws (or some of all three) can also be used. The table saw is essential for ripping the stock to size and for grooving the sides of the seat and back frames.

2. Construct the bending jig. The jig is made of five pieces of ½-inch plywood cut to the arms' curve. The pieces are stacked and fastened to a plywood base. This provides a strong form on which to bend and laminate the arms.

Enlarge the pattern and lay it out on a sheet of plywood. With a saber saw, cut out the five curved plies and the jig base. From the plywood scrap, cut a dozen 2½-inch-square clamping blocks.

Using carpenter's glue and underlayment nails, attach one of the curved plies to the jig base. Glue and nail another curved ply atop the first and so on, until all five plies have been fastened together, forming the jig. When the glue has dried, smooth the outside convex face of the jig with a belt sander. Apply a heavy coat of paste wax to the jig to

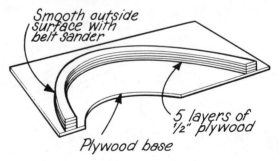

LAMINATION JIG

Smooth outside surface with belt sander

5 layers of ½" plywood

Plywood base

prevent glue from adhering to it. Finally, screw or clamp the jig to a workbench or a couple of sturdy sawhorses.

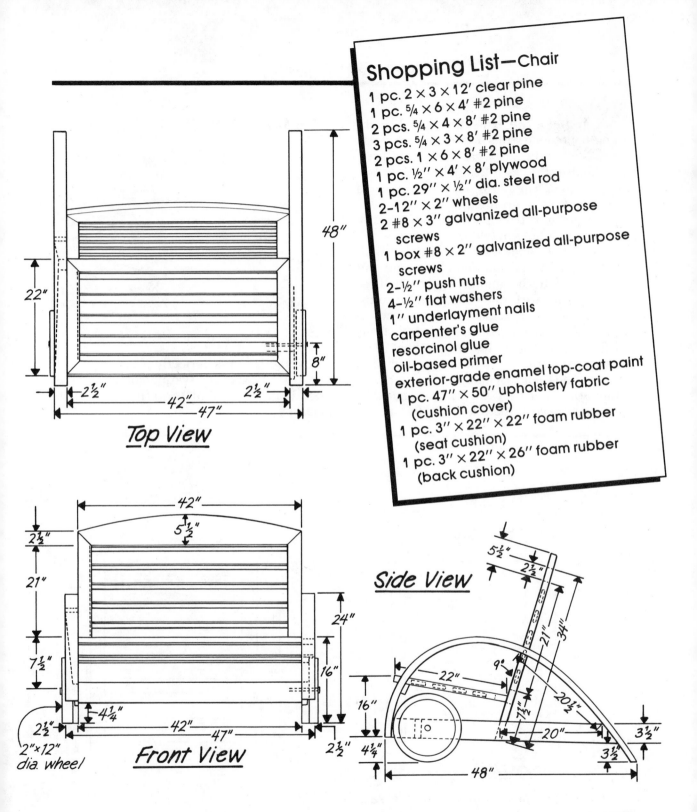

Top View

22"

48"

8"

2½"

42"

47"

2½"

Shopping List—Chair

1 pc. 2 × 3 × 12' clear pine
1 pc. ⁵⁄₄ × 6 × 4' #2 pine
2 pcs. ⁵⁄₄ × 4 × 8' #2 pine
3 pcs. ⁵⁄₄ × 3 × 8' #2 pine
2 pcs. 1 × 6 × 8' #2 pine
1 pc. ½" × 4 × 8' plywood
1 pc. 29" × ½" dia. steel rod
2–12" × 2" wheels
2 #8 × 3" galvanized all-purpose
   screws
1 box #8 × 2" galvanized all-purpose
   screws
2–½" push nuts
4–½" flat washers
1" underlayment nails
carpenter's glue
resorcinol glue
oil-based primer
exterior-grade enamel top-coat paint
1 pc. 47" × 50" upholstery fabric
   (cushion cover)
1 pc. 3" × 22" × 22" foam rubber
   (seat cushion)
1 pc. 3" × 22" × 26" foam rubber
   (back cushion)

Front View

42"

5½"

2½"

21"

7½"

4¼"

2½"

42"

47"

24"

16"

2½"

4¼"

2" × 12"
dia. wheel

Side View

5½"

2½"

9°

22"

7½"

21"

34"

20½"

16"

20"

3½"

3½"

48"

3. Laminate the arms. Rip eight ¼-inch-thick, 6-foot-long strips from *clear* pine stock. The width of the strips can vary slightly; on our chaise, they are 2¾-inches wide, but they can be 2½ inches wide, allowing you to rip them from 2 × 3 stock.

Select four strips, and spread resorcinol glue on both sides of two and on one side of the other two. Stack the strips together with the unglued faces out, and clamp one end of the stack to the laminating jig. The best clamps to use are the so-called quick clamps; use the plywood blocks under the jaws to spread the clamping force. Start at the front of the arm and work toward the back. The individual strips will tend to slip and slide as they find their respective positions in the lamination, but they are long enough that you don't need to be too concerned about

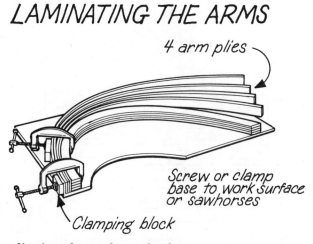

LAMINATING THE ARMS

4 arm plies

Screw or clamp base to work surface or sawhorses

Clamping block

aligning the ends perfectly.

Ideally, this is a two-person job, one to bend the strips and the other to set the clamps.

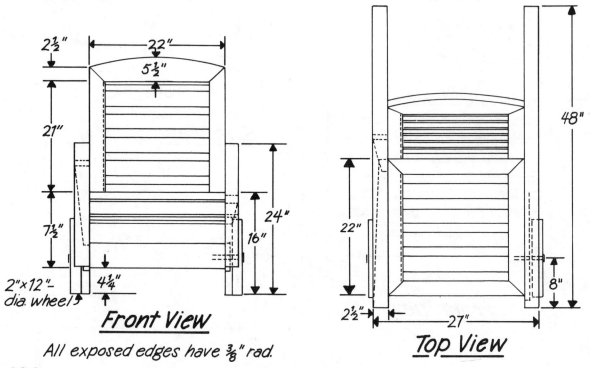

Front View

All exposed edges have ⅜" rad.

Top View

Allow the glue to dry for 24 hours, then remove the clamps and glue up the second arm.

Trim the laminated arms to 2½-inch width on a table saw with a carbide-tipped blade. Rest the arm on the saw table with the concave face up, and support the end on your shoulder as you feed it into the blade. Having a helper guide the outfeed end of the workpiece is prudent. (You can also use a belt sander or block plane for this, though the resorcinol glue is abrasive on the plane's blade.) Trim the ends of the arms so they will be parallel to the ground.

4. Cut and install the rails. The remainder of the chaise is made of #2 pine. Cut the rails from 5/4 stock. Trim the ends of the rails to fit their respective laminated arms. Glue and screw the rails in place. It's best to drill pilot holes for the screws. Note that the rails are flush with the inside edge of the arms, so you must make left and right arm assemblies, which will be mirror images of each other.

5. Build the seat assembly. From 5/4 stock, cut two sides, a front, and a back for the seat frame. Miter the ends at 45 degrees. Plow a ¾-inch-wide, ⅜-inch-deep groove along the inner edge of each side for the seat slats.

Cut the seat slats from 1 × 6 stock. With a router and a ⅛- to ¼-inch round-over bit, break the edges of the slats.

Assemble the seat with glue and screws. Drill pilot holes for the screws, and countersink the screw heads. Space the slats evenly within the seat frame.

After the glue has dried, rip a 9-degree bevel along the back edge of the assembly. Do this on a table saw.

6. Build the back assembly. From 5/4 stock, cut two sides, a bottom, and a top for the back frame.

Using a dado cutter in a table saw, plow a ¾-inch-wide, ⅜-inch-deep groove in the inner edge of each side for the back slats. Then miter the top ends of the sides.

On each end of the bottom, form a tenon by cutting a ⅜-inch-wide, 5/32-inch-deep rabbet across both faces. You can do this with a router or a table-saw-mounted dado cutter. The tenons fit into the grooves cut in the sides.

Lay out and cut the arc along the top edge of the top. The radius of the arc is 80 inches, so you can strike the arc with a string compass—a pencil at the end of an 80-inch length of string. But it is probably easier to use a thin strip of wood—say about ⅛ inch thick—as a guide. Hold the strip by the ends and flex it. Hold it against the face of the top so a helper can trace the curve. You can adjust the curve by moving your hands closer together or further apart. Cut the curve with a saber saw. Finally, miter the ends.

Cut five back slats from 1 × 6 stock. Radius the edges of the slats, as you did the seat slats.

Assemble the back with glue and screws. Drill pilot holes for the screws, and countersink the screw heads. Space the slats evenly within the back frame.

7. **Assemble the chair or settee.** To complete the assembly, you must make the seat support and extensions, the back support, and the cross member. These pieces provide structural support and enhance the design by filling spaces and lending a smooth appearance to the whole.

Join the arms together first. Cut the seat support from 5/4 stock. On a table saw, rip a 12-degree bevel along the top edge. Glue the seat support to the arms, then drill pilot holes and drive screws through the support into the arms.

Mount the back next. First, cut the two back supports, trimming and tapering them to fit between the arm and the rail. Cut the tapers with a saber saw or on a band saw. Locate these supports, as shown in the Seat Extension/Back Support Detail. Glue them in place, then drive screws through the arms into the supports. Fit the back assembly in position, and glue and screw it to the back supports. Trim the bottoms of the back's sides so they are flush with the bottom of the rails.

Next, place the seat assembly in position, and glue and screw it to the back and to the seat support. From 5/4 stock, cut two seat extensions. Taper these pieces to fit between the back support and the front of the arm

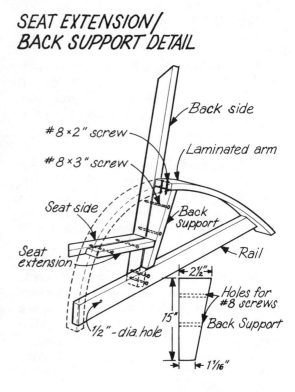

SEAT EXTENSION/
BACK SUPPORT DETAIL

#8×2" screw

#8×3" screw

Back side

Laminated arm

Seat side

Back Support

Seat extension

Seat

Rail

2½"

Holes for #8 screws

Back Support

15"

½"-dia. hole

1 1/16"

atop the seat support. Cut the tapers with a saber saw or on a band saw. Glue and screw the extensions in position.

Cut the cross member and install it between the rails. Drill a ½-inch hole through each rail, as shown, to accept the axle.

8. **Sand the assembly and apply a finish.** Radius all exposed edges with a router and round-over bit, or break the edges with sandpaper if you prefer. Sand all surfaces smooth. Cover the screws with wood filler and resand where necessary. Pay particular attention to the areas where the seat extensions and the back supports abut other parts in the same plane.

Prime the whole assembly with oil-based primer, and when dry, apply a finish coat, using your choice of paint and color. Place the ½-inch steel axle rod through the rails, mount the wheels with flat washers on either side, and install push nuts over the ends of the axle.

MAKING THE CUSHIONS

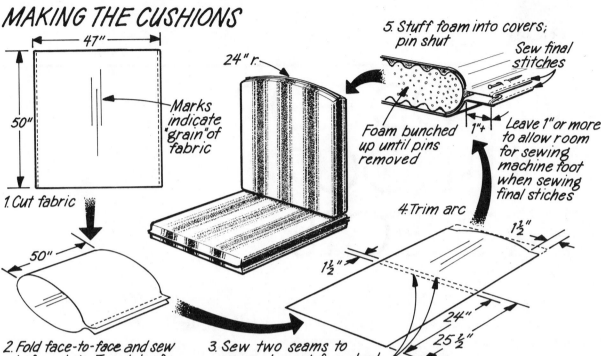

47"

50"

Marks indicate "grain" of fabric

1. Cut fabric

50"

2. Fold face-to-face and sew to form tube. Turn tube face out; center seam on bottom.

24" r.

3. Sew two seams to separate seat from back. Turn ¼" in and hem each end of tube.

5. Stuff foam into covers; pin shut

Sew final stitches

Foam bunched up until pins removed

1"+

Leave 1" or more to allow room for sewing machine foot when sewing final stitches

4. Trim arc

1½"

1½"

24"

25½"

9. **Make the cushions.** Cut two 47 × 50-inch pieces of upholstery fabric for the cushion covers. The pattern should parallel the larger dimension. Fold each piece once across the short dimension, with the back of the fabric exposed. Stitch a seam along the 50-inch dimension, ½ inch from the edge. Turn the resulting tube right side out, so the fabric's face is now on the outside, and center the seam on the bottom.

Flatten the tube and sew two seams across it, as shown, 24 inches and 25½ inches from one end. These seams create two separate seat-cushion compartments. Trim the top end of the cover to a 24-inch radius arc. Turn under the fabric edges at both ends of the cover and hem them.

Cut the cushions from 3-inch-thick foam rubber. The seat is 22 inches square; the back is 22 × 26 inches. Cut an arc on one short edge of the back cushion to match the cover.

Stuff the foam cushions into the covers. Pin the ends of the covers shut with a row of straight pins about 1 inch from the hemmed edge of the covers—you may have to temporarily bunch up the foam to get the pins in. This allows enough room to guide the layers of fabric under the foot of the sewing machine. Fold in the corners of the top and bottom layers of fabric about 1¼ inches. Sew a line of stitches through the hemmed edges of both layers of fabric, closing the ends of the covers. Remove the pins, allowing the cushions to unbunch. Place the cushions on the chair.

WOOD FOR OUTDOOR PROJECTS

Selecting wood for an outdoor project involves a lot of considerations.

First, there are the usual woodworking considerations: The wood must be strong, warp-free, attractive. It's got to be available in the dimensions and quantities you need.

But wood used outdoors must stand up to additional tests. It faces at least two natural enemies: rot and weather. If the wood is anchored to the ground, it faces threats from wood-eating insects, such as termites and carpenter ants. To complicate things, some woods stand up well to one threat, but not to another. Some species are resistant to rot but have a pronounced tendency to crack and twist from the effects of rain and sun.

Armed with information about the strengths and weaknesses of various woods, enemies of woods, and products intended to protect wood from those enemies, you'll be better equipped to choose the best wood for whatever outdoor project you intend to build.

Lumber

Lumber is the wood that comes from the sawmill. Solid wood. No glue, no fillers, no additives. There are two basic kinds of lumber: hardwood and softwood. The category in which a wood is placed has nothing to do with the actual hardness or softness of the wood itself. It has to do with the tree. If the tree is deciduous, dropping its leaves annually, then the wood is a hardwood. If the tree is evergreen, bearing needles and cones, then the wood is a softwood. In fact, some hardwoods, like poplar, are softer than some softwoods, like fir.

What's important at this point, perhaps, is the difference that these two categories make to you. Softwood is widely available, and is sold in a predictable, standard way throughout the country. Hardwood is less easy to find and is sold in a less predictable way.

Defects

Lumber—hardwood and softwood—has defects. Would that all of it was clear and unblemished, straight and true. But it isn't. Some of the defects affect the grading, but others don't. Thus, you can avoid getting boards with knots and pitch pockets by purchasing high grades of lumber. But warping and some other defects don't enter into the grading, and you can pay premium prices and still get stuck with defective boards.

The most obvious defects you'll run into are those lumped together under the term warp. A warped board simply isn't straight and flat. It may be bowed or crooked, which means it is curved from end to end, either in the plane of the width (bow) or of the thickness (crook). It may be cupped, which means that it is curved from edge to edge across the width. Or it may be twisted, which is worst of all.

The best way to deal with warped boards is to avoid them, by selecting individual boards very carefully at the lumberyard. If you have to, you can sometimes work around warpage. For example, a bowed, crooked, or twisted board will usually yield many small, usable pieces, even though it would be totally unsuitable for use in one piece. Cupping can be minimized by ripping the board into narrower, less obviously cupped lengths.

LUMBER DEFECTS AND KNOTS

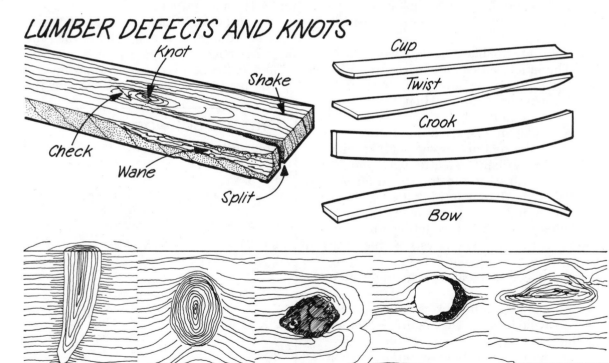

Knot · Shake · Check · Wane · Split · Cup · Twist · Crook · Bow

Spiked knot · Intergrown knot · Encased knot · Knot hole · Pitch pocket

Splits, checks, and shakes are in another family of defects. All are separations in the wood. All usually occur at the end of a board, and crop up during drying. The end grain gives off moisture better than the edge grain. Occasionally, a check will develop after you crosscut a board that wasn't as dry as you thought it was.

The most common defects are knots and pitch pockets. All woods have knots. Pitch pockets are specialties of the softwoods, particularly pine, fir, and spruce.

Knots are so commonplace that a whole lexicon has grown up around them. There are dimensional definitions for small, medium, and large knots. There are encased, intergrown, not-firm, and loose knots. There are red knots and black knots. There are spikes and branch knots.

Knots are the black holes of woodworking. The grain eddies and swirls around a dense, dark spot. Any saw strains to cut it. It resists cleaving. Nails bend in it. Resins and pitch ooze from it.

And all a knot is, is a branch.

Pitch pockets are crevices filled with pitch, a sticky resin. No matter what you do, the pitch will continue to ooze from the pocket longer than you think it ever possibly could, and it will spoil many finishes, including paint. The best solution is to clean the pocket as thoroughly as possible with turpentine, then shellac it before finishing the board. This will seal any remaining pitch inside the pocket.

Knots and pitch pockets are relatively easy to avoid because they figure in lumber grading systems. The absence of knots makes a board more valued, thus winning it a higher grade than one with knots. For most outdoor furniture projects, knots are not a major consideration.

Softwood

The building industry is the biggest user of softwood. Your house surely is framed with softwood. The windows and doors are cased in it. The place is trimmed with it.

The softwoods are species like pine, fir, spruce, larch, and hemlock. Most of these trees are cut into framing materials, lumber with a 2-inch or greater thickness, which is commonly called dimension lumber. But the pine is cut into boards that are nominally 1 inch thick (actually ¾ inch thick). This material is commonly called board lumber. Some lumberyards stock a third thickness of softwood; it's called five-quarter ($5/4$) and is nominally 1¼ inches thick.

Regardless of the cross-sectional dimension, board lumber is delivered to the lumberyards in lengths ranging from 8 feet up to 20 feet, in 2-foot increments. It may be sold by the board foot in some places, but the

Dressed Softwood Sizes

Nominal	Actual
1 × 2	¾" × 1½"
1 × 3	¾" × 2½"
1 × 4	¾" × 3½"
1 × 6	¾" × 5½"
1 × 8	¾" × 7¼"
1 × 10	¾" × 9¼"
1 × 12	¾" × 11¼"
2 × 2	1½" × 1½"
2 × 3	1½" × 2½"
2 × 4	1½" × 3½"
2 × 6	1½" × 5½"
2 × 8	1½" × 7¼"
2 × 10	1½" × 9¼"
2 × 12	1½" × 11¼"

most widespread approach is to sell it by the running foot.

The nice thing about board lumber, from the standpoint of the occasional woodworker, is that it is in as predictable and uniform a state as wood is ever likely to be. The sizes are the same from board to board. The surfaces are flat, square, and parallel, as are the edges. It is entirely possible to build attractive, durable outdoor furniture using board lumber without ever having to rip a board or plane an edge.

Lumber Grades

Class	Grade	Characteristics
Softwood		
Select	B and Better (or B & Btr, or Clear)	Practically clear on both sides; no knots; virtually no blemishes
	C	Slightly more blemishes than B & Btr; perhaps a few very small knots
	D	One side finish quality; recognizable defects on back
Common	No. 1 (or Construction)	Smooth grain; evenly distributed knots no more than 2 inches in diameter; no knots near edge
	No. 2 (or Standard)	Similar to No. 1, except knots up to 3 inches in diameter in wide boards
	No. 3 (or Utility)	Some coarse or loose knots or other major blemishes; sometimes a single defect surrounded by good wood
	No. 4 (or Economy)	Numerous knots, knotholes, and other defects; some usable wood
	No. 5 (or Economy)	Poor quality; use only if neither appearance nor strength is required
Hardwood		
	Firsts and Seconds (FAS)	Usually at least 6 inches wide and 8 feet long; over 81 percent clear on both sides
	Select	At least 4 inches wide and 6 feet long; one side as good as FAS
	No. 1 Common	Narrower and shorter than Select; 66 percent clear
	No. 2 Common	50 percent clear
	No. 3A Common	33 percent clear
	No. 3B Common	25 percent clear

Hardwood

Working with hardwoods makes some extra demands on the woodworker, but it may be worth the trouble if you're after a classy appearance. Pine is a poor match for the beauty of oak or other hardwoods. They are excellent woods: attractive, reasonably easy to work, and quite commonly available, if you look in the right places.

Hardwoods are sold by the board foot, a volumetric as opposed to a linear measure. This is due at least in part to the nature of hardwood sizing. There's no uniformity of thickness, width, and length, as there is with dimension and board lumber. To eliminate waste, hardwoods are cut to "random widths and lengths," meaning that in any given lot of hardwood, you may not find even two boards of like dimensions. Thicknesses likewise vary. Though nominal thicknesses are expressed in uniform increments of quarters of an inch, actual thicknesses may vary from one lot of lumber to another.

Traditionally, hardwoods were stocked in a rough-sawed state, then planed to the buyer's specifications. More and more, however, hardwoods now are stocked already surfaced. As this trend spreads, more uniformity of thickness, anyway, is likely to prevail. At any rate, if the wood isn't surfaced, you should have it planed at the lumberyard.

Enemies of Wood

Regardless of its grade or dimensions, regardless of whether it is a hardwood or a softwood, wood has enemies. The more the backyard builder knows about these enemies, the better equipped he or she will be to deal with them.

Rot

Rot must be wood's Outdoor Enemy Number One. Fence posts rot in the ground. A corner of the deck collects water and rots. Lawn chairs develop foot rot after a summer or two under that shady tree.

The actual enemy is fungus. The earth is full of hungry fungi, looking to make a meal of your project. One sure way to defeat them is to poison their food. This is what chemically treating wood does. But chemical treatment is not the only way to protect wood. Indeed in many cases, it is not the best way.

In addition to wood to eat, these fungi need warmth, oxygen, and moisture. Different fungi need different amounts of water, but none will grow if the moisture content of wood is kept below 20 percent.

For most outdoor projects, it is impossible to eliminate oxygen and impossible or

---

The Board Foot

A board foot is a cubic foot of wood. Here's a simple formula for calculating board feet:

Thickness in inches × width in inches × length in feet ÷ 12

For example, calculate the board feet in a 10-foot 2 × 8:

$2 \times 8 \times 10 \div 12 = 13.3$ board feet

---

impractical to eliminate warmth. Usually, it's much easier to make sure that the wood never reaches a moisture content of 20 percent. Of course wood that never gets rained on, such as the framing of your garden shed, is protected. But even wood that's rained on regularly can endure for decades if the water cannot collect and soak in. If the water runs off or evaporates, fungi don't have a chance to grow.

Keep this principle in mind when joining wood that will be exposed to the weather, whether you are building a fence or a bench. Orient the boards so they shed water. Where possible, make joints that will dry out quickly when the rain stops.

Naturally rot-resistant woods. Fortunately, fungi have food preferences, so you can build with wood they don't like to eat. Significantly, fungi prefer sapwood—the pale wood on the outer part of a log. Much less appealing to fungi is the heartwood, the darker, more resinous wood in the middle of a log. Fungi will eat the sapwood of any species, even the most rot-resistant, such as redwood or cedar. If you are buying wood for its natural resistance to rot, make sure you get heartwood. Actually, fungi eventually will eat the heartwood of any untreated wood if moisture, warmth, and oxygen are abundantly available, as is the case, for example, when you set a post in the ground.

Treated woods. Fungi can't digest it. Insects won't eat it. The treatment doesn't come off on your hands or smell bad, and it won't leach out of the wood. It can be cut with the same tools as other wood, and you can nail it or screw it easily. It's no wonder this material has become so popular. It's so widely used for outdoor structures that practically everyone is familiar with the green tinge of wood that's been pressure-treated with chromated copper arsenate (CCA).

The drawback of pressure-treated wood is its color. Many find that green tinge unattractive. But if left to weather for a couple of years, it will—since it's still wood—turn silvery gray. Moreover, it can be painted or stained without problem.

The Forest Products Laboratory of the United States Department of Agriculture set CCA pressure-treated stakes in the ground around the country nearly 40 years ago. Stakes that were treated to retain 0.44 pounds of preservative per cubic foot have shown no sign of rot. If you install a properly treated post in the ground it might never rot; no one knows for sure. But in any case, chances are you won't be around to replace it if it does.

Rot-Resistant Woods

Bald cypress, old growth	Oak
Catalpa	Bur
Cedar	Chestnut
Cherry, black	Gambel's
Chestnut	Oregon white
Cypress, Arizona	Post
Juniper	White
Locust, black*	Osage orange*
Mesquite	Redwood
Mulberry, red*	Sassafras
	Walnut, black
	Yew, Pacific*

SOURCE: *Wood Handbook: Wood as an Engineering Material*, U.S. Department of Agriculture Forest Service, Forest Products Laboratory, Madison, Wis., 1987.

*These woods have exceptionally high decay resistance.

That 0.44 pounds of preservative per cubic foot is significant, because stakes treated to half that level did begin to rot after 15 years. This research is the basis for the American Wood Preserver's Association retention standards for CCA-treated lumber and plywood:

Retentions (lbs./cu. ft.)	Uses/Exposure
0.25	Aboveground
0.40	Ground contact
0.60	Wood foundation
2.50	Salt water (marine)

Grading Redwood and Cedar

Redwood and cedar have their own grading system based on the fact that the heartwood is much more decay-resistant than the sapwood. The best grade is Clear All Heart—clear indicates no knots, all heart means it is all heartwood. The next grade is Clear, which can contain sapwood. If you are looking for rot-resistance but don't care what the wood looks like, bump down to Construction Heart—an all-heartwood grade that permits large knots. Between Clear and Construction Heart you'll find B Heart—an all-heartwood grade that permits a limited number of small knots —and B Grade, which permits sapwood and limited small knots. The lowest grade is Construction Common, which permits sapwood and larger knots.

Make sure the CCA-treated wood you buy is marked with the retention level appropriate for its intended use.

When you buy CCA-treated wood, it's a good bet you'll be getting southern pine. That's because southern pine is a relatively inexpensive, plentiful wood with sapwood that is easily penetrated by pressure-treatment. Other species that readily accept pressure-treatment include other pines, coast Douglas fir, western larch, Sitka spruce, western hemlock, western red cedar, northern white cedar, and white fir.

Creosote. Railroad ties—they've been finding their way into garden landscapes for years—are preserved with coal-tar creosote. Though it usually is applied by pressure treatment, creosote sometimes is applied by soaking the lumber. It's also available in brush-on form, which is good for maintaining creosote-treated wood.

Creosote-treated wood resists rot in the ground for several decades, but creosote has not proven to have the staying power that CCA is showing. Its biggest advantage is low cost, a big plus to railroads that need a lot of treated wood and don't care that it is sticky, smells bad, can't be painted, and gives off vapors that are toxic to growing plants. But for home landscaping, these can be big disadvantages.

Pentachlorophenal. For decades pentachlorophenal—often called simply penta—was the most popular wood preservative. You could buy it at any hardware store. But a 1985 federal Environmental Protection Agency ruling restricted its use to licensed applicators. It's still used on pilings, manufactured windows, and other manufactured products, but its use for outdoor projects has been supplanted by CCA-treated wood.

Weather

The paint wore off the old barn years ago, and the barn boards have turned a silvery gray. The grain is raised, and you can't run your hand over it without getting splinters. There are deep cracks, often called checks, in many of the boards, and many are cupped. Most of the nails are so loose you could pull the boards off the barn with your bare hands.

Yet the boards are still strong.

If you scrape just below the surface you'll find richly colored, beautifully seasoned wood. These boards have weathered without rotting.

There was warmth, oxygen, water, and wood to eat; all that fungi need to thrive. But because the wood was, in effect, hung out to dry on the barn frame, water ran off and evaporated too quickly for fungi to grow.

In a process called photodegradation, the ultraviolet rays of the sun turned the wood gray and caused its exposed surfaces to disintegrate. In most applications, this surface erosion is too slow to worry about— about ¼ inch per century for softwoods and about ⅛ inch per century for dense hardwoods. Low-density softwoods, some of which are very rot-resistant (western red cedar is one), can erode as much as ½ inch per century.

Paint is an excellent deterrent to photodegradation. Its pigment blocks out ultraviolet rays. Stains, depending on their pigmentation, can help, too. CCA treatment greatly slows the process of photodegradation. The wood cells turn gray, but they disintegrate much more slowly.

But photodegradation did not cause the warping and deep cracks in those old barn boards. The sun needed the help of rain and humidity changes to do that. Exposed wood is like a sponge, soaking up moisture and releasing it with changes in humidity. This causes wood to expand and contract and creates tension between the cells. This tension can cause the board to cup, and if the tension is great enough, to crack. (Wood's movement also loosens nails, which is why the old barn boards are so easy to remove.)

In general, the denser the wood, the more prone it is to cracking and cupping. Heft a piece of redwood: It's very light, not dense. It's also very rot resistant. These reasons are why redwood is so popular for decks.

CCA-treated wood has become a popular alternative to redwood decking because it is resistant to rot and photodegradation. *But CCA does absolutely nothing to block the effects of moisture on the wood.* If you buy CCA-treated southern pine, it will crack and cup just as readily as nontreated southern pine. Southern pine is denser and more subject to cupping and checking than are redwood and cedar. For this reason, it is recommended that a water repellent be applied to CCA-treated wood (unless it will be given some other sort of finish). The repellent must be reapplied each year or so, and no repellent is 100 percent effective. This is something to keep in mind, especially if you live in an area that has extremes of dry and wet weather.

Termites

Few native North American woods are significantly resistant to termites. The heartwood of redwood offers some resistance, especially when used aboveground. Very resinous heartwood of southern pine is practically immune to attack, but it's not available in large quantities and is seldom used.

But termites will not eat chemically treated wood. So the principal line of defense is: *Don't use wood in contact with the ground unless the wood is pressure-treated.* This will not only protect the wood from the ground contact, but it will deny the termites a route to other wood in a structure. A redwood deck erected on CCA-treated posts, for example, would be well protected.

Plywood

Plywood is graded by the American Plywood Association (APA). Each sheet bears a stamp with all the information you need to know to use this material appropriately.

For building outdoors, it is most important to understand the difference between plywood rated "exterior" and plywood rated "exposure."

"Exterior" plywood is intended to be permanently exposed to the weather and includes many styles of plywood siding. This is a great material for siding a garden shed or playhouse.

"Exposure 1" is designed to be used as sheathing (the layer beneath siding). While it will withstand fairly long-term exposure, it isn't intended to be used as siding.

"Exposure 2" is for sheathing, but it won't withstand much exposure. If you are building a small outdoor project that will get done in a few weekends, you can save a few dollars on the plywood by using Exposure 2.

Plywood is also graded for appearance of its face veneers, with "A" indicating the best and "D" the worst. Each sheet has two veneer grades, one for each side. CDX, the stamp on the most commonly used sheathing plywood, means one side is C grade—good enough to provide solid nailing and temporary weather protection—and the other is D grade—nothing better is needed because this face will be covered and never exposed to the weather. The X stands for exposure.

Wood Finishes

Exterior wood finishes used to be simple: paint, stain, or varnish. These broad categories still exist, but they are not as clear-cut as they once were. What is the difference between paint and solid stain, anyway?

The ideal exterior finish would never need maintenance, would keep moisture out to prevent cracking and cupping, would prevent photodegradation, and would stop fungi in their tracks. No such finish exists. All finishes provide some protection from moisture, the sun, and fungi, but each different type is better at some of these jobs than at others. Frequency and ease of maintenance also vary.

Three prime considerations in choosing an exterior wood finish (in no particular order) are:

■ What the finish looks like
■ The conditions under which the wood will be used
■ The kind of wood you are finishing

Keep them in mind when choosing a finish.

Paint. Paint does the best overall job of protecting wood outdoors. It is best for preventing erosion. Paint has more pigment than other finishes, and pigment blocks out the sun's degrading effects. Also, paint forms a film on the wood (instead of soaking in, as does stain), which further retards erosion.

The disadvantage of any film-forming finish is that recoating causes a buildup, which eventually has to be removed.

In general, oil-based paints are more resistant to moisture than latex paints, so you may want to use oil-based paint on your fence or garden shed.

The advantage of latex paints is that they are easier to apply, dry faster, and clean up with water. Cleanup for oil paints requires mineral spirits.

Solid-color stains. Solid-color stains completely obscure the natural color and grain of the wood. These stains are quite similar to thinned paints and can, in fact, be used over old paint or stain. They can be water-based (latex) or oil-based, and they have a lot of pigment, much more than other stains. As a result, they form a film like paint, and the oil-based stains can even peel like paint. The film layers will build up, but because the stain is thinner than paint, the surface can be recoated many times before it needs to be stripped.

Solid color stains are not recommended for areas that will be walked on. They can wear off and adhere to shoes.

Semi-transparent penetrating stains. Semi-transparent stains are only moderately pigmented and, thus, do not totally hide the wood grain. They penetrate the wood surface, are porous, and do not form a surface film like paints. As a result, they will not blister or peel, even if moisture moves through the wood. Penetrating stains are oil-based or alkyd-based (synthetic oil), and some may contain a fungicide. Semi-transparent stains are not inherently resistant to moisture, but some have a water repellent such as paraffin. Moderately pigmented latex stains also are available, but they do not penetrate the wood surfaces as do the oil-based stains.

Stains are most effective on rough lumber or rough-sawed plywood surfaces, but they also work well on smooth surfaces. They are an excellent finish for weathered wood. They are not effective when applied over paint or solid-color stain.

Stains come in an ever-increasing variety of colors, but not as many colors as paint or solid-color stains. White is not available.

Water-repellent preservatives and water repellents. Water-repellent preservatives are popular for decks. When you want to retain the natural appearance of wood while protecting it from cracking and warping, water-repellent preservatives are the choice. They contain no pigment and darken the wood only slightly. To prevent mildew and fungi that can discolor the surface, these preservatives contain a fungicide, but because this is only a surface treatment, the fungicide will not prevent rot.

The first application to smooth surfaces is usually short-lived. When a blotchy discoloration starts to show, the wood should be cleaned with a liquid household bleach and detergent solution, then re-treated. During the first few years, re-treatment will be an annual affair. But after the wood has weathered to a uniform color, it will need refinishing only when it becomes discolored by fungi.

Inorganic pigments can be added to the water repellents to provide color. The resulting mixture is classified as a pigmented penetrating stain. As with semi-transparent stains, the addition of pigment to the finish

Plywood Veneer Grades

Grade	Characteristics
A	Smooth, paintable. Not more than 18 neatly made repairs permitted (boat, sled, or router type, and parallel to grain). May be used for natural finish in less demanding applications. Synthetic repairs permitted.
B	Solid surface. Shims, circular repair plugs, and tight knots to 1″ across grain permitted. Some minor splits permitted. Synthetic repairs permitted.
C Plugged	Improved C veneer with splits limited to ⅛″ width and knotholes and borer holes limited to ¼″ × ½″. Admits some broken grain. Synthetic repairs permitted.
C	Tight knots to 1½″. Knotholes to 1″ across grain and some to 1½″ if total width of knots and knotholes is within specified limits. Synthetic or wood repairs. Discoloration and sanding defects that do not impair strength permitted. Limited splits allowed. Stitching permitted.
D	Knots and knotholes to 2½″ width across grain and ½″ larger within specified limits. Limited splits allowed. Stitching permitted. Limited to Interior, Exposure 1 and Exposure 2 panels.

SOURCE: *Wood Handbook: Wood as an Engineering Material,* U.S. Department of Agriculture Forest Service, Forest Products Laboratory, Madison, Wis., 1987.

helps stabilize the color and increase the durability of the finish.

Water-repellent preservatives may also be used as a treatment for bare wood before priming and painting. This reduces moisture movement through the wood, which reduces shrinking and swelling. As a result, less stress is placed on the paint film and its life is extended.

Water repellents also are available. These are water-repellent preservatives with the preservative left out. They should not be used as a final finish, only as a stabilizing treatment applied before priming or painting.

Varnishes. Varnishes, including urethane, provide a beautiful natural finish, but unfortunately, they don't hold up outdoors unless protected from direct exposure to sunlight. Varnish forms a film which can peel and, when used outdoors, generally requires refinishing every year or two.

Photography Credits

Ernest Braun, courtesy of the California Redwood Association: page 295 (both photos)

Kim Brun: pages 4 (both photos), 271 (bottom)

Courtesy of the California Redwood Association: pages 229 (top), 267 (top, and bottom right)

Jim Collins: page 96

John Connell, courtesy of the California Redwood Association: page 10 (both photos)

Stephen Cridland: pages 3, 31 (top), 192, 202 (top right), 220 (top)

Rufus Diamant, courtesy of California Redwood Association: page 16 (bottom left)

Carl Doney: pages 8 (top), 21 (top left), 29 (bottom left), 33 (bottom right), 73 (top), 80 (left, and top right), 135 (both photos), 141 (both photos), 161 (middle), 170 (top right), 179 (top), 220 (middle and bottom), 397 (middle), 473, 483

Thomas L. Dunn: page 114

Barbara Engh, courtesy of the California Redwood Association: page 30 (top)

Richard Fish: pages 20 (bottom left), 153 (both photos)

T. L. Gettings: pages 7 (both photos), 20 (bottom right), 32 (middle and bottom), 85 (both photos), 99, 112 (top), 161 (top), 170 (middle), 171 (both photos), 178 (top), 179 (bottom), 196 (both photos), 200 (right), 202 (bottom left and bottom right), 303 (bottom right), 417 (bottom)

Karlis Grants: pages 13 (top left and top right), 118

Joe Griffin: pages 423, 425

Chris Grover, courtesy of the California Redwood Association: pages 11 (both photos), 393 (both photos)

John P. Hamel: pages 200 (left), 417 (top)

Donna M. Hornberger: page 33 (bottom left)

Hursley & Lark (R. Greg Hursley, Inc.), courtesy of the California Redwood Association: page 299

J. Michael Kanouff: pages 9 (all photos), 12 (all photos), 14 (all photos), 15 (all photos), 18 (all photos), 19 (all photos), 20 (top), 21 (bottom left), 23 (both photos), 49 (right), 148, 178 (middle), 245 (both photos), 267 (bottom left), 274 (top), 275 (all photos), 297 (both photos), 370 (top)

Phil Kantor: page 27 (top)

Michael Landis, courtesy of the California Redwood Association: page 229 (bottom)

Mitch Mandel: pages 5 (top), 8 (bottom), 13 (bottom), 17 (bottom), 24 (all photos), 25 (both photos), 26 (all photos), 27 (bottom), 28 (bottom right), 29 (bottom right), 33 (top), 34 (all photos), 39 (both photos), 53, 56, 60, 63 (bottom), 67, 86, 88, 105, 123 (bottom), 128 (both photos), 136, 143, 149, 161 (bottom), 170 (top left), 178 (bottom), 179 (middle), 181, 186, 188, 224, 242 (both photos), 252 (both photos), 271 (top), 285 (both photos), 293, 309, 314 (both photos), 332 (both photos), 329 (both photos), 333 (all photos), 348, 350 (all photos), 372 (both photos), 374 (both photos), 426, 430 (all photos), 440 (both photos), 446, 452, 457, 468

Courtesy of Matarazzo Design, Concord, N.H.: pages 22 (bottom right), 235

Andrew McKinney, courtesy of the California Redwood Association: pages 16 (right), 258 (both photos)

Alison Miksch: page 6 (bottom)

Mike Moreland: pages 22 (top), 170 (bottom)

Diane Petku: pages 21 (right), 194, 222

Tom Rider, courtesy of the California Redwood Association: page 31 (bottom)

Karl Riek, courtesy of the California Redwood Association: pages 16 (left top), 210

Rodale Stock Images: pages 22 (bottom left), 27 (middle), 28 (top, and bottom left), 63 (top), 73 (bottom left and bottom right), 80 (right bottom), 81 (all photos), 112 (bottom left and bottom right), 123 (top), 202 (top left), 205, 207, 208, 303 (top, and bottom left), 359 (all photos), 397 (top), 421

Courtesy of Stevenson Projects, Del Mar, Calif.: page 385 (both photos)

Marilyn Stouffer: pages 5 (bottom), 6 (top), 370 (middle)

Sally Shenk Ullman: pages 17 (top), 29 (top), 32 (top), 49 (left top and left bottom), 274 (bottom), 370 (bottom), 397 (bottom)

Jeff Weissman, courtesy of the California Redwood Association: pages 30 (bottom), 190

INDEX

Page references in *italic* indicate illustrations. **Boldface** references indicate tables.

Rodale Press, Inc., publishes AMERICAN WOODWORKER , the magazine for the serious woodworking hobbyist. For information on how to order your subscription, write to AMERICAN WOODWORKER™, Emmaus, PA 18098.